Movements and Parties

How do social movements intersect with the agendas of mainstream political parties? When they are integrated with parties, are they coopted? Or are they more radically transformative? Examining major episodes of contention in American politics – from the Civil War era to the women's rights and civil rights movements to the Tea Party and Trumpism today – Sidney Tarrow tackles these questions and provides a new account of how the interactions between movements and parties have been transformed over the course of American history. He shows that the relationships between movements and parties have been central to American democratization – at times expanding it and at times threatening its future. Today, movement politics have become more widespread as the parties have become weaker. The future of American democracy hangs in the balance.

Sidney Tarrow is Emeritus Maxwell M. Upson Professor of Government at Cornell University and Adjunct Professor at the Cornell Law School. His recent books include *Power in Movement*, 3rd ed. (2011), *War, States, and Contention* (2015), and *The Resistance: The Dawn of the Anti-Trump Opposition Movement* (co-edited with David S. Meyer, 2018).

Cambridge Studies in Contentious Politics

General Editor

Doug McAdam, Stanford University and Center for Advanced Study in the Behavioral Sciences

Editors

Mark Beissinger, *Princeton University*
Donatella della Porta, *Scuola Normale Superiore*
Jack A. Goldstone, *George Mason University*
Michael Hanagan, *Vassar College*
Holly J. McCammon, *Vanderbilt University*
David S. Meyer, *University of California, Irvine*
Sarah Soule, *Stanford University*
Suzanne Staggenborg, *University of Pittsburgh*
Sidney Tarrow, *Cornell University*
Charles Tilly (d. 2008), *Columbia University*
Elisabeth J. Wood, *Yale University*
Deborah Yashar, *Princeton University*

Rina Agarwala, *Informal Labor, Formal Politics, and Dignified Discontent in India*
Ronald Aminzade, *Race, Nation, and Citizenship in Post-Colonial Africa: The Case of Tanzania*
Ronald Aminzade et al., *Silence and Voice in the Study of Contentious Politics*
Javier Auyero, *Routine Politics and Violence in Argentina: The Gray Zone of State Power*
Phillip M. Ayoub, *When States Come Out: Europe's Sexual Minorities and the Politics of Visibility*
Amrita Basu, *Violent Conjunctures in Democratic India*
W. Lance Bennett and Alexandra Segerberg, *The Logic of Connective Action: Digital Media and the Personalization of Contentious Politics*
Nancy Bermeo and Deborah J. Yashar, eds., *Parties, Movements, and Democracy in the Developing World*
Clifford Bob, *The Global Right Wing and the Clash of World Politics*
Clifford Bob, *The Marketing of Rebellion: Insurgents, Media, and International Activism*
Robert Braun *Protectors of Pluralism: Religious Minorities and the Rescue of Jews in the Low Countries during the Holocaust*
Charles Brockett, *Political Movements and Violence in Central America*
Marisa von Bülow, *Building Transnational Networks: Civil Society and the Politics of Trade in the Americas*
Valerie Bunce and Sharon Wolchik, *Defeating Authoritarian Leaders in Postcommunist Countries*
Teri L. Caraway and Michele Ford, *Labor and Politics in Indonesia*

(continued after index)

Movements and Parties

Critical Connections in American Political Development

SIDNEY TARROW

Cornell University

CAMBRIDGE
UNIVERSITY PRESS

CAMBRIDGE
UNIVERSITY PRESS

University Printing House, Cambridge CB2 8BS, United Kingdom

One Liberty Plaza, 20th Floor, New York, NY 10006, USA

477 Williamstown Road, Port Melbourne, VIC 3207, Australia

314–321, 3rd Floor, Plot 3, Splendor Forum, Jasola District Centre, New Delhi – 110025, India

103 Penang Road, #05–06/07, Visioncrest Commercial, Singapore 238467

Cambridge University Press is part of the University of Cambridge.

It furthers the University's mission by disseminating knowledge in the pursuit of education, learning, and research at the highest international levels of excellence.

www.cambridge.org
Information on this title: www.cambridge.org/9781316515556
DOI: 10.1017/9781009028905

© Sidney Tarrow 2021

First published 2021

A catalogue record for this publication is available from the British Library.

ISBN 978-1-316-51555-6 Hardback
ISBN 978-1-009-01396-3 Paperback

Cambridge University Press has no responsibility for the persistence or accuracy of URLs for external or third-party internet websites referred to in this publication and does not guarantee that any content on such websites is, or will remain, accurate or appropriate.

To Aziz, Doug, David, Eitan, Eric, Lis, and The Other Sid;
Patient Teachers and Fast Friends

Contents

Tables

Figures

Preface and Acknowledgments

On a chilly October morning in 2008, on the way to celebrate the life and work of our friend and mentor Charles Tilly at Columbia, Doug McAdam and I sat down for breakfast in a Starbucks in New York City. It was the first time in a decade that we had been together without Chuck to encourage our advances and wisecrack at our inadequacies. Our meetings with Chuck had begun almost ten years earlier over another breakfast when we started work on what we came to call "the DOC project" – short for *Dynamics of Contention* (McAdam et al. 2001).

Over the intervening decade Doug, Chuck, and I had met regularly: first at the Center for Advanced Study in the Behavioral Sciences, where the Mellon Foundation and the Center sponsored the efforts of "the contentious gang;" then in Chuck's office at Columbia, where we argued endlessly over the book; and, finally, in Aurora, New York, where we sorted out our differences. When Chuck left us in the summer of 2008, he left a yawning gap in our professional and personal lives.

At that breakfast on West 86th Street, the silence was palpable until Doug broke it by declaring: "We should do something to let Chuck know we are still 'DOC-tors.' I have an idea," he continued. "How about exploring a gap that we left unexplored in *Dynamics of Contention* on the relations between movements and parties?" "What a great idea!" I responded, "but it's probably impossible, since no one has laid the groundwork for such a study in a systematic way, and each of us has a full docket of unmet obligations." To do it right, I warned, would involve looking at "big structures" and "large processes" through "huge comparisons" – a combination that Tilly had warned of in his 1984 book by that title. "True," said Doug, "but what if we began by slicing off a small piece of the onion – for example, the role of movements in *elections?*"

This still sounded like too vast an undertaking, but when Doug offered to take the lead, my ears pricked up. I had been obsessed with the relations between parties and movements since the 1960s, when I found myself in Rome with a failing dissertation topic. In desperation, I went to see a Communist historian, Franco Ferri, who suggested I drop the topic I had designed in Berkeley and focus on the relations between his party and the southern Italian peasant movement. Wary of being politically exploited, I asked him whether he had made this suggestion to highlight his party's successes in the south. "On the contrary," he explained. "It is because of our *failure* to organize the peasants in the region that I'd like to encourage an outsider to look at it!"

My curiosity piqued, I looked into a Communist party journal, *Cronache Meridionali* (Southern chronicles) and found there a searing series of self-criticisms of the party's failures in the south. This was a puzzle: Between the end of the war and 1951, and with Communist support, the southern peasants had fought a series of battles with landowners and the militarized Italian police and won an agrarian reform (Tarrow 1967: ch. 11). Yet outside of a few industrial enclaves and areas of commercial farming, the party's position in the South remained static. Trying to explain this puzzle led to a dissertation topic and to *Peasant Communism in Southern Italy* (1967), the book that began my career as a historical political sociologist who focused on party/movement relations (Tarrow 1967).

But specializing on Italian parties and movements placed me in a lonely backwater in the mid-1960s, alongside my mentor, Joseph LaPalombara, and some of his students, like Steve Hellman and Robert Putnam. In those days, the discipline radiated outward from the sun of the United States, with comparative politics, IR, and political theory being seen as supporting players. And although voters and parties occupied a substantial place in the political science firmament, there were few hardy souls, like Frances Fox Piven and Richard Cloward (1977), who dared to study their relations to social movements. So, when McAdam proposed that we write an article on movement/electoral relations in the United States in 2008, I lit up. If he would do the initial spadework and we left the larger project for a vaguely defined future, why not take it on?

That effort never came off, but we did attack the more limited problem of the role of movements in elections, first in a 2010 article aimed at political scientists; then in a book with a team of sociologists edited by three Dutch colleagues in 2013; and finally in a volume in honor of Chuck's contributions put together by our Spanish colleague, Maria Jésus Funes, in 2016. No one could claim that we had gone back on our initial commitment, but by the tenth anniversary of our agreement, I had the distinct feeling that we were spinning our wheels without having made much progress on the larger project.

In the meantime, a group of scholars were beginning to fill the gaps in the study of American politics that McAdam and I had identified. I knew the names of Andy Andrews, Joseph Luders, Sidney Milkis, Eric Schickler, Danny Schlozman, and Dan Tichenor, but I had not realized that a growing firmament of experts were beginning to explore the connections between movements and parties that I had explored all those years ago in Italy. This book builds on their work, but from the perspective of a comparativist who has mainly studied parties and movements in Europe.

In this book, I try to bite off a bigger chunk of the movement/party apple than McAdam and I did in our earlier effort, but it is still limited: limited by my imperfect knowledge of the vast expanse of work on parties and interest groups in the United States; limited by the absence of any original empirical material of my own; and limited by the absence of some important episodes of movement/party relations.

But despite these limitations, I had three incentives for taking on this project. First, as I began to think about it, the interface among movements, interest groups, and parties was taking new forms in America. This country was in the midst of a strange interlude in which a charismatic movement leader not only won a presidential election but took effective control of one of the two mainstream parties. Parties and movements are emerging from this juncture but will probably take different forms after the country's adventure with elective authoritarianism.

Second, although many scholars have looked at how movements gain access to and seek advantages from government (see, for example, Gamson 1990), they did not exhaust the ways in which movements interact with parties. In this book, I will propose a number of other mechanisms of party/movement interaction that have become common in the last few decades.

Third, living in an age when the very fundamentals of liberal democracy are under threat (Levitsky & Ziblatt 2018; Mettler & Lieberman 2020), I thought I might contribute to our understanding of the role of movements and parties in challenges to democracy. If democratic systems emerged historically from the encounters between movements and parties – which I think most of them did – can they be undermined through the same channels?

This has proven to be a daunting project not helped by the constraints of being stuck at home during the coronavirus pandemic. Taking it on would not have been possible without the help of many friends and colleagues. Eitan Alimi, Lis Clemens, Doug McAdam, David S. Meyer, Sidney Milkis, Aziz Rana, Eric Schickler, Danny Schlozman, and my adored wife, Susan Tarrow, read every chapter – some of them more than once – and helped me to avoid some egregious errors. I thank them warmly for their loyalty and their help.

As a Johnny-come-lately to the study of American politics, I called on the help of a number of friends and colleagues to read and comment on specific chapters. At the risk of leaving anyone out, they are Glenn Altschuler, Andy Andrews, Kristi Andersen, Julia Azari, David Bateman, Karen Beckwith, Lance Bennett, Rachel Blum, Donatella della Porta, Mike Dorf, Megan Ming Francis, Dan Gillion, Peter Gourevitch, Michael Heaney, Swen Hutter, Jeff Isaac, Joseph Luders, Matt Karp, Mary Katzenstein, Kathrine Krimmel, Holly McCammon, Mona Morgan-Collins, Gerardo Munck, Chris Parker, Ken Roberts, Leila Rupp, Elizabeth Sanders, Virginia Sapiro, Martin Shefter, Daniel Schlozman, Verta Taylor, Dawn Teele, Chloe Thurston, and Christina Wolbrecht.

Friends and colleagues who shared unpublished work with me are Julia Azari, Lance Bennett, Rachel Blum, Alex Hertel-Fernandez, Dana Fisher, Dan Gillion, Anton Jäger, Joseph Luders, Liliana Mason, Holly McCammon, Suzanne Mettler, Sid Milkis, Mona Morgan-Collins, Chris Parker, Paul Pierson, Charles Postel, Lara Putnam, Ken Roberts, Eric Schickler, Danny Scholzman, Dawn Teele, and Theda Skocpol.

I had precious advice in sketching the three comparative vignettes in Chapter 9 from Santiago Anria, Ruth Ben-Ghiat, Paul Chang, Steve Hellman, Jai Kwan Jung, Sun-Chul Kim, Ken Roberts, and Chan Suh. Susan Tarrow, my "editor-in-chief" and my best friend since we met in Berkeley in 1961, read every chapter at least twice and offered gentle but pointed critiques. Jonathan Tarrow Rhudy helped make the book accessible to bright undergraduates like himself. Jerry Goldberg served as a volunteer design consultant. More than anyone, I am grateful to the late Charles Tilly, who never recognized a problem that was too big for him to tackle. I'm no Tilly, but his love of intellectual adventure is what inspired this book.

Introduction

Between November 3, 2020, and January 20, 2021, the United States experienced a combination of events that will be remembered as a tragic episode in American history. In the midst of a devastating pandemic, one president was soundly defeated and another sworn in; the first one refused to accept the results of the election while the second calmly took the reins of a government that was struggling to cope with the pandemic and the resulting economic crisis. In the midst of all this, the country was shaken by an attempted coup and by an attendant riot.[1] Although it may not be the case that this political and institutional shock "changed everything," it certainly marked the peak – or the nadir – of what will surely be remembered as a "critical juncture"[2] in American history. But another "critical connection" that was exposed by the events of those two months was the enduring, but ever-changing, and often overlooked juncture between political parties and social movements. That critical connection is the subject of this book.

When Donald Trump lost the presidency on November 3, 2020, he claimed that the election had been "rigged" against him and that he had actually triumphed over his Democratic opponent, Joseph R. Biden. "Dead people" and individuals under the voting age had been dredged up to defeat him, Trump argued, and "voting by mail" (a method he himself had used to cast

---

[1] For a reading of what happened that day as the combination of a coup and a riot, see Jeff Goodwin, "The Eighteenth Brumaire of Donald J. Trump." www.pwsc.us/conflicted-the-pwsc-official-blog/blog/the-eighteenth-brumaire-of-donald-j-trump?fbclid=IwAR0NuirjoSzaH7Dc_ZbsA4t-N-v2g2OCACYrug_YrAWUl-j3jkWkAXbwOMU

[2] The concept of "critical junctures" comes out of a tradition in comparative politics, first in the work of Seymour Martin Lipset and Stein Rokkan (1967) and then in that of David and Ruth Collier (1991). Working with Gerardo Munck, David Collier revived the study of critical junctures in their 2022 edited volume, Critical Junctures and Historical Legacies: Insights and Methods for Comparative Social Science. Lanham, MD: Rowman & Littlefield.

his ballot in Florida) was used in many states to aid a massive electoral scam, even in states – like Arizona, Georgia, Michigan, and Pennsylvania – whose legislatures were in the hands of Republicans. Hundreds of Republican legislators – many of them elected in the same states that Trump was accusing of having rigged the presidential election – rose up to join a campaign that Trump and his supporters labeled "Stop the Steal."

Over the next month, employing millions of dollars in donations from supporters and a tribe of apparently willing lawyers, Trump proceeded to take state election authorities to court over the electoral improprieties he had claimed were used against him. Supported by his personal lawyer and former New York City mayor, Rudolf Giuliani, the Trump campaign took more than eighty cases to court against six different states. They lost them all, spectacularly so in the Supreme Court, which did not even deign to consider his brief.[3] So far-fetched was Trump's legal campaign that it was bound to fail, but its real intent was to undermine the legitimacy of the election that Biden had won by more than seven million votes. In that goal, Trump succeeded: By mid-November, half of Republican voters believed that the election had been stolen;[4] by early December, the proportion had actually increased to 77 percent.[5] In response, and across the country, a social movement began to mobilize around the demand to "Stop the Steal!"[6]

The success of Trump's campaign to convince Republican voters that Trump had won the election had a feedback effect on the party's elite, which had long been terrified of what he could do to their political futures if he turned against them. On December 11, 126 Republican members of the House of Representatives signed an amicus brief in support of the State of Texas' complaint that the votes of four other states should be declared invalid because of electoral irregularities. Although Texas' suit was slapped down by the Supreme Court,[7] the effect was to convince a number of Congress members to "object" to the certification of the election in a number of "swing states" that had voted Democratic. Led by presidential wannabees Josh Hawley of Missouri and Ted Cruz of Texas, the dissenters forced congressional leaders to schedule debates on the "objections" on January 6, 2021, in both houses of Congress.

That was the day when President Trump had called a "March to Save America" rally in Washington, DC, where he emerged from the White House to support his claim of election fraud. Encouraged by the president and by his sons, Don Jr. and Eric, and by his lawyer, Rudy Giuliani, the rally was organized

---

[3] www.reuters.com/article/us-usa-election-trump/u-s-supreme-court-swiftly-ends-trump-backed-texas-bid-to-upend-election-results-idUSKBN28L2YY

[4] www.reuters.com/article/us-usa-election-poll/half-of-republicans-say-biden-won-because-of -a-rigged-election-reuters-ipsos-poll-idUSKBN27Y1AJ

[5] www.courant.com/politics/hc-pol-q-poll-republicans-believe-fraud-20201210-pcie3uqqvrhyvnt7geohhsyepe-story.html

[6] On January 10, 2020, I found 427 million hits on Google for the phrase "stop the steal!"

[7] www.nytimes.com/2020/12/11/us/politics/supreme-court-election-texas.html

by a nonprofit group called "Women for America First," which was headed by a former Tea Party leader, Kylie Jane Kremer, who tweeted, "The Cavalry Is Coming, Mr. President!"[8] A number of other movement groups supported the initiative.

This was not just a movement-based event: Supporting the rally was a policy arm of the Republican Attorneys' General Association and the Rule of Law Defense Fund, which sent out robocalls inviting recipients to "march to the Capitol building and call on Congress to stop the steal.[9] Parties and movements congealed behind the claims of a president who seemed intent on overturning the results of a repeatedly certified election.

As the "March to Save America" got underway, parallel events were mounted around the country. In Phoenix, a mysterious group brought a guillotine to a gathering outside the Capitol; in Sacramento, a right wing militia, the Three Percenters, and the street-fighting group, the Proud Boys, confronted counterprotesters in a violent melee; in Tallahassee, another Proud Boys detachment rallied outside the capitol in support of stopping the steal; in Georgia, which had just elected two Democrats to the US Senate, the leader of a right-wing group called American Patriots USA roamed the Capitol, looking for Secretary of State Brad Raffensperger, who had refused Trump's demand that he "find 11,000 votes" to overturn the election; in St. Paul, more than 500 Trump supporters, many of them dressed in colonial-era costumes, cheered when they learned of the outcome of the protest in Washington.[10]

As the debate on the "objections" began in the Capitol, Trump addressed the demonstrators who had converged from around the country to support his claim that the election had been rigged. Warming up the crowd with his traditional diatribe against the media, he urged Vice President Mike Pence, who was presiding over the Senate debate, to overturn the election result. "We will never give up! We will never concede!" he told the cheering crowd, concluding with a rousing call for them to march down Pennsylvania Avenue to the Capitol to put pressure on Congress to support the objectors. "Now it is up to Congress to confront this egregious assault on our democracy," Trump declared.

---

[8] www.cnbc.com/2021/01/09/pro-trump-dark-money-groups-organized-the-rally-that-led-to-deadly-capitol-hill-riot.html. Kremer had served as president of the Tea Party Express, a minor group in the spectrum of the Tea Party movement that was founded in 2009. Go to http://teapartyexpress.org for its self-presentation.

[9] www.nbcnews.com/news/us-news/republican-ags-group-sent-robocalls-urging-march-capitol-n1253581. Officials of both organizations denied that they had approved of the call to march on the Capitol. Members of the Trump campaign also supported the rally but, in its wake, took down their social media accounts and tried to disappear into the political woodwork. For a report ten days after the rally and the riot, see www.nytimes.com/2021/01/16/us/capitol-riot-funding.html.

[10] These events are summarized from Fabiola Cineas, "The Insurrection is Happening at State Capitols Too," on *Vox*, January 6, 2021. www.vox.com/2021/1/6/22217736/state-capitol-stop-the-steal-protests-rallies

We're going to walk down to the Capitol, and we're going to cheer on our brave senators, and congressmen and women .... You have to show strength, and you have to be strong .... But we're going to try and give our Republicans, the weak ones, because the strong ones don't need any of our help, we're going to try and give them the kind of pride and boldness that they need to take back our country .... So let's walk down Pennsylvania Avenue.[11]

Trump's invitation to march on the Capitol would turn into one of the most explosive combinations of movement/party relations in American history, for among the demonstrators were organized groups that had come to Washington expressly to invade the Capitol, cause mayhem, influence the votes on the "objections," and do violence to congressional leaders like House Speaker Nancy Pelosi and even the loyal vice president, who had told Trump he did not have the power to stop the certification of the election. Pence and House Speaker Nancy Pelosi were marked as special targets of the invaders.

This was not the first time that a movement and a party had converged around an American election. Since the 1850s, where the accounts in this book will begin, the relationship between movements and parties has been both constant and changing. It has been constant because movements have repeatedly joined their forces with parties in elections and pressured them to make policy changes, sometimes aligning with these parties and often opposing them. All through American history, movements have been sometimes silent, often noisy participants at the gates of institutional politics (Tarrow 2012). In turn, movements have often been transformed by their encounters with parties, sometimes becoming what sociologists call "institutionalized" and sometimes becoming parties themselves.

At the same time, the relationship between parties and movements had also evolved. Compared to the plot to assassinate Lincoln as he made his way to Washington for his inauguration, movements today possess resources that could not have been imagined in 1861 or even when the labor movement rose to support Franklin Delano Roosevelt in the 1930s. The party system as an institution has been "hollowed out" even as the polarization between the two major parties has widened. These changes mean that we will have to examine two kinds of dynamics in this book: first, the changing dynamics *within* particular cycles of contention; and, second, *the long-term changes* that have led to our current conjuncture of parties and movements. These are the dynamics that I hope to understand through a comparative study of a number of key episodes in American history, beginning with the one that led to the Civil War and ending with the struggle between Trumpism and democracy today.

Political scientists have usually seen political participation operating along two registers: the articulation of interests/identities/ideologies and their aggregation to build electoral majorities. Analysts have sometimes assigned

---

[11] For the complete transcript of Trump's remarks, go to www.rev.com/blog/transcripts/donald-trump-speech-save-america-rally-transcript-january-6

these two functions to different types of political organizations (e.g., while movements and interest groups "articulate" interests, parties "aggregate" them). But as many of the cases in this book will show, this division of labor does not always map neatly into these two boxes. Particularly during cycles of contention like the one that peaked in January 2021, movements and parties engage in reciprocal relations, often cooperating – as congressional Republicans and the mob that invaded the Capitol did on January 6, 2021 – but sometimes clashing – as did the women who had demonstrated against Donald Trump four years earlier (Berry & Chenoweth 2018).

Although not all social movements are oriented toward electoral politics, when movements do turn to political engagement, the relationship is shaped in large part by their interactions with parties. Sometimes movements advance policy demands that can be integrated into parties or institutions, but movements can also champion transformative agendas, like the abolition of slavery or votes for women. Their success is shaped by both their ability to combine insider and outsider tactics and by the conditions of the parties themselves – whether they are vulnerable to outside influence, as the new Republican Party was in 1860, or are in need of new blood, as the same party was in 2016.

Whatever the situation of the party system at any given time, the impact of movement/party engagement is not limited to a particular election. This is why I will examine "long movements," like the Civil Rights movement or the long Republican Right, as well as shorter cycles of contention. Over time, movements seek rule changes that increase their influence on the party system – like expanding access to the vote for black southerners in the 1960s – and party leaders try to capture new constituencies by responding to their demands and, at times, coopting the movements that placed these demands on the agenda. Movement insurgencies also trigger reactive sequences (Mahoney 2000) that generate durable forms of backlash politics – like the reactions against Reconstruction that led to the Ku Klux Klan and the Jim Crow South or the movement for civil rights in the 1960s that turned white southerners into the core electorate of the Republican Party. We will see that the interaction between movements and the countermovements they trigger is one of the driving forces of American political development.

Of course, most episodes of movement/party interaction lacked the drama and the danger to democracy of what happened in Washington, DC, on January 6, 2021. When we examine movement/party relations in the broad sweep of American history, we will find long periods of relative stability and shorter episodes in which these dynamics have profound influences on the party system and the fate of future movements. In these historical moments, interactions sped up, new alliances and new axes of conflict developed, old institutions were threatened, and new ones were created; the very shape of the regime was often profoundly affected.

Sometimes these moments exploded – as in 1861, when the South seceded after the election of an abolitionist-backed Republican president – but more often, they were embedded in broader periods of contention. What Charles Tilly writes of revolutions is true of such periods of contention: "They do not resemble eclipses of the sun," he wrote, but "resemble traffic jams, which vary greatly in form and severity, merge imperceptibly into routine vehicular flows, develop from those flows, and happen in different circumstances for a number of different reasons" (1993: 7).

WHAT CAN THESE REFLECTIONS TELL US ABOUT THE RELATIONSHIP BETWEEN MOVEMENTS AND PARTIES TODAY?

First, we are living in what David Meyer and I called, in a book by the same title, a "social movement society," in which the lines between movements and other actors are more blurred than they once were (Meyer & Tarrow (eds.) 1998).

Second, we are now living in a country in which the parties have been "hollowed out" (Schlozman & Rosenfeld 2019). Although this occurred in other industrial countries as well (Mair 2013), in America, the decline was accompanied by institutional changes like the universalization of the direct primary and changes in campaign finance laws.

Third, this combination has opened spaces for new hybrid forms of activism to be created both within and on the boundaries of the traditional parties (see Chapters 5–7). These new forms of activism can provide candidates with an infrastructure during electoral campaigns – as they did during the Trump campaign of 2016 – but they operate independently of the parties and, to some extent, have impinged on their territory.

Fourth, these interactions have been increasingly influenced by the growing partisan coloration of the state – and particularly, of the executive. Although the antebellum state was so sparse that the Lincoln administration had to create new mechanisms with which to support the war (Bensel 1990), the national state has become the major site of both partisan and movement activity (Milkis & Tichenor 2019).

Finally, these changes in relative power and position have led to an intensification of movement/party relations over time. In 1860, observers would not have considered the young Wide-Awake movement that mobilized to support the Lincoln campaign as part of Lincoln's "base" (Grinspan 2016), but President Trump went into the 2020 elections with a support base that had essentially fused with the Republican Party (see Chapter 7). It was a part of that support base that produced the attempted coup and the riot at the Capitol in January 2021.

Taken together, these changes have led to a partial "movementization" of parties in which political polarization has reached down from the summit of the political system to meet insurgents from the grassroots. The evidence for this double movement will be seen in a number of ways. The participation of social movements in elections is the most obvious one (McAdam & Tarrow 2010), but it is not alone. As I hope to show in this book, the dynamics of movement/party relations have taken five major forms over the last century and a half:

- In the short run, movements *introduce new forms of contentious collective action* to influence election campaigns.
- Also in the short run, they can join electoral coalitions.
- In the slightly longer run, movements trigger *the formation of countermovements*, which can produce profound reactive sequences.
- In the longer run, *movements and parties affect each other.*
- They also affect the future of political institutions and of the regime itself.

Though some of the movement/party linkages we will examine – like Reconstruction and the extension of the vote to women – "bent toward justice," others led in the opposite direction – toward the creation of authoritarian enclaves, the embedding of white supremacy in the South, and the disenfranchisement of vast sectors of the citizenry (Bateman 2018). The broadest question I will raise in this book is whether and how, by entering, challenging, or altering parties, movements have helped to reconstruct key features of the American political regime.

In Chapter 1, aimed mainly at specialists on parties and movements, I will examine a number of traditions of research on parties, movements, and on their interactions before turning to a series of studies of these relationships during crucial periods of American history. In Chapter 2, I will examine the Civil War juncture, beginning with the passage of the Kansas-Nebraska Act and ending with the collapse of Reconstruction. In Chapter 3, I will turn to the farmers' insurgency in the South and West in the 1880s and 1890s, which ended with their failed effort to enter national politics as the Populist Party in 1896. In Chapter 4, I will turn to the women's movement and to the franchise campaign that succeeded in 1920 but failed to put a female stamp on national politics in the years that followed.

That period was followed by the decades from the Great Depression to the 1960s, when both the labor movement and civil rights entered a new phase of relations with the party system, relations that I will examine in Chapter 5. Chapter 6 turns to the "long" New Right and its relationship to the Republican Party between the failed Goldwater campaign of 1964 and its conquest of power under Ronald Reagan. Chapter 7 shifts to an examination of the "hybrid" forms of organization that have both seconded and challenged the party system since the 1960s before turning, in Chapter 8, to the interaction between Trumpism and the anti-Trump movement. In Chapter 9, I will draw on my experiences as a comparativist to examine three countries in which movement/party relations also intervened in threats to and in transitions to democracy: Italy after World War I; South Korea during the 1980s; and Chile in the thirty years that followed the fall of the Pinochet dictatorship. Although these three cases are very different than the United States, they each hold lessons for the defense of democracy in this country. The conclusions recapitulate the findings of the study and reflect on their implications for the defense of democracy in America today.

There have always been threats to American democracy, but they did not randomly occur. "Rather," write Suzanne Mettler and Robert Lieberman, "they developed in the presence of four specific threats: *political polarization, conflict over who belongs in the political community, high and growing economic inequality, and excessive executive power*" (2020: 5–6, italics added).[12] America finds itself today in a situation in which "all four threats to democracy loom large simultaneously .... What's more," these authors warn, "they have begun to combine with each other in ways that intensify their destructive power" (pp. 237–38), which is what we saw in the events of November 2020 to January 2021. Mettler and Lieberman conclude their book by pointing out that deliberate choices by political leaders either promoted or opposed each of the four threats they detail.

Mettler and Lieberman are not wrong, but this book should add an important element to their analysis – social movements. Just as particular configurations of parties and movements have sometimes advanced "the arc of history" toward democracy, different configurations of movements and parties have taken the country in the opposite direction – as we saw on January 6, 2021. Beginning with the abolitionist/Republican alliance of 1860 and ending with the Trumpian/Republican collusion of 2020–21, this book will seek to deconstruct important episodes of movement/party interactions in American political development and construct "superior stories" that both reveal their dynamics and their outcomes for democracy.

---

[12] I am grateful to Professors Lieberman, Mettler, and their colleagues in the *American Democracy Collaborative* (https://americandemocracycollaborative.org) for including me in their deliberations. In addition to Mettler and Lieberman's *Four Threats*, see Robert Lieberman, Suzanne Mettler, and Kenneth Roberts (eds.). *Democratic Resilience: Can the United States Withstand Rising Polarization?* (2021).

I

Movements and Parties in Contentious Politics

Political scientists have often seen participation operating in two main modes: articulating interests/identities/ ideologies and aggregating them to build electoral majorities. Although analysts have sometimes assigned these two functions to different types of political organizations (e.g., while movements and interest groups "articulate" interests, parties "aggregate" them), as many of the episodes in this book will show, that division of labor does not always neatly map onto these two functions. This somewhat artificial distinction results in part because, though parties are constants and provide regular measures of their strength and duration by their electoral performances, another important part of the reason is the inveterate habit of academics of dividing their terrain into neat circumscriptions, each with its own rules, measures, disputations, and rules of engagement. Before turning to the historic episodes in this book, it will be important to survey the literatures in the study of parties and movements and the important efforts to bring them together in recent years.

I BETWEEN MOVEMENTS AND PARTIES: A CURIOUS LACUNA

Historical, social movement, and political party research are all well-developed traditions in the United States. But until quite recently, disciplinary barriers hampered a synthesis among them. Although the study of parties has been seen as the proper province of political scientists, research on movements has largely been left to sociologists (Gamson 1990; Goldstone (ed.) 2003; McAdam & Tarrow 2010). And while students of movements mainly focused on the phenomenology, the origins, and the discourse of movements, political scientists have been more interested in the effects of the protest wave on elections than on the movements that trigger them.[1] Historians, until quite recently, divided their efforts neatly between political and social history.

Why such a disjunction? As Jack Goldstone observed in the introduction to his edited book, *States, Parties, and Social Movements*:

There has been a persistent tendency to see this interaction [between movements and the state] as distinct from normal institutionalized politics occurring through voting, lobbying, political parties, legislatures, courts, and elected leaders. (2003:1)

Coming from the European tradition in which research on movements and parties has never been as separate as in the United States, Donatella della Porta and her collaborators complained that

research on parties moved away from concerns with the relations between parties and society ... and social movement studies mainly framed them as a social phenomenon whose political aspects had to be located outside of the political institutions". (della Porta et al. 2017: 3)

In this section, I will examine the reasons for this divided reaction to these relations before examining three recent efforts to "fuse" research on movements, parties, and institutions.

Coming from History

Although historians have given a great deal of attention to both movements and parties, for many years they divided neatly into "political" and "social" historians, the former focusing mainly on elite politics and the latter examining "history from below." This meant, for example, that while a fine political historian like Joel Silbey focused on the role of parties in the Civil War (1977), equally talented social historians, like Eugene Genovese, were delving into the world the slaves made (1972).

This divide was first transcended by two historians – Glenn Altschuler and Stuart Blumin – in their in-depth study of American local politics in the nineteenth century (2000). But it took a historical sociologist, Elisabeth Clemens, whose *People's Lobby* was published in 1997, to effectively show how associations from above and below came together in such movements as the agrarian revolt

---

[1] Although memories of the 1960s suggest that ordinary white voters will be turned off by the violence that can occur during protest movements, Daniel Gillion's work suggests that this connection has been overblown: "Both the people marching in protests and those observing them," he writes,

are inspired to contributed to candidates who are perceived as being committed to change .... Protests likewise increase voter turnout .... On average, a district that sees 50 liberal protests in an election year sees the Democratic candidate in that district increasing his or her vote share by 2 percent and the Republican decreasing by 7 percent compared with the previous election.

www.theatlantic.com/magazine/archive/2020/09/protest-works/614182/election

and the women's suffrage movement. More recently, the divide was transcended by a new generation of historians who blended political and social history in ways that illuminate the dynamics of both.[2]

More recently, Clemens' *Civic Gifts* (2020) melded America's tradition of civic association with state structuring of civil society, beginning with the Civil War creation of benevolent societies (see Chapter 2). Writing of the same period, Steven Hahn broke new ground with his study of black abolitionism (2003), while Matt Karp has focused on the mass politics of antislavery (2019) and Gregg Cantrell examined the relations between the agrarian movement and the People's Party (2020). The once canonical divide between political and social historiography seems to be coming to an end.

Coming from Movement Studies

Movement scholars, especially in the United States, long avoided interaction with the tradition of political party research. One reason was because much of the early research on movements was carried out by Marxists, who long regarded politics as the "superstructure" of society beneath which "real" structural change occurs. Another was the authoritarian involution of movements of Europe during the interwar period, which led European exiles and those influenced by them to regard movements as dangerous (Arendt 1966). This helped to produce a "collective behavior" approach in which movements were seen as the outer edge of unruly crowd behavior (Smelser 1962). Finally, the 1960s produced a leftward lurch of movement scholarship that led many scholars to regard parties as cranky conservative institutions (Melucci 1980; Offe 1985; Touraine 1971), which could not be considered alongside movements that were seen as emergent actors (Alberoni 1984).

Indifference to parties and elections continued into the new century. The index to the first edition of *The Blackwell Companion to Social Movements* (Snow et al. 2004) – until recently the definitive American sourcebook on the subject"[3] – included exactly two page listings for the term "elections." As Daniel Gillion writes: "Historians and sociologists have explored protest and social movements, but they have largely focused on movements' origins or what sustains them; they rarely draw political connections to electoral outcomes, leaving this terrain for political scientists" (Gillion 2020, p. ix).

During the 1970s, Charles Tilly (1983) and John McCarthy & Mayer Zald (1977) began to study protest events and social movement organizations (SMOs). Although voter surveys focus on individual decision making,

---

[2] Among those whose work is closest to this spirit of this book are Meg Jacobs et al. *Democratic Experiment: New Directions in American Political History* (2003); Gary Gerstle et al. *Beyond the New Deal* (2019); and Brian Cebul et al. *Shaped by the State* (2009).

[3] The second edition of the *Blackwell Companion* – (Snow et al. 2018) is far more ecumenical in this respect than the first, a volume that was far more "social movement-centered."

contentious event analysts like Tilly focused on collective actions (also see Rucht & Olemacher 1992; Hutter 2014; Bremer et al. 2020; Kriesi et al. 2020) while students of movement organizations studied the mobilizing structures that enable such actions (Minkoff 1995; Zald & McCarthy 1987).

Coming from Political Party Research

For decades, sociologists and political scientists studied parties and movements without much of a conversation between them. While the former tended to focus on "protest," the latter gave their attention to movements and, increasingly, to social movement organizations (McCarthy & Zald 1977). To some extent, this gap was a natural outcome of diverging methodological practices. After the appearance of *The American Voter* (Campbell et al. 1960), electoral studies were reshaped around survey methodology, which can only tap into movements through the reports of surveyed individuals.[4] More recently, a few scholars have endeavored to use survey methods to study both protest and voting behavior (Aytac & Stokes 2019; Klandermans 2019), and a small but significant literature has adapted survey technology to study protesters during demonstrations (for representative examples, see (Fisher 2019). But there were also ontological differences between party and movement scholarship that made it difficult for the two groups of scholars to intersect, except around the attitudes of activists and voters.

With their habitual practice of slicing the study of politics into neat and manageable sectors, political scientists mainly elided the role of movements in studies of elections. For example, when Doug McAdam and this author searched the index of the *Oxford Handbook of Comparative Politics* (Boix 2009) for studies of movements and elections, we found subject headings for elections and electoral systems – but none for social movements (McAdam & Tarrow 2010). Social movements have been "the phantom at the opera" of public politics (Tarrow 1990).

Although "party organization" was one of the three legs of political party scholarship that were examined by V. O. Key (1955), in recent decades the field moved away from this focus to define parties as the result of the calculations of individual office holders and office seekers. This was in part the result of the methodological and theoretical individualism that became fashionable in political science between the 1960s and the 1990s (Downs 1957; Aldrich 1995). John Aldrich, who best exemplified this approach, argued that parties are the solution to ambitious politicians' problems as they face election campaigns and attempt to build their careers. Voters, political institutions, groups, and movements hover uneasily outside of this elite-based model.

---

[4] A small but significant literature has adapted survey technology to the study of protesters in the act of protesting. For representative examples, see Fisher 2019.

In the 1990s, reacting to the near-hegemony of the Downs-Aldrich approach to party scholarship, political scientists working mainly out of UCLA reimported groups into the study of parties after the long, slow death of the pluralist tradition. David Truman, who had launched that tradition, had observed that interest groups are leery of becoming too closely associated to a particular party (1951). Unlike the pluralists, the UCLA scholars redefined parties as groups of "policy-demanders" who jostle for control of party coalitions (Bawn et al. 2012; also see Cohen 2008). As two close observers of the UCLA school summarized:

In making nominations, the groups that constitute parties define basic party positions, decide how much risk to take in pursuit of those positions, and choose which candidate to put forward under the party banner. Where Downs and Aldrich give primacy to office holders, the [UCLA-based] theory of parties sees successful politicians primarily as reliable agents of the groups that constitute the party". (McCarty and Schickler 2018:176–7)

For the UCLA group, parties were essentially "long coalitions" of groups that compose and compromise their differences through "invisible primaries" in order to win elections.[5]

But the UCLA model elided the third leg of Key's definition of parties – their *organization* – and the brokerage role they play between the state and civil society. As McCarty and Schickler put it: For the UCLA group, rather than being a separate, intermediary institution, the party is the sum of the bargains made by the groups that compose it" (p. 184). The UCLA model gestured toward "activists" (Bawn et al., p. 575) but sidestepped the role of ideology, making it a product of the interaction between its internal groups rather than something distinct and variable within the party system (Grossmann & Hopkins 2016).

Largely absent from both of these frameworks were social movements. Although interest groups dovetailed nicely within the UCLA framework, movements were harder to integrate within it. The reason is that though interest groups are *transactional*, movements are held together by their *ideological missions* and *collective identities*. One of the recurring divisions between interest groups and movements is that, while the former are built to bargain with opponents and allies, the latter are more deeply committed to their beliefs and identities and are likely to interpret bargaining as betrayal. As Gregg Cantrell writes of the relations between the agrarian movement and the People's Party, to which we will turn in Chapter 3:

Movements create an ideology and then set concrete goals that their adherents believe can and must be achieved .... By contrast, parties, or at least successful ones, create more

---

[5] To the categories of "policy seekers," Hans Noel added ideologies (2012; 2014), and Rachel Blum added "insurgent factions" (2020: ch. 1), by which she means something like internal movements.

or less stable bureaucratic structures that address the needs of individuals and of the various interest groups that comprise the electorate (Cantrell 2020: 254–5).

In this book I will argue that the missing intervening variable between social identity and the increase in partisanship has been the rise of a movement society and the growing interpenetration between movements and parties that has resulted from it.

II MOVING TOWARD FUSION

The first moves toward fusion among these streams of scholarship came from movement scholars. Early pathbreakers were Doug McAdam, Frances Fox Piven, and Richard Cloward. McAdam's history of the civil rights movement was packed with evidence of that movement's relations to the party system (1999b), while Piven and Cloward moved from an emphasis on the weight of public policy on the poor (1972) to analyzing the costs and benefits of political involvement on social movements (1977). Earlier, this author drew on the European tradition to examine the links between the Italian Communist Party and the peasant movement between the end of World War II and the 1960s (Tarrow 1967).

In the 1990s, Edwin Amenta and his collaborators developed the concept of "political mediation," which signified the intervening institutional agents that either make it possible for movements to influence policy or stand in their way (Amenta 1999; 2005; 2006). Amenta was persuaded that, starting with the New Deal, the growing diffusion of movements like the Townsend Clubs, which attempted to influence old-age pensions, produced a convergence between movements and institutional actors. "The Townsend Plan," writes Amenta, "had its greatest influence when it was able to match its action appropriately to the political situation at hand" (2006:11). But the same was true on a grander scale for the labor movement, which, during the period of formation of the Congress of Industrial Organizations (CIO), grew closer to the Democratic Party (Schickler 2016).

The systematic analysis of the policy outcomes of movement activity has led to a vast literature, best summarized in the work of Marco Giugni and his collaborators (Giugni & Yamasaki 2009; Giugni, McAdam & Tilly 1998; 1999). But specifying the interaction of movements and parties in terms of policy outcomes narrows the range of their possible consequences. While Amenta's "political mediation" model focused on the regime in power and on the domestic bureaucracy as "mediating" factors (ibid., p. 8), we need to know more about the specific role of parties as interlocutors in the struggle of movements to achieve collective goods.

The new century brought a number of new moves toward the fusion of political party and social movement studies both in the United States and elsewhere. An important part of the reason was the advent of "movement-parties." This concept has grown popular among political scientists in Europe in recent decades, as the work of Herbert Kitschelt (2006) and Donatella della Porta and her collaborators (2017) attest. But after the rise of the Worker's Party (PT) in Brazil, the relations between parties and movements in Central America (Almeida 2010), and of a group of indigenous-based parties in the Andes in the 1990s, it was already familiar to scholars of Latin America.[6]

These experiences in Europe and Latin America illustrate one of the main mechanisms that trigger sequences of party/movement relations. When party systems are weakened or when they are committed to an outdated alignment structure, political space can be filled by new or revitalized movements (Roberts 2015). The weakening of the party structure leaves space for movements to move into the space previously occupied by parties, while the advent of new alignments provides opportunities to bring new voting blocs into the political community.

Some of these movements – like the Brazilian PT – transformed into conventional parties, although they retained their basis in the labor movement. Others – like the Bolivian MAS – retained enough of their decentralized organization to maintain close ties with their movement base after coming to power (Anria 2019) without fully transforming into conventional parties. Still others – like the right-wing groups that appeared in American politics from the 1960s on – dislodged traditional party elites from their position in the Republican Party and became the source for what I will call "the movementization" of party (see Chapter 8).

But the phenomenon of the movement-party is not an entirely new one in the United States either. Think of the abolitionist movement that we will examine in Chapter 2: It survived long after the formation of the Republican Party, and it maintained close relations with that party's radical branch. In Chapter 3 we will examine another movement-party – the People's Party – which grew out of the agrarian movement in the rural periphery in the 1880s. In both cases, we will see that movements that produce parties in their image do not automatically vanish when the party opens its doors.

In a different form, the Republicans in the twenty-first century moved toward a movement-party model both by capturing much of the energy of the Tea Party movement and then by the capture of the party by the Trumpian movement (see Chapter 8). That shift increased the ideological valence of the party and made its leaders ever more reluctant to negotiate with their opponents (Grossmann & Hopkins 2016). It is from the continuing link between movements and the parties they produce that both the energy and the conflicts within these parties

---

[6] In additional to the foundational work of Paul Almeida on Central America, see Hunter (2007) and Keck (1992) on the Brazilian PT. On indigenous movement-parties in the Andes, see Van Cott (2005) and Anria (2019). Roberts' work (2015) comes closest to the theme of this book in connecting the rise of movement-parties to different patterns of party system alignment.

are drawn, as I will argue on the post-2020 struggle for the identity of the Republican Party.

III PATHBREAKERS: TILLY, SCHLOZMAN, AND MILKIS AND TICHENOR

As the UCLA school was moving beyond elite-centered models of political parties and movement scholars were exploring "political process" approaches to contentious politics, other scholars were exploring the links between movements and parties in a developmental framework. This was, in part, a result of impatience with the "presentist" bias of survey-based research but also of the changes in party/movement relations in the early twenty-first century.[7] These American Political Development (APD) scholars were also influenced by research in what came to be called "comparative historical analysis," best represented in the field of contentious politics by the work of Charles Tilly, most of whose work centered on Europe.

Tilly and "Contentious Politics"

The most ambitious effort to bring together movements with other forms of political conflict came within the broad framework of "contentious politics" founded by Charles Tilly (1995), who was later joined by his collaborators McAdam and this author (McAdam et al. 2001) and by a group of scholars led by Jack Goldstone (2003). By contentious politics, these authors meant "interactions in which actors make claims bearing on other actors' interests, leading to coordinated efforts on behalf of shared interests or programs, in which governments are involved as targets, initiators of claims, or third parties" (Tilly & Tarrow 2015: 7). Contentious politics thus comprises a wide range of actors and forms of action, ranging from revolutions and Civil War on one side to relatively contained forms of action like legal suits, petitions, and leafletting on the other.

Within that broad range of action, movements were defined as *sustained campaigns to advance causes, using repeated performances that advertise these causes, based on the organizations, networks, traditions, and solidarities that sustain these activities* (ibid., p. 145). That is the definition that will inform this study: Movements are a part – but only a part – of the broader field of contentious politics, which can range from anomic groups to civil society

---

[7] From an insurgency against the largely ahistorical orientation of the mainstream of American politics in the 1970s, this school has become so widely diffused that it is difficult to find a single literature review that effectively captures its main strands. For the best such effort, see Richard Vallely, Suzanne Mettler, and Robert Lieberman (eds.). *The Oxford Handbook of American Political Development* (2016). For a treatment that takes the term "development" more literally, see Karen Orren and Stephen Skowronek, *The Search for American Political Development* (2004).

associations, nonprofits, NGOs, and even at times political parties. Though movements are most often associated with disruptive forms of collective action, they also engage in conventional behavior including, increasingly, in elections (McAdam & Tarrow 2010).

For Tilly, movements operate through a variety of "repertoires of contention," in which some performances are forbidden by the state, others are permitted, and still others are required. Repertoires are not only what people do but what they *know how to do* (Tilly 2006) and what their interlocutors will recognize. For example, after a half century of experience, college administrators, police forces, and entrepreneurs know the meaning of a sit-in, but their predecessors a century ago would not have recognized what has become a familiar protest performance.

Contention ranges on a spectrum from "no repertoires" to "weak repertoires" to "strong repertoires" to "rigid" ones. "Strong repertoires," writes Tilly, "imply great embedding of contention in previously existing history, culture, and social relations" (2006: 41). Movements are most visible when they engage in transgressive forms of contention, but they put a great deal of effort into recruiting members, creating networks with other groups, and educating the public. Many of these activities overlap with the activities of other collectivities, ranging from unorganized mobs to interest groups to political parties. Although traditional scholars tended to draw a sharp line between the performances of movements and parties, as we will see, this line is increasingly blurred, and some of these performances overlap (Borbath & Hutter 2020; Bremer, Borbath & Kriesi 2020). And although movement activities are usually viewed as operating outside the range of institutions, some of their activities take place within institutions, which is where they are most likely to overlap with parties.

Particularly in times of crisis, like the 2007–8 financial crisis, protest politics serves as a "signaling mechanism" for electoral punishment for decision makers and "highlights the *political dimension* of deteriorating economic conditions" (ibid., p. 231). At a minimum, this can lead party leaders to make procedural concessions to accommodate pressure from the streets; at a maximum, pressure from the streets can result in destabilization of the party system as occurred in several Latin American countries following the adoption of neoliberal economic policies (Roberts 2018).

Something important was missing in the work of Tilly and his collaborators on contentious politics – oddly enough, the state, to which Tilly had devoted a great deal of attention in previous work (1990; 1995). Another way of putting this is that their book, *Dynamics of Contention* (2001), was so focused on the mechanisms that drive contentious politics that it elided how political institutions direct movements either to ally with parties or to challenge them.[8]

---

[8] In a subsequent book in 2006, *Regimes and Repertoires*, which he called an "orphan" of the *Dynamics* project, Tilly tried to fill this lacuna, but that book operated at too high a level of

More recent work by Sidney Milkis and Daniel Tichenor (2019) has brought social movement scholarship into dialogue with work on the presidency and with the expansion of the executive in general.

A lacuna as big as "the state" could not be easily ignored, and in work that also came out of the *Dynamics* project, Jack Goldstone and his collaborators endeavored to embed the relations between movements and parties in an institutional framework. For example, in his contribution to that book, Joseph Luders showed that local officials responded to the sit-in movement in the South to end segregation in local businesses "less to the general interest in defending Jim Crow against federal incursion and more to their specific local political incentives" (2003, p. 211). But Goldstone and his collaborators did not offer any general mechanisms for how movements, parties, and the state intersect in American political development. Efforts to do so had to await the work of scholars in the field of American political development.

Schlozman and the "Anchoring" Mechanism

Daniel Schlozman's landmark study of the "anchoring" of movements into parties took the form of a comparative-historical study, *When Movements Anchor Parties* (2015). The two main examples he used to illustrate such "anchoring" were the links between organized labor and the Democratic Party during the New Deal era (ch. 3) and between the Republicans and the Christian Right in the 1980s (ch. 4). Schlozman also looked at a number of "failed" and partial anchorings between parties and movements, some of which will be examined in this book.

In companion efforts to his book, writing with Sam Rosenfeld, Scholzman argued that the "anchoring" process has been favored by the "hollowing out" of political party organizations (2019), a phenomenon that will be examined in Chapter 7 of this book. They also argued that the interactions between a particular party and the movement sector need to be seen over a longer historical period that what we typically find in either the social movement or the political party fields. They also examined the "long" conservative movement in the United States, beginning in the 1950s with the McCarthy anti-Communist crusade, continuing through the Goldwater and Christian Conservative movement and its relations to the Reagan administration, to the latest generation of "Tea Party" and Koch network–related right-wing groups (2018).

These movement/party linkages exerted a long-term influence on party organizations and ideologies and – more broadly – on the development of the American political regime. "Repeatedly," writes Schlozman,

comparison to specify how particular institutions – like parties, legislatures and executives – intervene between movements and institutions.

movements have redefined the fundamental alignments of political parties and, in turn, the organizable alternatives in national politics. The alliances between labor and the Democrats, and the Christian Right and the Republicans have defined parties' basic priorities, and exerted long-term influence away from the median voter .... Still more important, they diverged sharply from those of major social movements that *failed to find and to maintain* a stable place inside political parties. (2015, p. 3, emphasis added)

I have italicized "failed to find and to maintain" in Schlozman's summary because of what seems to me his excessive narrowing of the mission of social movements – whether or not they forge an alignment with a political party. This seems to me to be a very "American" way of looking at the relations between movements and parties (e.g., in a two-party system, movements that do not forge an enduring alliance with a party tend to "fail"). This elides the decision that movements make about whether or not to aim at such an alliance. Many movements do not have political aims in the first place and, for many that do, their aim is to *channel* party elites rather than combine with them. Moreover, Schlozman's "anchoring" mechanism leaves uncertain which agent is the "anchor" and which is the "ship" in movement/party relationships.

Finally, Schlozman's account pays little attention to the role of particular institutional configurations in shaping the relations between movements and parties. As argued by Nicholas Jacobs and his collaborators (2019), the longer-term increase in the power of the executive has shifted the axis of partisanship from the party system to the state, weakening the former and empowering both Democratic and Republican administrations (Jacobs, King, & Milkis 2019). These institutional factors have shifted movements' efforts away from parties toward the administrative state (Lieberman 2005). This takes us to a third effort to link parties and movements to one another.

Milkis and Tichenor on Presidents and Movements

In their important book, *Rivalry and Reform: Presidents, Social Movements, and the Transformation of American Politics* (2019), Sidney Milkis and Daniel Tichenor have also turned to American political development to fuse the movement and institutional literatures. Taking off from the relationship between Lincoln and the abolitionists – which they call "the Crucible" of movement/president relations (Chapter 2) – their book moves steadily toward the present, with substantial chapters on the Progressives' relation to President Theodore Roosevelt (Chapter 3); on the relationship between Lyndon B. Johnson and the Civil Rights movement (Chapter 4); on Ronald Reagan's relationship to the new Christian Right (Chapter 6); and on the interactions between movements and the Obama presidency. Not only that: Unlike the "movement output" literature, which focuses on the one-way street from movements to policy, the authors answer Tilly's (2006) call for a relational analysis of states and social movements.

The overall argument of the book follows from its title. While "Lincoln and the abolitionists collaborated in a political order of highly decentralized and intensely mobilized political parties that animated a party realignment and circumscribed national administrative power" (p. 283), they write, from the Progressive Era onward innovations in both the presidency and social movements reshaped their relational dynamics. These innovations

have made modern presidents a more prominent and regular target of insurgents and, in turn, gave the White House fresh incentives to stay on top of potent social movements, to try to control them, and sometimes to partner with them (pp. 6–7).

Along the way, for Milkis and Tichenor, the "worlds of movements and the executive increasingly overlapped as the size and scope of presidential power and particular movements grew" (pp. 6–7).

Milkis and Tichenor did their historical homework well – with forty-eight pages of densely sourced endnotes covering both the secondary literature and original archival work. But more important, their narratives are shaped by a theoretically honed typology linking the type of movement challenge to different forms of institutional involvement (p. 19). The movement/presidential relations that they find in their histories are motivated by the variations and combinations that emerge from their typology. Table 1.1 adapts their typology to the broader issue of the relations between movements and institutions.

Each of the four cells of Milkis and Tichenor's typology can be illustrated by different examples of movement/presidential relations that we will encounter in this book:

- An example of what they call a *marginal movement,* one to which there was only a cursory presidential response, was the Occupy movement of 2011–12;

TABLE 1.1 *Linking conventional and disruptive movement capacities*

	Significant Tactical Challenge	Insignificant Tactical Challenge
Insignificant conventional Political leverage	Militant Movements	Marginal Movements
Significant conventional Political leverage	Formative Movements	Institutionalizes Movements

Source: Adapted from Sidney M. Milkis and Daniel J. Tichenor, *Rivalry and Reform: Presidents, Social Movements, and the Transformation of American Politics,* University of Chicago Press, 2019, p. 19.

- the case of a *militant movement* that triggered a forceful presidential response was the Animal Rights Militia of the 2000s;
- that of an *institutionalized movement* that led to a cooptive presidential response was the New Christian Right of the 1980s;
- and that of a *formative movement* that produced a forceful presidential response was the LGBTQ rights movement of the last few decades.

Milkis and Tichenor's most important contribution is to show how the growing power of the executive in the twentieth century both built upon and advanced changes in movements that made claims on presidential power. For example, as president, Lyndon B. Johnson forged an alliance with Civil Rights leaders like Martin Luther King Jr., which gave the movement leverage within the circles of power but also created factional divisions between leaders like King and a new generation of (mainly northern) younger leaders. If Milkis and Tichenor are right, then we will find an increasing presence of "formative movements" as we move through American political development toward the twenty-first century in this book.

IV MOVEMENTS AND PARTIES IN THE TWENTY-FIRST CENTURY

Throughout American history, movements have both shaped and been shaped by changes in institutions – and not always in cooperative ways. But during key crises, movements' ties with parties became more frequent and interactive. From Lincoln's intermittent relationships with activists like Frederick Douglass, president/movement interactions evolved toward Woodrow Wilson's tentative relations with the NAACP and the moderate branch of the women's movement, to FDR's deep alliance with organized labor, to Lyndon Johnson's partly cooperative and partly competitive interaction with Civil Rights leaders. From there they evolved to Reagan's carefully staged alliance with the New Christian Right, to Obama's efforts to create his own movement infrastructure around Organizing for Action (Milkis & York 2017), and to Donald Trump's barely disguised alliance with white nationalists.

The strengthening of the executive that Milkis and Tichenor traced was not the only trend leading to more intimate interactions between parties and movements. The weakening of the party system was also a source of increased interaction between movements and institutions, as I will argue in Chapter 6. As the executive grew in power and new forms of participation grew up alongside parties, the parties themselves were increasingly "hollowed out" (Schlozman & Rosenfeld 2019), leaving space for the partial "movementization" of the party system (Tarrow 2018) and for outsider groups like the Koch network to infiltrate the Republican Party (Skocpol & Hertel-Fernandez 2016). Another major trend – political polarization – also was produced by movements operating as "hinges" between parties and society.

Polarization and Its Roots in Society

As long as parties were seen as the product of elite preferences or interest groups, interactions, the links between parties and movements, would remain underexplored. But the growing polarization of the American party system since before the turn of the century has opened a route to bringing together the two fields of study. Early treatments of the phenomenon saw polarization as a *lateral* phenomenon (i.e., a function of the ideological distance between the parties). But as comparativists have long known, polarization also has a *vertical* dimension (i.e., the degree to which social identities and social signals map onto party identifications. As Robert Leiberman and his collaborators write:

The problem is not only that the Republican and Democratic parties have *moved further apart* in their programmatic stands (e.g., polarization), but that *they represent very different sectors of the American electorate, divided on lines of race, ethnicity, gender, religion, and place* (Lieberman et al. 2021).

Political scientists with a psychological bent, like Liliana Mason, have done excellent work in charting this split and its source in social identities (Mason 2018; Mason & Wronsky 2018; Mason & Kalmoe 2021). As Mason put it in her book, *Uncivil Agreement*:

As the parties have grown racially, religiously, and socially distinct from one another, a new kind of social discord had been growing. Partisan battles have helped organize Americans' distrust for "the other" in politically powerful ways. American partisans today prefer to live in neighborhoods with members of their own party, expressing less satisfaction with their neighborhood when old opposing partisans live there (2018: 3).

What remains to be demonstrated, however, is how American parties *became* so socially sorted. Social sorting is clearly not written into Americans' genes, since earlier periods of history did not demonstrate anything like the same depth of partisan identity (Altschuler & Blumin 2000). What behavioral studies of partisan attitudes largely ignored was the role of movements in translating social identities into political ones. In their book, *Deeply Divided* (2014), Doug McAdam and Karina Kloos provide a wealth of evidence that movements were key players in the polarization of the post-1960s decades. The late twentieth century saw the beginning of the generalization of the social movement form and the translation of movement activity into the polarization of the party system. This takes us to the thesis of "the social movement society."

V   TOWARD A MOVEMENT SOCIETY

Is the interaction between parties and movements that we see today only a repeat of what occurred during other historical junctures: the "anchoring" of abolitionist and free soil activists in the Republican Party in the 1850s (Foner 1995); the insertion of the Populists into the Democratic Party in 1896 (Sanders

1999); or the merger of labor radicals and civil rights advocates in the Democratic Party during the New Deal (Schickler 2016: ch. 3)?

This question is of theoretical as well as historical interest: In the late 1990s a group of European and American scholars noted what they saw as the generalization – indeed, the "normalization" – of contentious forms of politics in western democracies. They called this trend the emergence of a "movement society" (Meyer & Tarrow eds. 1998). By this term they meant not only that protest and collective action were becoming more common but also that these performances were becoming more familiar, more expected, and even legitimated.

In other words, public forms of contentious politics have become familiar, standardized, and "modular" – that is, adaptable to a wide variety of sites and sectors and are recognized as such by supporters, opponents, elites, third parties, and even the police (McCarthy & McPhail 1998; Tilly & Tarrow 2015: 16–17). This is not the same as saying that they had become "institutionalized" but, hovering on the border between transgressive and routine repertoires, movements are ripe for interaction with the party system – as we will see in the case of the Tea Party movement in Chapter 6.

After the turn of the twenty-first century, the domestication of protest began to give way to more threatening performances. As Erica Chenoweth and her collaborators concluded from an exhaustive global data analysis, "The decade from 2010 to 2019 saw more mass movements demanding radical change around the world than in any period since World War II."[9] First, in a series of "global justice" events beginning with the anti-WTO protest in Seattle, transnational groups turned to more transgressive forms of protest against international institutions. Meanwhile, right-wing extremists struck out at immigrants, authorities, and places of worship. This was followed by the rise of anarchist-leaning "black blocs" and "antifa" groups determined to gain attention for their goals by fomenting violence against opponents. It was not long before police and authorities moved back to tradition by shifting from protest management to physical confrontations.[10]

These trends suggest that the thesis of a "movement society" may have been too simplistic (Soule & Earl 2005; Soule & Davenport 2009). For although protest – assisted by the Internet and social media – has mainly diffused in conventional forms, it has taken highly disruptive and violent variants, too. Even more interesting, some "formative" movements employ both conventional and transgressive forms. And least predicted at all by

---

[9] Erica Chenoweth, Austin Choi-Fitzpatrick, Jeremy Pressman, Felipe G. Santos, and Jay Ulfelder, "The Global Pandemic Has Spawned New Forms of Activism – and They Are Flourishing," *The Guardian*, April 20, 2020, at www.theguardian.com/commentisfree/2020/apr/20/the-global-pandemic-has-spawned-new-forms-of-activism-and-theyre-flourishing.

[10] See Soule and Davenport 2009 for data and analysis that show that the shift to protest management could be scuttled when police face violent or highly disruptive protesters.

"movement society" authors was the growth of hybrid groups with some of the properties of a movement but piloted by deep-pocketed ideological groups like the Koch network that intervene in the party system without becoming part of party organizations (Skocpol & Hertel-Fernandez 2016). We will examine some of these groups in Chapter 5.

The weakness in the "movement society" thesis was that it did not take sufficient account of what was happening to the party system at the same time: the hollowing out of party organizations; their partial displacement by nonparty forms of interest articulation; and the internalization of movement logics into the party system. This combination of changes is what has produced the peculiar combination of a high level of polarization in the presence of a decline in the parties' capacity to manage ideological conflicts and "civilize" the ideological groupings that have made their way into the heart of partisan conflict.

VI WHAT'S COMING?

During periods of polarization and intense political conflict, institutional and noninstitutional conflicts converge, *people who enter public life through movements veer into parties, and parties shift their ground to embrace new issues and attack the cleavages exposed by the conflict.* Throughout this book, I will examine a number of such periods, beginning in Chapter 2 with the Civil War and how it connected the antislavery movement to the Republican Party and to the presidency.

But if we were to focus only on how organized actors reshape political parties, we would elide a second issue: *how interaction with the party system transforms movements.* Think of the European labor movements in the late nineteenth century, many of which were transformed – we may even say "institutionalized" – through their relations with the Social Democratic parties of the age. Chapter 3 will focus on the agrarian-based movements in the Gilded Age and how the party system reshaped –and ultimately emasculated – agrarian radicalism.

A third question is *how movements use elections to gain their claims.* Chapter 4 argues that both the implantation and the competitiveness of the party system in the West gave women suffragists greater advantages there than in the rest of the country, empowering the strategy of the movement's leaders to win their cause by moving eastward by degrees. How the strength, competitiveness, and strategic flexibility of parties intersect with the shift of movements toward institutions is the third question the book will examine.

A related question is *how movement/party relations affect changes in institutions.* Chapter 5 will turn to the legacies of the civil rights movement and its effects on the party system. If there is something new in my account of that movement, it will be to see civil rights as a "long movement," one that we foreshorten unduly if we identify it with "the sixties." In the language of "critical junctures," we will need to look as well at its antecedent conditions and at its legacies for the party system, many of which did not ripen until successive decades.

Chapter 6 will focus on one of these legacies – *the growing movementization of the party system* as the Republican Party absorbed a series of right-wing movements, becoming an ideologically driven party in the process. At the same time, the Democrats were bombarded with a series of movements based on race, gender, the environment, and sexual preference but remained the coalition of competing interest groups it had become in the New Deal. Both parties were transformed by their relations with movements, but while the Democrats added new constituencies to its phalanx of interest groups, the Republicans ejected its moderate wing and were transformed into an ideological party (Grossmann & Hopkins 2016).

Chapter 7 focuses on three examples of *movement/party hybrids*: the relations between the Democrats and the antiwar movement during the first decade of this century; the rise and diffusion of the Koch network of more conventional movements; and the rise of the Tea Party and its anchoring in the Republican Party. How a full-fledged movement intersected with a top-down one like the Koch network and intersected with the growing insertion of the media within movement/party relations is one of the signs that the "movement society" is more complicated than Meyer and I thought at the turn of the century.

Chapter 8 will take us to the most recent case of a *movement-countermovement interaction* – the rise of the "Trump movement" and the *anti*-Trump countermovement that arose to challenge it after Donald Trump came to power. It is always risky to hazard conclusions about a historical episode that is not yet closed[11], but the combination of extreme polarization, the "movementization" of the party system, and the challenges to American institutions represented by the Trumpian movement – even after Donald Trump's defeat in November 2020 – make it clear that the country had not yet closed this episode of party/movement interaction when this book went to press.

Threaded through these chapters is the question of *how movement-party relations changed* between the middle of the nineteenth and the early twenty-first centuries. Between the era of party centrality in the nineteenth century and the recent period, I will argue that movements have become more deeply engaged in intimate relationships with the party system and that this is the ultimate source of the polarization that is the hallmark of American politics today. In today's "movement society," I will argue, the boundaries between movements and parties are more fluid than they were in the past and a wide range of "hybrid" organizations have developed in the space between ideologically motivated movements and transactional parties.

---

[11] For an early but premature effort of mine, see www.dorfonlaw.org/2020/12/126-legal-novices-or-new-republican.html.

As I have argued in this chapter, the study of American political science has been obstructed by an artificial distinction between parties and movements. But it has been limited by another closure as well: the assumption that American political development is "exceptional." If American political development is "exceptional," it is because it has survived numerous crises that have put democracy at risk. But is it so exceptional? After leading the democratic countries of the world in civil liberties and democratic contestation for decades, in 2020 Freedom House reported that "Democratic processes in the United States are under threat, as shown through its failure to uphold a nonpartisan impeachment process, ensure the fair and equal treatment of refugees and asylum seekers, and safeguard electoral integrity."[12] Will the United States survive its current crisis as a constitutional democracy?

One of the benefits of the current crisis in American democracy is that it has made American scholars aware of the fragility of exceptionalist readings of American history and of the lessons that comparative studies can offer. In an effort to utilize this comparative experience, *Chapter 9 will examine movement/ party relations in three episodes of democratic crisis*: the failed experience of the democratization of Italy after World War I; the successful one in Korea in the 1980s; and postdictatorship party/movement relations in Chile after 2000. None of these countries looks anything like the United States in the first part of the twenty-first century, but their experiences with democracy highlight four of the features that we will see in this book:

- That party/movement relations are central to the critical junctures that produce democratic resilience or decline – as all three case studies will show;
- That polarization and the social sorting that underlies it play a key role in crises of democracy – as the Italian experience proves;
- That coalitions of parties and movements can be critical in producing democratic breakthroughs – as we learn from the democratic breakthrough in South Korea in 1987;
- And the suppression of movements can be dangerous for the party system and for democracy itself, as the Chilean experience will show.

The Conclusion will return to the episodes with which I began the Introduction – the attempted coup and the riot at the Capitol in January 2021, and will recapitulate the findings of the book with a fundamental question in mind: How can the varied experiences of party/movement interaction in American political development help us to understand the conditions in which the arc of history bends toward justice?

---

[12] "Freedom in the World, 2020." https://freedomhouse.org/sites/default/files/2020-03/FINAL_FIW_2020_Abridged.pdf

PART I

THE "PARTY PERIOD"

2

Mass Politics in the Civil War Crucible

On May 22, 1856, Congressman Preston Brooks (D-South Carolina) marched onto the Senate floor and brutally beat Republican Senator Charles Sumner (R-Massachusetts) with a cane. The immediate reason for this eruption was that Sumner had insulted Brooks' cousin, Andrew Butler, for his role in what Sumner called "the crime against Kansas" – the Kansas-Nebraska Act[1] – which allowed part of the western territory to enter the Union as a slave state. The assault, which incapacitated Sumner for months, gave quiet satisfaction to southern observers but shocked northerners, who regarded it as an attack on the heart of American institutions.[2]

Sumner recovered from his wounds, becoming one of the leaders of the radical wing of the Republican Party before emerging as an adviser to President Lincoln in the Civil War[3] and then a fierce advocate for the rights of African Americans during Reconstruction (Trefousse 1991: 214–2) But before he did, the Republican-leaning *New York Tribune,* which promised to distribute three million copies of Sumner's speech (Karp 2019: 153),[4] wrote that the assault on Senator Sumner

reverberates through the land, causing throughout the Free States the intensest excitement and indignation. Other men have been as causelessly assailed, and as wantonly, if

---

[1] The full text of the final bill will be found at https://www.ourdocuments.gov/doc.php?flash=true&doc=28&page=transcript.

[2] Sumner's speech can be found in Joel H. Silbey (ed.). *The Transformation of American Politics, 1840–1860,* 1967, pp 79–81.

[3] Students of the war often highlight the fact that the radicals were far ahead of Lincoln in insisting that the war was being fought to emancipate the slaves, but it was actually Sumner who helped convince the president of the contributions that freed slaves could make in fighting the war. See Klinkner and Smith 2002, p. 62.

[4] New York *Tribune,* June 13, 1856. http://history.furman.edu/editorials/see.py?sequence=sumenu&location=Sumner%20Caning&ecode=nytrsu560524a

not as savagely, beaten; but the knocking-down and beating to bloody blindness and unconsciousness of an American Senator while writing at his desk in the Senate Chamber is a novel illustration of the ferocious Southern spirit.

Sumner's caning was more meaningful than a particularly nasty personal encounter. The Kansas-Nebraska Act that he railed against was a key hinge between the passage of the Missouri "Compromise" in 1820 and the Civil War (Garcia-Montoya & Mahoney 2020). In between, the antislavery movement had bubbled beneath the surface as antislavery advocates like John Quincy Adams filed countless petitions before Congress, only to see them unceremoniously dismissed by a "gag rule" passed under southern pressure. The act deepened the gulf between northern and southern elites, helped to destroy the Whig Party, weakened the Democrats, and opened political space for a new party – the Republicans – to begin the rise to prominence that culminated in Abraham Lincoln's election victory in 1860 (Gienapp 1987). But none of this would happen as long as antislavery was restricted to the politically marginal abolitionist movement, and there was no political party able and willing to take up its challenge. Between the former, which were just emerging from their religious origins, and the latter, which were still organized around cliques of notables and local machines, there was no established recipe for collective action. It was only in the 1850s that people like Sumner, William Seward, and Thaddeus Stevens merged the idea of party with the antislavery impulse to create the first movement-party in American history.

As I argued in Chapter 1, movements and parties have almost always been seen as separate worlds in American political discourse. What the 1850s produced was a coupling between a party and a movement around a distinct set of policy promises that upset the equilibrium of American politics for decades. That merger brought the country to its worst crisis since the founding, but it also established the regional cleavage as the major axis of alignment in American politics for decades and set a baseline for what Elisabeth Clemens calls "the consolidation for the conditions for movement/party interactions in later periods."[5]

In this chapter, I will examine the Kansas-Nebraska Act as the opening phase of a sequence of conflicts that roiled, and eventually reshaped, American mass politics. Antislavery had both structural and "eventful" antecedents, involved intersecting actors engaging in both conventional and transgressive conflict, and produced a social movement that helped to create the first modern American Party. It also led to a major strengthening of the central government and the emancipation of four million individuals from the status of property. Put simply, in the words of Matt Karp, "The largest and strongest slave society in the modern world history also produced the largest and strongest antislavery political movement in modern world history" (Karp 2019: 132).

---

[5] I am grateful to Lis Clemens for suggesting this locution, which synthesizes the message of this chapter better than I could have done myself.

Many scholars have seen the Civil War as the result of a conflict between elites, and indeed, as we will see, the failed Missouri Compromise left Congress divided and the party system in a shambles. Others have seen it as an episode in capitalist development, "the subordination of merchant-to-industrial capital in the US economy" (Post 2011; Karp 2019: 135) or as a species of bourgeois revolution (Moore 1966). But as Karp writes, "The triumph of the Republicans cannot be reduced to the victory of industrial capitalism, either in material or in ideological terms. On the eve of the Civil War, over 70 percent of Northerners lived in rural areas and made a living from agriculture: this distinctive society of small farmers, which formed the bedrock of the Republican Party, certainly sought economic development but hardly organized itself around the accumulation of capital" (Karp, ibid.).

But although the Civil War had both elite institutional and underlying structural roots, it was the result of political struggle that had two interlaced strands – the antislavery movement and the Republican Party. As Karp argues in his seminal essay:

The fusion of antislavery sentiment and mass democratic politics in the 1850s has often been regarded as a diminution of the more radical abolitionist movement that preceded it. But in crucial ways the emergence of the Republican Party as a major political force only deepened the radical potential of the antislavery struggle as a whole (Karp, ibid.).

This does not mean that the Republicans simply picked up the gauntlet that had been passed on by the weak and widely despised abolitionist movement, but that radical abolition, political antislavery, and mass electoral politics intersected to produce the greatest crisis in American history. As Karp put it: "The fusion of antislavery struggle and electoral politics . . . meant that the scale of antebellum popular mobilization against bondage was . . . quantitatively greater than anywhere else in the Atlantic" (Karp, p. 146). Returning to movement/party interactions that I sketched earlier, the Civil War juncture revealed all five of them:

First, the movement against slavery introduced new forms of collective action to influence election campaigns;

Second, it initiated and shaped a new electoral coalition in the form of the Republican Party;

Third, it triggered the formation a countermovement in the form of the southern secession movement and produced a profound reactive sequence after secession was defeated;

Fourth, it changed the shape of the party system and America's political institutions;

Finally, through this complex of interactions among parties, movements, and institutions, the American political regime was threatened, almost destroyed, and ultimately reshaped.

I will make no attempt in this chapter to offer a new narrative of this enormously complicated period, probably the most studied one in American history. Instead, I will focus on the role of party/movement interaction in the crisis that produced the lineaments of the modern American state. I will characterize the changes in these relations in the antecedent period of the 1850s, during the war itself, and in the Reconstruction period to show how each period affected the growth, transformation, and ultimately the shaping of movement/party relations in nineteenth-century America. Here is a roadmap of what is to come.

The antecedents of the Civil War were almost as complicated as the war itself: They involved a sequence of new movements and parties, the unraveling of one party system and the creation of a new one, and an institutional crisis that led to the "anchoring" of the antislavery movement to the party system (Schlozman 2015). Abolitionism was probably the first modern American social movement, defining that term as I employed it in the Introduction, and the Republicans were the first modern American party to combine elite coalition politics with grassroots mass politics (Karp 2019). But their alliance was neither firm nor enduring and only lasted as long as the Civil War lasted.

When war broke out, the shock brought the abolitionists – a suspect minority before the war – to the center of the political system. Although the war was the result of long-brewing conflicts, it was also a source of new contention. In both North and South, new conflicts and organizations emerged, ranging from antiwar Democrats in the North to pro-Unionist groups in the South, from draft evaders in both regions to a guerrilla war on the frontier. War makes states, as Charles Tilly famously declared (1990), but it also makes and remakes movements (Tarrow 2015).

Though the war succeeded in its immediate aims of defending the Union and freeing the slaves, its legacies transformed the American state. What had been a loose federation since the passage of the Constitution grew into a far more centralized capitalist democracy (Bensel 1990); what had been a subject population – African American slaves – gained their first experience of political activism. But the war also led to the white power structure reconstituting itself, as the Republicans turned their backs on Reconstruction, and the political victors of the war – the radicals in Congress and the abolitionists outside – divided and declined.

I ELITE POLITICS, STRUCTURAL CHANGE, AND MOBILIZATION

In his theory of political parties, John Aldrich argued that parties are groupings of political elites whose behavior can be best understood as rational efforts to get elected and remain in office (1995). When we turn to the antebellum period, Barry Weingast, working in a similar tradition, focused on the efforts of party elites to keep slavery off the political agenda through a thirty-four-year-long political transaction – "the balance rule." Their incentive was plainly electoral:

to avoid a conflict that would end each party's representation in the region in which it was in the minority (Weingast 1998; 2002).

The Balance Rule and Its Collapse

The "balance rule" was an informal agreement that had maintained the number of slave and free states in uneasy equilibrium since the passage of the Missouri Compromise in 1820. That compromise was triggered by the controversy over whether Missouri should be admitted to the union as a slave or a free state. The issue became more pregnant after the Mexican-American war, which promised that a vast new territory would gain statehood in the near future. Would its components enter the union as free or slave states? Congress tried to resolve the dilemma by an agreement to balance Missouri's admission as a slave state with Maine's admission as a free one. This produced an ongoing commitment among political elites that the entry of each free state into the union was to be matched, either immediately or soon afterward, by the entry of a slave state – the balance rule.

But this could not be a permanent solution, and it was rife with risk. As the aging Jefferson wrote when he learned that Missouri was to enter the union as a slave state, "This momentous question, like a fire bell in the night, awakened and filled me with terror. I considered it at once as the knell of the Union. It is hushed indeed for the moment. But this is a reprieve only, not a final sentence."[6] It was at once the glue that kept the parties from losing their intersectional support bases and a cork that kept popular passions over slavery from exploding.

Because the country was expanding westward and the slave states were eager to expand their "great southern empire" (Karp 2016), slaveholders saw the lands of the West as ripe for colonization. Conversely, because the North was the more dynamic region, it was from there that the majority of westward-seeking immigrants came, many of them were small farmers with few means and a dread of having to face the competition of slave-run agriculture (Foner 1995). They provided a potential constituency in the North and the West against the expansion of slavery.

The breakdown of the balance rule came – as the "electoral incentives" model would predict – from the desire of ambitious politicians to increase their power and prestige. In 1854, Illinois Democratic Senator Stephen A. Douglas attempted to satisfy both southern and northern interests and build a national constituency for his presidential ambitions by pushing the Kansas-Nebraska Act through Congress. In the name of popular sovereignty, he reasoned, the law would give slave and anti-slave forces the incentive to settle the new territories in the West with their respective socioeconomic systems

---

[6] www.monticello.org/site/research-and-collections/fire-bell-night-quotation

(Gienapp 1987: 70–1). The Kansas-Nebraska Act declared the Missouri Compromise null and void and divided the new territories into two parts.

Douglas' maneuver was almost certain to lead to conflict. Opposition to the bill first arose in a manifesto signed by six senators and representatives from the Free Soil Party – most of them future Radical Republicans – who denounced it as "a gross violation of a sacred pledge" that would create "a dreary region of despotism, inhabited by masters and slaves" (ibid.).

The overt conflict over the Kansas-Nebraska Act was between elites, as the Sumner/Brooks incident testifies, but tension over its implications quickly radiated to the grassroots. Abolitionists held mass meetings throughout the North; New England clergymen circulated petitions and gave sermons from their pulpits against it; accusations circulated that the bill was nothing more than a clandestine effort to extend the empire of slavery into the West at the cost of free soil and free men (Foner 1995: 58–65). This was the period in which the metaphor of "The Slave Power" gained wide currency throughout the North and West.

The immediate result was not heartening for democratic development: a series of violent confrontations in Kansas, where well-armed settlers converged from North and South, hoping to add the territory to their respective sociopolitical regimes. This led to vicious guerrilla conflicts and to competing constitutions, offering an opportunity for radical abolitionist John Brown – who was later to attack a federal armory – to prove that violence was a possible weapon in the dispute over slavery. This was the origin of the rallying cry "bleeding Kansas" among northern abolitionists and western settlers who would form the core of a new Republican Party.

Structural Antecedents

The Kansas-Nebraska Act was a critical event, in Garcia-Montoya and Mahoney's apt term, but it also revealed a deep socioeconomic cleavage between the two regions. Economic and population growth rates tell a story of blossoming northern business and expanding western farming. It also tells a story of how the "West was won" – mainly by northern settlers and immigrants leaving the northeast for the rich granaries of the west. As the North expanded westward, settlers also brought with them a religious culture that prized enterprise, individualism, and (relative) equality – a set of values that clashed frontally with the plantation culture of the South.

The conflict also deepened a cultural chasm between a South that felt itself besieged by money-grubbing northerners and northerners who saw a growing threat of "Slave Power" expanding to the West. Before this episode, the concept of the South as "a tightly knit body of slaveholders united in a design to expand slavery and maintain their control of the nation's destiny" (Gienapp 1987: 76) had currency only in abolitionist circles. In the face of the movement to repeal the Missouri Compromise, "the anti-Nebraska protest gained a much wider audience than the abolitionist movement had ever enjoyed" (ibid., pp. 76–7). As George Fredrickson observed, "It took the assault of the abolitionists ... to force the practitioners of racial oppression to develop a theory that accorded with their behavior" (Fredrickson 1971: 3).

Loosely Coupled Episodes of Mobilization

Against this background, two loosely coupled episodes combined around the issue of slavery that had effects on both elite and mass politics.

Escaping and Fugitive Slaves: Although Article IV, Section 2, of the US Constitution required the return of runaway slaves, many northern states ignored it, and by the 1840s, several hundred slaves a year were successfully evading their masters and making it to the North, where they were welcomed by a small but effective antislavery organization. In response, a new Fugitive Slave Act was passed in 1850 that penalized officials who failed to arrest a runaway slave and empowered slave catchers to go after them – even within the North.[7] Some northern states, like Vermont and Wisconsin, responded by passing laws to assist runaway slaves. Abolitionists like the poet John Greenleaf Whittier and the author Harriet Beecher Stowe wrote against the law and ministers preached against it from the pulpit.

Because of the outrage it caused among antislavery groups, the Fugitive Slave Act encouraged the growth of a network of clandestine organizations – the famed "underground railroad" – whose "conductors" surreptitiously passed escaping slaves from one "station" to the next and eventually across the Canadian border. At its peak, the network transported nearly a thousand escaped slaves a year. Between 1850 and 1860, the black population of Canada grew from 40,000 to 60,000.

The Dred Scott Case: In 1846, a slave by the name of Dred Scott, who had moved back and forth between North and South with various members of the same white family, went to court in St. Louis to claim his freedom on the basis of the fact that he had spent considerable time in a free state. The Missouri courts were divided on the issue, but in 1852, the state supreme court decided against him and returned him to bondage. But the case attracted the attention of antislavery lawyers, who encouraged Scott to take the case to the US Circuit Court in St. Louis. He lost, but in 1856, his lawyers brought the case to the US Supreme Court, where, the next year, slave-owning Justice Roger Taney wrote a momentous decision against him, triggering a national debate that further polarized positions on slavery (Fehrenbacher 1978).

Taney's decision signaled that decades of temporizing over slavery were over. For rather than holding that the Court lacked jurisdiction over a case involving state law, Tawney declared that African American descendants of slaves were not citizens and therefore had no rights. This meant that free blacks in the

---

[7] www.history.com/topics/black-history/fugitive-slave-acts

North – as well as escaped slaves from the South – were vulnerable to reenslavement. Taney's decision also meant that Congress had no power to prohibit slavery in the territories. It also potentially reduced the value of free land in the West and of the investments of northerners in the region.

"Any one of these convulsions would have sullied the Court's reputation," writes Christopher Eisgruber. "Together they were a disaster" (2009: 155). Between them they spread uneasiness among ordinary citizens in the North and alerted antislavery advocates to the danger of the "Slave Power" emerging outside its redoubts in the South. This takes us to the expansion of the antislavery persuasion from within the narrow precincts of the abolitionists into the wider political system.

Abolitionism was never more than a minority movement, derided for its utopianism and regarded as an irritant even in the North. Like sabbatarianism, anti-Masonism, and, ultimately, the women's suffrage movement, it had grown out of the Second Great Awakening, especially in the "Burnt-Over District" of northern New York and western New England (Cross 1950: 221–3). Its religious background gave the movement a stirring moral fervor, but it also made it anathema to northerners who had trade ties with the South and saw dangers in the extremism of these "utopians." The "immediatist" strand of the movement was led by firebrand William Lloyd Garrison, who had famously burned a copy of the Constitution because it abetted slavery.

Less disliked but more widely diffused were varied antislavery groups both within and outside the party system, most of which shied away from immediatism and cohered around the idea that slavery was regional while freedom was national and could, and ought to, be defended outside the South (Oakes 2012). As Corey Brooks details in his historical reconstruction (2016), many of these "political" antislavery groups came out of the short-lived Liberty Party and the more vigorous Free Soil Party (Brooks 2016; Foner 1995). But it was ultimately in the radical wing of the new Republican Party that they gained a purchase.

The differences between outsiders and insiders were highly visible and were frustrating to both. As the title "abolitionist" signifies, the outsiders called for an immediate and complete end of slavery, while political antislavery advocates focused on keeping slavery out of the West and the District of Columbia and on opposing slavery in Congress and the courts. If the South could be surrounded by restrictions and discouragements that would keep slavery from expanding, they reasoned, the institution would be strangled and eventually die out (Oakes 2012). This was why the Kansas-Nebraska Act was seen as a threat by even the most moderate of abolitionists.

Although there were sharp differences between outsiders like Garrison and insiders like Sumner and Thaddeus Stevens, as fear of Slave Power diffused these lines began to blur. There had always been personal ties between insider and outsider advocates against slavery (Milkis & Tichenor 2019: 42–3; Gienapp 1987: 78). In response to Douglas' bill, petitions were drawn up, protest meetings were held, and antislavery candidates became confident of success in local elections across the North. "In the struggle to prevent passage of Douglas' measure opponents welcomed support from whatever quarter and for whatever reason," writes Hans Trefousse (1969: 77).

Dissention from the Right

It was not only runaway slave legislation and territorial disputes that were shredding the party system. At the same time as the Kansas-Nebraska Act was roiling Congress, a new movement-party – the American Party – emerged in the northeast. This was a combination of a secret society that opponents called the "Know-Nothings"[8] – complete with secret oaths and rituals – and a party that grew out of that society (Anbinder 1992). In the South the new movement-party provided a temporary home for voters who disliked the proslavery Democrats, while in the North its election campaigns were aimed at immigrants and Catholics. By the end of 1855, the new party had elected 8 governors, more than 100 congressmen, the mayors of Boston, Philadelphia and Chicago, and thousands of other local officials.

What explains the rapid growth of the Know-Nothings? A partial answer is that, as immigration grew, there was widespread intolerance of immigrants and Catholics.[9] But the Know-Nothings were more than an ethno-nationalist movement. On the one hand they profited politically from the budding temperance crusade, which was partly an anti-immigrant movement but was also a product of religious conviction (Anbinder, pp. 42–3; Gusfield 1986; Szymanski 2003).[10] On the other hand, the party opposed the repeal of the Missouri Compromise and the passage of the Kansas-Nebraska Act, attracting antislavery advocates because many native-born citizens believed that Irish immigrants supported slavery (ibid., p. 43). The combination transformed the Know-Nothings from a small fraternal group to a national party, which – though fleeting – helped to dissolve the antebellum party system.

Republicanism as a Composite Coalition

These diverse currents converged in the formation of the Republican Party. The political acumen of the party's future leaders, the errors of their opponents, and

---

[8] The reason was that when activists in the secret society were asked about it, they would regularly say they "knew nothing" about it.

[9] By 1854, immigrants outnumbered native-born citizens in Chicago, Detroit, and Milwaukee. In Boston, Pittsburgh, Albany, Rochester, and Troy, more than a third of the inhabitants had come from abroad (Anbinder, p. 8). The vast majority were Catholics – mainly Irish – who were widely suspected of wanting to put the country under papal hegemony (ibid., pp. 9–10).

[10] In two states that held referenda on prohibition in the 1850s – Ohio and Pennsylvania – the Know-Nothings cooperated closely with the anti-alcohol movement (Gienapp, pp. 98–9) and gained much of their support in those states from temperance supporters.

the roiling of the political waters by the Know-Nothings were the most visible causes of Republican emergence (Sewell 1976: 260). The new party drew from the ranks of Democrats, Whigs, Free Soilers, and Know-Nothings, but the rise of the Republicans was more than a reshuffling of political elites: In its appearance there was a link to abolitionism that went beyond electoral advantage. As Gienapp writes, it was the Kansas-Nebraska Act that "weakened the Democratic Party throughout the North, disrupted the sectional balance within the parties, gave additional momentum to the ongoing process of party disintegration, and fundamentally altered the nature of the anti-Democratic opposition" (Gienapp 1987: 81).

From the outset, the new party was a composite coalition containing deep fissures on tactics and even on its strategy toward slavery. Although the moderates and conservatives who entered the party would have been happy with no more than the reinstatement of the Missouri Compromise, as Gienapp writes, "Advanced antislavery men wanted a platform that demanded the exclusion of slavery from all the territories, opposed the admission of any new slave states, and advocated the repeal of the fugitive slave law" (p. 91). In the run-up to the Civil War, these differences were papered over in the interest of furthering the new party's hopes of gaining power. The differences between radicals who had come to the party from the antislavery movement, moderates like Lincoln, and conservatives with strong market-oriented instincts were deep and would last through the war and destroy the party's unity during Reconstruction.

II   WAR MAKES STATES – AND MOVEMENTS

In his wide-ranging book on war and state building in Western Europe (1990), Charles Tilly had little to say about the United States, but Richard Bensel took up Tilly's aphorism and applied it to the American Civil War (1990). Taking the Tilly/Bensel thesis a step further, I will argue that war also affects contentious politics, spurs the creation of new movements, and *re*makes existing ones (Tarrow 2015). This was not the only place where war and social conflict brought about a challenge to slavery, but elsewhere, as Karp points out,

antislavery gains *followed* violent revolution and military conflict – struggles that often originated over issues far removed from the question of slavery itself. Only in the United States, from 1854 to 1865, did an explicitly antislavery political victory precede, produce, and in a critical fashion sustain an abolitionist military revolution. (Karp 2019: 141)

The Civil War not only defeated the seceded southern states and the socioeconomic system they stood for, but it also loosened the boundaries of behavior, turned resentments into violent conflicts, and gave existing movements the resources with which to make bolder claims. As Sidney Milkis and Daniel Tichenor argue in their *Rivalry and Reform*, "the quest to end slavery became a crucible that began to redefine the relationship between top-down and bottom-up politics" (2019: 42). The war raised the temperature of contentious politics within both North and West. The most extreme episode was the revival of the guerrilla war that had broken out during the Kansas-Nebraska dispute. In 1862, the Confederate army tried and failed to gain control of the state of Missouri. What followed was a running armed conflict between rebel guerrillas and the Union army. The guerrilla, writes Mark Neely, "constantly threatened to break down the customary distinction between soldiers and civilians" (Neely 1991: 47).

In the East there was a wave of antiwar protests, beginning in Baltimore before Lincoln took office, but increasing when he turned to conscription in 1863. The draft stirred up resistance especially among urban immigrants who couldn't understand why they should have to fight for southern slaves. The worst violence occurred in New York, where 105 people – most of them free blacks – were murdered in the July 1863 draft riot, but there were riots over conscription in Boston, Chicago, Newark, Albany, and Milwaukee. The provost marshals who were appointed to round up recruits were often the objects of resentment and violence. "Across the union," writes J. Mathew Gallman, "sixty local provost marshals were wounded performing their duties" (1994: 148).

The war also produced resistance within the political class. In Ohio, ex-Democratic Representative Clement Vallandigham was arrested for advocating in public that young men should refuse to serve in the army. Vallandigham was brought before a military commission and charged with publicly expressing sympathy for those in arms against the government of the United States and declaring disloyal sentiments and opinions with the object and purpose of weakening the power of the government in its efforts to suppress an unlawful rebellion (Stone 2004: 98–120). Vallandigham filed a petition for a writ of habeas corpus before Judge Humphrey H. Leavitt, who denied it in an opinion that read more like a speech defending the president than the attempt of a jurist to find the law (p. 103).

The most spectacular effect of the war on activism was the spur it gave to the abolitionists. As Lincoln began hostilities with his customary caution and pragmatism, abolitionists like Garrison and Wendell Phillips saw an opportunity to urge the public to see abolition as a necessary compliment to the military effort. Together with former-slave Frederick Douglass, in November 1861 they founded the Emancipation League to coordinate efforts to turn the war into a quest for emancipation (Milkis & Tichenor, pp. 56–7). Reasoning that only a mature public opinion would compel the president to free the slaves, they crisscrossed the North, giving speeches and holding rallies on behalf of abolition. "The New York *Tribune* estimated that during the winter and spring of 1861–2 more than five million people heard or read antislavery speeches of Phillips and other Emancipation League agitators. The White House was also beleaguered by a steady stream of antislavery petitions, letters, and delegations" (ibid., p. 56).

As the crisis deepened, the hand of the Radical Republicans was strengthened. "From the very beginning," writes Trefousse, "the radicals' influence on the new administration was great." Seward, the new Secretary of State, called for compromise with the Confederacy, but a majority of Lincoln's cabinet supported the radicals and they gained the chairmanships of the most important committees in the Senate. "Almost overnight," writes Trefousse, "they became the most determined advocates of relentless warfare, the most insistent proponents of unconditional surrender of the South" (1969, pp. 158–9, 169). Their hand was also strengthened by the activism of free African American communities in the North and by the need to strengthen the army in the South. The combination of antislavery pressure and military necessity put emancipation front and center on Lincoln's agenda.

Emancipation as a Fulcrum

Early in the war, the Radical Republicans used their now dominant position in Congress to advance the cause of freeing the southern slaves. Meeting often with Lincoln, radicals like Sumner "worked to force the president's hand amid the constant drumbeat of external abolitionist criticism" (Milkis & Tichenor, pp. 56–7). They were helped both by the weakness of the Democrats, whose ranks had been decimated by secession (Silbey 1977), and by divisions among moderate and conservative Republicans who hesitated to take a position that would risk defeat in a war that was still going badly.

But it was the army that set off a wave of informal emancipations by welcoming slaves who crossed the battle lines. In May 1861, when three escaped slaves crossed the James River to Fort Monroe, asking the fort's commander, Benjamin Butler, for their freedom, he decided to regard them as "contraband" and keep them safe in the fort. When a Confederate officer politely asked for their return, Butler replied, "I mean to take Virginia at her word. I am under no constitutional obligation to a foreign country, which Virginia now claims to be" (quoted in Goodheart 2011, p. 314). By the next week escaped slaves were appearing at the fort almost hourly; by the end of the year, this trickle became a torrent.

Concerned that he might lose the support of border states, which had remained in the Union despite the existence of slavery, Lincoln at first hesitated to formally declare emancipation. But the combination of military necessity, abolitionist agitation, and pressure from the radicals and his generals led the president to support it – at least in parts of the South that had not been liberated. "Lincoln did not cooperate directly with the Radical Republicans," write Milkis and Tichenor, "and he sometimes resisted their most zealous abolitionist tendencies." But they "grew adroit at framing emancipation as consistent with Lincoln's self-proclaimed duty to do whatever was necessary to preserve the union" (p. 59). By the end of 1862, the Republicans had united with the abolitionists in calling for emancipation. This process of coalition formation by accretion culminated in the Emancipation Proclamation in 1863 and in congressional passage of the Thirteenth Amendment, which freed all the slaves, in 1865.

War and Organization

The war not only shook up alliances and created incentives for Lincoln to adopt a mild version of the abolitionists' platform; it also created new forms of organization that linked the government to private efforts to achieve victory and free the slaves. The formation of an Emancipation League by experienced abolitionist leaders in 1862 was part of an organizational revolution that swept the North by combining private charity with governmental responsibilities and partisan motivations (Clemens 2020). "In New York City, the elite-dominated Union Defense Committee raised volunteer regiments, collected funds to support soldiers' wives and families, and eventually took charge of public funds to support their voluntary effort," notes Elisabeth Clemens (p. 50). It was "a fundamentally Whig project that would long outlive the Whig Party," harnessing social status and community organization to national purposes (p. 51).

The New Yorkers were not alone. In the course of the war, the United States Sanitary Commission organized medical relief and other services for soldiers and for freedmen after the war. In her work on Civil War voluntarism, Clemens shows how a country with an "anti-state" political culture managed, in a remarkably short time, to mobilize networks of volunteers offering "civic gifts" to soldiers, the wounded, the infirm, and ultimately to former slaves set adrift by emancipation (ibid., ch. 2).

Women, Wide-Awakes, and the Union Leagues

The participation of women was the most remarkable innovation in the army of volunteers who mobilized to assist the war effort and help the wounded. Eric Foner has calculated that some 200,000 women were mobilized by local societies throughout the North in the course of the war, raising money and gathering supplies. The experience of volunteer work during the war led many of these women into postwar activism, for example, in the Women's Christian Temperance Union (WCTU) (Clemens, p. 70) and in the struggle for women's suffrage (see Chapter 4).

Women abolitionists were among the first to mobilize in support of the war effort because they saw a parallel between the plight of the slaves and the denial of women's rights. Although they would later split from the movement on the issue of black suffrage, Elizabeth Cady Stanton and Susan B. Anthony both saw abolitionism as inextricably joined to women's suffrage. In response, they formed the Woman's National Loyal League in 1863 and launched a massive petition drive to support the war effort and pushed for a constitutional amendment abolishing slavery.

Other organizational efforts were less sedate. During the 1860 election campaign, the "Wide Awake" movement began to march through the streets of northern cities. Beginning in Hartford, Connecticut, more than a thousand Wide Awake companies – and perhaps 100,000 young men – were thought to have been organized during the campaign and were soon recognized as an important electoral bulwark for the Republicans. "While everything else about American politics seemed to be crumbling in 1860, the Wide-Awakes established a model for youth-oriented campaigns that would be copied by most parties, in most major elections, over the next few decades" (Grinspan 2016: 199; also see Karp 2019: 154).

Less dramatic but more lasting in their influence, beginning in 1862, patriotic clubs were formed across the North to support the war effort. After the Republicans suffered losses in the congressional elections of 1862, these clubs combined under a National Council of what would become the Union League. Activists adopted the trappings of a secret order, vaguely Masonic in ritual, suitable for mass agitation in support of the war. The Council sought participation from working-class northerners but was supported financially by upper-class Union League clubs in New York, Philadelphia, and Boston. "By 1864, the organization was potent enough to play a role in the reelection of President Lincoln" (Fitzgerald 1989: 10).

As the war moved south, Union League organizers followed the troops, attempting to mobilize a future black electorate to support the Republican Party. Offering victuals and literacy efforts alongside electoral support, Leaguers formed the core of a Republican Party machinery in a region where none had existed. With many of its leaders holding patronage posts in the federal government, it was a para-political, quasi-governmental political action group not unlike the partisan-led civil society groups that we see today (Milkis & York 2017) and gave a preview of the "government out of sight" that would grow up later in the century (Balogh 2009).

The war did not change everything in American politics, and, as we will see, there were serious "reactive sequences" that followed it both during and after Reconstruction. However, it produced an intersection of social movement and political party activism that – despite internal rivalries and conflicts – helped to turn a war that had begun to save the Union into a mass movement for democracy (Karp 2019). As Milkis and Tichenor conclude:

The confluence of direct action, inside lobbying, and prudential presidential leadership ultimately made it possible to accomplish what Garrison and other radical abolitionists had once thought impossible: a closing of the vast divide between the Declaration of Independence and the Constitution". (Milkis & Tichenor 2019: pp. 69–70)

III   AFTER THE REVOLUTION

If "war makes movements," the *ends* of wars both transform existing movements and open the space for new ones to develop. We know from the history of women's suffrage in both Europe and the United States that support for war-making can help existing movements to gain their demands (see Chapter 4). But the ends of wars can also *un*make movements or at least remove the source of their strength. This was the case for abolitionism and the Radical Republicans after the Civil War, but it also created incentives for a reactionary countermovement that sought to roll back the outcome of the war and return to a real or imagined past.

As for the abolitionists, no sooner was the war over than Garrison declared his long career over and retired from the American Anti-Slavery Society at its May 1865 meeting. At the same meeting, Douglass disagreed, arguing that "Slavery is not abolished until the black man has the ballot." Phillips took over as the Society's president and changed the motto on the masthead of the Society's newspaper to "No Reconstruction Without Negro Suffrage" (quoted in Foner 2014: 67). The Society sputtered on until 1870, when it closed its doors, but with its main goal apparently fulfilled, it became politically irrelevant after war's end.

The situation in the Republican Party was more complicated because that party was a composite institution. "If the war against slavery had united Republicans who otherwise differed, especially on fiscal matters," writes Brenda Wineapple, "those differences threatened to splinter the same party or cost them votes in the coming elections" (2019: 221–2). Particularly after political competition returned to the South, the coalition that had given Lincoln political leverage while he lived began to fragment.

Impeachment and Dissolution

If this fragmentation was not immediately apparent, it was because the Republicans were temporarily almost united in opposition to the new president, Andrew Johnson, whom they had foolishly made vice president on the mistaken apprehension that he was one of them. Johnson was popular with Republicans because he had supported the Union during the war and regarded supporters of the Confederacy as traitors.[11] But as president, he not only refused to countenance votes for the former slaves, but he also replaced administrators who had come south to support black rights with former Confederates, assaulted the legislative branch of government by ignoring the Tenure of Office Act, and fired Secretary of War Edward Stanton. When Stanton refused to leave his office and Johnson hinted that he might take military action by creating a new "Atlantic" Department of the Army, the Republicans decided that their only recourse was to impeach him. Johnson,

---

[11] As wartime governor of Tennessee, Johnson had attacked landowner-based politicians and supported the Union (Foner 2014: 176–7). He writes, "Long dissatisfied with their partly cooperative, partly antagonistic relationship with Lincoln, Radical Republicans initially viewed Johnson's accession as a godsend" (p. 177).

writes Wineapple, "'brought the party together' on the contentious issue of impeachment, of all things" (ibid., p. 259).

But the long and tortuous process of impeachment in the House and the Senate trial that followed exposed long-hidden cracks in the Republican coalition. For one thing, Chief Justice Salmon Chase, who presided over the trial, wanted to be president himself and gestured toward creating a new party, "sprung out of Republican ruins" (Wineapple, p. 347). For another, the Radical Republican who argued the impeachment case in the Senate was former General Ben Butler, who was cordially disliked by many of his colleagues. But most portentous for the future of the party, Senate conservatives saw in defeating impeachment the opportunity to crush the radicals and restore a laissez-faire government (Wineapple, p. 396). All of this took place in the context of the military occupation of the South, disputes over how and when to bring the southern states back into the Union, and the struggle over the passage of the Fourteenth and Fifteenth Amendments (Ackerman 1998).

Created by the newly strengthened Congress and widely associated with Republicanism, Reconstruction prescribed continued military occupation of the ex-Confederacy through the Command of the Army Act. This act was intended to combat the violence that was targeting the freed slaves, assure Republican political control of the region, and oppose Johnson's plans to reinstate white power. With sweeping determination and using techniques of "constitutional hardball" (Tushnet 2004), Congress pushed through the Reconstruction amendments, made citizens of former slaves, gave them the (theoretical) right to vote, and created the bare bones for a welfare system.

Even as it was creating new rights for African Americans, Congress expanded the reach of the central state, presaging the combination of the "Second Reconstruction" of the 1960s (Orren & Skowronek 2004; Vallely 2004). It was, in Orren and Skowronek's words, "the outstanding example in United States history of dismantling of an entrenched political order" (p. 114). But there was a major difference between the two: Authority over enfranchisement and all that followed from it was expressly given to Congress by the Thirteenth Amendment, curtailing "the states' hitherto undisputed jurisdiction over domestic relations. The Civil Rights Act of 1866, the reauthorization of the Freedman's Bureau, the Fourteenth Amendment, the Reconstruction Act, the Civil Rights Act of 1875 – all were a gloss on the original authorization" (ibid., p. 136). If implemented, this would have constituted an institutional revolution.

But there was a problem: Vesting so much power in a Congress that the Republicans controlled exposed, and exacerbated, the original divisions among radicals and conservatives in the party over giving the vote to the Freedmen, maintaining an occupying force in the South, and, ultimately, defending the constitutional rights the party had created in the thrill of victory. Once the unity of the Republicans broke open over the vote for African Americans, maintaining the occupation of the South, and economic issues like the tariff, congressional supremacy no longer translated into the power of the party.

America would remain a system of congressional governance until the rise of executive predominance in the following century.

Not only that: It was one thing to insist that, in order to reenter the Union, the southern states would need to extend the vote to black men; it was quite another to support black enfranchisement in the North, where fifteen state referenda on the issue had been soundly defeated (Bateman 2018: ch. 4). While radicals like Sumner and Stevens argued that black male suffrage followed logically from the victory of the Union, "moderates wanted to keep the suffrage a southern issue, something Republicans could legislate in the former rebel states while leaving the others alone" (Wineapple, p. 397). When Republicans looked at the electoral future of the South, the freed slaves were the only large voting bloc they could count on. Hence, the rights of the former slaves were crucial to the future of the party's control of national politics, but free blacks in the North were not.

In the course of the war, northern blacks had mobilized on behalf of black rights. In October 1864, they called a national convention in Syracuse, New York, to advance abolition, equality before the law, and the suffrage. Following a stirring address by Douglass, the convention created a National Equal Rights League to advance these goals. But in the South, the situation was completely different. The freed slaves had every motive to try to advance their rights, but in the disorganization and displacement that the war imposed on them, there were few resources with which to organize (but see Hahn 2003), that is, until the Republicans and the Union Leagues descended on the South, offering physical and organizational succor. Only by turning the formers slaves into an electoral clientele could the party hope to become a truly national one and prevent the recreation of plantation hegemony in the former Confederacy.

As long as the white power structure was suppressed, sponsoring a black electorate in the South was attractive to the Republicans. After all, Congress had banned ex-Confederate officers from serving in the Senate; the military was officiating over elections in the region; and the former slaves – especially those who had served in the Union army – were not lacking in resources (Hahn 2003). But with no indigenous antislavery movement to draw upon, the party was hard-pressed to build an organization in the region. Instead, it relied on newly created and transplanted networks and organizations to defend their gains and assure the party's future in the region.

These networks and organizations had three main sources. First, many black soldiers returning from the battlefield became activists and elected officials (Hahn 2003: ch. 5; Klinkner & Smith 2002: 64; Parker 2009: 29). Second, newly independent black churches served as foci for election rallies, and many of their ministers became political leaders (Foner 2014: 92–5). Third, black fraternal, benevolent, and mutual-aid societies began to spring up throughout the region. "In early Reconstruction," writes Foner, "blacks created literally thousands of such organizations. Often spawned in black churches, they quickly took on lives of their own. By the 1870s, over 200 such organizations existed in Memphis, 400 in Richmond, and countless others were scattered across the rural South" (2014, p. 95). For a while, it looked as if the Republicans would be able to create a class to represent in the South, but not for long.

A Movement/Countermovement Interaction

The most effective organizational networks created in the former Confederacy were those created by the Union League (Valelly 2004: 33). League agents had followed the troops as they moved southward, attempting to organize both freed slaves and poor whites, offering assistance as well as organizing skills to both groups. But they increasingly focused their energies on new black voters and eventually became the basis for a Republican electoral machine in the region. As Foner writes, "By the end of 1867, it seemed, virtually every black voter in the South had enrolled in the Union League or some equivalent local political organization" (2014: 283).

But this organizational revolution triggered the rise of white vigilantism, the most ferocious expression of which was the Ku Klux Klan. Founded in 1866 as a Tennessee social club, the Klan spread into nearly every southern state, "launching a 'reign of terror' against Republican leaders black and white" (Valelly, p. 342). The Klan was most active at night, especially during election campaigns, where it focused on blocking blacks from voting or preventing polling places from opening. By the end of 1867, the Union League was in disarray, its infrastructure destroyed by white violence and its activists either fleeing or dead (Fitzgerald 1989: 83–4). This was the beginning of a politics of private violence and state repression that culminated in the widespread lynching and the destruction of black rights after the army returned to the barracks.

Giving Up on Reconstruction

For a time, the new black electorate met the Republicans' expectations. By 1867, the Bureau of the Census reported that between 85 percent and 100 percent of adult black males in Florida, Georgia, Mississippi, the Carolinas, Alabama, Louisiana, Texas, and Virginia had registered to vote (Valelly 2004: 33). Almost all of them supported Republican candidates, many coming from among their own race (p. 77). But growing white resistance destroyed black voting power both in the state legislatures and in Congress. In 1876, there were 162 black state legislators and members of the House of Representatives; by 1878 this number had been cut in half and, by 1890, only a handful remained. By the turn of the century, Jim Crow was in full control.

Much of the work of reducing black voting rights was carried out by a combination of electoral chicanery, poll taxes, and literacy requirements (Valelly 2004: ch. 3); some of this was accomplished by outright intimidation and repression and some, eventually, by suborning black voters by bribery (see Chapter 3). But shifting alignments in national politics also played a key role. In one of the shadiest deals in American electoral history, following the disputed presidential election of 1876, a deal was struck between the two parties that allowed the Republican candidate, Rutherford B. Hayes, to enter the White House in exchange for agreeing to the end of Reconstruction. This began of a period of white southern ascendancy in the region and in Congress that would last through the New Deal and into the 1960s (Katznelson 2013).

In part as a consequence and in part as a result of the decline of the antislavery movement, the Republicans grew to rely ever more closely on their conservative support bases in the North and on farmers in the West. Once white intransigence had begun to whittle away black rights in the South and northern voters grew weary of the costs of Reconstruction, GOP leaders realized that they could hold onto power with a pro-business, pro-farmer coalition of northerners and westerners. As Valelly concludes, "The black-white, North-South coalition of 1867–1868 was supplanted by a new white-white North-West coalition. The enormous growth of the Republican Party in the late 1890s outside the South substituted for lost black voters at the margin" (2004, p. 135).

The Republicans' abandonment of southern black voters took on deeper importance given the future role of the Supreme Court in interpreting the Fourteenth Amendment in ways that left the former slaves in a position that was, in some ways, "worse than slavery" (Oshinsky 1996). The nadir, of course, came in the case of Plessy v. Ferguson (163 US 537), in which the Court held that whites and blacks could be kept apart by facilities that were "separate but equal." "Negro suffrage," wrote W. E. B. Du Bois, "ended a civil war by beginning a race feud" (Du Bois 2005: 52).[12]

CONCLUSIONS

None of this legacy negates the profoundly revolutionary implications of the Civil War crucible for American political development. That war liberated millions of people from the status of property and – in the form of the Reconstruction amendments – gave future generations the constitutional tools with which to establish their rights and those of other minorities (Ackerman 1998). Moreover, unlike the French Republicans, who used terror as well as "virtue" to hold onto power, the Republicans retained a commitment to constitutional forms and chose to operate through electoral competition. But the way Reconstruction was implemented and then abandoned as the antislavery impulse waned left the road open for the resurgent white power

---

[12] Du Bois' essay "Of the Dawn of Freedom" remains one of the most balanced analyses of the promise and the pitfalls of Reconstruction. First published in the *Atlantic Monthly* in March 1901, it appears as chapter 2 of *The Souls of Black Folk* (2005: 29–58).

structure to wipe away the gains that abolitionists and the Radical Republicans had fought for in the Civil War.

In introducing this chapter, I first argued that the antecedents of the Civil War were deeply important for the depth of the crisis that followed. These antecedents involved not only the breakdown of comity between elites, but the transposition of a once-marginal movement to the center of institutional politics, which together produced a mass democratic movement. That movement was a "formative movement," in Milkis and Tichenor's lexicon, one that combined external and internal components and a broad repertoire of contention, both institutional and extra-institution; that model would be adopted by future movements – particularly by the twentieth-century Civil Rights movement, as we will see in Chapter 5.

Second, I tried to show that when war broke out, outsider abolitionists gained new leverage through the Republican Party. Although the war was the result of long-brewing contention, it was also a source of *new* contention. In both North and South, new conflicts and new organizations arose, ranging from antiwar Democrats in the North to pro-Unionist groups in the South, from draft evaders in both regions to a guerrilla war on the frontier. Most important, the radicals in Congress gained supremacy within the Republican Party and in Congress, as Lincoln and the country moved toward a position that accorded greater importance to liberating the slaves than anyone had expected when war broke out. Mass politics "fused the fanfare of mid-nineteenth-century democracy and the fervor of antislavery commitment" (Karp 2019: 153).

Milkis and Tichenor summarize the complex and contradictory dynamic of this crucial period of American history in this way:

Radical movement activists kept abolitionism before the nation and ultimately played a critical part in reshaping public debate over slavery during the war. The confluence of direct action, insider lobbying, and prudential presidential leadership ultimately made it possible to accomplish what Garrison and other radical abolitionists had once thought impossible: a closing of the vast divide between the Declaration of Independence and the Constitution. (2019, pp. 69–70)

The legacy of this period was decidedly mixed, combining both path dependency and what James Mahoney called a "reactive sequence." Path dependency included most famously the freeing of several million individuals from bondage. With the support of the Union army and a civilian army of administrators, charitable organizations, and the Union League, the freed slaves broke through the cultural bounds of slavery and developed the infrastructure – churches, civic associations, electoral experience – that would take them through the worst days of Jim Crow and prepare the way for the Civil Rights movement that followed.

But path dependency also produced a model for the emergence of future political parties through the merger between politically oriented elites and a social movement. As I suggested at the outset of this chapter, the

Republican/antislavery merger around a program of political change created a model for movement/party consolidation in future periods of American history. Rather than parties and movements succeeding each other in neat sequences, movements coupled with emerging parties to create a foundation for campaigning on the basis of policy promises.

Like many other cases that we will examine, the Civil War created a "reactive sequence" that was less liberatory. Faced by an objective coalition between white southerners who were working to rebuild the world they had lost and Republicans who had shifted to a strategy of constructing capitalism in the North, newly liberated African Americans were cut adrift. As the Republican Party turned away from Reconstruction to the more profitable task of constructing a robust capitalist economy, both Radicals in Congress and abolitionists in the country divided and declined. Sectional partisan divisions remained in place until the end of the century, even as new cleavages between capital and labor were surging.

Triumphalist historiography has tended to see the sorry fate of African Americans in the South after Reconstruction as an exception to the triumph of liberal constitutionalism. For example, in *Lincoln at Gettysburg,* Garry Wills saw Lincoln's achievement as the creation of "a new Constitution." "He [Lincoln] altered the document from within," writes Wills, "by appeal from its letter to its spirit, subtly changing the recalcitrant stuff of that legal compromise, bringing it to its own indictment" (Wills 1992: 38). Maybe so. But with the end of Reconstruction and the disappearance of the Radical Republicans and their abolitionist allies, the rights that Lincoln and the Republicans added to the Constitution went into abeyance and would not be implemented until the next century through an alliance between a new formative movement and a different political party. But that, of course, is another story and one to which we will turn in a later chapter.

3

The Agrarian Revolt, Populism, and the Gilded Age Party System

Not all social movements bend the arc of history toward justice or advance the cause of democracy. But some, despite their failures, help to shift the bases of the party system, as the 1896 election did (Burnham 1970). In this chapter we will turn from an ultimately successful movement – abolitionism – to a more broadly based but unsuccessful movement of poor farmers. Using the tools of cooperation and other institutional tactics, the agrarian movement of the 1980s and 1990s tried but failed to find a purchase in the two-party system that had taken root between the Civil War and the end of the century. Failing to gain advantages from either of the major parties, the agrarians attempted to build their own party, the People's Party – or Populists – but were tripped up when they attempted to merge with the Democrats in the dramatic but ill-starred presidential campaign of 1896.

This chapter tells that story but it also tells three others:

First, it describes how hard it was to form a multiclass, biracial coalition in the conditions of late nineteenth-century America, especially in the South, which was one of the bedrocks of populist fervor;

Second, it shows how the absence of twentieth-century organizational tools impeded the movement's effort to shift from local cooperative organizing to statewide and national political mobilization; and

Third, it shows how hard it was to insert an ideological movement into a transactional party system like the American one without either compromising its beliefs or merging with one of the two mainstream parties.

All of this came to a head at the Democratic Party national convention in summer 1896, when William Jennings Bryan, at the time a little-known Nebraska congressman, made a speech advancing the free coinage of silver, in which he famously accused the Republican Party of wanting to "crucify mankind upon a cross of gold."[1] To embody the metaphor, when he finished speaking, he extended his arms straight out from his body and held that pose for about five seconds as if offering himself as a sacrifice for the cause of free coinage of silver (Bensel 2008). As he left the podium, the audience burst into pandemonium and then raised him to their shoulders and carried him around the hall in triumph while the gold faction of the party quietly filed out. The next day, Bryan was nominated as the party's candidate in the 1896 presidential election.

Drawing on years of soft-money thinking, Bryan argued that putting the currency on a silver basis would offer relief to debt-laden farmers in the South and West. He adopted part of his platform from the People's Party and was even accused of being a Populist by his conservative opponents (Cantrell 2020: 28). But Bryan was never a Populist, and in fact, he refused to run with a Populist-nominated vice-presidential candidate. Bolstered by both Democratic and Populist voters, he swept much of the South and West, but the Populists, with their dispersed agrarian following and their lack of a national organization, failed to win a single state. Bryan went on to run two more times on a platform with a call for free coinage of silver, but he lost both elections. But the 1896 election marked the collapse of the People's Party and of the agrarians as a national movement.

The People's Party arose out of a Texas agrarian movement that was a response to farmers' late-nineteenth-century economic distress, before it spread like a tidal wave across the South, the Midwest, and the West (Goodwyn 1976: ch. 1). The Populists ran on a broad platform of reform, ranging from not allowing foreigners to purchase American farmland to the creation of cooperative, government-subsidized subtreasuries to free silver. Although there was hesitation from many farmers about the subtreasury idea, and keeping foreigners from buying farmland was a no-brainer, free silver was a program that had a long history among peripheral farmers and could gain support in many parts of the country where credit was scarce.

It would occupy an entire chapter to explain how "free coinage of silver" became the linchpin of a major presidential campaign. Suffice it to say that it arose in reaction to the federal government's shift back to the gold standard in the 1870s after printing paper money – "greenbacks" – during the Civil War. The move led first to the formation of the Greenback Labor Party before being taken up by every agrarian movement in its wake. The call for what opponents called "fiat money" took on renewed steam in the wake of the depression that followed the Panic of 1893, but it condensed into the more popular call for silver after President Grover Cleveland pushed for the revocation of the Sherman Silver Purchase Law. For obvious reasons, the call for "free silver"

---

[1] The text of Bryan's speech, which has been described as "the most famous speech in the history of American politics," can be found at http://historymatters.gmu.edu.

also appealed to silver mining states in the mountain West, like Colorado and Nevada.

The 1896 election has sometimes been called a "critical election," a term that was coined by V. O. Key (1955) and added to by E. E. Schattschneider (1960). It was used to describe elections that produce a major realignment of the party system.[2] But why would 1896 be counted as "critical" when the victor was a conservative Republican from a party that supported the gold standard, and the candidate who put forward the "radical" platform of free silver lost the election? Schattschneider offered two justifications: first, because of the tremendous reaction of conservatives in both parties to the advent of the Populists; second, because of Bryan's negotiation of a fusion with that party and his nomination on what seemed to many to be a radical platform (1960: 78–80).

Something important *was* stirring in American politics, but we will need to look beyond electoral politics at a social movement to grasp it. The People's Party, on which Bryan's margins depended in a number of states, had come out of virtually nowhere in the early 1890s, electing legislators "from counties both rich and poor, urban and rural, agricultural and lumber." Elisabeth Clemens points out that "in 1890 and 1892, populist governors, congressmen, and state representatives were elected in a number of states, and the organization enjoyed growing membership" (Clemens 1997: 157). If we follow the conclusions of scholars from Lawrence Goodwyn (1976), to Michael Schwartz (1976), to Elizabeth Sanders (1999), and, more recently, to Charles Postel (2007) and Gregg Cantrell (2020), we will see that what was "critical" in 1896 was not McKinley's win and Bryan's loss, but what lay *behind* the rise of the Populists: the growth of a vast farmers' movement coming from the country's rural periphery with a program that combined both traditional and reformist claims (Jager 2020).

To summarize what will be laid out in greater detail in this chapter, the Populists arose at a moment when the party system was still organized around its post–Civil War sectional bases while the country was shifting to a nationalized industrial/financial structure. Their inability to gain purchase in the party system was, in part, a result of the strategic error of tying their chariot to the Democrats' star, in part the result of the sectional bases of party loyalty, but, most important, it was the result of the failure to mediate effectively between its movement and its partisan identities. The Populists were both a movement and a party, but unlike the Republican/antislavery movement combination of the 1850s and 1860s, they came on the scene in the absence of a crisis like the one that had fused antislavery with the Republicans' partisan ambitions.

---

[2] The theory was elaborated by Walter Dean Burnham in his landmark book, *Critical Elections and the Mainsprings of American Politics* (1970), for American electoral history. Burnham's expansion of the concept into a virtual law of American political realignment was roundly criticized, for example, by David Mayhew, who devoted an entire book to its demolition (2002).

In Section I, I will sketch the broad lines of the economic crisis that spread across the country's rural periphery during the Gilded Age. In Section II, I will describe how the agrarian movement arose in the South and West with a strategy of local cooperation and geographic diffusion. In Section III, I will explain why the movement's goals led it into politics, where its organization would be inadequate to the task of competing with the two main parties. Section IV describes the movement's complex relations with two critical allies as it moved toward politics: the Knights of Labor (KOL), a union movement that peaked around the same time; and African American voters, who had emerged from Reconstruction still loyal to "the Party of Lincoln." Section V returns to the collapse of Populism. In the conclusions, I will turn to the mixed heritage of agrarianism and populism for the future of American political development.

I   THE AGRARIAN PERIPHERY IN THE GILDED AGE

In the late 1880s, as the nation passed its constitutional anniversary, southern and western farmers faced three orders of problems: the growing and largely unchecked power of corporations; the problem of getting their crops to market without turning over their profits to middlemen and railroads; and the underlying problem of debt that arose from a long agricultural depression, from the demonetization of silver and the retirement of paper money, and from the scourge of the crop-lien system. Among them, these three problems led to a widespread and nearly simultaneous effort of farmers' groups to organize, especially in the West and South.

The Corporations and the Railroads

As the country entered the "Gilded Age," the informal power of corporations began to infiltrate and counter the institutional power of political parties through their ability to secure legislation conducive to their interests. This was especially true of banks, which had gained a central place in economic governance during the Civil War (Bensel 1990) and of the railroads. What historians have remembered as "the Gilded Age" was consolidated as northern bankers and industrialists expanded their power into what Goodwyn characterized as "the first great gathering of American wealth, of the consolidation of new forms of power, and of experiments in ostentatious consumption" (pp. ix–x).

For poor farmers, whose need for getting their crops to market and to the ports of the north and east made them wholly dependent on freight rates, the railroads were the most visible symbols of corporate power. Americans' rush to settle the West had led to favorable legislation and enormous subsidies to the railroad companies, which used the government's power of eminent domain to gain control of broad rights-of-way and owned many of the warehouses where farmers stored their crops. On top of this, for each mile of track built, the railroads were granted 12,800 acres of public land, along with any coal or iron they contained, eventually totaling some 113 million acres (Cantrell 2020:120). Farmers were the major victims of this growing corporate empire.

The companies charged more for short hauls than long ones, and their rates remained high even as farm prices continued to decline (Cantrell 2020: 121). Farmers whose products – like wheat and cotton – were involved in international commerce were uniquely dependent on the railroads and could be ruined by even a small increase in freight rates. The companies' rapid reach across the country and their competition for lines led to a wave of mergers that gave individual companies monopoly power over particular areas of the West. Particularly powerful in the Southwest was the Gould trust, which, by 1879, controlled more than 10,000 miles of track (Borneman 2014).

The Crop-Lien System

The farmers' problems arose not only from the monopolies and the railroads. Since the 1870s, farmers had suffered from declining farm prices, indebtedness to banks and local provisioning merchants, and from the government's move to the gold standard after retiring the greenbacks that had been printed during the war years. The first problem was largely due to the fall of global commodity prices; the second, to the power of the eastern financial interests who had bought up great amounts of paper money at a discount and wanted it to be redeemed in gold-backed currency at face value (Goodwyn 1976: 11–12); and the third was the crop-lien system, which became "for millions of farmers, white and black, little more than a modified form of slavery" (ibid., pp. 25–31; Schwartz 1976: 36–9).

That system arose out of the economic devastation of the war when the rural states of the ex-Confederacy had little capital and few banks that could provide it (Goodwyn, p. 27). Capital-starved farmers were obliged to purchase the commodities they needed from "furnishing merchants," who supplied them on credit at high rates of interest and imposed a "two-price system" – one for cash customers and a second and higher one for customers who depended on credit (ibid.). It followed that more and more farmers lost their land to their furnishing merchant, who gradually acquired title to steadily increasing portions of the country's land, turning more and more farmers into tenants.

Although midwestern farmers had not fallen as far as desperate southern tenants and sharecroppers, in that region as well the proportion of tenant farmers grew rapidly during the 1880s and 1890s. Although there were far more banks in the Midwest, and they were better capitalized than in the South, "significant structural constraints limited the supply of funds available for loans, thus keeping short-term interest rates high in the Midwest" (Ostler 1993: 19, 22). It was thus no accident that the rise of the agrarian movement corresponded roughly to the territorial extent of the crop-lien system, to mortgages on land, and to tenantry (Schwartz 1976: ch. 3).

But although farmers in the two main agricultural regions shared subjection to these problems, they were divided on politics, race, radicalism, and commodity issues. While midwestern farmers were mainly Republican, southern farmers were largely Democrats; while the Northern Alliance favored the production of butter, southerners sold cottonseed oil. And northern farmers developed stronger state organizations and were less likely to back new national regulations, a difference that would be crucial when the southern agrarians proposed their "subtreasury plan" that would depend on subsidies from the federal government.

The power of corporations, the iron grip of the railroads, and the crop-lien and credit scarcity situation were common to many areas of the country. But as Elizabeth Sanders shows in her elaborate statistical analysis, peripheral farmers faced all of these pressures at once. They were

more bound to the fate of a single crop (whose price was set in a world market);

more distant from crop marketing, storage, and distribution centers;

more likely to be dependent on a single rail line and monopolistic or oligopolistic purchasers;

more starved for credit in the long months between planting and harvest; and

more vulnerable to drought and, especially in the warm and humid South, to insect damage (1999: 29).

"These were the conditions," concludes Sanders, "that predisposed periphery farmers to define their interests as antithetical to those of large industrialists, bankers, and railroads and to look to the national state for solutions to their difficulties" (ibid.). Those solutions turned on cooperation.

II COOPERATION, DIFFUSION, AND SCALE SHIFT

Insurgency began in the peripheral farming areas mainly in the form of cooperative ventures, which first arose in the Southwest. As Cantrell writes of Texas populists, "The proper response to the newfound power of corporations was for the people to exercise a countervailing power" (Cantrell, p. 15). But how could this revolt be knitted together? Farmers were divided by region, by the different demands of the crops they grew, by race, religion, and the habits of party identification. Party identification divided the North and Midwest, which had been dominated by Republicans since the Civil War, from the South, with its stubborn loyalty to the Democrats – "the party of the fathers."

A first wave of collective action was reflected in the Granger movement, which was built on the ritualized traditions of the Masons and other fraternal groups and offered the advantages of socialization among isolated farm families as well as a template for organizing collective action (Hild 2007: ch.1). Adopting a version of the British Rochdale system, the Grangers tried to offer farmers the means to cooperate. However, when their cooperative methods failed, a second wave of organizers whose epicenter was in the Texas Farmers' Alliance worked to build a cooperative commonwealth through the creation of cooperatives of consumption, marketing, and storage.

There was ritual in the Alliances too, and a great deal of socializing, but it was economic cooperation that gave the new movement its impetus – even among the farmers of the Midwest. In that region, writes Ostler, "By bidding farewell to their old party [i.e., the Republicans], Populists were not merely joining another party but were participating in a new kind of political movement, one of 'democratic promise'" (p. 130).

Cooperation had the potential to solve a number of problems. It could free the indebted farmer from the yoke of the furnishing merchant, provide a way to collectively store and market cotton, help control the prices of consumption goods by competing with private sources of supply, and bring dispersed and independent farmers together around their common interests. It was no wonder that the idea of cooperatives spread rapidly, first across the South and then into the upper Mississippi valley and into the West (Ostler, p. 94).

Lecturers as Agents of Diffusion

The Texas Farmers' Alliances were built around an ingenious network of local and state-level lecturers who spread the idea of cooperation first to neighboring Louisiana and then further afield through a capillary process of diffusion. It was not only the idea of cooperation that was spread by Alliance lecturers; traveling through desperately poor communities; they became – willy-nilly – agents of socialization and radicalization. "Slowly, one by one – and in many instances unknown as yet to each other – local Alliance lecturers came to form a nucleus of radicalism inside the Texas Alliance" (Goodwyn, p. 74).

This capillary model of diffusion expanded far beyond the borders of Texas. A Southern Alliance lecturer brought the message to Kansas in 1888 by explaining the advantages of cooperative purchasing and selling. "This was a sermon to the converted," writes Ostler (p. 96). As Goodwyn writes, "Six lecturers were initially dispatched to Mississippi, six to Alabama, seven to Tennessee, five to the border state of Missouri, and three to Arkansas. Others moved into the Carolinas, Georgia, Florida, Kentucky, and Kansas" (p.91).

Because poor farmers in the South and Midwest suffered from many of the same problems, the results of this diffusion were spectacular. Under the leadership of Charles Macune, a gifted young organizer (ibid., pp. 83–6), Alliances spread through word of mouth and through the evangelism of the traveling lecturers (ibid., pp. 94–102). Even more encouraging was the Alliance's merger with the Arkansas Agricultural Wheel, which had already spread into Tennessee and Missouri. "The Wheel," observes Goodwyn, "provided numbers, certainly; it also provided a political militancy beyond Macune's" (p. 148; also see Schwartz 1976: 95–9).

At first, the Alliance's cooperatives aimed only to escape the hold of the furnishing merchants, but they soon expanded to cooperative marketing, which allowed farmers to sell their cotton in bulk and wait for prices to increase before putting it on the market. Both forms of cooperation triggered the ire of local merchants and bankers, who did what they could to undermine their efforts. Faced by competition from Alliance stores, merchants began to cut prices to undersell the Alliance's coops, and banks would refuse to take the notes of the Alliance exchanges because their business clients wanted them to go under. "Cooperatives," writes Goodwyn, "encountered trouble because of the implacable hostility of the financial and commercial world" (p. 112).

But rather than responding to these pressures by retreating on cooperation, the Texas Alliance moved in the opposite direction. Under Macune's leadership, the Alliancemen proposed a bold solution, "the creation of a statewide Alliance Exchange that would collectively market Texas Alliance members' crops, purchase supplies in bulk direct from manufacturers, and perhaps most important, offer low-interest credit to farmers who would use their collectively pledged crops as collateral cooperation" (Cantrell, p. 48).

But although the statewide exchange plan was theoretically plausible, it never attracted sufficient dues to get off the ground, "even as the Exchange had authorized loans of $200,000 and had begun to sell equipment and supplies on credit" (ibid., p. 49). The Democrats, an antediluvian but powerful party in the state and hand-in-glove with the financial interests, were hostile. By September 1888, the Texas Exchange had gone bankrupt (ibid., p. 50). In the wake of this failure, Southern Alliancemen developed a broad new proposal to use the government as the instrument to protect their interests.

From Cooperation to Politics

It was not to *replace* cooperation with government that the Southern Alliance entered politics but to *extend* it by bringing about federal intervention in a way that would expand the currency and the public financial system as a whole. The instrument designed to enlist the national state on the side of the farmers was a scheme called "the subtreasury plan." Proposed by Macune in 1889, the plan "proposed that the federal government would build warehousing and elevator facilities for nonperishable crops like cotton and tobacco throughout the nation's farming regions" (Cantrell, p. 129). These warehouses would store farmers' crops at harvest time, extending loans to those who needed them for up to 80 percent of the value of their property at very low interest.

Macune's plan was designed at one and the same time to address the long-standing problem of credit, raise farm prices, and free farmers from the yoke of the furnishing merchant and the middleman. And because the loans would be payable in paper currency, it would "effectively take the nation off the gold standard, reversing the deflationary contraction of the currency and making the country's money supply more flexible and adapted to a modern economy" (ibid, pp. 129–130).

This was an ingenious and far-reaching proposal but it had three major flaws. First, it raised the hackles of both the cotton middlemen and the banks, which – in the late nineteenth century – controlled the currency. Second, it threatened the gold standard, which was supported by both major parties and, of course, by Wall Street. And third, it hadn't a prayer of gaining the support of the Democrats who controlled Macune's home state, who were hand-in-glove with the banks and the railroads.

Not all of the Alliancemen were equally enthusiastic about the subtreasury plan. For one thing, although periods of storage in state-run warehouses could work for crops like cotton or tobacco, it would be ruinous for producers of fruits and vegetables. "During a visit to Kansas in March 1891," writes Ostler, "Macune was alarmed to hear alliance members saying that his plan was a 'very good thing for the cotton and tobacco growers in the south, but it would not work so well in the wheat growing districts'" (Ostler, p. 105).

Moreover, the subtreasuries would need to be publicly run, funded by the federal government, and controlled by Congress. To accomplish that, the Alliance would either have to gain the support of one of the two major parties or go into politics themselves. Because the scheme smacked of state control during an era in which laissez-faire capitalism was in its heyday, neither party would offer its support. Particularly in conservative districts, there was deep suspicion of government intervention.

As a result of the failure of the subtreasury idea, the Alliancemen ended up choosing the second route – the formation of a third party – an idea that had been gaining support from insurgent groups since the 1870s but that had repeatedly failed since the creation of the Republican Party in the 1850s. In doing so, they faced the difficult task of moving into national politics, where they lacked the experience or the resources to deal with a party system that relied heavily on patronage. As Elisabeth Clemens wrote, the organizational tools needed to effectively organize either as a lobby or as a party were not yet available to a widely dispersed and poorly financed population group like farmers (Clemens 1997). These problems were heightened by the nature of the American party system during the Gilded Age. Let us turn to that system now.

III   THE POST-BELLUM PARTY SYSTEM

From 1838 to 1893, writes Joel Silbey, "political parties all but dominate the political nation. After 1838, the distinguishing elements of that particular nation gave way to ... regularized impersonal institutions of political activity, the political parties" (Silbey 1991: 2). Of course, this does not mean that Americans lived, ate, and slept party; in fact, there is evidence that there were "important elements of public life in American political communities that the political parties could not and did not reach," such as town meetings, some local elections, and religious, benevolent, and reform activities. But the two major parties, as Glenn Altschuler and Stuart Blumin agree, "quickly assumed the organization of what virtually everyone in the nineteenth century referred to when they used the term 'politics'" (Altschuler & Blumin 2000: 6).

After the Civil War, the parties became major structuring institutions of American public life. They nominated and ran candidates for office; they distributed patronage to reward these candidates' supporters; and they enacted policies in the state legislatures and in Congress – often in response to the pressures of special interests. America may not have been a party democracy like those that were developing in Europe in the nineteenth century, but it was a republic *by* party.

In many communities parties were at the core of local elite networks. In their studies, Altschuler and Blumin found that "in each town or city, small or large, high-level political activists were, as a group, the most likely to appear on the boards of benevolent and reform societies, churches, clubs, lodges, local companies, and whatever else was offered by the many voluntary organizations of post–Civil War America to men with a desire to join or lead" (p. 238). Parties were also the heirs and defenders of sectional loyalties. Although the bipolar structure of the party system went back to the early part of the century, it was the Civil War, and memories of that war's divisions, that soldered party identifications into enduring regional cultures. In the South, writes Goodwyn, "the Southern Democratic Party responded to the needs of 'New South' entrepreneurs – even as the farmers who had fought in the Confederate Army continued to provide their dazed allegiance" (p. 8).

There was greater interparty competition in the North and Middle West but even there the scars left by the war lay just beneath the surface. As Goodwyn noted, "party professionals, more interested in election results than in theories, found the politics of sectionalism – 'waving the bloody shirt,' in the contemporary expression – to be far more persuasive to voters than defending black rights" (Goodwyn, p. 7). As he concluded, "The politics of sectionalism contained a reserve of partisan firepower that could be used against any candidate or any party attempting, through an innovative appeal to 'issues,' to rearrange the nation's basic postwar alignment" (ibid., p. 9).

The West was different because most of the states in that region were young, and party machines had not become established there (see Chapter 4). The result was greater volatility and more competitive elections in that region than in the other two. This left space for grassroots movements to arise, but it also made it difficult for them to harness the population groups – like farmers – across regional lines into a national party (ibid., p. 9).

There was a paradox in the agrarians calling for state intervention through the subtreasury plan. Such a scheme assumed the existence of a national state with the wherewithal and the interest to intervene forcefully in local economic activity. In the absence of such a state, farmers would either have to organize as lobbies that would be strong enough to counter the power of the special interests or they would need to organize through a third party. There were problems with both alternatives. The problem with the lobbying strategy was that legislators were often in the pocket of special interests with far greater resources than farmers could muster; the problem with the third-party strategy was that sectional loyalties to the Democrats in the South and to the Republicans in the North and West ran too deep to be dislodged by a new party lacking deep roots in the political class.

Partisan Competitiveness and Third-Party Emergence

Although farmers across the South and the Midwest suffered from the power of the corporations, from the deflation of the currency, and from the weight of their mortgages, their organizations could only translate into political strength in some parts of the country. We can see the results in the election of 1892, when the Populists ran their own tickets. The results were dramatically different across the regions in which the movement had arisen. In the South, where the Alliance was strong, the only state in which the People's Party gained more than 30 percent of the vote was Alabama; nowhere else did the Populists gain as much as 20 percent. The heartland of Populist voting strength was in the Plains and mountain states, where the party gained more than 40 percent of the vote but "failed entirely to achieve meaningful levels of support east of the Missouri River" (Ostler, p. 2 and map 1–1 on p. 3).

What explains this difference in states that suffered from roughly similar agricultural crises? Jeffrey Ostler, who has done some of the most detailed demographic and electoral analysis of the agrarian movement and its political offshoots, carried out a carefully paired comparison of Nebraska and Kansas, where the new party surged in the 1992 elections, and Iowa, where it was largely stillborn. What is curious about this comparison is that in all three states, the Alliances were strong, with 2,630 suballiances in Kansas; 1,849 in Nebraska; and 1,835 in Iowa (ibid., Appendix A).

The explanation, in Ostler's view, was not the degree of farmers' hardship or of their organization but the varying degree of competitiveness of these states' party systems. In competitive Iowa, "where the Democratic Party had become a genuine threat to the Republicans in the 1880s, a competitive party system was responsive to Alliance demands" (ibid., p. 10). In Kansas and Nebraska, in contrast, where the Republican hold on the electorate remained firm, the situation was different (ibid.). As Ostler concludes, "State political environments were crucial in determining whether agrarian radicalism took a third party turn" (ibid.).

If these state-level variations made it possible to gain political strength in some states, but not in others, the farmers' locally based cooperative network could only with difficulty reach into national politics. When Alliance leaders tried to mobilize support in Congress for the subtreasury bill, they tried to use their cooperative network to circulate "copies of the bills and sample petitions to the suballiances, along with instructions for signing the petitions at local meetings and returning them to national headquarters for distribution to congressmen" (McMath 1975: 93). This way of operating was poorly adapted to convincing Congress of the wisdom of their proposal.

The logical implication of the successful diffusion of local cooperation across state lines was to go into politics. But success also meant forming coalitions beyond the range of poor white farmers who were at the core of the Alliance. Two groups in particular – workers and African Americans – were logical targets for such alliances. However, each one posed particular problems to Alliance leaders: the first, the problem of dealing with a workers' organization that was past its peak, the KOL, and the second having to navigate the treacherous shoals of racism.

IV   CLASS, RACE, AND POPULISM

One of the greatest costs of the sectional structuration of the post-bellum party system was that it left little space for bringing together the two most populous groups in American society – farmers and workers – across regional lines. Though northern and midwestern farmers were largely Republican, the South was governed by a "Democratic planter-industrial axis" that controlled much of the vote of southern small farmers and tenants. Southern elites also suppressed the vote of African Americans wherever they could not be bought or corrupted, and without them, a farmer-labor coalition in that region could never be constructed.

Class and Populism

Of course, neither farmers nor workers were socially or economically cohesive groups. As Matthew Hild writes, "The most common types of industrial workers in the early New South included coal miners, lumber and sawmill workers, textile mill workers ... and railroad workers" (p. 6). Among farmers, the divisions were even wider, ranging from planters, whose holdings varied from a few hundred to several thousand acres, to small landowning farmers who worked between 100 and 200 acres, to renters, tenants, sharecroppers, and farm workers (ibid., p. 5). When race is added to these divisions, it becomes clear that constructing a unified farmer-labor coalition would have been virtually difficult to imagine.

Drawing on Sanders' well-documented work (1999), there was evidence that a farmer-labor coalition was not impossible.

> First, many industrial workers were only a half generation or less away from the countryside, and many still had ties to the farm, "either having tilled the soil themselves or having relatives who did. Those ties, in certain parts of the South at least, would facilitate farmer-labor coalitions" (Hild, p. 6).

Moreover, farmers and workers had a common enemy in the railroads. Though many worked for the rail companies or in the mines that were owned by some of these companies, the great railroad trusts were deeply resented from both sides. As Sanders notes, "It was the railroads that occasioned the first national uprising of labor as well as the earliest confrontations between workers and the state" (p. 34). A major farmer/worker alliance was attempted during the great southwestern rail strike against the Gould rail empire in 1885–86. Not only did these strikes lead to tremendous growth in the membership of the Knights, but "they also laid the groundwork for farmer-labor unity in fighting a common enemy" (Hild, p. 69).

Second, the ideology of the KOL overlapped considerably with that of the farmers' movement. Both regarded themselves as "producers,"[3] both had ideas that were closer to classical republicanism than to modern socialism, and both despised the power of those who produced nothing – purchasing agents, middlemen, bankers, and industrialists. When the Farmers' Alliance came to the assistance of the railroad men in the southwestern rail strike, it was in the name of their common identity as producers (Ostler, p. 107). The producer ethic was the foundation of an entire panoply of populist ideas. As Anton Jäger writes, "Populists now thought seriously about the state and progress and reflected on the American republican heritage. Like good republicans, they were suspicious of standing armies, celebrated agrarian laws, and opposed monopolistic land tenure" (2020: 13).

Third, the encounter between farmers and workers had a history to build on – and it had begun in politics! In the 1870s, the Greenback Labor Party "presaged both the Knights of Labor and the Populists in attempting to bridge the farmer-labor chasm and in its platform and, to a lesser degree, leadership" (Hild, p. 11). The GLP showed that farmer-labor third-party politics had genuine potential in certain parts of the South, especially in Alabama and Texas, two states where the Populists would attract significant support from both farmers and laborers a decade later.

Finally, as the KOL began to recruit more and more members in heavily rural counties of the South, its programs shifted to a greater emphasis on rural issues (Sanders 1999). For example, in 1886, the Knight's Legislative Committee came up with a list of bills they wanted to press on Congress, many of which were designed to appeal to rural workers (ibid., p. 46). Conversely, many of the planks in the Knights' platform reappeared in the demands passed by the Texas Farmers' Alliance. Their demands would also factor in the platform of the future Populist Party (Hild, p. 47).

---

[3] See Jäger 2020, for the elemental political theory that underlay the concept of "producerism" for Populist thinkers.

These farmer-labor interactions soon took the form of third-party or independent political organizing (ibid., pp. 86–7).

But there were clouds on the horizon. First, these steps toward political coalition with the Knights caused a serious rift in the ranks of the Texas Alliance. From the beginning, there had been a strong antiparty strain in the Alliances, especially among those, like Macune, who believed the formation of a third party was antithetical to the goal of creating a cooperative commonwealth. In the months following the Clebourne convention, the organization nearly split over its relations with the Knights, forcing President Andrew Dunlap, who opposed all third-party activity, to resign over the issue (ibid.). Conversely, the Knights were cool to Macune's subtreasury proposal, going along with it for the sake of comity but unwilling to have their Washington office lobby on its behalf.

There was also a serious disjunction between the growth cycles of the two organizations. Though the second half of the 1880s was a period of growth for the Alliance, the failure of the strikes against the Gould empire marked a downward turn in the Knights' membership. In the ruins of the campaign, 80 percent of the strikers were left without a job and "very little was left of the KOL on the southwestern railroads" (Sanders, 1999: 49). In reaction to its failure, Knights General Secretary Terence Powderly insisted on a "no strike" policy, which "did untold damage to the KOL's standing among workers" (ibid., p. 50).

Then, of course, there was growing competition between the Knights and the newly formed American Federation of Labor (AFL), which was led by conservative unionist Samuel Gompers. Gompers' nonpolitical strategy was bolstered by his observation of the failures of the "political" adventures of the Knights, his insistence on organizing higher-skilled craft workers in place of the Knights' "industrial" strategy, and his relatively friendly relations with the Republicans. These choices redounded to the growth of the AFL and to the sinking fortunes of the Knights. By 1890, KOL membership had dropped from more than 700,000 in 1886 to about 100,000 (Sanders, ibid.). It was ironic that just as the Farmers' Alliance was gaining membership and diffusing from its Texas base into the South and across the Plains states, its closest partner was becoming both more rural and weakening.

Race and Populism

We saw in Chapter 2 that, following emancipation, black southerners had formed a network of self-help, religious, and political organizations. By the 1880s, thousands of African American farmers had formed agricultural mutual aid societies, very much like what their white neighbors were doing (Ali 2010). And although they were closest to the Republican Party, most of these activists steered clear of politics until their debts grew as the prices of the commodities they produced collapsed. The same economic currents that led white agrarians to turn to politics had a similar effect for their black neighbors.

In their 1992 election campaign, the Populists made a determined effort to appeal to black voters, who had not yet been formally disenfranchised by the state legislatures, as they would be around the turn of the century. Populist leaders were sincere in their desire to represent black as well as white economic interests, but the party did have a race problem. Cantrell, writing of the Texas Populists, puts the dilemma precisely:

White Populists who held relatively enlightened views on race, or who simply recognized the political reality that electoral success required cooperation across racial lines, faced a fundamental problem. They had to fashion policies that would genuinely appeal to African American voters, but they had to do so in ways that would not alienate large swaths of the white electorate (Cantrell, p. 185).

Although the Farmers' Alliance "operated in segregated farmer institutions," writes Sanders, "the political movement that grew out of it required broad collaboration across racial and occupational lines" (p. 128). And while the party's leaders carefully skirted around the issue of racial equality, the settled racism of post-bellum southern society left them open to charge from the Democrats that the new party was attempting to bring back the "horrors" of Reconstruction.

African American voters could have been a sizable electoral force in many southern states. For example, in Mississippi and South Carolina, they constituted almost 60 percent of the population; in Louisiana and Georgia, 47 percent; and in Alabama, 45 percent. In that state, writes Burton Wechsler, "the black vote always remained a force," despite the efforts to suppress, intimidate, or corrupt black voters (2002: 28).[4] In North Carolina a coalition of black and white Republicans and Populists actually came to power at the state level in 1894. They were driven out in the infamous Wilmington insurrection of 1898, which left 60 dead and more than 300 wounded.

Bringing African Americans into a fusion ticket with the Republicans was not an issue of racial fairness coming up against the ingrained prejudices of white voters. There was an electoral incentive for the party to appeal to black voters, which terrorized the Democrats. In parts of southern Texas, where African Americans were in the majority, large landholding Bourbons were accustomed to bringing "their" black workers and tenants to the polls to vote for "the Party of the Fathers." In such districts, it was hard for the Populists to convince black voters to vote for a new and untried party led by white farmers' representatives.

The limitations of the Populists' dedication to equal rights arose in 1891 in a controversy over what southerners disparagingly called the "Force Bill." Led

---

[4] The crucible of black/white agrarian relations was in Texas, where a Colored Farmers' Association was created in 1886 along the lines of the Farmer's Alliance. Though the two Alliances remained distinct, as the white Alliance moved toward politics the pressure became inexorable to combine its efforts with those of black farmers (Cantrell, pp. 50–1).

by a young Massachusetts congressman, Henry Cabot Lodge, the Republicans proposed a Federal Elections Bill that would provide for federal supervision of elections to defeat the suppression of African American voters in the South (Keyssar 2000). The Democrats, of course, opposed the bill, but so did Populist presidential nominee James Weaver (Cantrell, p. 91). The bill passed the House, although not the Senate, but not before it exposed the ambivalence of the Populists' support for African American voting rights.

In liberal historiography, the Populists have been remembered for their racist tinge, but this was mainly true after its failure as an insurgent party when the Populist governor of South Carolina, Ben Tillman, sponsored a state constitution that imposed prohibitive poll taxes that poor African Americans could not hope to pay. At the same time, he castigated the conservative white elite and supported the interests of poor white farmers with a combination of racial bias and populist policies. Tillman's policies laid the foundation for a tradition of southern populism that would find its most powerful representative in Huey Long of Louisiana in the 1920s and early 1930s.

An even more dramatic evolution toward racism was that of Tom Watson, a firebrand Georgia populist who had been nominated by the party for the vice presidency alongside Bryan. Watson was embittered by his loss and returned to Georgia where neither the ruling Democrats nor the minority Republicans would accept him as a leader. When it emerged that poor black voters – to whom Watson had tried to appeal – were in the pay of upper-class white Democrats, his attitude toward African Americans underwent a transformation. By 1904 he was publicly calling for support for any gubernatorial candidate who would commit to disfranchisement. "The Populists of Georgia," he wrote, "indorsed (sic) the pledge made, *in my own name and theirs* to support whatever legislation was thought to be necessary to insure the State of Georgia against Negro domination" (quoted by Fingerhut 1976: 337–8). Georgia was an extreme case, but by the turn of the century, African Americans had been essentially removed from the political life of the South.

V   THE SUDDEN COLLAPSE OF POPULISM

What happened to reverse the fortunes of this insurgent party between its electoral surge in 1892 and its effective collapse by the end of the century? The simplest answer – and the one embraced by most observers – is that the party bet that supporting Bryan in the 1896 election would lead to a foot in the door of national politics – but they bet wrong. Slightly more subtle is the theory that the Populists – never imagining that the Democrats would come forward with a Free Silver platform – expected to be able to nominate their own candidates who would push forward their broader reform platform behind the entering wedge of free silver.

Both of these hypotheses capture part of the truth, but only a part, because they are limited to *electoral* calculations and ignore the fact that the People's Party was a *movement-party,* in which a substantial portion of its mass base had come to activism with a sense of purpose that set them apart from both Democrats and Republicans. They also ignore the fact that internal debates over fusion exposed a deeper dichotomy between two visions of the party that had widened since its formation – between a grassroots movement based on cooperation and a political party with a broad program.

Michael Schwartz's work in Richmond County, North Carolina, illustrates the cleavage within Populist ranks. Richmond was a poor rural area whose farmers had joined together to engage in collective action and, especially, collective purchasing (Schwartz, p. 249). Through coops and trade agreements, cotton and tobacco "bulking" agreements, and other collective actions, they were able to negotiate discount agreements and purchase goods at fair prices from wholesalers and manufacturers (ibid., p. 255). In short, building on the Alliance experience in Texas, poor yeomen farmers in the Richmond area were working to create a cooperative commonwealth.

However, at the same time, more prosperous North Carolina farmers had created a state organization that devoted itself to less contentious activities, like education. One of the collective actions that the state alliance supported was a "jute boycott," organized to oppose the sharp rise in prices by the producers of the jute packing that was commonly used to ship cotton.[5] But they were leery of cooperative enterprises, which were inimical to their free enterprise ideology and their desire to put their energies into politics. By 1890, the state organization had abandoned all interests outside of lobbying and electoral politics (ibid., p. 267). "But as soon as politics became a possibility, it could compete with any economic action for the resources of the organization" (Schwartz, pp. 277–8). Out of such movement/party divergences came the cleavage that would divide the People's Party over support for Bryan and for fusion with the Democrats in 1896.

On a Cross of Silver

At first, many Populists thought of the silver plank as little more than an adjunct of their opposition to the gold standard and to the monopoly of eastern banks over the money supply. Until the panic of 1893, free silver had mainly been advanced by representatives of silver-producing states in the West. But when President Cleveland urged the reversal of the Sherman Silver Purchase Act, silver "suddenly became the leading issue in American politics." The call for free silver "blossomed into a full-fledged social movement, taking on a symbolic and even moral quality in the minds of many Americans ... a sort of force unto itself,

[5] For the region-wide jute boycott campaign, see Goodwyn, pp. 144–5. For the North Carolina experience in the jute campaign, see Schwartz, pp. 262–5.

a political and cultural tiger that the Populists would find themselves riding" (ibid., p. 136). By the time of the 1896 party conventions it outshone the more traditional – and more deeply held – parts of the Alliance reform program. To Populists who saw a chance of their party becoming a national contender, embracing silver seemed a way of chipping away at the monopoly of the two main parties. "Free silver" also seemed like a way to attract the votes of workers skeptical of greenback money and had already been adopted by the AFL at several of its conventions.[6]

Through a combination of smooth coalition building and parliamentary sleight-of-hand, at a meeting before the Democratic convention, Populist President Taubeneck maneuvered the leadership into a position in favor of silver. He also scheduled the party's convention *after* the Democrats' on the theory that either a "goldbug" takeover of the Democrats or a new split among them would provide the Populists with the opportunity to monopolize the silver issue in the coming election. The hope was that silver Democrats and silver Republicans would defect from their traditional party ties and end up supporting the Populists (ibid., p. 352).

Bryan's clamorous success at the Democratic convention overturned those schemes (Bensel 2008). When the Democrats adopted a pro-silver platform and Bryan looked as if he might actually defeat the Republicans, the Populists had to retreat into a position as his camp follower, with the peculiar codicil that they refused to accept his vice presidential nominee. What was left of Populist independence was their nomination of Tom Watson of Georgia as a Populist candidate for the vice presidency. Bryan never formally accepted Watson as a running mate, so this was not a true fusion. The result, for the Populists, was a defeat: Even in Texas, the heartland of the Populist insurgency, the Bryan ticket carried the state with 54 percent of the votes; it is estimated that 40,000 voters who had supported the People's Party in 1892 returned to the Democrats four years later (Cantrell, p. 389).

So far, this sounds like a standard electoral story, full of errors, misjudgments, and misplaced ambitions. The "superior story" only comes into focus when we look beyond interparty relations to what was happening within this "movement-party." At its 1896 convention, the party divided between "fusionists" and those who called themselves "mid-roaders," who attempted to claim a central position in what had become a heterogeneous collection of regional, ideological, and sociological groups. They also put forward "proposals" that called for measures of direct democracy, like the initiative and the referendum, and a one-term limit on the presidency. However, these were listed as "sentiments" that were a bow to the party's movement origins and could not be expected to appeal to a broader constituency. What united the Populist forces in 1896 was the focus on silver that had emerged after the 1893 panic; a retreat from the broader Omaha

---

[6] I am grateful to Elizabeth Sanders for pointing this out to me.

Platform that followed from it; and the dismissal of the subtreasury proposal that was the last whisper of the dream of a cooperative commonwealth.

This was the same kind of division between agrarian movement goals and political ambitions that Schwartz found in North Carolina. As Cantrell concludes, "That sense of purpose helped make the People's Party not just a political party but also a movement, with its own movement culture" (ibid., p. 184). Over time this would prove to be both a strength and a weakness of Populism: while their idealism and esprit de corps created great devotion and dedication, "it would also expose them to the dangers of disillusion and alienation if they ever perceived that the party had surrendered its purity or compromised its ideals" (ibid).

After the Fall

Although remnants of the People's Party survived in one form or another until 1908, by the end of the decade it was effectively dead as both a movement and an electoral machine.[7] Did it have an influence on the future? Surely it did, as a number of scholars have argued.

In Sanders' important book, *Roots of Reform,* she sees the agrarian movements of the late nineteenth century as the forerunners of the expanded national state that emerged from the Progressive Era. And in his 2007 study, *The Populist Vision,* Charles Postel frames the Populists as modernizers who accepted large-scale enterprise and tried to develop business principles to oppose corporate power. In his article, Jason Frank also emphasizes "the institutional improvisations and formative praxis of populism, its robust but often unexamined experimentation with different forms of political cooperation and democratic enactment" and "as an exemplary instance of radical democratic praxis and prefiguration" (2018: 629). And in his book, *The People's Revolt,* Cantrell sees in Populism the realization that modern forms of capitalist enterprise "rendered the classical liberal model obsolete" and required a large state to protect Americans against economic tyranny (p. 13).

These new interpretations have excavated populism from the intellectual backwater of the mid-twentieth century. But in some ways they elide the world in which the Populists were trying to maneuver. This was a world

---

[7] Elizabeth Sanders, whose work has inspired much of this chapter, disagrees. In a personal communication to the author, she writes that:

1896 was far from the end of Populism. Even in the 1930s, much of the reform legislation was rooted in Populist demands from the 1880s: a strong regulatory state and antitrust policy, a government-controlled paper currency and end to the domestic gold standard, the great new legislation for labor in 1932, 1935, and 1938, new laws on banking, a land reform plan for sharecroppers and tenant farmers, easy credit, government support for mortgages, and so much more.

governed by a party system that was both regionally based and deeply corrupt and in which there was nothing resembling the kind of administrative state that would have been necessary to implement their programs.

Even more negative, the Populist experience had a countermovement effect on southern politics, as the southern power structure – seeing the danger of a biracial insurgency – turned the screws on African American rights and effectively disenfranchised blacks from the electoral system. It is distressing to recall that the same decade that saw the height of the Populist insurgency also brought a wave of disenfranchisement of African Americans. Indeed, following the Populists' defeat in 1896, in Texas "the first item of business for Democrats was to disrupt local Populist organizations by mounting a concerted effort to end black voting" (Cantrell, p. 398; Kousser 1974; Winsboro & Musoke 2003). In North Carolina, the Populist-Republican coalition was destroyed both by violence and constitutional change, while in Alabama, in the best-documented case of disenfranchisement, a new constitution that excluded blacks from the vote that passed in 1901 was the direct result of the perceived threat of Populism to white supremacy (Taylor 1949).

Perhaps the Jim Crow–ruled one-party South would have come about in any case, but the Populists, who had gestured toward building a coalition of poor white farmers and even poorer black citizens, induced the Democratic power structure to institutionalize a legal way of depriving African Americans of their rights. The Populist insurgency both briefly threatened the hegemony of the two mainstream parties and also completed the "redemption" of the South as a white-dominated racist subculture in American politics.

CONCLUSIONS

As both the agrarian movement and the Populist Party dispersed after the losses of 1896, American politics was changing. First, the global economy was expanding, and with it the long agricultural depression that had ground down southern farmers began to ease. Second, under the aegis of the Progressive movement, the monopolies and railroads at which the Populists had aimed so much of their fire began to come under state control. Third, a series of reforms[8] ushered in the kind of activist state that the Populist platform would have required but which the Populists never seriously contemplated.

Particularly damaging to the old party system were the progressive electoral reforms that arose around the turn of the century, when Americans adopted the

---

[8] For example, the Pure Food and Drug and Meat Inspection Acts (1906), the Hepburn Act regulating railroad rates (1906), the Federal Reserve Act (1913), the Clayton Antitrust Act (1914), the constitutional amendments providing for the direct elections of senators (1913), and the graduated income tax (1913). The agrarian movement, according to Monica Prasad, also had an effect on the federal tax system and on the central place of credit in the organization of social provision/economic policy (Prasad 2013).

Australian ballot, the initiative, the referendum and recall, commission forms of government, nonpartisan local elections, and the direct primary – not to mention the expansion of the suffrage, to which we will turn in Chapter 4. But although these reforms eventually produced the "fourth American party system," like every other major change in American history they took time to be reflected in practice.

The reasons for this delay were, in part, the same as those that contributed to the failure of the Populists – the fragmentation and multiple veto points in the American constitutional system. But the Populists also failed because the organizational practices that would have been needed to gain traction for their reforms did not yet exist. Of organized lobbies, large corporations doling out cash to legislators, and institutional interest groups there were plenty, but the kind of organized groups that could mobilize *"people's lobbies"* were still in their infancy (Clemens 1997). It was only by turning from a movement into an interest group with corporatist ties to the Department of Agriculture that farmers gained a purchase on the American state (McConnell 1953; 1966).

Afterword to Part I

A comparison of the agrarians/Populists with the story of antislavery/Republicanism will both complete this chapter and summarize the message of Part 1 of this book. Why was the agrarian movement unable to repeat the kind of breakthrough that antislavery had accomplished in the 1850s? Beyond the tactical mistakes that the Populists made in the 1896 election, there were three reasons why they failed:

> *The antecedents*: As we saw in Chapter 2, antislavery activists cashed in on the collapse of the Whigs and the rise of a new party to which they could hitch their wagon. In contrast, by the 1890s, the two-party system was well entrenched, with sectional cleavages that a cross-sectional party like the Populists found difficult to bridge. Railroad moguls knew how to work that system and – at least in the North (Bensel 1990); so did the banks.
>
> But farmers were a different story. They were geographically and culturally dispersed, they were perched uneasily between the status of workers and small businessmen, and they were subject to the main sectional cleavage in the party system. Moreover, without harnessing the votes of African Americans, they could not marshal a majority in the South, which was where they had their main source of support.
>
> *The Shock*: While the Republicans in the 1850s adopted a platform that had well understood ideological and economic facets, in policy terms, the agrarians were ahead of their time. We saw in the failure of their subtreasury proposal how poorly Southern Alliance leaders understood that they

could wrench very little from the political parties with the tools adapted from their cooperative practices at the grassroots (Schwartz 1976: ch. 16). The bigger story was that although abolitionism-Republicanism could use the military might of the Union army to advance their goals, the administrative state that would be needed to implement the agrarian program did not yet exist (Clemens 1997). In order to "work" the American system, twentieth-century farmers fashioned a "people's lobby," which depended on cooperation with the agricultural experiment service and the Department of Agriculture, institutions that were in their infancy in the 1890s (Clemens, pp. 174–5). Most important, there was no shock equivalent to the conflict over slavery and the Civil War to create a solid bloc of farmers and workers and solder that bloc to a political party.

The Legacy: We saw in Chapter 2 how the Union's victory and the freeing of the slaves produced a rabid and well-organized countermovement in the South, while, in the North, the Republican Party became the party of business, leaving the South in the hands of a white "Redemption" and the Democratic Party. A broader legacy of the war was the strengthening of the national state – and particularly of congressional government vis-à-vis the states.

When we look back at the agrarian/Populist experience of the 1880s and 1890s, we can see that the populists were both forward- and backward-looking. They were forward-looking in the sense that the programs they advanced presumed the existence of a strong administrative state that was still lacking. But they were backward-looking because their organizational model was ill-adapted to operate in such a society. It was not until the Progressive revolt, with its influence on such movements as suffrage reform, that such a model would appear but by then the Populists had gone the way of most third parties in American political development.

PART II

THE TRANSITIONAL PERIOD

4

Women, War, and the Vote

In March 1913, writes David Morgan, "Before tens of thousands of people, hundreds of extremely well-dressed women paraded in neat lines behind banners inscribed 'Votes for Women'" (Morgan 1972: 7). Under the leadership of two young women, Alice Paul and Lucy Burns, these women had turned a nearly moribund committee of the mainstream National American Women's Suffrage Association (NAWSA) into the National Women's Party (NWP) (Lunardini 1986). In the years that followed, they repeated the performance, even organizing pickets outside the White House in 1917 when the country was getting ready to enter World War I.

Is this a story about the courage and persistence of a small band of intrepid suffragists, as many scholars of the women's movement have argued?[1] This chapter will argue that such a story would ask too much of movements and say too little about their relation to parties and coalitions (Sapiro 2020:1574–77; also see Schlozman 2015: 45). It would also place too much of the focus on what Milkis & Tichenor (2019: 2–19) called a "militant movement," eliding the crucial role of more institutional groups. Between them, the various factions in the suffrage campaign constituted what these authors called a "formative movement" (see Table 1.1).

Kristin Goss points to the interaction of these forces with "the "larger social, economic, and political forces" that sustained women's efforts to gain suffrage (Goss 2012: 3–4) – forces like the entry of women into the workforce; the settlement of the western states, and the expansion of higher education. Goss is not wrong, but like many studies of the women's movement, hers elides *how* this

---

[1] The most recent survey of the literature on this long and complex movement can probably be found in the *American Historical Review*'s "Interactions" symposium published in the centennial year of the passage of the Fourteenth Amendment (*American Historical Review* 2019).

happened, which was through the interaction between a social movement, its allies, and the party system.[2]

The movement had always been multiple and was far from unified (Sapiro 2020). By 1920, it consisted of two main strands: the NWP, which organized the Washington demonstration; and the NAWSA, the larger and more institutional part of the movement – not to mention the many state and local organizations that supported the campaign. Although the two national groups would later diverge on strategy, their differences before the passage of the amendment turned mainly on tactics, with Paul and her comrades employing what seemed like radical performances at the time and the NAWSA preferring to work through lobbying, petitions, and more sedate marches. The movement also depended on a scattering of allies – those that were loosely coordinated in the progressive movement but also had roots in the abolitionist movement and its alliance with temperance advocates in the late nineteenth century.

Finally, the "heroic" story of the suffrage campaign elides its links to the party system, which was undergoing major changes, in part due to electoral reforms that had been instituted since the turn of the century and in part to the shift from the sectionally based partisan alignment that had stymied the Populists to one that was structured more along class lines. If nothing else, the Progressive Party – which had split off from the Republicans to allow Wilson's win in 1912 – supported votes for women (Corder & Wolbrecht 2016: ch. 5; Teele 2018a: 444).

None of these factors could have brought about the doubling of the electorate that the Nineteenth Amendment produced on their own, but it was their interaction that made a reform that had seemed impossible for decades come to seem entirely natural – and even uneventful once women had begun to enter the mainstream of American politics. As Karen Beckwith writes:

[The] combination of institutional structures . . . the availability of alliances and coalition possibilities, generally increasing access to politics, and a prevailing state strategy of inclusion . . . constructed relatively conducive political opportunities for women's mass participation (Beckwith 2008: 185).

I will begin this chapter with the diversity of women's views and actions during the run-up to World War I. I will then turn to the relations between the suffrage campaign and the network of women's and progressive groups of which it was a part. In Section III, I will turn to the factors in electoral and party politics that offered increasing incentives for women's participation. The chapter will close with what happened to women's activism after suffrage reform, when their major goal had been achieved and they faced a more diverse and changing political landscape.

---

[2] Although Goss has a keen sense of the policy process in which women's groups participated, the term "political party" does not appear in the index of her fine book.

I THE DIVERSITY OF WOMEN'S ACTIVISM

Paul and Burns' group mounted its first march in Washington the day before Wilson's inauguration. It had begun as a committee of the NAWSA that was supposed to work in Congress to advance the goal of votes for women. But frustrated by the indifference of Congress to a reform they considered essential, the two women turned that committee into a party. Though it never ran for anything, the NWP employed a range of what were then considered contentious tactics to insist on the essential need for the reform. When Wilson arrived in Washington for his inauguration, he found the streets around the White House empty. "Where are the people?" he asked an aide and was told that they were on Pennsylvania Avenue watching a spectacle new to Washington: "Before tens of thousands of people, hundreds of extremely well-dressed women paraded in neat lines behind banners inscribed 'Votes for Women'" (Morgan 1972: 7).

Who were these women? Paul was a Quaker and a social worker who had gone to England to study and ended up participating in the suffragette movement there. She was not only jailed for her activities but participated in a hunger strike in jail for which she was threatened and force-fed. When she returned to America in 1910, she began to preach the lessons of the British movement to American women's groups, helping to organize open-air meetings in Philadelphia, where she was a PhD student. Burns was a Boston Irish Catholic who also studied in Britain where she too became active with the suffragettes.

Arriving in Washington in 1913, the two women had gathered a group of sympathetic allies and – within two months – had organized the parade before Wilson's inauguration. It was the first really large march on Washington in American history, followed by an even larger one on January 17, 1917, when the country was at war, adding pickets (the so-called "Silent Sentinels") outside the White House, which led to melees with male hecklers and the police. Mob violence broke out when envoys from the new Kerensky government in Moscow, calling at the White House, were welcomed with banners declaring that this country was a democracy in name only.[3]

In the meantime, under Carrie Catt's canny leadership, the NAWSA – the traditional women's suffrage organization – began to assemble support for the suffrage in a state-by-state series of campaigns before shifting to calling for a national referendum during the war. Federalism was always a constraint on – but also an opportunity for – the movement (Sapiro, 2020: 1566–68). The state-by-state strategy worked well in the West, gained partial success in Illinois, but failed several times in the key state of New York. When war broke out, while Paul and the NWP were stationing "sentinels" outside the White House, NAWSA leader Carrie Catt was meeting with Wilson and congressional

---

[3] As Eleanor Flexner recalls, some of the banners read "Democracy Should Begin at Home." Others referred to "free Russia," where women had received the vote after the overthrow of the czarist regime, "in invidious comparison with the United States and 'Kaiser Wilson'" (Flexner 1959: 284).

leaders to assure them of her organization's support for the war. Like other movements that ripen during and after wars, the move to support women's suffrage was in part the result of a grateful nation and in part the result of the transfer of mobilization from wartime to movement activism (Tarrow 2015).

Unlike Paul's and Burns' efforts, which were centered in Washington, the NAWSA had bases and alliances in many parts of the country. Of course, the opportunities varied from state to state and over time but so did the strategic intelligence of the leaders of the movement, who learned to employ a "separate spheres" argument to convince conservative men that they were not in danger of being engulfed by "new women" (McCammon et al. 2001: 57). The state-by-state strategy enabled the movement to take advantage of the weak party organizations and competitiveness of the party systems in the western states (Teele 2018a and b), win the endorsement of state party organizations in some of them, and forge links with sympathetic local officials where the movement was strong (Morgan-Collins 2021). This was not insignificant: Before the amendment passed, fifteen states had voted full voting rights to women and a handful gave women the right to vote in presidential elections. But it was a slow-moving, expensive, and exhausting process and was mainly successful in states in which party organizations were weak.

The strategic incrementalism of the NAWSA and the tactical radicalism of the NWP led to tensions between the two groups. But as Milkis and Tichenor argue in their work on "rivalry and reform," insurgent goals can be well served by leadership rivalries that produce strong moderate and militant wings (Milkis & Tichenor 2019: 46–47). The radical tactics of Paul and her comrades highlighted the reasonableness of Catt and the NAWSA in what sociologists have called a "positive radical flank effect" (Haines 1984). Confronted by the "silent sentinels" haunting the gates of the White House, Wilson and the Democrats looked with less hostility at the genteel lobbying of the NASWA – especially after the group supported the war effort. Between its two tactical variants, the women's suffrage movement was the kind of "formative movement" that we saw in antislavery in the 1850s.

Movement-Countermovement Interaction

Also like antislavery, the suffrage movement made enemies. No doubt encouraged by their husbands and frightened by the prospect of gender equality, a group of wealthy women formed the National Association Opposed to Woman Suffrage (NAOWS). In the South, these women mainly came from the planter class and were clearly worried that votes for women would disrupt a social order based on white supremacy. In the North, they were mainly the daughters or wives of wealthy businessmen, who were already active in charity or reform work that did not threaten traditional gender norms.

The NAOWS developed especially where the suffrage movement was strong, for example, in Massachusetts, one of the first states to mount an organized anti-suffrage campaign. New York City was also a center for both pro-suffrage and anti-suffrage mobilization.[4] Other anti-suffragists were less blunt in their desire to keep women from getting the vote, emphasizing the dirtiness of politics and the wish to keep women in the home, where their purity would be unsullied by contact with politics. Many anti-suffragists went on, during the war and after, to become members of antipacifist and antisocialist organizations.

II EMBEDDED SUFFRAGISM

During the first two decades of the twentieth century, the suffrage campaign was embedded in a broad network of women's groups that dated from abolitionism and the Civil War to the progressive movement that rose in the 1890s. Beginning with abolition and voluntarism during the Civil War, during this period women began to associate in a number of ways, forming charitable, social, educational, and, ultimately, political organizations (Sapiro 2020: 1578–86). As Elisabeth Clemens observes, "Whereas agrarian associations tended to expand and collapse, leaving an episodic trace of organizational activity, women's groups cumulated and were knit together by dense patterns of multiple membership" (Clemens 1997: 191).

Clemens has illustrated this growth and diversification through the "club movement" in three different states. From her research, she learned that although in California there were 17 such clubs in 1896, by 1908 this number had grown to 192. In Washington, the number of clubs grew from 7 in 1896 to 163 in 1915, while, in Wisconsin, they increased from 8 to 203 in the same period (p. 197) This grassroots expansion was matched, at the federal level, by the growth of the General Federation of Women's Clubs (GFWC), which was founded in 1890 amid the rising tide of progressivism that encouraged educational, social, and cultural activism.

Not only were women joining associations in large numbers during this period, but they were "knit together by dense patterns of multiple memberships" (ibid., p. 191). As Clemens notes,

the majority of women's associational activity was not linked directly to the demand for enfranchisement or other reforms of political institutions. Most women who joined associations during the late nineteenth and early twentieth centuries had rather different motives: alarm over moral decay, a commitment to aid the unfortunate, or a desire for sociability and self-improvement" (ibid., p. 190).

---

[4] We can gain a flavor of these women's culture from a meeting in New York City in 1894 whose organizers argued that "because the basis of government is force – its stability rests upon its physical power to enforce its law; therefore, it is inexpedient to give the vote to women. "Some Reasons Why We Oppose Votes for Women." National Association Opposed to Women Suffrage, New York City, 1894. Archived by the Library of Congress. www.loc/resource/rbpe .1300130

But this general growth in social participation was one of the secret weapons of the suffrage movement: Many women who had gained organizational experience in nonpolitical associations during and after the Civil War brought these experiences to suffragism.

The struggle for suffrage was never entirely separate from the broader women's movement that was beginning to germinate during the same period. Mobilization for enfranchisement of women was a *campaign*, part of a larger women's rights movement that addressed issues of divorce and marriage rights, contraceptive and reproductive rights, and the right to employment protections. Understanding women's suffrage as a long-term campaign helps to explain why the movement appeared to enter into abeyance in the 1920s – it left behind a mobilization vacuum.[5]

The early years of the suffrage campaign intersected with other causes, starting with abolitionism, then with the temperance movement of the 1870s and 1880s, leading to the broader progressive movement that arose in the 1890s. But these relationships were two-sided, offering organizational linkages to the suffragists but also earning them the dislike of these other movements' enemies. We can see these double-edged relationships in the case of the tensions over African American enfranchisement after the Civil War, in the relationship between the suffragist and temperance movements later in the century, and with the labor movement in the next one.

Abolition and Temperance

Both abolitionism and the suffrage campaign began outside of politics but were drawn into the political system to pursue their aims. But though in both cases there was a move toward electoral politics, the antislavery movement was made up of enfranchised men during a period when the party system was breaking down, while the suffragists were trying to wedge their influence into a party system that was still solidly structured around the two major parties. In itself, this difference in movement/party structuration can tell us a lot about the rapid success of the former and the slow and halting progress of the latter.[6]

Women's involvement in abolitionism began in "prayer circles," which brought women together to discuss the Bible and thence political issues. The religious base of their meetings provided justification for their collective endeavor and their standing in the abolition movement (McCammon et al. 2001). Male abolitionists were at first not happy to admit women to full status in their movement, but, as Eleanor Flexner writes, "It was in the abolition movement that women first learned to organize, to hold public meetings, to conduct petition campaigns (Flexner, 1959, p. 41).

---

[5] I am grateful to Karen Beckwith for this astute observation.

[6] I am grateful for this observation to Elisabeth Clemens who, as usual, puts more clearly something that is inherent in my thinking but which I have not been able to articulate.

From the antislavery movement suffragists adopted the tactic of the mass petition that had been central to the antislavery crusade since its founding in England in the late eighteenth century (Carpenter & Moore 2014). Women were also prime movers in the American Sanitary Commission, which worked to help the wounded in the Union army during the Civil War (Clemens 2020: ch. 2), and in the Women's National Loyal League (WNLL), which was "dedicated specifically to abolition and founded in 1863 by well-known women's rights activists" (Sapiro 2020: 1585). Many of these women would go south after the war to work with and help educate newly freed ex-slaves.

The most important interorganizational linkage was with the WCTU, which arose at about the same time. At first, the state Unions of the WCTU were deeply invested in a "separate spheres" argument, but as they experienced the disappointments of going it alone against well-funded opponents, they moved closer to the goals of the suffragists, eventually supporting the idea of a "family vote," which allowed them to forge an alliance with the NAWSA around a framing of women's "separate spheres" (McCammon & Campbell 2002). We can see the interactions between the two movements, first, in the overlapping careers of women who were members of both movements, in the political impact of this interpenetration, and in the career of Frances Willard, who led the WCTU for many years. Clemens' and James Cook's research shows that 37 percent of suffrage activists had held office in the WCTU at some time in their careers (1999: 623). But this interorganizational penetration declined among suffragists who were born after 1850, as each movement gained its own organizational identity (p. 627).

Although not every member of the NAWSA was an advocate for temperance, the owners of breweries and saloons did not make so fine a distinction, using their close ties to political party machines to fight off votes for women. From that point on, every effort of the suffrage movement to gain a foothold was vigorously opposed by the liquor lobby and by its well-paid cronies in the urban machines and state legislatures. Although prohibition did not follow automatically from suffrage reform, the suffrage and temperance movements profited from their alliance but earned unified opposition from the liquor lobby.

Opposition from producers of alcoholic drinks and saloon owners solidified in the period following the dramatic, but largely unsuccessful "anti-saloon crusade" of the 1870s. Beginning in the Midwest but spreading rapidly across the country, "Bands of singing, praying women held meetings, not only in churches but on street corners, penetrating into the saloons themselves and closing them by the thousands" (Flexner, 182). The crusade was short-lived but it led to the creation of the WCTU and to the leadership of Frances Willard. By the turn of the decade, the WCTU had gained support in every state in the country, claiming a membership of more than 200,000 and winning the enduring enmity of saloon keepers and producers of alcohol (ibid., p. 184).

Of the WCTU's commitment to suffrage reform there is no doubt, but it is not as clear that passion for the vote was universal among these largely conservative women. Much depended on the personality and determination of Frances Willard, who led the WCTU from 1879 until her death in 1898 (McCammon & Campbell, p. 237).[7] Willard's approach was indirect. As Flexner writes,

She began by herself espousing woman suffrage openly at the WCTU convention in 1876. She achieved success by a series of tangential moves, in the course of which women as yet unready for the brand of forthright argument employed by a Susan B. Anthony were gradually led to understand that they could not protect their homes and families from liquor or other vices, without a voice in public affairs (Flexner, p. 183).

More important than the ideological proximity of the two movements was their common relation to party politics. The connection was at first indirect: Though not all suffragists were as dedicated to stamping out alcohol as the WCTU, anti-alcohol convictions had a progressive side – protecting the family – which rubbed off on the suffrage movement too. But it also won for the suffrage movement the robust opposition of the liquor lobby, which had close ties with many of the party machines that dominated state and local politics. Given the corrupt nature of many of the party organizations of the time, making an enemy of the liquor lobby was tantamount to gaining the dislike of the political parties.

Labor and Progressivism

Politics, association, and suffrage intersected in the labor movement too. Coinciding with and supporting the suffrage movement was a loose conglomeration of intellectuals, publicists, dissident politicians, and public officials who never formed a central organization but whose influence on progressive reform was considerable. In some cities and states, like Chicago, New York City, and the states of the upper Midwest, progressives became a political party able to exercise marginal power between the two major parties. Many of them – like Jane Addams, Carrie Catt, and Florence Kelley – were also associated with women's suffrage, making it possible for the movement to use its progressive ties to put forward legislation that its leaders favored.

Consider what happened in Illinois in 1913, where the Women's Trade Union League (WTUL) was a vigorous advocate for women's rights in the factory. The city of Chicago had an active settlement house movement, which had a hand in brokering an alliance between the WTUL and the state suffrage

---

[7] Willard's biographer, Mary Earhart, even argued that her devotion to temperance arose "less from an overriding interest in that cause than from a belief that it could be the means of drawing large numbers of women hitherto not receptive to the issue of greater rights for women, into activity that could lead them in that direction" (quoted by Flexner, p. 183).

association. "The overlap between the reform interested middle-class women who pursued labor rights in partnerships with working women and those who organized for women's voting rights in the state's suffrage organization led to an increasingly strong link between woman suffrage and labor protection," writes Corinne McConnaughy (2013: 155).

By 1909, in a coincidence of interests, the two organizations were providing support for one another's campaigns in the state legislature. But soon after the legislature passed a suffrage bill, "IESA leaders made choices that put their desire for full suffrage rights above the WTUL's commitment to working women's goals." This included a deal with the notoriously anti-labor publisher William Randolph Hearst, who offered to produce a suffragist version of his Chicago newspaper. To the consternation of their labor allies, the suffragists accepted. As McConnaghy puts it; "For the WTUL, it was a stark symbol of the lack of concern the suffragists held for working women's labor rights" (ibid., p. 168). The movement's strategic imperative to do everything it could to advance women's voting rights worked against its long-term mutuality of interest with women's labor rights.

III   AN ANTIPARTY MOVEMENT IN THE PARTY SYSTEM

At first, the suffrage campaign was determined to avoid what Clemens calls "the fraternal world of nineteenth-century politics" (1997: 185). In addition, male politicos – particularly those who staffed the party machines that ran many of America's cities – were leery of the moral rigor that women threatened to bring into politics. As a result, women activists were obliged to invent alternatives to electoral politics, "if only as a means of gaining the vote for themselves" (p. 187). "Precisely because American women initially pursued their political goals without the benefit of the vote or access to the patronage system, they developed methods of influence distinct from partisan politics," concludes Clemens (p. 214). But try as they might, suffragists could not avoid the sordid world of party politics, a connection that was evident shortly after the Civil War ended.

Anthony, Stanton, and the Democrats

David Bateman writes, "The strength of racism had always acted as a constraint on legislators, who were aware that favoring black rights could leave them vulnerable to attacks from challengers" (2018: 185). When addressing the Republicans who controlled Congress, Elizabeth Cady Stanton described the former slaves as "ignorant, degraded, depraved, but yesterday crouching at your feet, outside the pale of political consideration" who "are to-day, by your edicts, made [woman's] rulers, judges, jurors and lawgivers "(quoted in Free 2015: 157; also see the account in Sapiro 2020).

There were more than enough racial stereotypes in these statements to lead to a split in the movement and to the formation of the American Women's Suffrage

Association, which broke from what became the NAWSA over the issue of African American enfranchisement. The NAWSA supported the Fifteenth Amendment. The split would last until 1890, when the two branches of the movement reunited. But the real targets of Stanton's venom were not the freed slaves but her former allies in the Republican Party, whose support for women's rights was no more enduring than their support for black rights.

We can see this cleavage in both New York State and Kansas after the war. In New York, a convention called in 1867 to rewrite the state's constitution fought over whether to admit blacks and women to suffrage. On the grounds that African Americans had served in the Union army – but that women had not – the convention, led by former radical publisher Horace Greeley, worried that giving women the vote would disrupt all gender differences and – as one delegate indicated – would "defeminize women" (Free, p. 146).[8]

A deeper break came in Kansas, where the Republicans had put a referendum on black suffrage on the ballot. While some Kansas Republicans argued for universal suffrage, others "feared that the association of women's suffrage and black male suffrage would defeat both" and worked to separate the two issues (ibid., p. 147). The danger of dividing the two causes soon became clear as Kansas legislators defeated both initiatives by a significant margin. Anthony and Stanton knew that they could not win enough Republican support to constitute a majority of almost any state and that they needed Democratic votes to succeed. Kansas was to be a testing ground for this strategy.[9]

Bruised by their defeats in New York and Kansas, Anthony and Stanton were offered an alternative by railroad mogul George Francis Train, who was eager to run for president with an appeal to Democrats and racists. Train offered to finance a new suffrage newspaper, *The Revolution*, which he invited the two women to edit and manage. "In the next few years," writes Laura Free, "their articles and editorials continued to appeal to Democrats, adopting Democratic arguments, rhetoric, and racism" (ibid., p. 151). Anthony's and Stanton's alliance with Train soon broadened into a general connection to the Democrats (ibid., p. 156).

The story of Anthony's and Stanton's desertion of the alliance with black allies over suffrage is well known in feminist circles but is usually told to underscore the contradictions between abolitionism and the suffrage movement. But it also suggests that, try as they might, it was impossible for these suffragists to accomplish the movement's goal without making alliances with parties where they could and work to defeat them where they couldn't. Despite finding such a move distasteful or anchoring themselves permanently to

---

[8] It was not lost on the suffragists that many male politicians had bought their way out of fighting in the Civil War but were ready to exclude women from the vote on the grounds that they did not serve in the military.

[9] I am grateful to David Bateman for pointing this out to me.

either of the two parties, the suffragists were increasingly drawn to interact with the party system.

Suffragists and Elected Politicians

Suffrage campaigners were mainly active in state and local politics, which was still the center of gravity of the party system in the late nineteenth century. In a careful district-level analysis, Mona Morgan-Collins (2021) found significant "negative incumbent effects" that coincided with the campaign for women's suffrage. This was not simply a function of the size of the female population or of its urban-rural mix; Morgan-Collins found that in districts in which state-level suffrage organizations were strongest, conservatives tended to lose office when women entered the electorate. "This electoral retaliation against conservative incumbents was particularly notable," she observes, "with respect to incumbents' opposition to bills that enhanced women's welfare, namely the establishment of the Women's Bureau and an increase in veteran pensions." Like the Populist movement before them, but with far greater success, suffragists had their strongest impact on politics at the state and local levels, which is why we need to look at the intersection of the movement and the party system at the grassroots.

This system was still at the center of politics but toward the end of the century, as new forms of participation blossomed across the country (Clemens 1997), the parties began to lose their monopoly of representation. Between the late nineteenth century and passage of the Nineteenth Amendment, there was a levelling off and then a decline in voting turnout. Part of the reason for this decline was undoubtedly due to the passage of Jim Crow laws disenfranchising African Americans in the South, but another part was a decline of support for the parties of what political scientists call "the third American party system." The new "fourth" party system would have to share political influence with organized lobbies, using the tools of mobilizing public opinion (Clemens 1997).

Spurring the declining popularity of the mainstream parties was the rise of the progressive movement, which brought powerful voices to demand reform of the party system and its practices. During an age in which readership of relatively inexpensive press outlets was growing, both the tabloid press and higher-level journals like Herbert Croly's *New Republic* specialized in exposés of corruption. It was during his period that suffragists began to turn with greater frequency to state and local governments – where the progressives aimed much of their firepower – as the appropriate arenas for political action (Clemens 1997: 207). These developments opened opportunities that astute suffrage leaders – despite their distaste for politics – were happy to exploit.

Political Competition and Partisan Instability

Two recent scholars, Corinne McConnaghy (2013) and Dawn Teele (2018a and b), have found innovative ways to examine the interactions between suffrage activism and the party system. In her 2013 book, McConnaghy focused on two variants of the relationships between parties and the movement: what she called *strategic enfranchisement* and *programmatic enfranchisement*. By the former term she meant "when a single party acts to enfranchise a new group of voters expecting to reap electoral rewards from that group" (p. 32); by the latter she pointed to where "suffrage expansion occurs not as a consequence of a search for new supporters from the ranks of the disenfranchised, but in accommodation to the demands of existing voters" (p. 37).

The strategic model – which McConnaghy sees as dominant in historians' approaches to the process – requires a substantial level of information, incentive, and capacity, requirements that are difficult to satisfy, especially when a political party lacks information that a group, if enfranchised, would actually deliver its votes (p. 35). In the programmatic model, in contrast, it is the perceived threat of the defection of *existing* voting groups if the party in power fails to deliver voting rights to the disenfranchised that drives support for reform (p. 37). As McConnaghy concludes, "Women were granted voting rights when state lawmakers had reason to believe that such action would win approval from important groups of existing voters" (p. 207).

Although she did not delve very deeply into the relations between the parties, McConnaghy points to a corollary of the model: "Politicians' vulnerability to those constituent demands was even greater when elections were more competitive" (p. 208). That competition for votes was sharper in the West is the main reason why the vote was granted to women more readily in that region than in either the Northeast or the South.

This takes us to the more recent work of Dawn Teele, whose analysis of state-level political competition meshes with McConnaghy's hypothesis but goes a step further by relating various measures of competitiveness to the level of suffragists' mobilization in different states. In the absence of modern forms of protest data on which to draw,[10] Teele relied on the NAWSA membership data presented in Figure 4.1 as a measure of movement strength. The membership data are weighted by population, which produces a fair proxy for mobilization.[11]

Teele finds that taken on their own, both voter mobilization and electoral competition correlated with the probability of the passage of suffrage legislation

---

[10] I refer here to the tradition of "protest event analysis" (PEA) developed in the United States and Western Europe from the 1970s on by Tilly (1995), McAdam (1982), and others. This tradition relies heavily on the existence of systematically reliable media coverage of protest events and also on the reliance of movement organizers on contentious performances – which was not the case for the more institutional wing of the suffrage movement. For a general introduction to protest event analysis, see Hutter (2014).

[11] I am grateful to Dawn Teele for allowing me to reproduce the data in Figure 4.1 from her original research. See Teele (2018a and b).

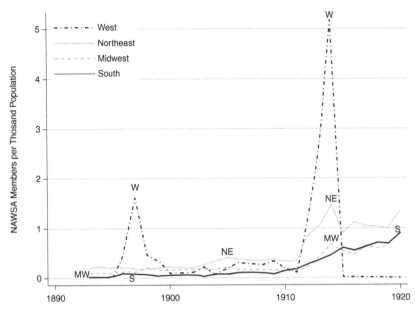

FIGURE 4.1 National American Women's Suffrage Association membership by region

in a state before passage of the Nineteenth Amendment.[12] Low levels of party competition reduced the probability of passage of suffrage laws from 9 percent to 4.5 percent while the share of seats held by a third party – Teele's best measure of competitiveness – increased the probability of passage from 9 percent to 14 percent (2018b: 452–4). An increase in NAWSA membership from its national mean of 0.34 members per thousand to 0.96 per thousand increased the probability of passage from 9 percent to 14 percent in a state.

Teele also found a positive interaction between competition and support for women's suffrage at high levels of movement mobilization (2018b: 454). If we can generalize from McConnaghy's and Teele's findings, "strategic choices made by politicians and the strength of the suffrage movement together form a logic of suffrage reform" (p. 445). "Winning the vote," observes Teele, "depends on the alignment of interests between elected politicians and suffragists" (2018a: 6).

---

[12] For her measures of party competition, Teele used voting data, measuring high and low levels of competition separately. She measured high competition by the ratio of runner-up votes to those of the winning party by a split in power between the two houses of the legislature and by the fraction of the vote won by third parties. She measured low competition by the length of the ruling party's electoral dominance, the fraction of the seats it held over 50 percent, and whether or not there was a dominant political machine in the state (2018a: 42). Taken together, she shows, heightened competition provided an impetus for politicians to seek new rules of play, while mobilization provided politicians with information about the preferences of excluded groups – like women (2018b: 445–6).

The Role of Third Parties

In a political system like the United States, the emergence of stable third, fourth, or *n*th parties is impeded by political institutions that encourage bipolar contests. As a result, such parties have most often been seen as flash-in-the-pan products of temporary disputes over policy or personality, or as way stations on the way to a new stage of party development. But the shortness of a third party's life is not the same as a lack of political importance at the time it emerges, as the election of 1854 showed, when the short-lived Know-Nothing Party surged, splitting the Democrats and leaving the Whigs to disappear from electoral politics.

The rise of the Progressives was no ordinary third-party insurgency. Like the advent of the Republicans sixty-eight years earlier, it was powered by activists, many of whom had come out of social movements. Women like Jane Addams, Carrie Catt, and Florence Kelly first saw in Theodore Roosevelt a possible vehicle for the achievement of women's suffrage and convinced him to include votes for women in the platform of the "Bull Moose" campaign in 1912. But more important, after Roosevelt lost the election, votes for women had gained the legitimacy of having been made an issue in a national election.

This interaction between progressivism and votes for women could be clearly seen at the state level and especially in the state of Illinois. After T. R. left the scene and President Wilson turned away from his progressive platform toward support for the war, the Progressives both moved to the left and remained strong in the industrial states of the Midwest. This led to a suffragist/Progressive alliance in the state of Illinois. Like many such alliances, its life was brief, but while it lasted it brought gains to the cause of votes for women.

Between 1912 and 1914, Progressives held the balance of power in the Illinois state legislature, where they tabled a wide spectrum of reform proposals – including the initiative and the referendum, key reforms advanced by the Progressives. These "western" innovations were anathema to both the Democrats who controlled Chicago politics and to the "downstate" Republicans who ran the legislature (McConnaughy 2013: 160–1). Both measures failed, but they left more peripheral Progressive measures – including women's suffrage (ibid., p. 161) – standing. Women's suffrage thus profited from both the presence of a reformist third party and from the heightened competitiveness that the Progressives brought to state politics. In the event, a coalition of Progressive legislators, a group of Republicans with interest in defeating the Democratic Chicago machine, and the progressive wing of the Democrats came together to back a limited version of women's suffrage in Illinois.

What happened in Illinois was a harbinger of a shift in the party system from localized and patronage-based parties to national programmatic organizations, a shift in which Progressives and other social movements played a key role. This would become general after the 1932 election, which brought many progressives back into politics as "New Dealers" after the disappointments during the Republican-dominated 1920s. Progressivism, the women's movement, and changes in party structure combined to produce a major change in the axis of American politics.

IV VOTERS, PARTIES, AND MOVEMENTS AFTER REFORM

In their study of the women's movement after World War II, Leila Rupp and Verta Taylor designated the first two decades after that war as the "doldrums" of the movement (1987). Determined to oppose the idea that the "new" women's movement of the 1960s and 1970s was an "immaculate conception,"[13] Rupp and Taylor were at pains to show that, in previous decades, women's activism had not disappeared either but had entered a period of "abeyance." By that term, they meant "a holding process by which movements sustain themselves in nonreceptive political environments and provide continuity from one stage of mobilization to another" (Taylor 1989: 761).

Rupp and Taylor were writing about the women's movement in the 1940s and 1950s, but students of the women's movement in the 1920s were almost unanimous in defining that decade as a period of decline.[14] With the virtues of hindsight, we can see that the expectation for an electoral breakthrough as the result of women getting the vote was unrealistic, in part because women were "peripheral" voters (Corder & Wolbrecht 2016: 23) and in part because, once the suffrage was achieved, they would be as divided in their preferences as men. Moreover, once women began to utilize the vote, the focal point that had unified their movement before suffrage was undermined by exhaustion, organizational differentiation, and the dispersive currents of electoral politics. As Clemens writes, "Having mobilized around identities and organizational forms defined in opposition to party politics, women activists found it difficult to mobilize as a bloc within the electoral system" (1997: 232).

But that conclusion turns mainly on electoral politics. When we look beyond the first elections after the passage of the Nineteenth Amendment, as Kristi Andersen suggests, we find that

women's political participation ... served as a bridge between Progressivism and the New Deal and helped to solidify the movement from the highly partisan politics of the

---

[13] Rupp and Taylor begin their book with a quotation from a long-time member of the National Women's Party, who comments about the "new" women's movement: "Well, I'm sure there are people that would just love to think that when Betty Friedan wrote *The Feminine Mystique* that started the whole thing except for some ineffectual old ladies." See Rupp and Taylor, *Survival in the Doldrums*, p. 3.

[14] In 1924, Charles Russell asserted that "nothing has changed, except that the number of docile ballot-droppers has approximately doubled" (quoted in Andersen 1996: 5). A more recent observer, William H. Chafe, argued that "women's political standing plummeted [in the latter half of the 1920s] because the mass of female citizens failed to act in the cohesive and committed manner which the suffragists had predicted" (quoted in Andersen 1996: 7).

nineteenth century to the increasingly nonpartisan, candidate-centered, interest group politics of the mid-twentieth century. (Andersen 1996: 2)

Beginning with the Ballot

In their careful analysis of the outcome of the Republican surge in the 1920 elections in the ten states in which they carried out simulations (in eight of which women were voting for the first time), J. Kevin Corder and Christian Wolbrecht estimated that 60 percent of women who voted in that year chose the Republican Party, compared to 59 percent of men voters (ibid., p. 155). The results were not very different four years later, despite the surge in votes for Progressive presidential candidate Robert M. La Follette in that year (ibid., ch. 6). Then, in the 1928 "rum and religion" election, women's turnout in the states that Corder and Wolbrecht sampled increased by at least 5 percent but continued to favor the GOP (p. 202). Turnout rose again in the first New Deal election to an estimated 48 percent in 1932 and to 54 percent in 1936, as a majority of women voters switched to the Democrats, especially in the Midwest and the Northeast (ibid., Figure 8.24 on p. 247 of their book). Women were not voting en bloc nor did they throw their votes to a single party, but by the late 1920s, they were "learning the habit of voting" (Andersen, pp. 68, 71).

Moreover, much like the male vote, female turnout soon revealed itself to be deeply structured by state and local factors. In Corder and Wolbrecht's sample, women's turnout was highest in competitive states. Next highest was the turnout in one-party Republican states, while the lowest women's turnout was found in states where there were comfortable Democratic majorities (see Figure 5.2 on page 142 of their book) – which was mainly in the South. At the same time, variations in the legal framework of suffrage had significant effects on turnout: States with high residency requirements for voting had a much lower female turnout than those with more relaxed requirements (see Figure 5.3 on p. 143 of their book).

Party System Change

But blaming the minor impact of the female vote on the decline of suffrage activism after passage of the Nineteenth Amendment would ask too much of movements and say too little about parties and coalitions. The variations in women's voting were also affected by changes in the party system that had been occurring during the first two decades of the twentieth century.

First, there was a general decline in voting participation following the heights of voter mobilization in the late nineteenth century. The most precipitous decline came between the 1916 and 1920 elections, and lasted until mid-decade, when it began to rise towards its New Deal heights (Corder & Wolbrecht, figure 9.1 on page 255 of their book).

Second, and related to the first trend, while electoral participation was eroding, social participation was expanding to interest representation as the result of economic and organizational changes around the turn of the new century (Clemens 1997). Although the agrarians had depended on their cooperative networks when facing their opponents, the early twentieth century saw the beginning of what Clemens calls "people's lobbies," which combined outsider mobilization with "inside" pressure on policy makers and legislators.

Third, women's organizations did not decline as their voting turnout disappointed the supporters of suffrage. After passage of the amendment, numerous associations of interest to women were formed, ranging from the National League of Women Voters, successor to the NAWSA, to social welfare associations, to associations of professional women, like the National Federation of Business and Professional Women's Clubs (NFBPWC). These organizations "sprang from a sense of identity among those who possess a special skill and knowledge" (Lemons, pp. 43–6). Then there were organizations that were not technically addressed to women's needs but which were largely run by women, like the National Parent-Teachers Association (p. 57).[15] Many of these organizations were only peripherally involved in politics but as Lemons observes from his careful study of "social feminism," it was inevitable that "The organizational impulse moved in the direction of politics" (p. 49).

We know from organizational studies that membership in civic organizations tends to enhance political activism (Minkoff 2016), and in the course of the 1920s, a number of women moved from women's associations into politics (Andersen, chs. 4 and 5). Indeed, this was a move that Catt encouraged before the NAWSA turned itself into the National League of Women Votes (NLWV). But the move into the party system was extremely slow and was met with resistance from party officials who thought that bringing women into public office was a bridge too far. Sophonisba Breckinridge reported that by 1931, there were 146 women serving in state legislatures, an increase from 37 in 1921 (1933, data reproduced in Andersen, 116). Although this was an astronomical growth rate, there were roughly 7,500 state legislators in office across the country during the decade of the 1920, which meant that by 1925, women held only 1.8 percent of state legislative seats (Lemons, p. 104).

Finally, in the wake of the "red scare" following the shock of the Russian revolution, the country was moving into a reactionary period that would only be reversed with Roosevelt's election and the coming of the New Deal. The war had brought into prominence a small number of well-funded patriotic and anti-internationalist organizations. Some of these groups had emerged to "defend

---

[15] Lemons lists 29 new national professional women's associations or organizations of interest largely to women that were formed between 1912 and 1928. See chapter 2 and note 8 of his book, which provides a chronological list of these new organizations.

the constitution" (Rana in press, ch. 4); others, triggered by the events in Russia, arose out of a general fear of socialism; while still others came out of the NAOWS. Groups with names like the Sentinels of the Republic, the Woman Patriots, the Constitutional Liberty League, and the Citizens Committee to Protect Our Homes and Children attacked both peace-oriented women's groups and legislative efforts to protect women and children.

The women's movement probably also lost membership as a result of intramovement conflicts that grew out of a debate between those who wanted to focus on equal rights for women in general – mainly the NWP – and those who wanted to ameliorate the position of women and their families through legislation, which were women's groups associated with social welfare and labor.[16] Those conflicts went back to differences over tactics in the suffrage campaign, but the passage of the amendment exposed cleavages that had previously been suppressed by the common struggle for the vote.

It was not inevitable that these competing sectors would end up in a "feminists against Feminists" struggle (Lemons, ch. 7), but Alice Paul's autocratic personality exacerbated ideological differences that were first exposed when the NAWSA supported the war while Paul and the future NWP picketed outside the White House. The dispute over a women's rights amendment was only healed in the 1970s, when the idea was embraced by the National Organization of Women (NOW) before being defeated by a new movement – the Christian Conservatives (see Chapter 6).

Bringing Women into the Parties

The lack of unity in the women's movement after the passage of the Nineteenth Amendment left the field open to political party efforts to capture the women's vote. This was unsurprising because parties are, after all, vote-seeking organizations, but it was striking that they got in early by recruiting women members and officers. "Both parties," writes Kristi Andersen, "though they had been lukewarm in their support of suffrage, saw the benefits of mobilizing the votes of women." Moreover, believing that women were the best mobilizers of other women, they "proceeded to set up distinct structures within the party organizations for that purpose" (Andersen, p. 80). At the NAWSA's final convention, Catt had encouraged women to join the parties as a means of advancing their movement (Lemons p. 90).

But the roles that the parties reserved for women within their organizations were symbolic at best. The number of women delegates to national party conventions did increase right after 1920, but it remained static at 10 percent to 15 percent of the delegates and about 25 percent of the alternates through the next decade (see figure 4.1 in Lemon's book). And while the Republicans allocated women to mostly appointive roles (appointed by men!), they also

---

[16] See, in particular, Cott (1977: chs. 2 and 3); Lemons (1973: ch. 7).

introduced a gender equity rule for state party organizations. In contrast, the Democrats created a Women's Bureau to prepare women for the franchise. In the words of a *New York Times* article, they "flung open all its doors, front, side, back and cellar, and wrote 'Welcome!' on each doormat" (quoted in Andersen, p. 85).

Progress in getting women elected to public office was just as glacial. Almost no women were elected to Congress in the 1920s, and the rise of women representatives was slow even during the early years of the New Deal. It was only after World War II – and especially during the 1960s and 1970s – that there was a significant surge in the number of women elected to Congress and especially to the House of Representatives (Beckwith 2003, 2008). As of 2016, as is well known, Americans were not yet ready to elect a woman president – even one as experienced and as moderate as Hillary Clinton.

The Policy Outcomes of Votes for Women

The policy landscape of the 1920s and early 1930s was too complex and too shifting to easily summarize, but, in short, when they came to power, the Republicans, fearing the danger of a unified women's vote, were eager to attract women's votes by supporting social reform measures. Pressured by groups like the Congressional Women's Caucus, the Republican Congress passed a number of bills of interest to women. Lobbying by women's groups increased during this decade, reflecting both the shift in women's activism from suffrage to concrete policy issues and the range of issues that Congress considered that touched on women's policy concerns (Goss 2013: 24–39). For example, Goss found that the number of women's groups testifying before Congress more than doubled between the decade of the 1900s and the 1910s (Goss 2013).

In 1921, Congress passed the Sheppard-Towner Maternity and Infancy Protection Act, which provided matching grants to the states for pre- and postnatal care. In the same year, it passed a bill that established federal regulation of the meat-packing industry – a historic demand of the Progressive movement. During the next year, it passed the Cable Act, which assured that women (like men) would not lose their citizenship if they married foreigners. In 1923, it passed one bill that prohibited the interstate shipment of adulterated milk and another that established the principle of equal pay for men and women in the civil service. Finally, in 1924, Congress passed a bill establishing separate women's federal prisons and supported a child labor amendment, which, however, was never ratified by the states.[17]

In accounting for these successes, Anna Harvey gives great emphasis to the efforts of the women's organizations, especially the NLWV (Harvey 1998: 4).

---

[17] This list of congressional actions on behalf of women's policy goals is summarized from Harvey (1998, ch. 1).

But the League's early legislative influence was based on the perceived promise – or the threat – of the women's vote, which was still indeterminate. In 1920, even incoming president Warren Harding made noises supportive of women's welfare proposals. There was also a progressive fringe in the GOP that welcomed the welfare legislation backed by women's organizations – at least until the defeat of the La Follette campaign in 1924. And there was an ultimately successful women's jury movement that was launched in the same decade (McCammon 2012). However, with the Progressives' failure to break the monopoly of the two mainstream parties, Republican enthusiasm for social legislation soon lapsed.

As women's voting behavior settled into predictable patterns, the reformist instinct subsided and fragmented into different policy rivulets that were put forward by the interest group sectors into which these women settled. Besides, women had won a lot of the concessions they wanted as "special protections" even *prior* to winning the vote – like sole trader laws, property rights, pensions, and of course the Seventeenth Amendment. As a result, the need for something as abstract as the ERA was felt less acutely.[18] Not only that: The number of issues on which women's groups testified increased from an average of just over ten per year to more than forty between these two decades (Goss 2013: 37, 39).[19] Both the number of groups testifying and the number of issues they testified about increased only incrementally between the 1910s and the decade following passage of the amendment (ibid.). It was only after the tectonic shifts of the Depression and the New Deal that women began to make substantial gains in welfare, social policy, and political influence. But that is another story, one that we will examine in Chapter 5.

CONCLUSIONS

The 1920s were a political apprenticeship for a generation of women activists, some of whom had won their spurs in the long campaign for suffrage, while others came to women's politics with the fresh perspective of the war. To extend Rupp and Taylor's "immaculate conception" metaphor, the movement did not experience a "sudden death" after the passage of women's suffrage. On the contrary, theirs was a slow adaptation to a party system in which women could participate as voters but struggled to gain actual representation. But as suffrage disappeared as the focal point of women's politics, the movement shifted its energies into insider activities like lobbying and educational activities that

---

[18] I am grateful to Dawn Teele for pointing this out to me.

[19] Goss's dataset consists of four sets of original data developed from a rich and systematic source of information on the participation of groups testifying before Congress starting in the 1870s, when women began testifying, through 2000, when her study ends. The data capture more than 10,400 appearances by some 2,100 local, state, and national organizations. For a detailed description of the dataset and of her coding procedures, see appendix A of her book.

were less visible, less local, and more like the "people's lobbies" that Clemens saw as the hallmark of the new interest group politics of the twentieth century (1997).

But why were women so slow to take advantage of the opportunity for independent political action after achievement of suffrage? Part of the answer was surely the decline of commitment after they gained the reform that had been the movement's focal point for decades. But exhaustion cannot have been the determining factor because there was a growth in women's *organizations* after the passage of the amendment.

A second reason was the natural differentiation among political, welfare-oriented, and professional women's groups, many of which became engaged in lobbying on behalf of their sectoral interests. Once the vote was attained, the splintering focus between social benefits and equal rights left women with no national organization to represent them as a whole. Equal rights – energetically forwarded by the NWP – was offered as a new focal point, but it was unpopular, especially among conservative women and by labor activists who feared it would be used by conservatives to sweep away hard-won protective legislation.

A third reason was the disappearance of the unity that the suffrage campaign had lent the women's movement after the passage of the amendment. As Virginia Sapiro concluded from her careful study of an earlier period of the movement: "The organizational logic of a coalition or network is that they are challenging to launch and maintain. They are fragile. Without a very strong and specific shared goal they can easily dissolve or break apart" (Sapiro 2020: 1608).

A final reason takes us back to the central theme of this book: We cannot understand the career of a particular movement apart from the relation between the movement and the party system. Not only did these relations evolve during the course of the movement's history, beginning with the tangled history of its relations with the Republican Party after the Civil War (Sapiro 2020), but they changed even more after its central mission was achieved. Before World War I, women – especially those who lacked the vote – had few resources with which to influence the party system. The war and the mobilization it brought gave the suffragists and their allies success in the cause they had supported for decades, especially once President Wilson – no feminist! – came around to their side. But the war was not the kind of shock that, for example, had enabled the antislavery movement to achieve its goal. When World War I ended and the country took a conservative turn, the women's vote became a normal part of partisan and interest group politics.

This was not small beer. Women had shown that a social movement could bring about a major constitutional change, and the reservoir of votes they represented would turn out to be critical in the future (Beckwith 2008; Corder & Wolbrecht 2016). But in the absence of a major shock to the system (World War I lasted less than two years for the United States), it was difficult for women to become a major force in institutional politics. This was particularly the case because the reform they sought integrated them as *voters* – and not as a movement – into the political system and turned the movement into a spectrum of interest groups. The movements and periods we will examine next – the labor and civil rights movements in the Depression and the New Deal – will have a far more transformative impact both on social movements and on the party system and on the relations between them.

5

Labor and Civil Rights from the New Deal to the War on Poverty

We saw in Chapter 4 that women's suffrage took decades to mature, diversify, and take root in various parts of the country before it ultimately succeeded. Spurred by World War I and by its capacity to take advantage of party competition, the movement built on its regional growth and ultimately succeeded. We can argue – as feminist scholars have done for decades – about whether that was a pyrrhic victory, but when we take the long view, it becomes clear that many victories of the women's movement ultimately depended on the relationship between the movement and the party system, especially in places and periods of intense interparty competition. That relationship would grow more integrated in the two major movements that followed: the industrial workers' movement in the New Deal and the civil rights movement from then into the 1960s, when it became a major "anchor" of the Democratic Party.

I will begin this chapter with an analysis of the brief, electrifying, and complicated relationship between the industrial workers' movement and the Democrats during the New Deal (Piven & Cloward 1977). This will serve as a useful comparison to the longer discussion of the civil rights/Democratic Party relationship to follow. Section II describes civil rights as a "long movement" that built on migration and associational growth from South to North. Section III surveys the movement's links to the courts and the parties up to the 1960s, while Section IV examines the repertoire of contention it developed in the latter decade. Section V examines the movement's triggering of a violent and legal countermovement and the effects of their interaction on the national government's support for the movement's goals. Section VI focuses on the movement's ultimate link to the Democratic Party and on the issue of whether that was a simple "anchoring" of a movement to a party like that of the labor movement in the 1930s or was it a "movement capture."

I   LABOR, THE NEW DEAL, AND MOVEMENT/PARTY RELATIONS

The industrial workers' movement of the 1930s provided a model for movement/party relations for the remainder of the twentieth century. The movement had advantages that African Americans lacked – mainly the capacity to use the strike weapon – but it had the long-term disadvantage that it depended for its success on the vagaries of the business cycle and on the presence of a reformist party in power. But it was the first movement to develop the tools for fashioning a modern party/movement coalition – for example, inventing the political action committee (Schlozman 2015: 70–4) – and it led the Democratic Party from a coalition of southern segregationists and northern machine politicians and their followings to the coalition of interest groups that it remains today.

Until the 1930s, industrial workers lacked a solid legal basis for collective bargaining; they were subject to vigorous employer and state repression when they struck and to wage pressure and internal competition when they didn't. Under its longtime leader, Samuel Gompers, the AFL had adopted a nonpartisan strategy, but this benefited mainly white craft workers and excluded the bulk of industrial workers in the mass production industries that were at the core of American economic growth during the first half of the century.

The New Deal changed all of that – at least temporarily. Other things being equal, workers are more likely to exert strike pressure in boom times than in hard times.[1] This underscores how unusual it was that mass strikes of industrial workers broke out in the coalfields, in steel, and in the auto and rubber industries during the Depression – the polar opposite of "boom times." It was in this period that the long-repressed energies of unskilled and semiskilled industrial workers were mobilized by a new union confederation, the CIO, and were "received" by a party leadership with the will and capacity to establish worker rights.

Which of these factors was the determinant one has been the object of dispute among social scientists for decades. In a spirited analysis in the "statist" tradition, Kenneth Finegold and Theda Skocpol put forward a capacious "state autonomy" explanation that placed great emphasis on the expansion of the New Deal state, the creation of a number of instruments for construction of labor rights, and the presence of determined reformist leaders in Congress like Senator Robert Wagner and his talented staff (Finegold & Skcopol 1984). The centerpiece for these authors was the passage in 1935 of the Wagner Act, which

---

[1] A long and somewhat technical literature deals with the relationship between economic conditions and strikes. A thorough summary and assessment is found in John Kennan's "The Economics of Strikes" (1986). In Orley Ashenfelter and Richard Lloyd (eds.). *The Handbook of Labor Economics* and, referring to the strike wave of the 1960s, David Soskice (1978). "Strike Waves and Wage Explosions, 1968–1970." In Colin Crouch and Alessandro Pizzorno (eds.). *The Resurgence of Class Conflict in Western Europe Since 1968* .

"embodied the culmination of the New Deal's break with the officially repressive, antiunion policies of the 1920s." This led to "a turnaround from the industrial labor policies of the early New Deal," which had encouraged all sorts of worker associations in the framework of the corporatist National Industrial Recovery Act (NIRA). The Wagner Act, as these authors later summarized their argument, "represented a triumph for a new approach to industrial labor disputes and unions within the evolving New Deal itself" (1990:1297).

In a vigorous critique of the "statist" model, Michael Goldfield placed far more emphasis on the confluence of labor militancy against a backdrop of a wave of social movement activity in the early 1930s as the ultimate causes for the passage of the Wagner Act and New Deal labor reformism in general (1989). As he summarizes his argument, Goldfield writes: "I will attempt to highlight the important effects of the interaction between labor militancy, social movements, and organized radicalism in the policy process" (p. 1266). Insofar as parties entered Goldfield's causal analysis, it was the surprising strength of the Communist Party, interacting with the labor movement, other radical organizations, and liberal reformers and government officials, that was mainly responsible for assuring the success of the turn to labor rights in the mid-1930s (ibid., p. 1269).[2]

Goldfield is correct that the Depression saw the rise of a major wave of worker and social movement mobilization, while Finegold and Skocpol are also correct that there was a good deal of party/political maneuvering in the passage of the Wagner Act and other pro-labor legislation during the New Deal. But as historian Jefferson Cowie writes:

The depth of the Depression and the crisis of World War Two forced clear realignments of American politics and class relations, but these changes were less the linear triumph of the welfare state than the product of very specific, and short-lived, historical circumstances (Cowie 2016: 9).

In addition to the qualitative changes in the labor movement that Goldfield details in his work, there was also a fundamental realignment in the Democratic Party that produced "an enduring alliance that safeguarded the policy achievements of the Rooseveltian era and sharpened the class divide between the parties" (Schlozman 2015: 49). Though never again would labor enjoy such support for collective economic rights as what it gained under the New Deal, its alliance with the Democrats set the template for a party that would develop into a coalition of interest groups and social movements (Grossmann & Hopkins 2016). The labor/Democratic Party alliance of the 1930s set the template for

---

[2] I will not consider here Goldfield's view of the Wagner Act as an instrument for the regulation of industrial conflict that would "preserve order, prevent high levels of strike activity, slow the spread of communism, and diffuse serious challenges to the capitalist system" (1989: 1276).

party/movement relations in the future – culminating in the civil rights movement.

Of course, no alliance is eternal, and there were hiccups in the "anchoring" of the labor movement to the Democrats: First, it was the newly-formed CIO, led by John L. Lewis and the two main garment workers' unions, and not the more conservative unions of the AFL – that forged the alliance between labor and the Democrats in the 1930s. Second, there remained a strong conservative faction in the party in the "Solid South" that was wary of any alliance that could increase the weight of African Americans within the party (Schlozman, p. 63). Third, the alliance depended on policies implemented by the expanding administrative state (Milkis & York 2017). Once the Democrats lost control of that state, labor's long slide to irrelevance in national policy making began. Nevertheless, it is safe to say that as long as the New Deal continued in power, labor and the Democrats constituted the most concentrated model of movement/party alignment that the country had yet seen.

Three features of this alliance provided models for movement/party alliances in the future:

First, the CIO unions essentially invented the kind of "hybrid" organizations that we will examine in detail in chapter 7. These groups established a permanent alliance with the Democratic Party. This was the beginning of what would turn into a long-term trend for both parties – the external-ization of fundraising and political influence to outside actors (Charnock 2020).

Second, that alliance was not exclusive: In the course of the New Deal, despite FDR's reluctance to do so and with the powerful support of part of the labor movement, the Democrats began to embrace the cause of civil rights for African Americans (Schickler 2016).

Third, although it was an organic relationship, the Democrat/labor alliance was buffeted by the variations in the business cycle and by the unwilling-ness of future Democratic administrations to delegate industrial policy to its labor allies. Though labor gained the support of the Supreme Court in the pivotal case of *Youngstown Sheet and Tube Co. v. Sawyer*[3] against President Truman's seizure of the steel industries during the Korean War, this was only a shot across the bows. A more important turning point was the Taft Hartley Act, passed in 1947, which rolled back many of the gains that labor had made (Cowie 2016: ch. 6). The Cold War, the country's anti-Communist turn, and the revival of entrepreneurial power combined to drain the strength that labor had gained in the New Deal.

Between the end of World War II and the 1980s, union density declined from 35.5 percent of nonagricultural employees to under 20 percent, while strike rates fell to the lowest levels they had reached for a century (Goldfield 1987: 8–22; Tilly & Tilly 1998: 250–52). The movement never succeeded in

[3] 343 US 579 (1952)

unionizing the South and, under President Ronald Reagan, the NLRB, which the Wagner Act had created, became an anti-labor instrument in the hands of a conservative administration (Cowie 2010).

The New Deal/industrial labor coalition was the result of a brief critical juncture that depended upon a particular political configuration of a movement and a political party during a period of national crisis (Piven & Cloward 1977). In contrast, the civil rights movement was a "long movement" whose fate was entangled with the development of party system as a whole and with the growth of the administrative state.

II CIVIL RIGHTS AS A "LONG MOVEMENT"

Like the industrial workers' movement, the civil rights movement also made its entry into national politics through an alliance with the Democrats. But its struggle was far more extended; it faced greater handicaps, based on the enduring racial undercurrent in American society, and it enjoyed no single moment like the 1934–1936 strike wave to anchor the movement to the party. But it had the advantage over the CIO upsurge that it was not dependent on a particular political-economic conjuncture; that it was sufficiently diverse in its organizational armature and its capacity to develop a varied repertoire; and that its leaders had the strategic vision to adapt to the changing alignments of American politics.

At first, the relationship was less organic than the anchoring of labor to the Democrats. For one thing, it took time to wean African American voters from their traditional fealty to "the party of Lincoln." For another, there were important elements in the Democratic Party – starting with President Roosevelt – that were unwilling to allow African Americans within the broad tent of the Democratic Party (Katznelson 2013). As a result, the anchoring of the civil rights movement to the Democrats took much longer and had to overcome more obstacles than the connection between the labor movement and that Party during the New Deal. The progress of the civil rights movement was slow and painful (Hall 2005), but its power to influence the party system grew even as the strength of organized labor declined. Though both movements benefited from political opportunities – the New Deal's reformism for the industrial workers and the Cold War for civil rights – the opening and closure of opportunities was much briefer in the case of the former and longer in the case of the latter. The National Association for the Advancement of Colored People (NAACP) campaign to oppose the plague of lynching shows how long it took and how many hurdles needed to be crossed for the movement to gain the support of the Democratic Party.

Anti-Lynching: An Unpopular Cause

In July 1916, *The Crisis*, the paper edited by W. E. B. Du Bois, published a pictorial supplement dedicated to the lynching of a black man, Jesse Washington, in Waco, Texas (Francis 2014: 46–7), who had been accused of raping and beating to death a white woman for whose husband he worked. After a rapid trial with an all-white jury, he was carried off and lynched by a mob of white townspeople. The event was brought to the attention of NAACP Secretary Roy Nash, who asked a British suffragette, Elizabeth Freeman, who was traveling in Texas at the time, to go to Waco and gather information on the atrocity. Freeman's report, circulated to *The Crisis*'s 30,000 readers, was followed with a speaking tour, using the brutal pictures of Washington's lynching to emphasize her point, as the national press picked up the story and helped to raise public awareness of the scope and brutality of lynching in America.

Why begin a discussion of the relations between civil rights and the party system with the campaign against the South's perverted justice system? The main reason is that we need to remember how long it took for the movement to break through the determined silence of both parties about the cruel forms that segregation had taken since Reconstruction. But this took the movement along a long and circuitous route, involving the courts, the executive, and a large and sometimes violent countermovement before political leaders grudgingly took up the cause of civil rights. Even where African Americans began to make economic progress, that progress led to what Tesla Weaver calls a "frontlash" – efforts to stop black progress in its tracks through violent repression (2007).

Typical of an early frontlash was the violent attack on a black neighborhood in St. Louis in 1917, when "urban and racial tension resulting from African American migration out of the South exploded into a brutal race war in that city leaving hundreds of black corpses in the streets, many of them shot or lynched by angry white mobs" (Milkis & Tichenor, p. 107). In response, civil rights protesters marched down Fifth Avenue in New York City in a "Silent Parade" bearing banners that drew, ironically, on President Wilson's wartime call to "Make the World Safe for Democracy" (Francis: 108).

The march charted a pathway to the future in three ways. First, it was the first major demonstration against racial injustice in the North, establishing a precedent for future performances. Second, by using the slogan "Make America Safe for Democracy," civil rights activists used foreign policy for the first time to highlight the contradiction between the country's racial politics and its claim to be a beacon of freedom (Dudziak 2000; Parker 2009). And, third, it launched the NAACP as an authoritative voice for African American rights, although Marcus Garvey's UNIA (Universal Negro Improvement Association) almost certainly commanded more support. But before any of that could happen, there had to be a pathway out of the repressive practices of Jim Crow to national politics and the party system. That path took two connected routes – through mass migration and association.

The Great Migration

The 1930s was an important decade for the civil rights movement (Hall 2005; Schickler 2016). Though in the 1920s, three Republican administrations had kept their distance from African American claims, from the 1910s a change began in the geographic distribution of the black population that would ultimately have profound implications for the linkage between civil rights and party politics (Lemann 1991).

Beginning in the 1910s, the collapse of "King Cotton" in the southern economy and an increased demand for black labor in the North led to a massive migration to the North and West, climaxing in the war years and in the 1950s (McAdam 1999b: 73–7). Between 1910 and 1960, while the Black population in the South increased by only 29 percent, it grew by 530 percent in the North and an astronomical 2,043 percent in the Mountain and Pacific West (ibid., p. 78). Immigration was particularly great in New York State with almost 900 thousand migrants; in Illinois with more than 600,000; and in California with more than 700,000 (ibid., p. 80). These were all states that would become important voting centers for the Democratic Party in the 1930s.

At the same time, the decline of the cotton economy, alongside the beginning of textile and furniture industries, brought significant shifts of African Americans from the countryside to the cities within the South, creating the foundation for the growth of a black middle class in the region. Although black voter registration was still suppressed by both legal and illegal disfranchisement, in the cities African Americans could escape the worst expressions of Jim Crow and establish their own associations and institutions.

Another population shift came with the onset of World War II (Kryder 2000). Until 1940, black recruitment into the armed forces had been limited to four military units, with only about 3,600 black soldiers and five black officers in the regular army. After a successful pressure campaign by black leaders, President Roosevelt, worried about losing votes to Wendell Wilkie, who called for an assault on racism during the 1940 presidential campaign (Parker 2009: 42–3), pushed for a Selective Service Act that opened military recruitment to African Americans. "By the end of the war," writes Christopher Parker, "approximately one million African Americans had ultimately served, either voluntarily or through conscription, two-thirds of them from the South" (Parker, ibid., pp. 45–6).

Although many of these troops were relegated to auxiliary units and others were greeted with racist violence by white officers and soldiers, they earned 11 silver stars and 69 bronze ones during the war. In the Air Force, black pilots shot down 111 German aircraft and earned more than 1,000 medals (ibid., p. 47). Many of these soldiers were greeted with racist incidents when they returned to their hometowns, but even there, they were able to draw on their military experience for professional advancement and associational memberships.

Associational Growth

The black population of the South had always worshipped in black churches. The move of substantial numbers of rural blacks to the cities increased the number of churches, the size of their congregations, and the proportion of clergymen holding higher degrees (McAdam 1999b: 99). Although many congregants and pastors were conservative religiously and politically, by the 1950s, a substantial proportion had become involved in the civil rights movement. Just as important, the churches offered African Americans a focal point for social networks that emerged as crucibles for civil rights activism (Morris 1984).

The black college population, which served as the main base for the civil rights movement in the postwar period, was also growing rapidly. McAdam, drawing on a number of original sources, shows that the number of students enrolled in black colleges grew from approximately 15,000 in 1928 to 35,000 in the early 1940s, to 75,000 by war's end, and to more than 100,000 by the early 1960s (1999b: 101). "By mid-century," he concludes "the poorly supported, inadequately staffed black colleges of thirty years earlier had been transformed into some of the strongest and most influential institutions within the black community" (p. 103).

The NAACP and Other Organizations

More directly relevant to collective action than either the churches or black colleges was the remarkable growth of civil rights organizations between the wars (Morris 1984). As the most visible African American organization during the interwar years, the NAACP was at the heart of this process (Francis, p. 3). That organization was founded in the wake of another brutal race riot, this one in Springfield, Illinois, in 1908 (Francis: 37–9)[4]. The spate of anti-black violence around this time led the new organization to make anti-lynching its central policy mission (Bernstein 2006; Francis 2014). Between 1911 and 1923, Megan Ming Francis calculated from NAACP board meetings that criminal justice was far and away the most prominent topic in the organization's mission, far more than education, labor, or voting rights (ibid., 40).

Although the organization's growth was slow during the first two decades after its founding, in the decade following FDR's election, it enjoyed a fivefold growth in membership and an even faster one after World War II (Wolters 1970: 302). In 1936 it established a Youth and College Division, which would be a major source of activism in the following decades. But its most important move in the direction of its institutional strategy came in 1940, when its legal

---

[4] Of course, there were predecessors to the NAACP's anti-lynching campaign, the most important of whom was Ida B. Wells, whose anti-lynching activism began in 1892 when three of her friends were lynched by a mob of white men in Memphis, Tennessee. For a brief account, see Francis (2014: 31–4) and the short-lived Niagara movement, which was founded by Du Bois and William Trotter after a group of African Americans had been denied entry to a hotel in Buffalo. The movement was also challenged by Marcus Garvey's Universal Negro Improvement Association, which tried to link African Americans to the black diaspora.

department was turned into the Legal Defense Fund, which became the public face of the organization for most white Americans.

Even more remarkable than its general membership growth was the NAACP's expansion in the South, particularly in the cities, where members could feel protected from the more virulent forms of racism that still infested the rural areas (McAdam 1999b: 103). Although only 42 percent of the NAACP's units were incorporated in the region in 1919, thirty years later that proportion had risen to 63 percent (ibid.). The spread of this northern-born and northern-led organization into the South was a portent of increased activism in that region that party leaders would ignore at their peril.

The NAACP was not alone. In her systematic study of African American organizations after 1955, Debra Minkoff emphasized the importance of the growth of service-oriented organizations. For example, the National Urban League (NUL) and the United Negro College Fund were both created prior to the civil rights movement but nonetheless represented one dimension of black organizational efforts (1995: 33). By the 1960s, these organizations had been joined by such future stalwarts of civil rights as the Southern Christian Leadership Congress (SCLC), the Congress for Racial Equality (CORE), and the Student Nonviolent Coordinating Committee (SNCC), followed by a number of more radical groups in the late 1960s. By the time Minkoff collected her data for her book, *Organizing for Equality,* in the 1990s, she enumerated 277 African American–based organizations, which constituted 28 percent of the 975 groups she studied (p. 19).[5]

The Civil Rights/Labor Alliance

During the New Deal, African Americans began to form coalitions with other movements. Especially important was the rise of a new and more militant branch of the labor movement, the CIO. The CIO grew out of a schism in the conservative, skilled worker–based AFL, which had grown up under Samuel Gompers as a "business union" that largely avoided party politics (Perlman 1928). John L. Lewis, the fiery head of the United Mine Workers (UMW), and two garment worker unions led the way to a new confederation organized on industrial lines that quickly took advantage of the leftward shift in the Democratic Party under Roosevelt. As Eric Schickler writes: "The meteoric rise of the CIO gave African Americans an important ally within the Democratic coalition" (Schickler, p. 5).

---

[5] The largest proportion of the minority groups that Minkoff identified were either advocacy groups or advocacy/service groups, each of them constituting 29 percent of the total. Only 5.6 percent were identified as primarily "protest" groups, but this was more than double the proportion among other constituencies (see table 3.1 in her book). The growth in the number of African American groups was fastest in the 1960s, but tended to level off after 1970 (see figure 3.1 in her book).

The linkage between civil rights and labor, notes Schickler, "underscores the ways in which major political transformations can result from the intersection of multiple, partly independent trajectories" (p. 8). Militancy in steel and mining, where African Americans constituted a substantial proportion of the workforce, was encouraged by the passage of the National Labor Relations Act (NLRA), sometimes referred to as the Wagner Act, in 1935. The act was the first in American history to give workers the legal right to organize and bargain collectively on behalf of their interests. Alongside the unions' workplace efforts, CIO leaders Sidney Hillman and Lewis formed the Labor Non-Partisan League, which worked with local, state, and civil rights activists to support Roosevelt in the 1936 elections. The president's immense victory in that election increased labor's political clout (ibid., p. 57). This would have been of only minor interest for African Americans if the CIO had not also developed a commitment to racial justice (ibid., p. 53). "From the start," writes Schickler, the *CIO News* sought to link the issues of labor rights with policies against racial discrimination under the common rubric of 'civil rights'" (ibid., p. 59).

The CIO was formed to give low- and medium-skilled industrial workers representative institutions. Though not aimed specifically at African Americans because so many African Americans worked mainly in these industries, the link between militant unionism and civil rights was important from the beginning. Before long, a loose coalition of union-sponsored and civil rights organizations, including the NAACP, the Urban League, and the Communist-influenced National Negro Congress, began to cooperate on both labor and civil rights issues. The redefinition of liberalism to include civil rights, not always recognized at the time, was one of the most important political outcomes of the New Deal, beginning in the 1930s with the convergence of the CIO's progressive unionism and civil rights activism (Schickler, ch. 4).

III A MOVEMENT USING COURTS AND PARTIES

Until the 1930s, the NAACP lacked ties to either of the two main parties, each of which – for different reasons – steered clear of involvement in racial politics: the Democrats because their most reliable electoral base was in the segregationist South, and the Republicans whose major electoral base was the North. Northern Democrats in Congress had little incentive to challenge their southern colleagues, who controlled a reliable reservoir of Democratic voters and used their control of southern courthouses and legislatures to depress black voting in the region (Key 1984; Katznelson 2013).

The Republicans' concession of the South to the Democrats had a profound effect on national as well as regional politics. The fact that one party dominated the politics of the region gave southern Democrats a seniority advantage in Congress that translated into control of key congressional committees, a development that prevented even mild reforms in race relations from gaining a foothold. For example, even when anti-lynching legislation passed the House of Representatives, it was filibustered to death in the Senate (Schickler, pp. 58–9).

The Democratic Party's policies toward the South had changed little since Reconstruction, and when the party did gain power in 1912, it was behind Woodrow Wilson, a native of Virginia and a segregationist. Elected in large part with southern support, Wilson maintained a cool distance from the civil rights community and allowed his administration to actively promote segregation in the federal government (Schickler, p. 101). As for FDR, he was no racist, but he never proactively put forward an agenda for civil rights because the support of southern conservatives was important to his program – the southern wing of his party backed his banking and antitrust reforms, tax reform, and the even the Farm Security Administration and the NLRA. In his thirteen years in office, FDR never proactively embraced the need for civil rights reform, even refusing to publicly support anti-lynching legislation when it was brought before Congress.

The racial contradiction at the heart of the New Deal went deeper than FDR's desire to appease southern supporters. As historian Meg Jacobs points out, New Deal state building came from the top but also engaged ordinary citizens from the bottom up (2019: 36–7). The broadened set of legislative rights created by the New Deal "invited, relied upon, and responded to pressure from below" (p. 38).[6] From these partnerships, African Americans were largely excluded. For example, even as thousands of black troops were fighting in World War II, southern Democrats made sure to insert language in the G. I. Bill for veterans' benefits that would excluie them from much of the law's coverage (Altschuler & Blumin 2009). It was only toward the end of his second term that FDR was willing to come out against lynching (Francis, p. 95). In the meantime, and in large part because of its inability to gain leverage from the parties, the NAACP turned to the institutions that were furthest from representative politics – the courts.

To the Courts

Until the 1920s, the Supreme Court had shown no interest in racial justice, and in fact, in the case of *Plessy v. Ferguson* (163 US 537, 1896), it had sanctified

---

[6] As Brent Cebul and Mason Williams write, "Sometimes of choice and sometimes of political and institutional necessity, the New Dealers made state and local government, private contractors, and members of civil society their local partners in administering many of their initiatives" (Cebul & Williams 2019: 96).

the doctrine of "separate but equal."[7] But a turning point came in 1923 in the case of *Moore* v. *Dempsey* (261 US 86). The case resulted when a meeting of African American sharecroppers in a rural county in Arkansas was invaded by a posse of white landowners and sheriff's deputies, who attacked the meeting-goers before burning down the church in which the meeting was held. This event was followed by an invasion of the county by white vigilantes from neighboring counties who claimed that local blacks were planning an insurrection. This was followed by a torrent of violence, counterviolence, lynchings, and arrests, leading to the conviction of twelve African Americans for murder in a state court and was marred by threats against them from both inside and outside the courtroom.

In its Supreme Court pleading, the NAACP asked the court to establish the power of federal courts to intervene in such cases on habeas corpus grounds. With Justice Oliver Wendell Holmes writing for a 6 to 2 majority, the Court ruled that a mob-dominated trial had deprived the defendants of the due process guaranteed by the Fourteenth Amendment.[8] In Dempsey, the Court overturned Frank and "positioned itself as a major player in the politics of race in Jim Crow America" (Francis 2014:171).[9]

It was only in the 1930s that the Court began to stand up for the rights of African Americans with any consistency.[10] As Francis writes, beginning with these cases, "the Supreme Court ... sent a message to state governments that a criminal trial had to have more than simply the appearance of being conducted in a lawful manner" (p. 6). It was this shift in the Court's views on civil rights that inspired the NAACP to fashion its systematic campaign to gradually erode the legal basis of separate but equal. From that time on, the NAACP – despairing of engaging either party in defending black citizens against denial of their rights – turned to the courts in a campaign of legal mobilization.

---

[7] In a landmark case in 1915, it had denied the claim of a Jewish businessman that he had been denied due process of law in a Georgia case in which he had been accused of murder. In Frank v. *Mangum* (237 US 309), Leo Frank, one of the owners of the National Pencil Factory in Atlanta, was sentenced to death by a Georgia court amid an atmosphere of violence. Frank's request for a writ of habeas corpus in the Supreme Court was turned down by a vote of 7 to 2 with Justice Oliver Wendell Holmes dissenting.

[8] It is interesting that Holmes used the same reasoning he had developed in his dissenting opinion in *Frank*.

[9] In chapter 5 of her book, *Civil Rights and the Making of the Modern American State*, Francis recounts the grim history of this case and makes clear the key role of the NAACP in its legal history.

[10] In *Powell* v. *Alabama* (287 US 45), the court held in 1935 that defendants in capital cases have the right to state-appointed counsel. In the same year, in *Hollins* v. *Oklahoma* (295 US 392), the court ruled that the exclusion of African Americans from juries was unconstitutional. The next year, in *Brown* v. *Mississippi* (297 US 278), the court ruled that confessions extracted through torture violated due process under the Nineteenth Amendment, and in 1940, in *Chambers* v. *Florida*, the court held that confessions obtained under duress were illegal.

Turning to the Ballot

Much earlier than many people realize, African American organizations began to turn to politics at the local level. Harvard Sitkoff summarizes some of these developments in various southern states during the 1930s. In North Carolina, he writes;

> Raleigh blacks formed a Negro Voters' League in 1931 to fight for the franchise. Early in 1936 Durham blacks followed suit, organizing their own Committee on Negro Affairs and setting up branches in Charlotte, Greensboro, and Winston-Salem. In Georgia, the Atlanta Civil and Political League doubled the number of registered blacks from 1936 to 1939. In Savanna the Young Men's Civic Club organized in 1938 for the same purpose (Sitkoff 1981: 99).

It was not long before New Deal allies in state and local Democratic parties began to respond by allying with African Americans to spread some of the benefits of Roosevelt's programs beyond his white base (Schickler 2016). Added to the structural and demographic changes sketched earlier, this eventually translated into votes.

First, the move from countryside to the city took African Americans out from under the heavy burden of farm tenancy and the repression it produced. Second, the presence of a vast new population of color in the cities of the North alerted politicians there – including many machine politicians (Sitkoff 1981: 88) – that African Americans could be turned into an electoral clientele (McAdam 1999b: 82). Third, as McAdam infers, "the expansion of the northern black electorate introduced an element of political conflict into a northern-southern racial alliance already weakened by the economic conflict produced by the growing northern demand for black labor" (ibid.).

The historic attachment of African American voters to the Republican Party went deep, and in the 1932 presidential elections, a majority of black voters still supported the party of Lincoln (Sitkoff, p. 39). By the 1934 congressional elections, however, black voters began to defect from their Republican loyalties, and the Democratic Party – if not the president – was quick to respond. "For the first time," writes Sitkoff, "some Democrats campaigned in black neighborhoods" (p. 88). By the 1936 election, according to a Gallup Poll, an astounding 76 peorcent of Northern black voters turned out for Roosevelt. "In every northern city but Chicago," writes Sitkoff, "blacks voted at least 60 percent for Roosevelt (ibid., pp. 95–6).

Always acute to the benefits of patronage, Roosevelt's counselor, Jim Farley, helped to create a division of the Democratic Party dedicated to placing African Americans in government. There was also an informal "Black Cabinet Initiative" led by Robert Weaver and Mary McCloud Bethune. With Farley's help, FDR also ended the two-thirds rule for nominations at the 1936 Democratic Convention, which helped to shift the center of gravity in the

Democratic Party toward the North.[11] By the second half of the 1930s, the African American population in the North was part of the New Deal coalition, consisting of unionized workers, northern and midwestern ethnic groups, African Americans, and the South.

War and Movement Building

World War II, with its call for America to become the beacon of democracy, increased the incentive for African Americans to use the ballot, even in areas of the South where there were strong disincentives to do so. The end of the white primary, which resulted from the Supreme Court's *Smith* v. *Allright* decision in 1944,[12] boosted black electoral participation, which rose from roughly 250,000 before that decision to 500,000 by 1947 (Parker, p. 178). Extralegal disincentives to vote, like poll taxes, literacy tests, and other "legal" obstacles, remained, but by 1952 voter registration among blacks and risen to 20 percent before reaching an early plateau of 28 percent in 1960 (Matthews & Prothro 1966).

Black veterans were especially incentivized to use the ballot. All of the veterans interviewed by Christopher Parker for his study, *Fighting for Democracy,* cited their military service as a motivation for activism. Of course, many had experienced racism during their service, particularly those who were posted to southern army bases. But discrimination may have served as an incentive to participate in civil organizations and elections. This determination probably had a multiplier effect: As Aldon Morris reports, "Black soldiers returning from the wars began urging their relatives and friends not to accept domination" (Morris 1984: 80).

Their wartime experiences may even have served as an incentive for black veterans to participate in politics at war's end. Drawing on Donald Matthews' and James Prothro's Negro Political Participation Study (1966), Parker found that both voting behavior and nonvoting forms of political activism were strikingly higher among veterans than among the general African American population.[13]

Political Competition and Civil Rights

As long as FDR was in the White House, support for the war gave the Democrats a comfortable margin, and the African American vote was not

---

[11] I am grateful to Sidney Milkis for reminding me of these early moves toward integrating African Americans in the New Deal outside of congressional obstruction.

[12] 321 US 649 (1944), which overturned a Texas state law that had authorized parties to set their internal rules, including the use of white primaries

[13] The differential between the veterans and others was highest for voting in presidential elections (30 percent) and for attending meetings (a 23 percent differential). Black veterans were also 23 percent more likely to report talking to others about politics and 21 percent were more likely to participate in local elections (Parker 2009: 184).

crucial to the party's electoral success. But with FDR's passing, like the experience of the suffrage movement in the West, party politics became more competitive, as was evident from the results of the 1946 congressional elections, when the Republicans took control of the House of Representatives for the first time since 1932. The GOP used its new leverage to oppose every one of Truman's efforts to build on the New Deal heritage and launched the beginning of a savage anti-Communist campaign aimed indirectly at the Democrats. This was also the moment when the unions began to oust Communist Party members, depriving the confederation of some of its most effective organizers (Piven & Cloward 1977: 164–5).

In this competitive political moment, even while he softened his party's support for organized labor, Truman turned enthusiastically to courting the African American vote. In a crucial memorandum, two of his advisors, Clark Clifford and James Rowe, argued that the president could afford to ignore the Dixiecrats and should push hard for votes in the West and from African Americans. Clifford and Rowe argued that "the Negroes not only vote as a bloc but are geographically concentrated in the pivotal, large and closely contested electoral states such as New York, Illinois, Pennsylvania, Ohio, and Michigan."[14] The weight of the black vote was never greater than in this highly competitive electoral moment.

Genuinely concerned that the Soviet Union was actively criticizing its American rival for the hypocrisy of promoting democracy around the world while denying a substantial body of its citizens equal rights, Truman expanded the federal government's powers to advance African American rights. Though coming from a border state, Truman was a genuine New Dealer who saw in the black vote a necessary component of his coming electoral challenge. Soon after his election, the president delivered a controversial pro–civil rights speech to Congress, followed by a promise to establish a Fair Employment Practices Committee and end segregation in the military.

The most competitive moment in the relation of African Americans to the party system followed John F. Kennedy's election. In the course of his campaign, Kennedy made a highly publicized phone call to Coretta Scott King to assure her of his support for her husband, who had been jailed in Atlanta (Branch 1989). Elected with a razor-thin margin by a coalition of "strange bedfellows" – northern liberals, white ethnics, African Americans, and the "Solid South" – the new president was determined to avoid intervening in southern race relations. But the growth of African American militancy, together with the political and legal acumen of the NAACP and its more

---

[14] James Rowe, "Cooperation – or Conflict? – The President's Relationship with an Opposition Congress" (December 1946). Clark Clifford Papers, Truman Library. Quoted in Donaldson (1993): 751. That the Rowe-Clifford memorandum provided the strategic blueprint for Truman's successful 1948 campaign is clearly shown in Milkis' *The President and the Parties* (1993: 154–9).

militant competitors, forced Kennedy's hand as was evident soon after he took office. This was the result of a combination of institutional and noninstitutional actions that began even before his election.

In 1958, Bruce Boynton, a black student at Howard University Law School in Washington, DC, had taken a bus to his home in Montgomery, Alabama. During a layover at a bus terminal in Richmond, Virginia, Boynton entered the segregated restaurant, sat in the white section, and ordered a sandwich and tea. When asked to move to the colored section, he refused, saying that as an interstate passenger he was protected by federal anti-segregation laws. He was arrested by local police, charged with trespass, and fined $10. Following his conviction, lawyers for the NAACP appealed to the Supreme Court. Intervening as a friend of the court, the Justice Department agreed that the Interstate Commerce Act expressly forbade "unjust discrimination." On December 5, 1960, the Court decided 7–2 in favor of Boynton.

The Court's decision in *Boynton* (364 US 454, 1960) encouraged the Congress of Racial Equality (CORE) to organize a series of "freedom rides" to southern bus terminals to test the federal government's willingness to protect African Americans' right to travel between states.[15] The ride was organized by CORE together with the Fellowship of Reconciliation, which had overlapping memberships. In the most dramatic of these rides, CORE activists were attacked, beaten, and one of their buses was set on fire in the presence of FBI agents who, in deference to state law enforcement, refused to intervene. After their bus arrived in Birmingham, the confrontations escalated. As Joseph Luders writes, "Local police conspired with the Ku Klux Klan to permit a white mob to have an uninterrupted fifteen minutes in which to assault the riders" (Luders 2010: 165).

Soon after the Freedom Rides, Martin Luther King's Southern Christian Leadership Conference (SCLC) launched a series of efforts to oppose segregation, first in Albany, Georgia, and ultimately in Birmingham, Alabama. The Albany effort, which was met with a determined but nonviolent police response, was generally regarded as a failure (McAdam 1983), but the Birmingham experience was successful, largely because of the violent response of the city's police chief, "Bull" Connor, "a notorious racist and hothead who could be depended on *not* to respond nonviolently" (ibid.). In full view of the media, Connor trained fire hoses and unleashed attack dogs on the peaceful demonstrators.

King and the SCLC had not blundered mindlessly into this torrent of violence. Chastened by their failure in Albany, they chose Birmingham as their next target precisely because Connor's violent response could be

---

[15] Although the tactic was seen as unprecedented at the time, in 1947, a group of eight African Americans and eight white men undertook a "Voyage of Reconciliation" through the South to test the Supreme Court's recent decision, *Morgan v. Virginia* (328 US, 1946), holding that segregated seating on buses in interstate commerce was illegal (Catsam 2009).

predicted, as was the presence of the media to broadcast the brutality of his police against peaceful demonstrators. The resulting scenes of demonstrators being slammed into storefronts by the force of fire hoses and being attacked by snarling police dogs were broadcast nationwide on the nightly TV news.

The movement's goal was both local and national; at the national level, it was exquisitely political. As McAdam summarizes the outcome:

SCLC saw its task as destroying the political calculus on which Kennedy's stance of neutrality rested. It had to make the political and especially electoral benefits of support-ing civil rights appear to outweigh the costs of alienating Southern white voters and their electoral officials. This meant mobilizing the support of the general public, thereby broadening the electoral basis of civil rights advocacy (1999b: 350).

It did so through the combination of an inherited repertoire of using courts and parties and the invention of new performances that have inalterably changed the repertoire of contention in America.

IV THE NEW REPERTOIRE OF CONTENTION

Formative movements go through periods of innovation in the forms of contention that they deploy. Just as the industrial workers learned to use the sit-down strike in the 1930s to keep strikebreakers out of their factories (Piven & Cloward, pp. 137–40), in the 1960s, civil rights groups learned to employ a wide range of collective actions to expose the evils of segregation, trigger racist reactions, attract the attention of the media, and gain electoral leverage (see Andrews & Gaby (2015: 517). In doing so, Civil Rights became a genuinely "formative movement," one that was able to combine institutional and noninstitutional actions that used local struggles to invite federal intervention. To do so, it developed a rich and varied repertoire of contention that it used flexibly and strategically to achieve its aims.

Perhaps nowhere in American history do we find as broad a range of social movement tactics as in the civil rights movement. Even before its "classical period" in the 1960s, the movement developed a repertoire far more varied than the legal actions mounted by the NAACP. For example, between 1955 and 1960, McAdam uncovered from the *New York Times Index* 27 institutional actions *other than* court cases, 25 economic boycotts, 136 sit-ins or other forms of direct action, and 6 cases of violent actions (McAdam 1999b: 134). McAdam has adapted the preferences for different kinds of action among African Americans from Brinks' and Harris's survey in 1963. Table 5.1 shows that roughly half of the leaders and nonleaders interviewed were willing to march in a demonstration, take part in a sit-in, get arrested, or picket a store that practiced segregation (p. 163).

During the years between *Brown* and Kennedy's election, activists targeted a wide range of public and private concerns, ranging from public accommodations (55 percent) to transportation (13 percent), education

TABLE 5.1 *Percentage of African Americans in 1963 reporting a willingness to participate in various forms of collective action*

Form of Action	Percentage of Leaders	Percentage of Nonleaders
March in a demonstration	57	51
Take part in a sit-in	57	49
Go to jail	58	47
Picket a store	57	46

Source: Brink and Harris, 1963, p. 203, adapted by McAdam, 1999b, p. 163.

(11 percent), and political institutions, including voter registration drives, with 9 percent of the total (ibid., p. 137). Table 5.1, drawn from McAdam's research, shows how widespread the targets of the movement were even before Kennedy was elected.

Just as important as what protesters did was *how* they did it: though the use of a community organizing model that was inspired by Ella Baker, who counseled sending activists into communities to cultivate local leaders and create a local network. That was a tactic that built on traditions of labor organizing but that went much further than the unions (Payne 2007). The community organizing model was later emulated by other movements like the farm workers and by many contemporary community organizers. A new actor – African American college students – had meanwhile gained political consciousness and was spurred into contentious collective action.

Beginning in Greenville, North Carolina, in early 1960, students throughout the South initiated the first successful lunch counter sit-in campaign (Andrews & Biggs 2006; Schmidt 2018: ch. 1). This was followed by the attempt of James Meredith, a decorated army veteran, to register at the University of Mississippi, leading to a white racist riot and forcing President Kennedy to send troops to the campus. Not only did Kennedy have to face the tense drama of the Freedom Rides soon after coming into office, but he was challenged by a rapidly spreading brushfire of student protests across the South.

Sit-Ins and Their Aftermath

Much of the post-1960s scholarship on civil rights has contrasted the disruptive protest performances of the "new" part of the movement with the tried-and-true conventional methods of the NAACP and other traditional African American groups. Elided in this division was the interaction between the two varieties of contentious action. As Omar Wasow has recently argued, "nonviolent action, particularly when met with state or vigilante repression, drove media coverage, framing, congressional speech, and public opinion on civil rights" (2020). This process of "agenda seeding" was the most effective mechanism in the armory of the civil rights movement.

Perhaps the most influential disruptive performances employed by the civil rights movement in the 1960s were the sit-ins. Sit-ins were a variation on the "sit-down" strikes that CIO activists had employed in the 1930s and were already used by civil rights activists in the 1950s. But they gained new resonance from the variety of sites that activists chose for their demonstrations and from the availability of television to publicize their actions. If the public could see spitting thugs brutalizing well-dressed black college students sitting quietly at lunch counters, it would be hard to ignore the contradiction between the American idea of freedom and the reality of segregation.

Sit-ins appeared to be spontaneous, short-term performances mounted by small groups of intrepid, well-dressed students, but when examined over time and across the region, they showed clear patterns that depended in part on the concentrations of black college students, in part on the presence of major media markets, and in part on the presence of organized civil rights groups (Andrews & Biggs 2006). They also led to the involvement of civil rights lawyers who – after initially hesitating about supporting this uncontrolled form of protest – set to work defending the right of access to public accommodations (Schmidt, ch. 2). But going to court on behalf of students who had been arrested for sitting-in was complicated. As Christopher Schmidt shows, the law did not speak with one voice about access to public accommodation, and the legal precedents were uncertain. As a result, "judges were ultimately just one among many groups of influential actors" (Schmidt, p. 5).

The hundreds of cases sparked by the sit-ins dragged through the courts for three years, until the issue finally percolated into national politics. Because the very idea of a federal public accommodation law had seemed far-fetched, JFK's initial approach was to hope that the issue could be adjudicated at the state level. But it was quickly clear that neither the courts nor the state legislatures were interested in dealing with the issue. Pressure on the administration grew as Martin Luther King Jr.'s "Project-C" protest in Birmingham was gaining national media attention, and the administration worried that a negative decision on the sit-ins in the courts would only spark further protests (Schmidt, pp. 155–6).

The result was to push the Kennedys to include public accommodations in Title II of the Civil Rights Act that Bobby Kennedy was putting together with congressional moderates in the spring of 1963. Though opponents railed that Title II went beyond congressional power and infringed on individual liberty, the Supreme Court, in the case of *Hamm* v. *City of Rock Hill* (379 US 306, 1964), decided that "the peaceful conduct for which petitioners were prosecuted was on behalf of a principle since embodied in the law of the land" was legal, evacuating all the cases that had piled up in the courts since 1961 (Schmidt, ch. 6). Though it is remembered for the courageous efforts of small groups of African American students risking jail or beating, the sit-in movement was unusual for the wide diffusion of the practice, the length of its resolution, and the involvement of a variety of actors from protesting students, defending lawyers, the highest levels of government, and the courts.

Circling Back to Party Politics

Mississippi Freedom Summer was the most notable example of the marriage of disruptive and conventional tactics. The summer of 1964 was selected for an army of northern volunteers – most of them white – to register African Americans to vote in the state with the lowest level of black registraton in the South (McAdam 1988, p. 26). Freedom Summer played a crucial role in linking the movement to the party system, as activists insisted on the participation of Mississippi African American activists in the 1964 Democratic Convention (McAdam 1988: 77–9). It also had a long-term effect on the recruitment of veterans of the movement into other forms of activism – including the party system. In a series of studies on Freedom Summer, McAdam surveyed a group of veterans of that campaign and found that it had a profound biographical impact on their lives, leading many to later – and generally more conventional – forms of activism (1999a).

Intensive episodes like Freedom Summer served as a crucible out of which many participants moved into other forms of activism – like feminism (Evans 1980). But it was also a moment when a part of the movement made its peace with institutional politics, because the Democrats – torn between their long-standing dependence on the South and the disruptive tactics of the civil rights movement – chose the former in thieir 1964 and 1968 conventions. Yet even as the mainstream of the movement was anchoring itself to the Democratic Party, a separate trend in movement politics redounded to the benefit of the Republicans.

The basic strength of the movement was to trigger a wide variety of tactics – institutional and disruptive, local and national – to impose costs on their targets and sometimes on third parties. These tactics ranged from "litigation, lobbying, petitions, voter registration, political campaigns, marches, rallies, direct-action protests (such as sit-ins), economic boycotts, and on rare occasions violent actions, the last often in response to segregationist brutality" (Luders 2010: 23). Community organizing, the use of the media to highlight movement actions and repressive reactions, sit-ins and boycotts, the use of the courts and pressure on politicians overlapped and reinforced one another, congealing into a major cycle of contention that many Americans remember as "the sixties." They combined in a major cycle of contention that attracted media attention, legal action, and policy success (Biggs & Andrews 2015; Schmidt 2018). Figure 5.1, drawn from data collected by Craig Jenkins, shows that both total movement events and movement protests shot upward in the early 1960s in the largest wave of civil rights protest until that time.

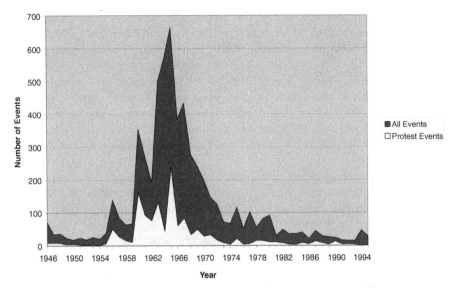

FIGURE 5.1 African American total movement and protest events, 1946–1994
Source: Data kindly provided by Craig Jenkins.

The Radical Turn and the Decline of the Movement

The wide variety of forms of contention employed by the civil rights movement in the South and its capacity for strategic innovation were important aspects of the success of the movement. But as occurs in many cycles of contention both in America and elsewhere (della Porta & Tarrow 1986), the variety of forms of mobilization eventually diverged into separate streams, with some activists moving wholeheartedly into institutional politics, others shifting into other movements like the anti-war and feminist movements, and others drifting into violence.

The shift toward institutionalization could be accounted partly to changes in the life cycle of activists, as younger people moved into adult professional lives. In part it was the result of exhaustion with life in the frenzied atmosphere of activism and, in part, it was the result of the advantages offered to civil rights activists by the new wave of nonprofit groups that arose in the 1970s. Especially important in this respect was the Community Action Program (CAP) of the Johnson Administration's Great Society, which sought to encourage the "maximum feasible participation" of community members in its poverty programs.

Repression – or the threat of it – also led activists to retreat from open forms of participation, especially in areas of the South where the Klan was particularly active (Luders 2010: 47–8). By 1960, the Anti-Defamation League reported the burning of more than a thousand crosses across the South (ibid.). But paradoxically, repression – or its threat – also had the effect of radicalizing a proportion of African Americans during the second half of the 1960s. "By 1970," writes McAdam, "insurgent activity had taken on a more diffuse quality with a veritable profusion of small groups addressing a wide range of issues by means of an equally wide range of tactics" (1983: 752). Both competition for political space and the radical import of some of these groups' claims led a minority to adopt tactics that shaded into violence. Inevitably, these groups attracted the attention of the police and the FBI and the fascination of the media, especially after the novelty of the earlier Freedom Rider and sit-in periods had worn off.[16]

Repression, radicalization, and urban violence culminated in a spiral of insurgency that was marked by a combination of tactical innovation and strategic impotence. All of this was exacerbated by the riots of the mid-1960s in the North. These were tangential to the movement in an organizational sense but also revealed the frustration among African Americans at the slow pace of reform. Omar Washaw's research on the impact of protest on voting shows that where protester-initiated violence drove media coverage, there was a 1.5 to 7.9 percent shift toward the Republicans (Wasaw 2020). These media, elite, and public opinion responses to violence helped to elect Richard Nixon in 1968 on a platform of defending the "the silent majority" and tilting the Republican Party's future toward the South (see Chapter 6). Movement activity and institutional responses shifted the field of contention from protest to politics. Another factor – countermovement reaction – was the mechanism that effected this transition.

V MOVEMENT/COUNTERMOVEMENT INTERACTION

Even before the civil rights movement began to bifurcate into institutional and violent strands, it faced a challenge from another direction. Beginning in the middle of the 1950s, there was a multifaceted white countermovement, less vicious perhaps than the "redemption" movement that accompanied the first reconstruction, but more effective because it combined insider and outsider methods. While Klansmen and white thugs were burning churches and beating protesters, semiofficial and official state commissions and local white councils were organizing legal resistance to integration.

The first organized reaction to the *Brown* decision was a wave of legislative enactments attempting to enforce "massive resistance," leading to the creation of a number of state "sovereignty" commissions intended to give an official voice to opposition to integration. Beginning in Mississippi and followed in Louisiana and Alabama, the commissions were state funded and spent much of

---

[16] In a personal communication, Joseph Luders points out that as the target of the movement shifted from segregated spaces, which could be targeted for physical occupation, to class inequalities, which are much harder to protest against and also tend to activate more oppositional mobilization, contention became more diffused and more likely to lead to violence.

their efforts in encouraging segregation and collecting information on civil rights activists. At least in Mississippi, they were suspected of complicity with repressive violence. As Luders summarizes:

sovereignty commissions churned out a torrent of segregationist propaganda, conducted surveillance, infiltrated civil rights organizations with paid informers, helped local law enforcement identify potential "trouble makers," and orchestrated various forms of economic intimidation and reprisals against movement participants and supporters" (2010: 30).

The state of Virginia went a step further than the sovereignty commissions. In the late 1950s, the General Assembly created the Virginia Commission on Constitutional Government (VCCG), which was formed to oppose school integration and encourage private schools to exclude all but a few black children. The commission then broadened its remit to "take aim at the entire structure of constitutional understanding on which federal regulation of organized labor's power and civil rights protections alike depended" (MacLean 2017: 84).

The VCCG gained the support of the state's flagship public institution, the University of Virginia, when its president, Colgate Darden, accepted a positon on its board. It gained intellectual firepower when James Buchanan, founder of the university's Thomas Jefferson Center, provided contract research for the commission, including a multiyear project on Virginia's tuition grant system to private schools. "The Study," writes Buchanan's historian Nancy MacLean, "reported the private school subsidies to be a great success and, indeed, a model for evading government control" (2017: 83).

More durable and less "official" than the sovereignty commissions were the Citizens' Councils, which were estimated at their high point to have enrolled 60,000 members, mainly in the deep South, which Neil McMillen estimates to have had 300,000 members at their height (McMillen 1971: 153). Although the council movement diffused across the South, it was strongest in the "black belt" where there were still strongholds of plantation agriculture (Luders 2010: 31) and where classical "redemption" sentiments were still widely diffused.

Although the councils energetically claimed to have a legal vocation, they advanced political polarization by putting pressure on moderate and integrationist groups and, at times, enforcing economic pressure against whites who they considered traitors to southern values. The Mississippi council, probably the most vigorous in opposition to desegregation, demanded, after the Meredith affair, that the University of Mississippi force its faculty to take an oath to support segregation or leave the University (McMillen, p. 246).The councils also put pressure on elected officials to hold the line against integration. "Fear of electoral reprisals," writes Luders, "doubtless impelled many legislators to adhere to the Council's orthodoxy, despite their own misgivings" (2010: 37).

As the council movement was taking a "legal" road to resist integration, a mass-based movement of lower-income and less-educated whites revived the

Ku Klux Klan, which had been moribund since the 1920s. These groups supported the most vehement segregationists for public office, intimidated opponents, and threatened and attacked civil rights activists (ibid., p. 46). Klan members revived the historical tactics of harassment, violence, and fear; only four years after the *Brown* decision, the Southern Regional Council (SRC) calculated that there had been 530 instances of "intimidation, reprisal, and violence" against African American civil rights advocates and white moderates, including 6 murders, 29 woundings, 44 people beaten, 5 stabbed, 30 homes bombed, 4 schools, 7 churches, and 4 Jewish houses of worship bombed.[17] "Reacting to what they perceived as the threat posed by black insurgency," writes McAdam, "these forces mobilized and grew increasingly active on two fronts during the late 1950s" (1999b: 142).

The combination of council activity and Klan violence – what we might call a "formative countermovement" – led to further forms of segregationist activity. In Mississippi in the latter half of the 1960s, the Supreme Court decided the case of Alexander v. *Holmes County* (396 US 19, 1969), which struck down the state's "school choice" statute that allowed white students to choose to attend an all-white school. After fourteen years of delay and obfuscation, the decision effectively required all school districts in the South to integrate. The response was to spur white families, churches, and other institutions to create a new instrument to preserve segregation – private academies (Andrews 2002: 921–2). To this day, conservative opinions on race are centered in the strongholds where segregation academies were created (Porter et al. 2014).[18]

These activities were not randomly distributed. As McAdam's *New York Times Index* event analysis shows, white supremacist activity rose in parallel with civil rights activity, first after the Brown decision came down and then in an even greater volume following the direct action campaigns of the early 1960s (ibid., p. 143; also see Luders 2010: 47–8 and Wasow 2020). Using county-level Freedom Summer activities as his measure of activism, Andrews found that counties with higher levels of civil rights mobilization in the 1960s had higher enrollments in white academies (Andrews 2002).

The relationship between movement activity and antimovement violence varied according to the political culture of various states. In Mississippi, there were almost as many anti-rights events as rights events, but in North Carolina, "Firm opposition to anti-rights violence limited the opportunities for Klan-type mobilization and reduced the amount of racial contention to a level below what

---

[17] Southern Regional Council, "Intimidation, Reprisal, and Violence in the South's Racial Crisis" (1960), results summarized from Luders 2010: 47.

[18] Andrews and Jowers also found that the countermovement stimulated legal action on the part of movement lawyers in Mississippi (2018: 23–6). Legal action triggered by a countermovement would also be a major response of the racial justice movement following a spate of police murders, civil rights protests, and countermovement responses.

might have been expected based on the prevalence of the Klan throughout the state" (Luders 2003: 32). This variation in the level of violence was not independent of public policy. In Louisiana, where state repression of anti-civil rights violence was largely lacking, private citizens initiated 144 anti-rights events, many of which involved disruptive crowd actions, shootings, bombings, cross burnings, and assaults" (ibid., pp. 37–8).

In contrast, in South Carolina, "after an initial period of support for 'massive resistance' to civil rights in the latter 1950s ... authorities eventually adopted a ... law-and-order stance" (ibid., p. 32). From these findings, Luders concludes that "social movement theory must be refined to better encompass the complex relationship among state actors, movements, and countermovements" (ibid., p. 44). Luders might have added that these movement/countermovement interactions were ultimately reflected in changes in the party system.

For example, the implantation of Christian (read: white) academies was at the origin of many parts of the Christian Right that developed in the next decade. These, in turn, became centers for the "southern strategy" of Republican leaders like Nixon and Reagan and added to outrage that the Internal Revenue System was planning to tax these institutions. Race, religion, and small-government anti-tax sentiment combined in the creation of a coalitional base for the Republican Party in the South, as we will see in Chapter 6.

VI   MOVEMENT ACTIVISM AND PARTISAN DYNAMICS

If Mississippi was the archetype for white resistance to desegregation, it was also the site of the clearest evidence that movement mobilization would have a profound effect on the electoral process. In his careful analysis of the correlates of voter registration in the 1968 elections, Kenneth Andrews found that both the number of Freedom Summer organizers and membership in the NAACP were better predictors of electoral change in that state than the presence of federal registrars sent to monitor election irregularities, with the presence of Freedom Summer volunteers the more powerful predictor of the two (Andrews 1997: 89). Andrews also measured the influence of prior mobilization on support for black candidates in 1967 and 1971 (also see Bullock & Gaddie 2014). Voter registration, voter turnout, and growing support for the Democratic Party were all direct or indirect outcomes of movement mobilization. There can be no more dramatic evidence of the impact of movement activity on the party system at the state and local level, but it also percolated upward to the national level of the Democratic Party.

"We didn't come all this way for no two seats ... "

The causal chain from movement mobilization to African American anchoring in the Democratic Party did not always run smoothly. This can be seen from the most highly charged episode in the relations between the movement and the Democrats. The episode began in the spring of 1964, when a group of SNCC volunteers, on the heels of a 1963 successful voter registration campaign, arrived in the state to assist the Council of Federated Organizations (COFO), which had been formed in 1961 in a voter registration drive (Carson, ch. 10). "Originally," writes McAdam (1988:77–8),

the plan was simply to use large numbers of white students ... to register as many black voters as possible. However, as long as the state Democratic Party was effectively closed to blacks, it was unclear how beneficial the simple registration of voters would be. To address the problem, SNCC spearheaded the establishment of the Mississippi Free Democratic Party. (MFDP)

The goal of the MFDP was to expose the segregated process of candidate selection in the Mississippi Democratic Party by putting up a slate of candidates of its own. Of course, the activists had no hope of prevailing in the fixed primary, but they wanted to expose the racial bias of the process. When their candidates were rejected by the (all white) State Board of Elections, they turned to a strategy they had used before – holding a mock election – to challenge the state's delegation to the 1964 Democratic Convention (ibid., p. 78). As they continued to register black voters for the November election, the activists also asked them to fill in a "Freedom registration form" to justify their attempt to wrest representation from the official delegation in Atlantic City.

It was at this point that the goals of the SNCC activists and their local colleagues clashed with the political imperative of the national Democratic Party and its newly installed president, Lyndon B. Johnson. As Democratic majority leader in the Senate, Johnson had successfully maneuvered between his southern colleagues in the party and its northern wing. Facing an election as a nonelected president against the ferocious attacks of Republican candidate Barry Goldwater (see Chapter 6), Johnson felt he needed to hold onto his southern base in order to preserve his presidency. Allowing an integrated group like the MFDP to displace the Mississippi delegation would, he feared, trigger the rage of the southern wing of his party and could cost him the election. To accomplish his goal, he called for a period of civil rights "cooling off" as the convention approached. But the young activists who were organizing Mississippi African Americans to register to vote had other plans. They wanted to gain national attention for the racial bias in the state's Democratic Party by triggering a confrontation at the convention.

As we now know, Johnson did not need to worry about his election. But at the convention in Atlantic City, he strove to tamp down the conflict with the all-white Mississippi delegation by offering the insurgents two seats at the convention. Rejecting this token concession, Fanny Lou Hamer, one of the "delegates" representing the MFDP, responded, "We didn't come all the way up here to compromise for no more than we'd gotten here. We didn't come all this way for no two seats when all of us is tired" (quoted in Dittmer et al. 1993: 20).

After shepherding the Civil Rights Act through Congress, refusing to seat the MFDP delegates to protect white separatists was a badge of dishonor for Johnson. Stung by the embarrassment having given in to the "lily white" political culture of the South, he made a little-noted concession to the insurgents that turned out to be crucial for the future of movement/party relations in America. Pressed by the publicity given to the controversy and worried about the longer-term future of his party, Johnson extracted a concession from the convention that no segregated delegation would be certified at the party's next convention. In 1968, Hamer and a biracial delegation were seated at the Chicago Convention.

In the event, the hemorrhage of southern white support for the Democrats could not be staunched. In both 1964, when the Democrats prevailed, and in 1968, when Richard Nixon defeated a wounded presidency, the transformation of the American party system was already underway (McAdam & Kloos 2014: ch. 3). But as the party lost ground among white southerners, it adopted the model of a coalition of group interests, largely under the pressure of the successive movements of the 1960s.

As the MFDP episode attests, this shift was neither painless nor unidirectional. By 1968, the country was deeply divided over the Vietnam War and the Chicago Convention of that year was scarred by the violent repression of a new movement – the anti-war movement – amid a general climate of fear and frustration caused both by the war and by the urban disorders of the middle of the decade. Not for the last time, the price for supporting a movement for racial justice was paid by the Democratic Party. The converse, of course, was that the end of the 1960s protest cycle crystallized the shift of southern whites to the Republicans and soldered them to the small-government, religiously embedded ideological core of that party, to which we will turn in Chapter 6.

CONCLUSIONS

As I argued in the Introduction, until recently, most social scientists respected a methodological and theoretical boundary between the study of institutional and noninstitutional politics. But both the short surge of the industrial workers' movement and the "long" civil rights movement tell a more complicated story. Rather than being in opposition to each other, movement and party intersected in both institutional and contentious arenas. It was actions taken by the least democratic branch of government – the Supreme Court – that triggered a widespread countermovement against integration, which was followed by the militant phase of the civil rights movement. Together, white reaction and civil rights militancy forced the federal government to come down strongly on behalf of African American rights. But these decision makers did so only following a sequence of movement insurgency and segregationist counterinsurgency that, between them, forced the Democratic Party to take a more forthright position on racial justice.

The lesson of the civil rights movement is not that movements are actors while governmental authorities are only *reactors*. It is, rather, that significant social change only occurs when formative movements – driven by structural and electoral change – mobilize both institutional and extrainstitutional resources to put pressure on governing authorities to do what they might otherwise be disinclined to do. Nowhere in the critical junctures we have so far examined do we find as broad a range of social movement tactics as we saw in civil rights. From legal mobilization to marching on Washington to community organizing to the use of obstructive tactics like the sit-in, the movement employed a broad, modular spectrum of contentious performances.[19] It was only when these performances bifurcated into an institutionalized and a more radical strand of contention that tactical diversity turned into a cost.

But that cost was not the responsibility of the movement alone. As we saw in Section 5, the movement's achievements triggered a violent countermovement in the South and an electoral one throughout the country. It was out of that movement/countermovement interaction and its political exploitation by ambitious politicians that the country's next "formative movement" – the New Right – would be born. That would turn out to be another "long movement," one whose broad range and electoral vocation partially disguised its origins in racial politics. As Vesla Weaver writes:

Civil rights cemented its place on the national agenda with the passage of the Civil Rights Act of 1964, fair housing legislation, federal enforcement of school integration, and the outlawing of discriminatory voting mechanisms in the Voting Rights Act of 1965. Less recognized but no less important, the Second Reconstruction also witnessed one of the most punitive interventions in United States history. (Weaver 2007: 230)

Some authors, like Paul Frymer (1999), see civil rights as a captive of the Democratic Party. But to me, that seems to be a hypothesis that fits the labor movement better than it does civil rights. For one thing, the labor movement was never able to conquer the growing industrial sector in the South (Goldfield 1987); for another, as unionization declined, the movement's dependence on its party sponsor grew. In civil rights, in contrast, the movement's broad range of organizations, its flexible repertoire of contention, and its capacity during key moments to forge alliances with other groups lent it autonomous resources that enabled it to hold its own within the extended coalition of the Democratic Party. This is in part because of the internal resources of the movement itself, but it is also because of the party's capacity to mollify its varied internal interests and manage the entry of new actors – like the women's movement – in response to new threats and new opportunities. Not so the relationship between the Republican Party and the "long" New Right, to which we turn in Chapter 6.

---

[19] For an interesting analysis of the effects of tactical diversity on movement success, see Piazza and Wang (2020).

PART III

HOLLOWING PARTIES IN A MOVEMENT SOCIETY

6

The Long New Right

In their introduction to the symposium on "Critical Junctures and Historical Legacies" that they edited in 2017, David Collier and Gerardo Munck observed that such periods can be a concentrated episode of "synoptic" policy innovation, as was the episode of neoliberal transformation that I will examine in Latin America in Chapter 9. Alternatively, the change may occur over a more extended episode and be *incremental, consisting of smaller steps that eventually add up to a major transformation* (italics added).[1]

In the New Deal and the Sixties we saw how a deep economic depression and a major protest cycle produced seismic changes in the party system and in movement/party relations. But what about periods in which there is no depression, and no major cycle of contention? At least for the Republican Party, and, I will argue, for the American polity as a whole, the period from Barry Goldwater's landslide loss of the 1964 election to the clamorous election of Ronald Reagan in 1980 constituted an "incremental" juncture because it brought together two major movements – Christian conservatives and the New Right – with the GOP in a coalition that produced the so-called Reagan Revolution. It was part of a cultural age of fracture, in historian Daniel Rodgers' words (2011). This is a period, as the cultural critic, Stuart Hall wrote, in which "old lines of thought are disrupted, older constellations displaced, and elements, old and new are regrouped around a different set of premises and themes" (1986:33).

---

[1] "Introduction to Symposium on Critical Junctures and Historical Legacies – Building Blocks and Methodological Challenges: A Framework for Studying Critical Junctures." www.researchgate.net/publication/319650770_Introduction_to_Symposium_on_Critical_Junctures_and_Historical_Legaci es_-Building_Blocks_and_Methodological_Challenges; A_Framework_for_Studying_Critical_Junctures, p. 1.

An important part of this disruption was the conquest of conservative economic thought by neoliberalism (Rodgers, ch. 2). But another was the "hollowing out" of the party system and its partial replacement by a myriad of semi-representative and downright *un*representative bodies, as this chapter will argue. Of course, as in polities across the democratic West, a series of slow-moving structural factors led to a weakening of party systems (Katz & Mair 1993) and brought a widespread entry of "new" social movements into politics (Kriesi et al. 1995). But in America, these trends were accompanied by political and institutional changes that reduced the centrality of party to representative politics. Even as partisanship deepened, parties as institutions declined. As Julia Azari puts it, "Although parties and partisanship are related, they have evolved in different ways" (2018:20).

These trends gradually opened the gates to successive waves of conservative movements that cumulated in an infiltration and takeover of the Republican Party. Like conservative movements in the past, they combined support for religious traditionalism, opposition to business regulation and taxation, anti-communism, and rejection of government interference in racial relations. Conservatives had been trying to take over the Republican Party since at least the McCarthy era. What was new was the fusion of racial, religious, and economic facets with a new, more aggressive style of politics that came out of the 1960s.

In this chapter, I will focus on different phases of the relationship between the "long new right" and the Republican Party. I will begin by briefly outlining the structural trends that have weakened the party systems throughout the democratic West. In Section II, I will turn to the political and institutional factors that rendered these changes more extreme in the United States than elsewhere in the developed world. Together, those changes produced both the New Right and the Christian conservative movements and the ultimate fusion of the two with economic conservatism, as I will argue in Section III. Two major policy issues – abortion and the fight over the Equal Rights Amendment (ERA) – brokered these movements' alliance with the Republicans, as I will show in Section IV. This laid the groundwork for the so-called Reagan Revolution of the 1980s, which I will examine in Section V, a development, I will argue, that was less a revolution than a consolidation of trends that began over the previous two decades. Section VI will examine the period of as a cycle of movement/party interaction.

I   STRUCTURAL SOURCES OF PARTY DECLINE

Almost every study of the American party system published over the last decade begins with the paradox that the weakening of the party system has been combined with strong partisanship. For example, writing in the *Washington Post* in 2018, Frances Rosenbluth and Ian Shapiro put the problem in this way: " ... none of this is because parties are 'unusually strong' ... On the contrary, our political system is dysfunctional and polarization is intense because parties are too weak."[2]

A solution to that puzzle was offered by Daniel Schlozman and Sam Rosenfeld, who argue that the parties are not so much weak as "hollow": Both parties have dedicated partisans at the base and party leaders at the summit, but as organizations, they have been hollowed out. "Our new Party Period," they argue, "features a nationalized clash of ideology and interests but parties that are hollowed out and weakly legitimized" (2019: 121). This was not so different from what was happening to European parties over the same period, as prime ministers gained primacy vis-à-vis their parliamentary parties and central offices (Mair 2013).

The strengthening of the American presidency had the unintended effect of reducing the role of party *qua* party in national politics (Milkis & Tichenor 2019). This was reinforced by the creation of a large administrative armature around the presidency. It had begun quietly with Warren Harding's creation of the Bureau of the Budget, with its move into the White House by FDR, and with its expansion into the Office of Management and Budget under Nixon. But Nixon went further, creating a Domestic Council to centralize domestic policy making in the White House and doubling the size of the White House staff (Jacobs & Milkis, 2020, ch. 5). As Jacobs, King, and Milkis write, "The dimension of conflict that divided Democrats and Republicans during the New Deal ... was displaced by a struggle for the resources and powers of the administrative state" (2019: 460).

Of course, through their legal authority to "see that the laws are implemented," their control of patronage, and their near-monopoly of expertise and information, presidents have always possessed the resources with which to control their parties. But from the New Deal onward, the welfare functions that were once centered in local and state party machines gravitated to the welfare state, leaving the parties bereft of what had once been a key resource in mobilizing voters (Shefter 1994).

Each party laid claim to a different aspect of the New Deal state – the Democrats centering their partisan-inflected policies on the welfare state and the Republicans on national security. The *locus classicus* of the former was the New Deal, which created administrative agencies by the dozen to implement its spcial policies, while the wartime and the postwar Cold War extended the expanded state to national security. It is interesting that despite the Republicans' endless evocation of the need to reduce the power of the national state, when they took power, they too expanded the size and scope of that state, reconfiguring it to suit their purposes (Jacobs & Milkis, ch. 1). The New Deal, World War II, and the Cold War increased the power of the executive but left the

---

[2] Frances McCall Rosenbluth and Ian Shapiro, "Political Partisanship Is Vicious. That's Because Political Parties Are Too Weak." *Washington Post*, November 28, 2018. www.washingtonpost.com/outlook/2018/11/28/political-partisanship-is-vicious-thats-because-political-parties-are-too-weak

parties' bases and their national offices increasingly outside the circle of political power.

From Clientele to Cartel Parties

Difficult as it is to make comparisons across different types of party systems, European parties were experiencing a similar increase in the power of what Richard Katz and Peter Mair call the "party in government" at the cost of the parties' central offices. From their comparative analysis of European party systems, Mair and Katz (1997) discovered that the weight of party central offices has declined in favor of the party in government (ibid., pp. 610–11). They also found a widespread tendency to strengthen the position of public officeholders within the parties' national executive bodies (ibid., p. 614). By the 1960s the once-mass parties and catch-all parties of mid-century had given way to what were called "cartel parties," which have gained resources from national states and increasingly lost their connections to party members and voters (Mair & Katz 1997; Katz & Mair 2009).

Of course, party membership never had the meaning for American parties that it had in Europe of "an encapsulated political community." But by the 1970s, in contrast to the "party period," Americans increasingly channeled their participation through organizations other than parties, weakening whatever claim party organizations had to control their representatives (Katz & Mair 1993: 616). As a result, observers have seen a clear decline in a variety of indicators of party strength, such as the grip of the parties on the loyalty of the electorate, a substantial decline in voter turnout, an increase in the proportion of independents – especially among younger voters – and an increase in negative attitudes toward parties (Everson 1982: 51).

As this was happening, new associations were springing up to fill the gaps in the parties' monopoly of representation (McCarthy & Zald 1973, 1977). At the same time, the nature of these associations was evolving from federated organizations with state and local roots to national organizations without local bases (Skocpol 2003). The professionalization of association that Mayer Zald and John McCarthy observed in the 1970s did not reduce the number of associations; on the contrary, associations mushroomed (Minkoff 1995), but it changed their character. Party decline and the professionalization of association left a gaping hole that new groups with more strident ideologies strove to fill. Among these were the New Right, whose origins dated to the 1960s, and the Christian conservative movement that arose in the next decade.

II INSTITUTIONAL SOURCES OF PARTY DECLINE

These changes stretched over half a century and were not always seen as weakening the party system at the time. There were three main institutional sources of change that reinforced the structural changes. The first, which began under the New Deal, was the practice of establishing direct lines between the executive and party constituencies. The second was the passage of campaign finance laws that were designed to reduce the influence of private money on constituency politics. And the third was the desire to capture the new energies of the activism of the 1960s through reforms in the parties' mechanisms for nominating candidates.

Executive Partisanship

As is well known, the New Dealers circumvented the urban political machines by establishing executive agencies that stood outside the domain of electoral and party politics (Shefter 1994: 95). These changes were justified by the economic crisis, but they dovetailed with the New Dealers' political project. New agencies like the Works Progress Administration (WPA) and the National Labor Relations Board (NLRB) were created to implement New Deal policies, but they also established direct ties with constituencies that FDR wanted to solder to the new Deal.

In the 1960s, the Johnson administration created a blizzard of new federal agencies. Led by White House advisers who thought they could capture the energy of the New Left, they offered new programs to local communities in the name of "maximum feasible participation," which threatened to sideline the traditional state and local party organizations. "These traditional party organizations," writes Robert Lieberman, "sought above all to keep control of federal programs that were channeled through local governments" (2005: 123).

The War on Poverty was ended prematurely by the demands of the Vietnam War, but not before it reduced poverty considerably – especially among older Americans. It also helped to form a new generation of black leaders who had come out of the civil rights movement. Between 1968 and 1975, thirteen African Americans were elected as mayors of cities of 50,000 or more population; by 1996, the figure had risen to sixty-seven (Colburn 2001: 25–26). "That cadre of striving leaders, instrumental both in the increasing election of black mayors in American cities and the growing influence of civil rights groups on social policy during the late 1960s and 1970s, developed political bases that were not tied directly to the Democratic Party or the White House" (Jacobs & Milkis, ch. 1).

As is well known, in his 1968 "law and order" campaign, Richard Nixon shifted the Republican Party away from its traditional support for civil rights. Best remembered for his "southern strategy," an important aspect of Nixon's approach was also to appeal to white northerners who had gone sour on civil rights – the so-called silent majority. That strategy drew many white working-class voters away from the Democrats and weakened the loyalty of white unionists to that party (Cowie 2010). "The dramatic demise of the Economic Opportunity Act came about because, in the end, white Southerners *and* urban Northerners equally resisted its nationalizing thrust – each for their own reasons . . . ." (Lieberman 2005: 124).

   After Nixon's election, federal spending on the cities did not decline but was redeployed from the welfare-oriented programs of the Johnson administration to policy measures that increased spending on law and order and moved the country toward an increased federal role in internal security (Button 1978). "Upon entering office," write Jacobs, King, and Milkis, "Nixon reorganized rather than curtailed the executive aggrandizement of the Johnson years" (2019: 459). As these authors conclude, "The waning of the traditional party system had the two-fold effect of nationalizing policy debate and centering that debate on the ends the newly empowered national State should serve" (ibid., pp. 459–60).

Reforming Campaign Finance

From the Progressive era onward, reformers have striven to direct money away from party machines. Throughout the twentieth century, the decline of patronage and the shift of welfare to the federal level supported this shift by taking leverage over campaigns and candidates away from the parties and opening opportunities for candidates to seek direct support from voting publics (Cain, Ferejohn & Fiorina, 1987). At the same time, the increase in personal income and the dispersion of the population to the suburbs and from the machine-dominated East to the "nonpartisan" West was depriving parties of the platoons of party workers who had carried out the routine tasks of electoral canvassing in the past.

   The ideological turmoil of the 1960s, and especially the abuses revealed by the Watergate scandal, impelled Congress to create a set of campaign finance laws between 1972 and 1974 that were aimed at advancing the institutionalization of candidate-centered electoral politics. "Under the Federal Election Campaign Act (FECA), the party committees were treated hardly better than political action committees (PACs), in that they were allowed to contribute no more than $5,000 per election to their candidates" (La Raja & Schaffner 2015: 63). Many states followed the FECA model, which diffused the party committees' loss of power.

   Readers may wonder why it made a difference that campaign finance went directly to candidates instead of passing through the coffers of party committees. The first, and simplest, answer is that especially as the cost of election campaigns began to mount, candidates naturally looked to nonparty sources for funding – PACs, labor unions, and corporations. But the second reason had to do with the different nature of party "insiders" and "outsiders." While the former are "transactional," social movements are held together by their ideological missions and their collective identities, benefiting what La Raja and Schaffner call "purists" over "pragmatists." The latter are activated in order to be right, while the former are in it to win. Rules that weakened the control of party organization over campaign funding allowed purist outsiders to play a large role in financing candidate elections and in nominating candidates to office. As La Raza and Schaffner conclude, limiting the role of parties in controlling campaign finance "gives issue groups additional leverage in deciding who runs for office and who wins" (ibid., p. 19).

In the wake of the Watergate scandal, FECA was designed to limit corruption in elections. But the new campaign financing rules benefited individual candidates and the groups and movements they turn to for financing. This has had the effect of giving advantages to more extreme candidates "because it allows ideological donors and factions to have disproportionate influence on which types of challengers and open-seat candidates run for office and win" (ibid., p. 65). The obvious correlate was to encourage the movementization of the party and the polarization of the party system that we see today.

The Adoption of the Direct Primary

In the 1960s and early 1970s, as the New Left emerged from the Civil Rights and anti–Vietnam War movements, the Democratic Party risked losing its reputation as a progressive party among a generation of young activists. As Jacobs and Milkis put it, "When Vietnam became a quagmire that overwhelmed the Johnson administration and fractured the nation, the idealistic, all-consuming Cold War that Kennedy exalted in his inaugural address was attacked by liberal activists as imperialism disguised as 'man's noblest cause'" (ch. 4).

The gap between the Democratic Party and the New Left, which had seemed bridgeable to Johnson and his advisers, only grew with the expanding military commitment in Southeast Asia. This worsened after the party's Chicago National Convention, when Hubert Humphrey won the party's nomination without competing in a single primary. While Fanny Lou Hamer was being seated as part of the all-white Mississippi delegation (see Chapter 5), Mayor Richard J. Daley was sending his police to attack the thousands of antiwar protesters who were gathered outside the Convention Center in the glare of national television (Gitlin 1980, 1987). Humphrey's nomination widened the breach between traditional Democrats and progressives, leading many of the latter to join the opposition and others to work to reform the party from the inside.

To advance the inclusion of African Americans into the party after the debacle of the 1964 convention, in 1968, the party created a special committee on equal rights headed by Governor Richard J. Hughes of New Jersey. That committee not only insisted on seating the insurgents in the Mississippi delegation, but it led to the creation of a reform commission that pushed for an abandonment of the binding state "unit rule" for voting at future conventions and created the McGovern-Fraser Commission, a move that, in Jacobs and Milkis' words, "sounded the death knell of the traditional party structure" (ibid., ch. 4).

McGovern-Fraser consisted of a series of reforms that did away with what reformers regarded as a system of "smoke-filled room" candidate selection and replaced it with a near-universal system of state-level primaries (Shafer 1983). Primaries had been used in state and local elections since the beginning of the century, but the goal here was to turn over the first instance for selecting candidates to grassroots groups, which would include African Americans, women, young people, and opponents of the war. For supporters of the reforms, their virtue was that they "deprived party leaders of the power they had exercised since the early part of the nineteenth century" (Jacobs & Milkis, p. 39). For Byron Shafer, who has written the most astute analysis of the reforms, they were nothing less than "revolutionary" (1983, p. 4). The Democrats were both committing themselves to inclusion as a principle and reconstructing party rules to allow for stronger ties to outside movements.

The impact of the move was almost immediate: The number of states with Democratic primaries grew from 17 in 1968 to 23 in 1972, and to 40 in 2000. The reforms made substantial progress in increasing the number of minorities, women, and younger delegates taking part in the Democrats' nomination process. Although women had comprised only 13 percent of the convention delegates in 1968 and African Americans constituted 5.5 percent, by 1972, the former had risen to 38 percent and the latter to 15 percent. In addition, young peoples' proportion of the delegates increased from 11 to 27 percent during the same 4 years (Harris 2012). In both parties, the reforms led to increased popular participation in the nominating process. In 1968, only 13 million Americans had participated in the process; by the year 2000, more than 30 million Americans voted in primaries or took part in caucuses.

Not everyone was happy with the reforms. For one thing, poorer Americans especially remained underrepresented among the delegates. For another, by increasing the weight of activists who had come out of the movements of the Sixties, the reforms deepened the cleavages within the party. Indeed, the 1972 convention witnessed power struggles between the new generation of delegates and older leaders. To some, it seemed like the old party structure, led by a stratum of experienced and thoughtful party leaders, had been more effective in uniting the party than the new arrangements. For example, to elder statesman David Truman, the McGovern-Fraser reforms destroyed almost all semblance of a federal national party and replaced it with another on a grand scale (Truman 1984–85: 638). When the Republican Party adopted a similar reform, many of the party's new elites would come from the New Right and the Christian conservative movements.

III   THE NEW RIGHT, THE CHRISTIAN CONSERVATIVES, AND THE GOP

"Movementization" affected both parties but took different forms in each. While the Democrats simply added new interest groups to their broad coalition, the Republicans were opened up to an ideological takeover. Grossmann and Hopkins summarize this development in this way:

> Whereas the organization of activists within the Democratic Party has tended to be divided into multiple social groups and issue areas – the labor movement, the civil rights movement, the antiwar movement, the feminist movement, the gay rights movement, the environmental movement, and so forth – the conservative ascendency in the Republican Party occurred via a broad mobilization of ideologically motivated activists who promoted an alternative philosophy that applied across a broad spectrum of policy domains. (2016: 9)

Sidney Milkis puts this point in metaphorical form: While the 1960s simply added to the number of interest groups in the Democratic Party, the same reforms helped to turn the Republican Party into an "ideological petri dish"[3] in which a succession of new actors fused together into a new form of radical conservatism, mixing together racial resentment; religious fervor; small-state, antitax ideology with an ideological cast; and an instinct for the jugular that had been lacking in its predecessors. This trend began with the insurgents who took over the Republican convention of 1964.

Goldwater and the Birth of the New Right

At the 1960 Republican convention, Senator Barry Goldwater had declined to have his name put forward for his party's nomination for the presidency. Explaining his annoyance at what he saw as a premature move, he made a blunt reference to what he hoped for the Republican Party's future: "Let's grow up, conservatives. If we want to take this Party back, *and I think we can someday*, let's get to work [italics added]."[4] When Goldwater was trounced by Lyndon Johnson in the 1964 election, that "someday" seemed distant indeed.

While Goldwater's campaign was a dismal failure, the 1964 election was a success of a different kind. Goldwater's victory over moderate Republicans Nelson Rockefeller and William Scranton at the Republican convention began the disintegration of the moderate branch of the party and laid the groundwork for a generation of conservatives to take it over (Kabaservice 2012). "Thus," write Daniel Schlozman and Sam Rosenfeld, "did the New Right arrogate to themselves the integrative role of the political party."[5]

Like much else in modern conservative politics, the trend began in the South. Recall from Chapter 5 that after the Supreme Court made segregation illegal in public schools, in many southern states, "white academies" were created to evade the court's judgment. But these were essentially *private* schools and were thus, in the judgment of the Internal Revenue Service,

---

[3] I am grateful to Sid Milkis for coining this term in a personal communication to the author.
[4] This part of Goldwater's withdrawal speech is reproduced in Perlstein (2009: 95).
[5] Quoted in Jay Nordlinger, "#ExGOP," *National Review* online, June 7, 2016. www.nationalreview.com/2016/06/exgop-shock-disaffiliation-leaving-gop

subject to taxation. As we saw in that chapter, this infuriated segregationists but allowed them to clothe their opposition to civil rights in an anti-tax and anti–federal power message.

Opposition to taxation and federal regulatory power were traditional features of economic conservatism. The key to the shaping of a new conservative majority was the fusion of this traditional conservatism with a new, more religious, more nationalistic, and more racially inflected set of elements. This ideological fusion was already presaged when Goldwater, at the 1960 party convention, urged a group of young supporters to form a permanent national organization, leading to the creation of the Young Americans for Freedom (YAF), one of the key movements in the party's shift to the right (Perlstein 2009: 95; Schlozman & Rosenfeld, 2018: 17–18). As Paul Weyrich, who was a crucial broker connecting the New Right to the evangelicals, explained, "We are radicals, working to overturn the present power structure" (quoted in Schlozman, p, 82).

The YAF and Other Groups

The rise of the New Left and its highly visible public protests in the 1960s obscured the rise of New Right organizations, starting with the highbrow *National Review,* founded in 1955 by William Buckley Jr., and the wildly anti-Communist John Birch Society, founded in 1958 by Robert Welch (Kabaservice, p. 127). Though Goldwater had insisted that he always supported party unity, "He would also give his blessing to the growth of a veritable infrastructure of conservative 'splinter groups', many of which would be actively hostile to the official Republican Party organization" (ibid., p. 60).

The YAF was created with the support of William Rusher, publisher of the *National Review* and a long-time collaborator of William Buckley Jr., at whose estate the group was founded. Its young activists were not adverse to protest, as their leadership of a counterdemonstration in favor of the House UnAmerican Activities Committee (HUAC) suggested (Perlstein 2009: 104), but most of their activities were carried out within the Republican Party. The YAF soon "claimed 24,000 student members on more than a hundred campuses" (Kabaservice, pp. 35–36), becoming one of the major sources in the launch of Goldwater's 1964 presidential campaign. After the failure of that campaign, one that the YAF blamed on Republican moderates, the group turned its firepower on them (ibid., pp. 173–4). Its "longer-term goal was to transform the Republican Party into an organ of conservative ideology and purge it of all who resisted the true faith" (ibid., pp. xvii–xix). From the beginning, the "thunder from the right" was aimed at an internal takeover of the GOP (Crawford 1981).

The YAF was not alone: Between the mid-1950s and the 1970s, a spectrum of conservative groups emerged on the perimeter of the Republican Party, ranging from the American Conservative Union (ACU), founded in the wake of Goldwater's failed campaign; the Heritage Foundation, created in 1973; and the National Conservative Political Action Committee, founded in 1975 (ibid., pp. 21, 31–32). These groups surrounded the Grand Old Party like besieging troops, not always troubling to show their respect for party elders, and eventually capturing the heights of that party. "Less the resemblance than the *interpenetration* of extremist and mainstream elements has defined conservative politics across the era," conclude Schlozman and Rosenfeld (2018: 10).

Although these new groups were not homogeneous, they were united by a shift in approach from the decorous conservatism of their predecessors in the Taft wing of the party to a take-no-prisoners attack on opponents both outside and within the party and an instinct for the jugular that won them the attention of the media. In this respect, they resembled Senator Joseph McCarthy far more than the traditional Taftite conservative branch of the party:

> The fervid demonization, the headlong transgression of institutional and behavioral norms, the suffusion of political debate with potent social resentment – all these hallmarks of the Wisconsin demagogue's style would become core elements of a broader, more durable political tendency." (Schlozman & Rosenfeld, ibid., p. 10)

Of course, the 1960s were a decade in which new groups were springing up all over the place and moderate Republicans strove to combat the takeover of their party by forming new organizations too, like the Ripon Society. But as Kabaservice points out, this group, which was inspired by the British Conservatives' "Bow Group," became more of a talk shop than an activist group, determined "to educate themselves politically through systematic study of policy problems" (ibid., p. 75). What the moderates lacked was the ideological intensity and the ruthlessness that enabled New Right activists to take over the Republican convention in 1964.

In its activists' willingness to employ underhanded, duplicitous, and near-illegal methods, the New Right was more like the classical Communist model for infiltrating other groups than the methods of "participatory democracy" being trumpeted by the New Left (Flacks & Lichtenstein, eds., 2015). While the New Left harbored a deep suspicion of parties that led them to keep their distance from the Democratic Party, the New Right had no hesitation in attempting a "Leninist" infiltration of the GOP.

The figure who best embodied this ethic was F. Clifton White, an army veteran who began his career as a graduate student at Cornell, where he helped form a chapter of the American Veterans' Committee (AVC), an association of World War II vets. When he ran for statewide chair of the organization in 1946, his candidacy was sabotaged by Communists in the organization. The irony was that "White saw in movement conservatism the vehicle through which to take over the Republican Party, using tactics he had learned from the Communists" (Kabaservice, pp. 49–50).[6]

---

[6] White later put these lessons to work in the YAF and then in the Young Republicans (YR), which he and an informal group calling itself "the syndicate" took over as a step to infiltrating the party

The activists of the New Right did not so much seek an "anchor" to the Republican Party as to capture it from the inside. This set a pattern for right-wing groups, which – unlike the accretion of new interest groups that we saw in the Democrats (e.g., labor, African Americans, women) – merged with economic conservatives to transform the party into an ideological instrument. "The moment," write Schlozman and Rosenfeld, "encapsulated a deep transformation in American party politics as the right's loose cannonballs came eventually to dominate and define the Grand Old Party" (2018: 1).

Why did it take so long for the New Right to capture the heights of the Republican Party? One reason was that nothing fails like failure, and party elders were wary of a group of insurgents whose tactics had pushed aside moderates like Thomas Kuchel, Nelson Rockefeller, and William Scranton and lost the party the 1964 election. But there were two other reasons: First, Lyndon Johnson's success in painting the Goldwaterites as dangerous extremists (Gerstle, Lichtenstein & O'Connor 2019: 6) and, second, the fact that these activists were a small group of political operatives without a coherent social basis. They found such a basis in the next phase of right-wing organizing – the Christian conservatives.

The Christian Conservatives

Richard Viguerie and Paul Weyrich were the most important brokers between the New Right and the Christian conservatives who bonded with the party in the 1970s and 1980s. Political professionals who "skillfully exploited events to build a diffuse conservative insurgency helped turn evangelicals into an advantageous partner as they marched into the Republican Party" (Milkis & Tichenor 2019: 215).[7] Weyrich, who had been the cofounder of the Heritage Foundation, allied himself with Jerry Falwell, whose Thomas Road church was a beacon for Christian conservatism. In a meeting with Falwell, Weyrich used the term "moral majority" to indicate people who agreed on principles based on the Decalogue but who had been divided by geographic and denominational differences. When Falwell heard this term, according to Rick Perlstein, he interrupted – "That's it!" he is said to have exclaimed. "That's the name of our organization!" In his next column in the weekly newspaper he published, Falwell announced a political crusade "against abortion-on-demand, pornography and sex and violence on television and government intervention ... . But I am especially concerned about the IRS attempt to legislate regulations that will control Christian schools" (Perlstein, p. 491).

---

itself. "In the black arts of convention trickery," writes Rick Perlstein, "there was no greater master than F. Clifton White" (2009, p. 314).

[7] Note that Viguerie and Weyrich also advised evangelicals not to tie their movement too closely to the GOP, but were repulsed. They wanted a strong conservative leadership that would make the party the servant rather than the master of right-wing aspirations. Most conservative ideological leaders had very different aims in mind, hoping to "position their followers as a significant voting bloc within the Republican Party" (Milkis & Tichenor, p. 216).

In 1978, Weyrich brought together a group of Christian conservative leaders with a range of New Right groups including the Heritage Foundation, the American Conservative Union, the National Conservative Political Action Committee, the Republican Study Committee, the National Association of Manufacturers, and Reagan's PAC, Citizens for the Republic (ibid., p. 486). The meeting decided on a fifty-state campaign in partnership with Falwell's Moral Majority to defeat the Carter administration's support for détente, "abortion on demand," and the taxation of Christian private schools. Viguerie, who was the editor of *Conservative Digest*, "solemnized the marriage between the New and Christian rights with an article titled "Mobilizing the Moral Majority" (ibid., p. 605).

The Christian conservatives fused four elements that had emerged earlier in the fight against civil rights:

> First, they adopted the rough-and-tumble tactics of the New Right, though in a more restrained form. Emblematic of this linkage were the figure of Viguerie and the strategy of the YAF that he headed. As Schlozman points out, "The YAF served as a prototype for the movement building para-organizations that would sustain the Christian Right" (ibid., p. 82).
>
> Second, from the fight to oppose the IRS's taxation of Christian academies, they took an anti-tax ideology that blended seamlessly with the views of Republican business circles. As Schlozman emphasizes, "The IRS episode politicized white churches, giving them a powerful narrative that cast evangelicals, rather than African Americans, as victims and wedding them to a program devoted to fighting entrenched liberalism" (ibid., p. 97).
>
> Third, they took from the fight against civil rights the fusion of race and religion. This could be seen as early as 1958, when Falwell preached that "the racial problem in this country is not one of hate – but one of biblical principle." Citing Acts 17:26 as his authority, Falwell pointed out that the Lord sets the "bounds for their habitation" for the nations of the earth. "The 'true Negro'," he intoned, "does not want integration. He realizes his potential is far better among his own race" (quoted in Perlstein 2020: 468).

Finally, institutional changes helped to effect the Christian Right's insertion into the Party. The most important was the Republicans' adoption of the direct primary along the lines of the McGovern-Fraser reforms. While the Democratic reform can be traced to the loss of the 1968 election, it was the backwash of the Watergate scandal that led the Republicans to adopt "a more candidate-centered, media-driven primary system." As Jacobs and Milkis summarize, "Reagan's 1976 primary challenge and his nomination in 1980 would have been less likely without the Republican Party's adaptation of progressive nominating reforms" (ch. 5).

These primary contests lent a more ideological tone to GOP election campaigns than was the case among the Democrats. This was not because of

TABLE 6.1 *Rhetorical asymmetry in presidential primary debates*

No. of Mentions per Debate Answer	Republicans	Democrats
Ideology or principle	.56	.26
Conservative (GOP)/Liberal (Democratic ideological principles)	.48	.18
Public policy	.58	.59
New policy proposals	.08	.10
Conservative (GOP)/Liberal (Democratic policy position)	.07	.08
Social group or interest group	.15	.24
Demographic group	.06	.12
American imagery	.32	.23
n. =	731	769

Source: Matthew Grossmann and David A. Hopkins, *Assymmetric Politics: Ideological Republicans and Group Interest Democrats* 2016, p. 233. Data, content analysis, codebook, and analyses of reliability can be found online at mattg.org

differences in the shape of the reform in the two parties but because grassroots evangelicals were heavily overrepresented in Republican primaries. When Grossmann and Hopkins content-analyzed a sample of candidates' responses delivered during presidential primary debates between 1996 and 2012, they found that "Republican presidential candidates were more than twice as likely than Democrats to mention ideology or principles in their debate statements and were nearly three times as likely to invoke conservative principles." Table 6.1 reproduces Grossmann and Hopkin's findings about the language of presidential primaries from their analysis of their original data.

Once entrenched in the Republican Party, Christian conservatives expanded their activities from primary campaigns to more general policy purposes – for example, contesting school board elections, agitating in the anti-abortion movement, in anti-gay rights referenda, and in the STOP ERA campaign. In this respect, they had a ready-made infrastructure to sustain them in local churches at the local level. As liberals were writing checks and signing petitions in favor of "pro-choice" positions, Christian conservatives were using their church networks to demand that policy makers adopt pro-life and pro-family policies (McCarthy 1987). Two of these policies – abortion and opposition to the ERA – were especially important in creating a cultural mood within the Republican Party that would last much longer than the decade in which they were fought out.

IV   ABORTION AND EQUAL RIGHTS

Our story about the "long" New Right has so far been dominated by men. Missing from this story have been the more than half of the electorate who are female. Two issues brought women to the head of the line in the issues that absorbed both Democratic and Republican movements in the 1970s and the 1980s – abortion and the fight over the ERA. Between them, they were a turning point in the explicit genderization of the party system. While the 1970s was the decade in which the concept of the "gender gap" entered party politics (Beckwith 2003; Goss 2013, ch. 3), this was also the decade in which "family values" emerged as a transverse meta-issue in partisan sorting.

Abortion: From Personal Religion to Partisan Polarization

In the late 1960s, spurred by medical professionals in California trying to establish their professional autonomy, the state legislature passed a law legalizing abortion in cases in which it would protect the physical and emotional health of the mother or in cases of rape or incest (Karol & Thurston 2020: 94). Opposition to the law came mainly from the Catholic Church, which was unable to prevent its passage but organized anti-abortion activists into a Right to Life League soon after. Support came from Catholics within both parties, until the religious Right turned abortion into a partisan issue. As David Karol and Chloe Thurston write, "Pro-life issues ultimately became linked to other positions also important to the conservative movement, as well as to the development of the religious Right and its incorporation into the GOP" (ibid., p. 97).

At the same time, on the Left, access to abortion was recast as a feminist issue rather than one of professional autonomy and became linked to Democratic Party politics. The movement was at first led by a California Association for the Repeal of Abortion Laws (ARAL) but helped trigger the rise of two new women's organizations: the National Organization for Women (NOW), founded in 1966, and the political action committee it formed, the National Association for the Repeal of Abortion Laws (NARAL). Both groups became allies of the Democrats. "In sum," write Karol and Thurston, "during the 1970s, interest groups arose on both sides of the abortion debate ... eventually became aligned with the two parties, pulling Democratic and Republican elected officials of all faiths in different directions on abortion" (p. 99). From a personal religiously based issue through the mediation of opposing social movements, abortion became a partisan issue that "coincided with the incorporation of groups focused on abortion in both parties' coalitions: feminists for the Democrats and the religious Right in the GOP (p. 105).

The ERA: Seizing Defeat from the Jaws of Victory[8]

Equal rights for women, as we saw in Chapter 4, had been the goal of radicals like Alice Paul within the women's movement since the 1920s. The "new"

---

[8] The following section is much in debt to the contribution of Jane Mansbridge, *Why We Lost the ERA* (1986).

woman's movement of the 1960s was, in general, much closer to those of the "social improvement" policies of the moderates of the earlier decade than to the single-minded equal rights mission of the NWP. But a central strand of the new woman's movement insisted that an across-the-board constitutional amendment could serve as a platform on which to build an architecture of specific rights for women. The result was the campaign for an ERA, which – along with abortion – dominated the debate about women's rights in the 1970s.

In the country as a whole, support for the ERA was virtually stable throughout the 1970s. "While responses differed according to the wording of the question," writes Jane Mansbridge, "the 'average' survey found 57 percent for the ERA, 32 percent opposed, and 11 percent with no opinion" (Mansbridge 1986: 14). Yet the amendment failed. Why? The major reason was the forging of a "coalition of the pro-family, anti-feminist and, to some extent, a pro-business coalition in Republican party." As Mansbridge concludes:

The battle against the ERA was one of the first in which the New Right used "women's issues" to forge a coalition of the traditional Radical Right, religious activists, and that previously apolitical segment of the noncosmopolitan working and middle classes that was deeply disturbed by the cultural changes – especially the changes in sexual mores – in the second half of the twentieth century. (p. 16)

For liberals, equal rights for women was an extension of the civil rights message, first during the Kennedy and then in the Johnson administration. That led to attacking the problem of unequal pay for women through Title VII of the Civil Rights Act of 1964. The inclusion of women's rights in that act was a complicated story, but linking women's to African American rights assured the opposition of anti-civil rights forces, as well as from anti-feminists.

Of course, in the American federal system, which was founded by men who wanted to make the Constitution hard to revise, the action moved to the state legislatures, where a number of states immediately voted for ratification. But Article V of the Constitution requires ratification by three-quarters of the state legislatures or by a constitutional convention, and this led to a knock-down drag-out fight in the fourteen states that had not yet ratified the Amendment. As the deadline for ratification approached, both ERA supporters and their opponents began to mobilize supporters in these states to either ratify the amendment or allow it to die.

NOW and its allies, who had focused their campaign on Congress, were less prepared for the debate over ratification in the states than their opponents. For one thing, the coalition of pro-ERA groups was a top-down federation of Washington- and New York–based nonprofits for whom ERA was far down their list of organizational priorities (Perlstein 2020: 81). In contrast, the anti-ERA forces were locally based and often avid Christians who were able to mobilize their church networks against ratification. Lending a religious component to the conflict, the debates in the states that had not yet approved of ERA tended to merge with agitation over the recently passed abortion decision in *Roe* v. *Wade* (Mansbridge, p. 13).

Phyllis Schlafly and Christian Conservatism

Opposition in the states was soon dominated by a single centralized organization, STOP-ERA, led by Republican firebrand Phyllis Schlafly. Schlafly had entered Republican politics as a Goldwater supporter with her book, *A Choice Not an Echo* (1964). Though not as extreme as those of the Birchers, her views were to the right of most Americans. "In her conspiratorial view," writes Kabaservice, "America's so-called democracy was controlled by 'secret kingmakers', a shadowy group mostly made up of internationalist New York bankers who dominated the media and worked through agents like Nelson Rockefeller, Henry Cabot Lodge Jr., and Robert McNamara" (Kabaservice, p. 89).[9]

Each year during the ERA controversy, Schlafly organized a "training conference" for members of her organization, The Eagle Forum, in which "the STOP ERA 'commander' formally addressed 'her lieutenants' to train them in how to fight off moderates at Republican conventions" (Mansbridge, p. 135). Her ruthless style was just the thing to bludgeon state legislators, who were already petrified by the fear generated by *Roe* v. *Wade*, to take no chances that wild-eyed feminists would be taking over their states in the name of equal rights, for which they would pay an electoral price.

With its exaggerated claims of the damage that ERA would do to women, to the family, and to children, Schlafly's campaign led the Republican Party, which had been supportive of ERA since 1940, to turn against it. Both the Republican platform of 1980 and candidate Ronald Reagan "gave every indication that they were committed both to making the GOP unabashedly conservative and to aggressively cultivating the new Christian Right vote" (Milkis & Tichenor 2019: 221). It was also a personal victory for Schlafly, who was welcomed back into the fold of the Republican Party and never looked back.

V THE REAGAN [NON] REVOLUTION

For many Republicans and others, the election of Ronald Reagan was the start of a "revolution" in American party politics and public policy. As in Britain, with the rise to power of Margaret Thatcher a year earlier, this was widely seen as the end of the New Deal coalition and the rise of neoliberalism as a guiding economic model. For others, it was seen as the substitution of the politics of personality for the politics of policy. After all, Reagan had first gained notoriety

---

[9] https://en.wikipedia.org/wiki/Phyllis_Schlafly#Women's_issues. Schlafly retained her party identification; when she supported John McCain in the 2008 election, she justified it by saying, "Well, I'm a Republican."

as a movie star and TV advertising figure, and his engaging personality was an important part of his appeal (McAdam & Kloos 2014: 192). For others, it was the result of the blunders and the bad luck of the Carter administration, which had had to deal simultaneously with an energy crisis, roaring inflation, and the Iran hostage crisis as the 1980 election approached.

But these interpretations elide the cumulative impact of the two movements we encountered earlier in this chapter and their merger with economic conservatism. Reagan's campaign was a natural outgrowth of this movement fusion. Long before the 1980 convention, Morton Blackwell, an adviser to Reagan campaign aide Lynn Nofziger, had pointed out that "the time was ripe to take over the GOP and forge a new party coalition of the new Christian Right, economic conservatives, and foreign policy hard-liners" (Milkis & Tichenor 2019, p. 220). Reagan had little history of links with the Christian Right and was not a visible churchgoer, but when he was asked, at a convention of the National Religious Broadcasters, what he would ask if he was transported to heaven, he replied: "I wouldn't give any reason for letting me in. I'd just ask for mercy" (ibid., p. 608).

In the election of 1980, Reagan gained an estimated two-to-one edge over the deeply religious Jimmy Carter in a political marriage between his economic conservatism and the Christian conservatism that was brokered by the New Right.[10] While economic conservatives like David Stockman worried that he was "aligning himself with Jerry Falwell, the anti–gun control nuts, the Bible-thumping creationists, folks obsessed with the threat of unisex toilets, the school prayer amendment and the rest of the New Right litany" (quoted in Perlstein 2020: 755), Reagan deflected these fears by telling an assembly of Christian conservatives that "'I know this is nonpartisan, so you can't endorse me, but I want you to know that I endorse you!' The recognition and access that Reagan bestowed upon conservative evangelicals was a powerful source of legitimation for a movement that for years was relegated to the US political wilderness" (Milkis & Tichenor 2019: 227, 230).

The most enduring result of the Reagan/New Right/Christian connection was to lay the groundwork for the "asymmetric polarization" that would only become visible to scholars in the new century (Mann & Ornstein 2012). But we cannot understand that dynamic as the result of party polarization alone: It was also the outcome of the movement/countermovement interaction between the long conservative movement and the even longer – but more evanescent – movement on the Left.

VI MOVEMENT/COUNTERMOVEMENT INTERACTION

The 1960s and early 1970s were a period of "movementization" on both left and right (Tarrow 2018). I have taken this concept from Doug McAdam and

---

[10] See the poll results summarized by McAdam and Kloos from a variety of surveys in their *Deeply Divided*, p. 185.

Katina Kloos's book, *Deeply Divided* (2014). They synthesize the tangled history of the period in this way:

[It] was one movement – civil rights – and one powerful *countermovement* – white resistance or as we prefer, "white backlash" – that began to force the parties to weigh the costs and benefits of appealing to the median voter against the strategic imperative of responding to mobilized movement elements at their ideological margins. (pp. 10–11)

McAdam and Kloos are correct, but the story of movement/ countermovement interaction is more complicated. Though the energy driving the polarization of American society came from the movement sector, it fed into the two major parties rather than through direct confrontation between movements of left and right, as had occurred between the civil rights movement and segregationists in the South in the previous decades (see Chapter 5). That case of conflict was *direct*, with a reactionary movement confronting a progressive one. But from the 1960s on, much of the movement/countermovement interaction we see in America was mediated through the party system.

Some of this interaction took institutional form. For example, the conservative legal movement that gave birth to the Federalist Society in 1982 was a reaction to what conservative lawyers thought they saw on the other side of the ideological divide from the 1960s – an organized *liberal* legal movement attempting to colonize the law schools and take over the courts (Teles 2008). That movement has had perhaps the most profound institutional influence of any recent movement on American politics, producing, among other things, the theory of the unitary executive that bolstered the claims of conservatives from George W. Bush to Donald Trump (Skowronek 2009).

Of course, the two sets of movement/party interactions were different because the two movement families had different repertoires of contention. With the exception of grassroots groups like Randall Terry's anti-abortion group Operation Rescue, the movements on the Right employed mainly institutional means that helped it to infiltrate the Republican Party. In contrast, the New Left's power was largely in the streets (Miller 1987). It was a lot easier for the Republicans to absorb a movement like the YAF, which was comfortable operating in the corridors of power, than for the Democrats to absorb the SDS, which employed a revolutionary discourse. While the New Left made it clear that it regarded the Democrats as hopelessly compromised with capitalism, racism, and imperialism (Flacks & Lichtenstein 2015; Miller 1987), the New Right's leaders used indirect language to state their goals (e.g., "defending states' rights" rather than opposing rights for African Americans). As William Rusher, publisher of the *National Review*, once said, "Conservatism is the wine; the GOP is the bottle" (Schlozman & Rosenfeld 2018: 2).

CONCLUSIONS

What can we learn from this telescopic excursion into the movement and party politics of the 1960s and 1970s?

First, that the 1960s represented a "cycle of contention" is widely accepted but less often noticed is that it fed into the party system through a process of movementization. The civil rights movement and the countermovement in the South; the urban disorders that followed in the North; the Vietnam War with its attendant controversies and protests; the killing of the Kennedys and of Martin Luther King Jr.; the defeat of the ERA by a movement led by a Republican activist: This fundamental change in the relations between movements and parties was a legacy of the 1960s that has endured into the new century. Compared to the European "1968," it is clear that we cannot understand the American "Sixties" without looking to its legacies. The McGovern-Fraser reforms and the ERA ratification struggles were not as dramatic as the Freedom Rides or the battle in the streets of Chicago during the 1968 Democratic convention, but they left a profound legacy for the future of American politics. And in the agitation against the IRS's taxation of Christian schools and its fusion with the "small government" ideology of economic conservatism, we see a "reactive sequence" that was every bit as powerful as the reaction against the urban disorder of the 1960s.

Second, the processes we have seen in earlier chapters drove the dynamic of the 1970s as well: the infiltration of the New Right and the Christian Right into the Republican party; the interaction of a movement and countermovement mediated by the party system; the impact of movement challenges on institutional rules and practices; and the reciprocal impact of party politics on the movements. Movements and parties interacted in a variety of ways during the decades of the 1960s and 1970s. It would be reductive to see this period as a simple causal chain from noninstitutional movements to institutionalized parties, as classical social movement scholars often have. Parties were present at every stage of the cycle – as initiators of collective action, as receivers of movement claims, and as the implementers of policies that were designed to respond to the demands of these movements. Not only that: Party politicians like Goldwater and Reagan encouraged the movementization of their party by broadcasting – and to some extent legitimizing – right-wing discourses in their presidential campaigns.

Third, in this chapter I emphasized the fundamental difference between one party – the Republicans – that has increasingly become a coherent ideological instrument and another – the Democratic Party – which has remained since the New Deal as a coalition of group interests. These contrasting characteristics greatly influenced how the two parties received the movement challenges of the sixties and seventies. While the Democrats changed through the accretion of new groups – women, African Americans, other minorities, and eventually LBGTQ Americans – the Republicans absorbed, and were transformed by, the ideological challenge of the New and Christian rights. As Grossmann and Hopkins put it, "[In the Democratic party] the various social movements of the 1960s became institutionalized in an array of interest organizations representing specific identities" (p. 100), while in contrast, "Conservatism was a vibrant intellectual movement that built institutions to promote broad principles and cultivated a broad base of popular support, establishing itself over the past 50 years as the main intellectual and popular engine of Republican politics" (ibid., p. 80).

The absorption of the New Right and the Christian conservative movement into the Republican Party, compared to the group-based structuring of the Democrats, has had profound effects on the party system. For one thing, its ideological structuring made the Republican Party a more coherent electoral force than the Democrats. For another, it led to greater ideological discipline in Congress and in the state legislatures. Dependence on a racially, religiously, and generationally narrowed electorate has sustained this internal ordering but has made it difficult for the party to appeal to a population that is increasingly diverse. The asymmetric polarization of American politics in the twenty-first century can largely be ascribed to this difference in the relationship between the movements and parties of the last decades of the previous century.

The new Republicanism is not an ideology that admits of a great deal of internal diversity. Driven by a mix of ideological dogma and self-interest and increasingly influenced by neoliberal economists and libertarian business groups (see Chapter 7), the party would become an instrument for what would otherwise be unpopular economic programs (Bennett & Livingston 2020: xvii, 18). This disjuncture has left it with an umbilical connection to right-wing media sources and reliant on a growing use of disinformation, resulting in "attacks on the press, the spread of hate and propaganda, efforts to exclude various minority groups and the rise of ethnic nationalism" (ibid., p. xiv).

Like the Democrats' group structuring, the Republicans' ideological structuration has been path-dependent, making the party susceptible to incursion by new waves of ideological insurgents, like the Tea Party, and ripe for takeover by the ideological adventurer, Donald Trump. This threatened to transform the party into something that the acolytes of ideological politics like Goldwater and White in the 1960s could never have imagined a movement-party. I will turn to these more dangerous incursions in Chapter 7.

7

The Hybridization of the Party System

I began this book with a definition of social movements as a form of contentious politics that combines sustained campaigns of claim making with arrays of public performances, adding up to public displays of worthiness, unity, numbers, and commitment (Tilly & Tarrow 2015: ch. 1). That definition has served us well through the last six chapters. From the abolitionists to the agrarian movement to the women's suffrage movement to labor and civil rights, movements used marches, rallies, strikes and demonstrations, public meetings, public statements, petitions, letter writing, and lobbying by specialized associations at the gates of conventional politics to put forward their claims (Tarrow 2012). But I also argued that, as the United States reached the second half of the twentieth century and the party system began to hollow out, the movement repertoire was expanding and increasingly overlapped with interest groups, nonprofit advocacy groups, and the party system. The results were the hybrid forms of collective action that populate the space between parties and movements today.

Does this mean that the distinction political scientists have employed for decades between articulating interests – the specialty of movements and interest groups – and aggregating them – the stock-in-trade of political parties – is no longer valid? I am not inclined to go that far but in examining party/movement intersections in the early twenty-first century, an additional distinction seems to be called for: Given the hollowing out of the political parties and the rise of what David Meyer and I called "a movement society" (1998), a variety of forms of collective action have filled the corresponding gap. To understand it, I will introduce the concept of "hybridity" that I have borrowed from the field of contentious politics.

This is a concept that has been employed to analyze the multiple forms of collective identity held by individual militants (Heaney & Rojas 2014); to designate the nested relationships of individual organizations in networks of organizations (della Porta & Diani 2006: ch. 6); and to describe movements that make multiple claims and aim to represent a variety of claimants (Rich 2019). I will employ it to examine organizations that maintain close ties with individual parties but that are not subsumed by those parties. An early example was the creation of the Labor Nonpartisan Action League in the mid-1930s, which we met in Chapter 5. Another was the Eagle Forum of Phyllis Schlafly, which was the instrument she used to defeat the ERA in the early 1980s. A third was the creation of the Moral Majority by Jerry Falwell in the 1970s.

Such relationships were relatively rare in the United States until the combination of the "hollowing out" of the parties and the strengthening of social movements after the 1960s. This suggests the need for a category that has some of the properties of movements – for example, their ideological "purism" (La Raja & Schaffner 2015) – and some of the characteristics of interest groups – their policy orientation and tactical flexibility. If the early twenty-first century is the age of "hollowed-out parties," it is also the age of expanded, politically connected associations using both conventional and movement-like tactics.

Looking at the broad array of groups that circulate around the party system today, we can identify three types of hybrid formations:

- *horizontal hybrids*, the traditional form of group/party relations that is based on common political interest and specialization of function;
- *vertical hybrids*, group/party relations based on the provision of resources to the party and the use of those resources to influence it; and
- *blended hybrids*, a combination of the first two types of hybridity.

We will see a prominent example of a "horizontal hybrid" in the relationship between the anti–Iraq War movement and the Democratic Party in response to President George W. Bush's plan to invade Iraq in 2002. The most prominent example of a "vertical hybrid" that we will examine is the Koch network of organizations that developed in the 1980s and 1990s outside the Republican Party but that became quietly influential in that party's political-economic policies. The most successful case of a "blended hybrid" was the Tea Party movement, which had grassroots origins but developed links to Washington-based advocacy groups. That movement ended up helping to elect a new cadre of Tea Party–linked candidates who brought the "take-no-prisoners" culture of the movement into the halls of Congress after the 2010 elections.

In this chapter, I will compare these three forms of party-movement interaction. I begin by reviewing some of the major changes in movement activism and the party system as the country entered the new century. In Section II, I will turn to the antiwar movement, which developed a symbiotic relationship to the Democratic Party base. In Sections III and IV, I will focus on what I will call a "blended hybrid" – the Tea Party – and its impact on the

Republican Party. In Section V, I will examine the Koch network, a "vertical" hybrid that may have ushered in a new phase of movement/party relations.

Focusing on two crowded decades of recent history has certain risks, including the risk of eliding important social movements.[1] But these omissions are inevitable if we are to focus on a central theme of this book – *the increasingly intimate relations between parties and social movements in the early twentieth century*. Although the antiwar movement's move into the grassroots of the Democratic Party and the Tea Party's entry into the GOP are familiar patterns from American history, the Koch network's interpenetration with the Republican Party, while maintaining its independent base, was a fundamentally new phenomenon. But before we turn to these variations, it will be important to at least gesture toward the general changes in contentious politics in the contemporary period. I will argue that the expanding resources of movement groups and the hollowing out of party organizations have led to a more intimate relationship between the two and contributed mightily to the current polarization of American society.

I PARTY/MOVEMENT CHANGE IN THE EARLY TWENTY-FIRST CENTURY

Contentious forms of politics have always appealed to groups other than classical social movements, but this trend has expanded enormously in what David Meyer and I called "the social movement society" (1998). By this term, we intended to demarcate two things: first, the expansion of contentious forms of activity from movements to other collectivities; second, the legitimation of these forms of action that allowed them to spread beyond classical social movements and to lose the elements of surprise and shock they possessed as part of the movement repertoire.

An example: When Alice Paul organized the first mass women's suffrage march in Washington in 1913, it shocked the public and challenged the more conventional parts of the women's movement (see Chapter 4). But by the second decade of the twenty-first century, a march led by women – like the anti-Trump marches in early 2017 – was a regular occurrence (see Chapter 8). It was only because that movement spread so widely and so rapidly across the country that it drew so much attention (Berry & Chenoweth 2018; Fisher 2019).

The expansion of contentious politics that Meyer and I discerned in the late 1990s has gone well beyond what we predicted then, for several reasons.

First, a technological revolution that we failed to predict has put access to the Internet and to social media within the reach of even the most informal

---

[1] I am thinking, in particular, of the Occupy movement, the "Me-Too" movement, and the young people's anti-gun movement that was touched off by the mass murders in Parkland, Florida.

groups of activists, as well as at the disposal of established groups and parties (Earl & Kimport 2011; Bennett & Segerberg 2013; Schradie 2019). As Dana Fisher points out in her book *American Resistance*, it was by using the mechanism of "distributed organizing" through the Internet that the anti–Trump Resistance was able to coordinate online with offline mobilization (2019: 85–86). In her book, *Twitter and Tear Gas* (2017), Zeynep Tufekci argues that social media make the staging of large-scale events much quicker and easier, but the organizing still needs to be done on the ground, which means that traditional methods of mobilization are unlikely to disappear.

Second, increasing inequality and the international financial crisis that exacerbated it led to a revival of the kinds of class-based movements that scholars of "postindustrial society" once thought were becoming obsolete (compare Inglehart 1990 with Inglehart & Norris 2017). Inequality has also created new strata of workers, those with short-term contracts, temporary workers, and workers in the gig economy, and has subjected them to new forms of exploitation. As the organizers of the "Gig Economy Data Hub" write: "Many data sources suggest the nature of work is indeed changing, with workers increasingly engaging in short-term and project-based work outside of, in or addition to, full-time, long-term employer-employee relationships."[2]

A sequence of critical events, both global and national, reflected these structural changes, helping to blur the lines between electoral and protest politics, as Endre Borbath and Swen Hutter (2020) point out.[3] Their research underscores the fact that party-sponsored protests are an important feature of contemporary protest politics. Sometimes these pairings take the traditional form of movement groups turning into parties, but parties are also mounting protests through the "civil society" groups they sponsor to advance their interests (Greskovits 2020).

Expanding the Movement Repertoire

During periods of rapid change, familiar claim-making routines have always dissolved in spurts of innovation (Tarrow 2011: ch. 10). Recall that the civil rights activists in the 1960s did not simply rely on the decorous performances inherited from the past – the march, the public meeting, the prayer service – but developed new kinds of performances that disrupted existing routines and put

---

[2] The "Gig Economy Data Hub" is a collaborative venture of the Aspen Institute's Future of Work project and the Cornell University School of Industrial Relations. For information, go to www .gigeconomydata.org/about-us.

[3] The major results of the study are found in Hanspeter Kriesi, Jasmine Lorenzini, Bruno Wieest, and Silja Hausermann, *Contention in Times of Crises. Comparing Political Protest in 30 European Countries, 2000–2018* (2020).

opponents off balance (McAdam 1983). New and old actors used new kinds of performances, culminating in extended cycles of contention – mostly peaceful but with outcroppings of violence alongside a trend to institutionalization (della Porta & Tarrow 1986; Meyer & Staggenborg 1996).

The period since 2001 has seen an increase in the use of contentious forms of collective action, their spread from movements to other collectivities, and their increasing penetration into parties. Although this has been true throughout the world (Chenoweth 2017), it has been aided in advanced industrial countries by the increasing organizational capacity of private associations and their amplification by the Internet and social media.

These interactions have produced movements that put pressure on parties but have also led to the formation of movements *within* parties and encouraged the growth of a new layer of conventionally organized groups that employ both traditional interest group practices (e.g., lobbying, supporting candidates) and movement tactics. As Mayer Zald and Michael Berger argued decades ago, "belonging to associations and networks eases the cost of information flow and mobilization" (1987: 208). As Rachel Blum writes of the Tea Party, "Insurgent factions are characterized by their willingness to destabilize their host parties in order to seize control of them" (Blum 2020: 6).

Some conventional lobbying groups have learned to sponsor groups that adopt some of the repertoire of social movements. For example, the Obama campaign created a new hybrid online/offline activism called Organizing for Action (Milkis & York 2017). On the right, the Heritage Foundation, an inside-the-beltway legal think tank dating from in the 1970s, created Heritage Action for America, which maintains a grassroots network outside of Washington based on coordinators who recruit and train "Sentinel activists." The new group's first campaign was to try to defeat Obama's Affordable Care Act (i.e., "Obamacare"),[4] while the most recent was to back the countermovement to defend the police against the charge of abusing African Americans (see Chapter 8). If these are not signs of the intrusion of the "movement society" on conventional politics, they are the next closest thing to it. They were advanced by a simultaneous decline of the central organizations of the two major parties and the growing resources of social movements.

Changes in Parties

While movements and movement-like performances were gaining greater purchase outside the traditional precincts of contentious politics, political parties were losing their centrality to institutional politics. In their research on European parties, Richard Katz and Peter Mair found in the 1990s that party systems were getting weaker as institutions for representation (Katz & Mair

---

[4] "The Fight to Repeal Obamacare," www.humanevents.com/20110/07/05/the-fight-to-repeal-obamacare

1993). As we saw in Chapter 6, these structural trends were accompanied by institutional changes – like the shift of partisanship to the executive, the near-universal adoption of the direct primary, and the evisceration of campaign finance legislation, which further reduced the centrality of party organizations to representative politics. While during the "Party Period" of American history, parties were effectively organized at the local level and maintained themselves through the distribution of patronage; parties today are focused on raising funds nationally. "A critical facet of contemporary polarization," wrote Nolan McCarty and Eric Schickler, "is that group alignments and issue stances appear to be far more consistent across states, as national-level cleavages permeate the fifty states" (2018: 189).

We could already see the decline of what David Mayhew called "traditional party organizations" in the 1970s and 1980s (1986). In the decades since Mayhew wrote, there has been a decline in the central funding of party organizations and a diffusion of campaign funding through nonparty organizations. In an original effort to compare the resources of extra-party consortia with party-linked organizations, Theda Skocpol and Alexander Hertel-Fernandez found that although the resources of party-linked groups have dropped sharply, those of extra-party consortia have sharply increased. Between 2001–2 and 2013–14, the resources controlled by these "nonparty funders" more than tripled, while the proportion controlled by Republican Party committees was almost cut in half. "Crucially," they conclude, "the resource shifts on the right ... have largely occurred through the rise of new far-right organizations instituted after 2002, not through increases in the resources controlled by older groups" (Skocpol & Hertel-Fernandez 2016: 683).

Institutional changes are partly responsible for this shift from party to nonparty funding. In striking down the Bipartisan Campaign Reform Act of 2002, the Supreme Court's *Citizen's United* decision (558 US 310, 2010) held that the free speech clause of the First Amendment prohibits the government from restricting corporations, labor unions, and nonprofit associations from making independent contributions to political candidates. This opened the gates to a broad spectrum of mainly moneyed groups inserting themselves between parties and candidates to office (La Raja & Schaffner 2015). However, short-circuiting of party organizations as brokers between corporations and policy makers has also been responsible.

Have the organizational cores of political parties declined so completely that they are no more than "coalitions of policy demanders," as members of the UCLA research group maintain (Cohen et al. 2008; Bawn et al. 2012)? That might be a step too far, because, as McCarty and Schickler note, "parties respond to particular group demands, *but only to the extent that the party's officials and candidates judge that doing so serves their interests, either as individuals or as partisans*" [emphasis added]. Parties are more than an aggregate of "policy demanders" and spend much of their time "making decisions about how to respond to the array of pressures emanating from both groups and voters" (2018: 184).

Of course, the ability of parties to make these decisions ebbs and flows, having reached its nadir in the failure of the Republican Party in the campaign of 2015 to block the "outsider" candidacy of Donald Trump. Subsequent to that, it also failed to prevent the infiltration of MAGA hat-wearing militants into its party organizations and the effective merger of the party with lunatic far-right networks like Q-Anon. The culmination of this trend came when Republican members of Congress fought to block a commission to investigate the insurrection of January 6, 2021.

In the rest of this chapter, I will argue, with David Karol (2014), that there have been fundamental changes in the party system, but I will also argue that the most significant developments have taken place *outside* traditional party organizations in the creation of intimate links among movements, nonmovement groups, and the party system. We will begin with a traditional kind of linkage that briefly created a horizontal relationship between the anti–Iraq War movement and the Democrats. From there, we will examine the better known example of the Tea Party, which created a mixture of horizontal and vertical ties with the Republicans, before concluding with the case of the Koch network, which has penetrated the policy-making levels of the GOP.

II   THE ANTIWAR MOVEMENT: A HORIZONTAL HYBRID

Almost by definition, antiwar movements arise during wars and threats of war. Thus, the anti–Vietnam War movement came at the high point of the development of 1960s activism, building on the Civil Rights and New Left movements but also drawing on traditional pacifist groups, religious activists, veterans' groups, and even members of the armed forces (Cortright 1975). But unlike that earlier movement, the anti–Iraq War movement was a coordinated transnational movement organized on the Internet, much like the global justice movement that preceded and fed into it (Walgrave & Rucht, eds. 2010; Hadden & Tarrow 2007).

More than most other movements, "antiwar movements" have never been unified collective actors. This is not only because more than one organization shares space within a unified movement – that would be true for the labor movement, the women's movement, the civil rights struggle, and the environmental movement – but because they bring together movement groups with broader claims. The antiwar movement not only attracted traditional pacifists, opponents of particular wars, and opponents of certain kinds of wars but also those whose primary commitment was to other forms of collective action. As David Cortright writes, "The term 'peace movement' refers not only or even primarily to the organized activities of specific groups ... . Of course, such groups are essential to the movement, but the movement extends far beyond traditional peace organizations to include people of all walks of life who commit themselves to the prevention of war" (Cortright 1993: 3).

Many different tendencies and political approaches, some at odds with one another, coexist within the same antiwar movements, but all contribute directly or indirectly to political pressures for arms restraints (ibid, p. 3). These organizational differences have not always fractured peace movements, but they do constrain their capacity for concerted collective action – as they did in the "freeze movement" of the 1980s (Meyer 1990) and in the movement against the war in Iraq.

Not only the heterodox nature of the coalition that arose in 2002 against the looming war with Iraq but the conditions in which it emerged limited activists' ability to mobilize large numbers of Americans. The country had been struck by the cruel massacre of 2001; the government was scrambling for an adequate response to it; and the public was thunderstruck by the vastness and brutality of the attacks and was ripe to "rally round the flag." When, in early October 2001, American special forces joined Afghan militants in attacking the Taliban government, the response from the peace community was therefore muted. Not so the attack on Iraq in early 2003. The Iraq War led to the most extensive peace mobilization since the Vietnam War.

George W. Bush's war not only left a long-term legacy involving the United States in a prolonged military involvement in the Middle East, but it also contributed to the defeat of the Republican Party in the November 2008 presidential election and to the election of the nation's first African American president, who campaigned as a peace candidate. If we think of critical junctures as often leading to "reactive sequences" (Mahoney 2000), the wars in Iraq and Afghanistan were reactions to 9/11 while the defeat of the Republican Party and Obama's election victory in 2008 were reactions to that reaction.

There were many causes for the reversal in party fortunes, the most fundamental of which was the 2007–8 financial crisis; the Bush administration stumbled badly in response. But Obama's victory was in no small measure due to his embrace of an antiwar position, first as a senator from Illinois and then as a candidate for the presidency. Of course, his victory was also due to an unusually high turnout of African American voters and to reactions to the financial crisis that had emerged during the waning days of the Bush administration. But his electoral edge also came from antiwar voters who had been animated by his early and determined opposition to the war, while competitors like Hillary Clinton and John Kerry had been hesitant to go on record against it.

The anti–Iraq War movement was born even before the attack on Iraq that was launched in March of the following year. It produced its largest turnouts between 2003 and 2006. Along with millions of protesters around the world, in what was probably the first global protest organized on the Internet (Bennett et al. 2010: 231–32), the movement began on February 15, 2003, when something like 2.5 million Americans (Verhulst 2010: table 1.1) protested against the impending attack. It was not only on the east and west coasts – where we find the usual suspects of progressive activism – but in the conservative heartland of the country that Americans turned out in force to oppose the war that President Bush had decided upon. This was the most broadly based antiwar protest since the Moratorium against the Vietnam War (Cortright 2008).

During a series of demonstrations between 2003 and 2006, the number of people turning out to protest remained at historic peaks, but the numbers began to decline during the electoral season of 2007–8 and even more sharply after Obama assumed office in January 2009. In their book, Michael Heaney and Fabio Rojas traced the average size of the largest antiwar protests by month between 2001 and 2012.[5] The movement peaked quite early – between the outbreak of war and the beginning of the 2006 midterm election – after which average participation declined from more than 100,000 in the early demonstrations to much lower proportions afterward, reflecting the gravitational pull of elections on the party, as we can see in Figure 7.1.[6]

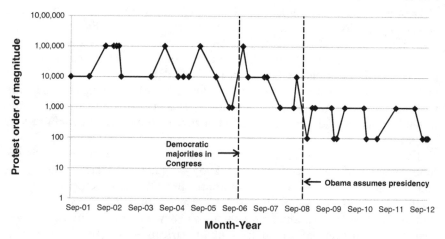

FIGURE 7.1 Size of national and nationally-coordinated antiwar protests, 2002–12
Source: Michael T. Heaney and Fabio Rojas, *The Party in the Street*, ch. 2 and Appendix D. I am grateful to the authors for allowing me to reproduce this data from their book, published by Cambridge University Press.

[5] The events they studied were mostly organized in Washington, DC, with some demonstrations held in New York, Denver, St. Paul, and elsewhere. These authors conducted surveys in Washington, DC, as well as in one city on the East Coast, one in the Midwest, and one on the West Coast.

[6] I am grateful to Michael Heaney for providing the data for this figure, prepared for his and Fabio Rojas's *The Party in the Street* (2015).

The movement was made up of a number of constituent organizations and coalitions (Heaney & Rojas 2014), some of which predated the outbreak of the war and had much broader missions than opposing this particular war. It drew heavily on recruits from the nascent global justice movement, the environmental movement, the women's movement, the LGBTQ movement, the labor movement, and other sectors of movement activism. A number of organizations that participated in the protests were themselves hybrid formations, such as Code Pink: Women for Peace, which combined peace and women's activism; US Labor against the War; and Veterans for Peace, which drew on veterans from the Vietnam War as well as from the earlier Gulf War. Heaney and Rojas found that such "hybrid" organizations played a key brokerage role in bringing together disparate strands of a movement that might otherwise not have held together.

As is the case for most hybrid movements, some participating organizations in this new movement were moderate, while others were more radical and couched their opposition to the war in a broad anti-imperial discourse. In the early years, animosity to President Bush and to a war they considered illegitimate helped keep the movement's different strands together. However, once Obama came into office, "they clashed on whether the administration represented a real change in US foreign policy or was simply another incarnation of more of the same" (Heaney & Rojas 2015: 134). Some groups – like United for Peace and Justice (UFPJ) – collapsed of their own weight, while MoveOn shifted the core of its interests from the war to health care organizing (Heaney & Rojas 2015: 134), becoming little more than an adjunct of the Democrats. As a result of these defections, space was created for more radical groups like End US Wars, the Black Is Back Coalition for Social Justice, and the National Assembly to End the Iraq and Afghanistan Wars and Occupations to become more prominent in the movement.

The slide toward radicalization after Obama's election was evident at events organized by these coalitions when speakers tended to frame their concerns in ways that were not likely to resonate outside the community of hard-core peace activists. As a result, the movement never again achieved the unity or the dimensions it had enjoyed between 2003 and 2005 (ibid., p. 135). A good part of the decline in the size of the demonstrations we saw in Figure 7.1 was due to this collapse in unity and from the defection of some of the largest and more moderate sectors of the movement (Meyer & Corrigall-Brown 2006).

Where did these activists go when they moved beyond their antiwar activities? We can get a hint of their destinations from the network analyses that Heaney and Rojas carried out for their book. Democratic Party–identified interests experienced a surge within the antiwar network during the 2007–8 period, but, after this period, as Heaney and Rojas observe in their book: "Democratically identified organizations – notably MoveOn and the Democratic party itself – moved to the sidelines (i.e., of the antiwar demonstrations) as a Democratic president assumed office" (ibid., pp. 145–47).

Heaney's and Rojas's individual-level analysis triangulates with their findings about organizational persistence and defection in the antiwar movement. As it settled into a more stable phase, movement and partisan identities "pulled activists in different directions after the election of a Democratic president" and "Democratic identities were associated with individuals who eventually withdrew from antiwar activism" (ibid., p. 116 and table 4.4). Antiwar activists with strong Democratic Party identities (i.e., those who had identified with the party during their youth) were more likely to defect after a Democratic president was elected.[7]

How much the antiwar movement contributed to Obama's victory is difficult to sort out from the survey data because, by 2008, opposition to the war was so widespread among Democratic voters. Antiwar sentiments were probably more important for white voters, because the African Americans who flocked to the polls in 2008 were more likely to turn out for identity reasons. What was certainly the case was that Obama's ability to gain the nomination over Hillary Clinton was helped by her early support of the war. The antiwar movement was a horizontal hybrid formation, one of whose main components was support for the Democratic Party. That left the movement adrift when a Democratic president was elected. By the time his administration had begun to consider intervening in the Syrian civil war, most of these antiwar Democrats who had returned to their Democratic roots were engaged in domestic concerns – like the passage of Obama's signature Affordable Care Act.

The dynamics of the relations between the antiwar movement and the Democratic Party illustrate the major weakness of horizontal hybrids. Once the events that create an incentive for activists to organize outside a party are past, the durability of the alliance subsides. More enduring are the vertical ties created by the dependency of a party on its external partners, especially when that party is dependent on external financial resources, as we will see in the relations between the Republican Party and two major networks that grew during the first decade of the new century – the Tea Party and the Koch network of organizations.

III   THE TEA PARTY: A BLENDED HYBRID

The growing intersection between party and movement activism in the early twenty-first century was not limited to the left. Soon after Obama's election, a new movement arose on the right, one that eventually became a key component of the Republican coalition – the Tea Party. In fact, the emergence

---

[7] From interviews they carried out at the US Social Forum in 2010, Heaney and Rojas found that even participants who were highly committed to movement activism were more likely to reduce their involvement in antiwar protests after 2008. Thus, even in the movement-leaning share of their sample, the authors found that partisan identities were a more powerful draw than movement identities (2015, p. 121).

of a mostly white, mostly comfortable movement on the right of the Republican Party had many of the properties of a countermovement to the election of this African American president. However, it was constituted at the base by grassroots groups and at the summit by national advocacy groups with deep pockets and a libertarian mission. True, it drew on traditional sources of conservative commitment, including religious faith, racial resentment, and status insecurity, but what was new about it was what the antiwar movement lacked – a combination of a grassroots base and a national organizational network.

We know how that movement began. Although there were early premonitions of turbulence on the right before 2008, the Tea Party's emergence was triggered soon after Obama's election when broadcaster Rick Santelli railed about the government's bailout of large firms following the financial crisis. Santelli's call for a Chicago Tea Party was picked up by the *Drudge Report* and "quickly scaled the media pyramid." Web-savvy activists saw Santelli's outburst as rhetorical gold. "Operating at first through the new online social networking site Twitter, conservative bloggers and Republican campaign veterans took the opportunity offered by the Santelli rant to plan protests under the newly minted 'Tea Party' name" (Skocpol & Williamson, p. 7).

Building on a vast "tax day" turnout, many of these participants created what seem to have been more than 1,000 local groups, "taking grassroots activism from the realm of occasional outbursts connected by Internet communications into sustained, face-to-face community organizing" (ibid., p. 8). The potential firepower of these activists was revealed at town hall protests before the 2010 midterm elections, when many thousands of them came out to shout at Democratic candidates. Their efforts were amplified by the mainstream media and by the alacrity with which moneyed groups – some of them coming from the Koch network – noted their potential and claimed their leadership.

Who Were the Tea Partiers?

Because of the attention of a group of intrepid social scientists, we know a great deal about the Tea Party's activists and sympathizers. From Michael Bailey and his collaborators' analysis, we know that they came disproportionately from the Midwest and the West, from areas with a high median household income, and from election districts dominated by Republicans (Bailey et al. 2012: 784). Although they should not be confused with the Christian Right that came before them, they were largely Protestant, came predominantly from evangelical denominations, and were for the most part regular churchgoers. We also know that they shared a dislike of immigrants and harbored a high degree of racial resentment (Jacobson 2011).

From David Kirby's and Emily Ekins' early analyses of Tea Party sympathizers, we also know that roughly half of them could be identified as "libertarians" while the other half were coded as "conservatives" (Kirby & Ekins 2012). This distinction is an important one, especially when racial resentment is included in the definition of social conservatism. In comparison, the national-level organizations that claimed leadership of the movement were mainly libertarian – especially those associated with the Koch network. As Bryan Gervais and Irwin Morris concluded from their exhaustive analysis, "Tea Party *organizations* tend to focus on policy objectives driven by fiscal conservatism. Tea Party *supporters* among the members of the mass public, however, tend to care far less about fiscal conservatism (apart from tax cuts) than Tea Party organizations" (Gervais & Morris 2018: 39).

The distinction between libertarians and social and racial conservatives was to some degree obscured by the fact that the media focused attention on the "business friendly libertarians" who tried to take hold of the grassroots insurgency from Washington and New York. These groups were within easy reach of the media and tried to emphasize the new movement's opposition to taxation, regulation, and the welfare state (Van Dyke & Meyer 2014: 15). In contrast, more than four-fifths of the grassroots Tea Partiers were social conservatives who were, for example, worried that "religion as a whole" was losing influence on government leaders and institutions (Kirby & Ekins 2012: 18). They also harbored deep racial resentments, fearing that they were "losing the America they have known and cherished" (Skocpol & Williamson, p. 32).

This fear was enhanced by the financial crisis of 2008–9, but it went deeper than economics. Their sense of dread was deepened when – after eight years of a Republican administration – Americans elected as president a mixed-race law professor with an African father and a background of community organizing in Chicago.

The merger of economic libertarianism and social conservatism among these groups of voters was a carryover of the fusion of ideological elements we saw in Chapter 6 and presaged the merger of populism and plutocracy we would see in the Trumpist movement later in the decade (Pierson 2017). However, the rejection of "the other" went deeper than antipathy for the new president. Many Tea Partiers looked with equal disdain at black and brown Americans, illegal immigrants, lazy young people, and "freeloaders" on government largesse. Based on in-depth interviews with activists in three states, Skocpol and Williamson concluded: "The nightmare of societal decline is usually painted in cultural hues, and the villains in the picture are freeloading social groups, liberal politicians, bossy professionals, big government, and the mainstream media" (p. 75).

Some scholars saw an authoritarian streak in many of these voters, a tendency that Donald Trump would later amplify with his attacks on immigrants and his bleak warning at the state of "American carnage" (Hetherington & Weiler 2009). In the same spirit, Inglehart and Norris (2017) see authoritarian orientation as a durable factor in American politics (Merciera 2020). More interesting: Many of the authoritarian supporters of Donald Trump also see themselves as defenders of the American republic (Parker 2021).

In their penetrating study *Change They Can't Believe In* (2013), Parker and Barreto tried to explain Tea Party sympathizers' attitudes. They began their book by quoting a speaker at a 2011 Tea Party gathering who claimed that President Obama was "a closet secular-type Muslim, but he is still a Muslim. He's no Christian. We're seeing a man who's a socialist communist in the White House, pretending to be an American ... he wasn't even born here" (Parker & Barreto 2013: 1). Leaving aside the speaker's casual acquaintance with the facts, Parker and Barreto saw in such statements an expression of the status anxiety of Tea Party supporters. They argue that

[P]eople are driven to support the Tea Party from the anxiety they feel as they perceive the America they know, the country they love, slipping away, threatened by the rapidly changing face of what they believe is the "real" America: a heterosexual, Christian, middle-class, (mostly) male, white country. (ibid., pp. 2–3)

Parker and Barreto tested their theory with a battery of interview items that led them to conclude that Tea Party activists were *"reactionary* conservatives: people who fear change of any kind – especially if it threatens to undermine their way of life" (p. 6). Although there were strong racial components to their suspicion of Obama, for these authors, he also *"represents* change in which the Tea Party, and their many supporters, cannot believe; change they don't support" (p. 11). After a series of empirical tests and "after accounting for a host of alternative explanations," their central claim was that "support for the Tea Party represents the reaction of its constituents to their perception that America no longer belongs to them" (p. 156).[8]

Along with their conspiratorial views, Tea Party sympathizers displayed an alarming indifference to facts, a property that would expand in the Trumpist movement to which many of them transferred their loyalty after 2016 (see Chapter 8). For example, when Parker and Barreto asked their respondents if they thought Obama was a Christian, 71 percent of Tea Party "true believers" disagreed; when they were asked if he was born in the United States, 59 percent disagreed (p. 209).[9] Gervais and Morris also found that "hyperbolic" (and in

---

[8] Parker and Barreto fortified their theory with an ingenious paired comparison between official Tea Party websites and the conservative website that guided the development of the New Right, *The National Review Online.* The authors examined a total of forty-two Tea Party websites from March 2009 through the midterm elections of 2020, selected based on official domain names and state or regional representation. For the list of the websites they examined and their geographic distribution, see the appendix to their book (pp. 280–81). In contrast to the economic conservatism of the magazine, the Tea Party websites revealed a tendency to promote conspiratorial views and antiminority sentiment, sharply different from what the authors found on the *National Review's* website (p. 160).

[9] On Tea Partiers' disdain for expertise, which resembles that of Donald J. Trump, see Skocpol and Williamson, pp. 52–54.

some cases apocalyptic) language about the effects of the stimulus package, bailouts, the Affordable Care Act, and other Obama policies was a hallmark of Tea Party rhetoric after 2009 and potentially a boon to congressional Republicans (Gervais & Morris, p. 158).

Was the Tea Party a true grassroots movement as many activists and some outside observers claimed? Or was it an "astroturf" expression of big-money groups, like the Kochs, who were hoping to use the movement to give their plutocratic aims a patina of populism? Or was the Tea Party a creation of the expanding right-wing mediascape, led by Fox News? In a period marked by the rise of "hybrid" mobilizations, for Skocpol and Williamson, it was all three of these things. Their conclusions are worth quoting in detail:

> Grassroots activism is certainly a key force, energized by angry, conservative-minded citizens who have formed vital local and regional groups. Another force is the panoply of national funders and ultra-free-market advocacy groups that seek to highlight and leverage grassroots efforts to further their long-term goal of remaking the Republican Party. Finally, the Tea Party cannot be understood without recognizing the mobilization provided by conservative media hosts, who openly espouse and encourage the cause. (ibid., p. 13)

As we have seen, the antiwar movement was a hybrid, too, but the Tea Party's hybridity was also *vertical*, with links to the polished operatives of the national advocacy groups that aimed to represent it. Much of the visibility of the Tea party came from above – from national advocacy organizations like FreedomWorks and newly formed groups like the Tea Party Express. These entities "suddenly saw fresh opportunities to push long-standing ideas about reducing taxes on business and the rich, gutting government regulations, and privatizing Social Security and Medicare" (Skocpol & Williamson 2011: 9). In short order, large, wealthy organizations had found an outlet to claim authorship of the kind of grassroots movement they had been unable to create themselves.

This was not the first time that national advocacy organizations had attempted to latch onto grassroots activism in order to advance their agendas. Remember how the Democratic Party in 1896 attempted to capture the grassroots energy of the agrarian movement behind the candidacy of William Jennings Bryan? What was unusual in the case of the Tea Party was the number of organizations that competed for sponsorship of the movement. Some, like FreedomWorks and Americans for Prosperity (AFP), had been in the field for years and maintained their activities after the Tea Party had disappeared as a distinct movement. Others, like the Tea Party Express, were founded by California Republicans to support the movement and advance their political interests. The Tea Party Patriots, begun in 2009 as a "citizens' group," organized many of the anti-Obamacare town hall protests in 2010 and also offered "training opportunities" to local Tea Party groups (Fetner & King, 2014: 40). A fifth group, calling itself Tea Party Nation, was largely a commercial enterprise that organized a Nashville conference featuring Sarah Palin, which failed to attract a large enough audience to justify continuing the practice (Meyer & Pullum 2014: 87). A sixth, founded by Glenn Beck, called itself the 9/12 Project and was designed to build national unity around nine principles and twelve values. Unlike FreedomWorks and AFP, whose goals were libertarian, Beck's group was the only national "Tea Party" group that endorsed religious principles designed to appeal to social conservatives (ibid.).

In summary, rather than an astroturf organization manipulated from the top or a true grassroots insurgency, the Tea Party was what Skocpol and Williamson call "a field of loosely interconnected organizations" in which each level attempted to "leverage" something – ideas, information, political and financial support – from the other.[10] These links helped the Tea Party "negotiate a far more rapid emergence and effective entry into mainstream politics than most social movements" (Van Dyke & Meyer 2014: 6).

The Mediascape and the Tea Party

But this would not have happened – or, at least, not so quickly – without availability of both free and paid media, as well as from the newly available online social media. "These resources added rapid growth, but created other dilemmas for the movement," write Nella Van Dyke and David S. Meyer. "Perhaps the most salient dilemma centered on political identity, as conflicts played out about both ultimate goals and tactics" (2014: 6).

In the lead for this affordance was Fox News, not only because it saw the potential of the movement for improving its ratings but because it saw an opportunity to shape the new movement's identity. By allocating prime space to Tea Party activities, Fox "served as a kind of social movement orchestrator, during what is always a dicey early period for any new protest effort." As a result, "a community of Fox-viewing Tea Partiers came to share a powerful, widely shared political identity, and the Fox News framing, in due course, shaped national perception of the Tea Party phenomenon" (Skocpol & Williamson, p. 135).

Fox was not alone. Apart from talk radio, where the new movement found homespun and religious broadcasters' support, the mainstream media soon felt a commercial need to join in – especially during the 2009 congressional recess,

---

[10] That these were not "astroturf" organizations appeared clearly from the links in local Tea Party websites. When Skocpol and Williamson carried out an analysis of Tea Party group websites, their results showed extensive digital connections between the local and national expressions of this movement. For example, AFP was cited on 206 local Tea Party groups' websites and FreedomWorks on 267. Tea Party Patriots was mentioned almost 500 times on local Tea Party websites, while the Heritage Foundation was mentioned on 345 (Skocpol & Williamson, p. 114). These findings, although persuasive, should be interpreted with caution. As anyone who has constructed a website knows, the "mention" of links to a national organization can be purely nominal.

when Tea Partiers began to attack Democratic candidates in their town hall appearances. As the 2010 midterms approached, coverage of Tea Party rallies heated up in both parts of the media landscape. In this unusually polarized midterm election, when thousands of conservative voters turned out to vote against President Obama and his health-care plan (Jacobson 2011), the media "began to portray the Tea party as a full-fledged independent political movement, and speculated about whether it might even be an alternative to the two parties" (Skocpol & Williamson, p. 142).

Of course, this was never going to happen. In addition to the powerful constraints that the American system imposes on third parties, Tea Party voters were basically Republicans, and their deep-pocketed backers would never have backed a move that would divide the Right. The 2010 election demonstrated the movement's independent clout, but it also showed that the Tea Partiers aligned themselves predominantly with the right wing of the Republican Party (Jacobson, pp. 10–12).

IV   OUTSIDERS INSIDE: TEA PARTIERS IN THE REPUBLICAN PARTY

We now know what happened to the Tea Party in the years that followed its appearance in 2009. Although the Tea Party was never a party, many of the activists who identified with the movement gravitated into an "insurgent faction" of the Republican Party, from which many of them had come (Blum 2020). But they were different than most Republican voters in that many were willing to support lost-cause candidates and embrace policy positions that were almost guaranteed to fail. As Rachel Blum writes, in her recent book:

Tea Partiers were willing to contest Republican incumbents in primaries, even if this meant later losing the seats to Democrats. They had no qualms about pushing Republicans to oppose popular legislation or obstruct government operations, even if doing so would damage the party's reputation. (ibid., p. 3)

These were *movement Republicans* with the kind of "purist" attitudes to politics that we saw in the Garrisonian abolitionists, Alice Paul's National Women's Party, and the radical wing of the civil rights movement.[11] This was evident in their willingness to take positions in Republican primaries that were so extreme as to virtually guarantee the failure of the candidates they supported, from their use of brash, uncivil language to their willingness to accept as fact

---

[11] In her book, Blum sees the Tea Party as an "insurgent" faction (2020, pp. 22–23). She contrasts the movement to the Christian Right, which, in her view, employed a "consociational strategy" to push the Republicans to prioritize religious traditionalism (pp. 21–22). Blum's distinction between an "insurgent" and a "consociational" faction is a useful way of distinguishing between "inside" and "outside" strategies of ideologically driven groups, as far as parties go. But when they rallied in the thousands against the income tax, shouted down congressional candidates at town halls, and – most importantly – organized an independent network of local groups at the grassroots of American society, the Tea Partiers were more "outsiders" than "insiders."

conspiratorial speculations that no rational individual could believe in. Probably the best way to characterize the Tea Party at its height was as a social movement on the boundary of an institution, one that reflected the dissatisfaction of many Republicans with the direction and the lassitude of their party (Almeida & Nella Van Dyke 2014, p. 61). They contributed mightily to the movementization of the party system.

In this development, congressional elites played an important part. In July, 2010, a Tea Party–inspired group in the House of Representatives was created by Congresswoman Michelle Bachmann under the label "The House Tea Party Caucus." "Its ranks swelled after the 2010 midterms, but by 2013 many of the caucus's founding members had left office or lost energy, and the caucus went dormant" (Blum 2020: 81). Bachmann's effort was followed by the creation of a "Liberty Caucus" in 2011, "which claimed kinship with the Tea Party and was even chaired by Tea Party favorite Justin Amash" (ibid.). The House "Freedom Caucus," founded in 2015, solidified the Tea Party's presence in the House. This new caucus avoided direct association with the Tea Party label but "carried on the Tea Party's obstructionism" (ibid.). Its early success was to oust House Speaker John Boehner from his post before turning into a loyal buttress of the Trump administration. The Tea Party, which began as a social movement at the grassroots with support from well-funded national right-wing groups and sympathetic media outlets, evolved into an "insurgent faction" within the Republican Party, laying the groundwork for the Trump movement that followed.

Sociologist Rory McVeigh made a linkage between the Tea Party and earlier right-wing movements. In his contribution to *Understanding the Tea Party Movement* (2014: 15–34), McVeigh saw the popularity of the Tea Party as the result of "power devaluation," a theory of movement emergence that he developed in studying the 1920s-era Klan. McVeigh notes that, much like the twentieth-century Klan, the Tea Party was based on the mobilization of predominately middle-class whites who already enjoyed some level of political access and resources. He argues that a threatened loss of power in three realms, politics, economics, and status, inspired their mobilization.

Although I am not sure we need to return to the Know-Nothings or to the Klan to understand the Tea Party, the movement certainly included familiar motifs of reactionary mobilization based on race, anti-immigration, suspicion of government, fear of the unknown, and a recurring alternative to the "liberal tradition" (Smith 2010). But as Gervais and Morris demonstrated in their 2018 book, the Tea Party also laid the foundation for a new and even more disruptive movement/party interaction – the presidential campaign and election of Donald J. Trump in 2016, to which I will turn in Chapter 8.

V THE KOCH NETWORK: A VERTICAL HYBRID

Some scholars, like David Karol (2014), have argued that, since the 1970s, there has been a revival of parties in a new form, based largely on the weight of the "outside groups" that support candidates under a variety of guises. Karol writes, "The groups that scholars saw replacing parties, political consultants, and interest groups work within parties to a great extent" (2014: 9) But while they carry out many of the functions once monopolized by party organizations – especially fund-raising and allocation to candidates – it is not clear what is gained by defining parties so broadly that "outside groups" are seen as evidence for "the revival of the party system."

To avoid misunderstanding, I agree with Karol that the weight of outside groups has increased, especially on the Right and particularly since the Supreme Court's *Citizens' United* decision. But to employ the language of Daniel Schozman (2015), it is no longer clear which is the "anchor" and which is the "ship" in this relationship. The enormous financial clout of the Koch network, the intellectual and organizational skills of its leaders – the Koch brothers – and their ability to create "purpose-built" organizations to surround and, to some extent, infiltrate Republican policy making made them a powerful challenge to the party system as a whole. Unlike traditional business-funded groups that focus on either lobbying or electoral activity, the Koch network created a full spectrum of organizational and educational endeavors.

Playing the Long Game

But it didn't start out that way. The origins of the network go back to the 1970s, when Charles Koch, the source of the intellectual firepower of the network, began to seriously study the work of the "Austrian school" of economics represented by Ludwig Von Mises and Friedrich Hayek. The intellectual broker of this filiation was public choice economist James Buchanan; Charles got to know him when Buchanan was teaching at Virginia Tech University in the 1970s. "In the eventual merger of Koch's money and managerial talent and the Buchanan team's decades of work monomaniacally identifying how the populace became more powerful than the propertied," writes historian Nancy MacLean, "a fifth column movement would come into being, the likes of which no nation has ever seen" (MacLean 2017: 127).

Accumulating money and resources and spending it to advance their companies' interests is what has gained the Koch brothers their notoriety and power. But it would understate the importance of their organizational model to reduce them to common or garden fat cats with a special talent for mobilizing other wealthy Americans into a well-oiled political and financial machine. What they began to fund in the 1970s was not an interest group but a movement – granted, mainly an *elite* movement but one with a high degree of ideological coherence and consistency. As Jane Mayer writes of Charles Koch, "His language was militant," demanding that "our movement must destroy the prevalent statist paradigm" (Mayer 2017: 66). "It is undeniable," wrote Koch, "that ideas do determine actions and that we should refine and apply our ideas. But ideas do not spread by themselves; they spread only through *people.* Which means we need a *movement*. Only with a movement can we build an effective force for social change."[12]

Charles Koch had the classical movement activist's disdain for parties and politicians. In his 1978 article, he hardly bothered to hide his dismissal of Republicans who sought to influence regulation rather than attacking the entire statist paradigm. And although much of the network's resources were channeled to Republican candidates, some of its affiliates – like AFP – had more than fifty paid staffers. "Other Koch-related advocacy groups, such as Generation Opportunity and the LIBRE Initiative, planted grassroots organizers wherever there were hotly contested elections" (Mayer, p. 454).

The Koch's long-game strategy of building up an intellectual brain trust was also familiar from the social movement playbook. They spent lavishly to create a network of students and academics who would support their ideas, spread the libertarian message, and eventually take up positions in the movement. This involved a long-term investment in educational institutions, including the creation of some two dozen privately funded academic centers. At George Mason University, they created the Mercatus Center and funded the law school. The Kochs also subsidized colleges that would promote the libertarian message and produce the shock troops for future battles. "The students that graduate out of these higher education programs," explained Kevin Gentry, vice president for special projects at Koch Industries, "populate the state-based think tanks and the national think tanks" and become the "major staffing for the state chapters" of the "grassroots groups." "Those with passion," he continued, "would be encouraged to become part of what he called the Kochs' *fully integrated network*" (quoted in Mayer, p. 449).

Building the "Kochtopus"

There have been plenty of big money pressure groups leaning into both political parties since the Gilded Age, but the Koch network is unusual, both for its extensive reach and for its long-term plan to instill a libertarian culture at the peak of American politics. This is not an old-fashioned lobby (although it spends lavishly on lobbying) nor is it a foundation (though it has that, too) but a conglomerate of foundations, special-interest pressure groups, educational initiatives, think tanks, and a billionaire's caucus that meets twice yearly in great secrecy to plan and collect donations for its initiatives. It is, as its libertarian allies characterized it, a *"kochtopus."*

For example, the Koch-funded keystone organization, AFP, which was created in 2004, combines lobbying and publicity efforts at the national level with mobilizing citizen activists in the districts. AFP has 38 statewide

[12] Charles Koch, "The Business Community: Resisting Regulation." www.libertarianism.org/publications/essays/business-community-resisting-regulation

chapters and claimed, in 2020, to have more than 3.2 million activists and 100,000 financial supporters. AFP can organize demonstrations in legislative hearings about legislation it supports or opposes (Skocpol and Hertel-Fernandez, p. 689). As these observers write of AFP, "It more closely resembles a European-style political party than any sort of specialized traditional US advocacy group or campaign organization" (ibid.). The network's power over the Republicans depends on both its financial clout and its ability to shape the policies of the party, as the following episode testifies.

John Boehner Goes to New York City

In 2011, in the course of the congressional conflict over raising the debt ceiling, Republican House Speaker John Boehner traveled to New York City to ask for the help of billionaire David Koch in convincing congressional Republicans to support the compromise he hoped to fashion with the Obama administration. As *New Yorker* reporter Jane Mayer recalls, "One former adviser to the Koch family says that 'Boehner begged David to call off the dogs. He pointed out that if the country defaulted, David's own investments would tank'" (Mayer 2017: 366). The plea would have been unusual for any member of Congress to make of a billionaire with no direct role in the Republican Party. "But the spectacle of the Speaker of the House, who was among the most powerful elected officials in the country, third in line in the order of presidential succession, traveling to the Manhattan office of a billionaire businessman to ask for his help in an internecine congressional fight captures just how far the Republican Party's fulcrum of power had shifted toward outside donors by 2011" (ibid., p. 367).

In the event, Boehner failed, and after his return to Washington, opponents to the deal that he had laboriously worked out with President Obama – many of them who had recently arrived in Congress with Tea Party support – prevailed, and Congress was forced to agree to indiscriminate spending cuts, mysteriously called "the sequester." The sequester caused enormous economic damage and made clear that a new and radical group of Republicans were now in the saddle in Congress.

The writing was on the wall for Boehner, who was forced to resign in 2015 after his next encounter with the radical right of his party in another fight over funding the government. "I got overrun, that's what happened," Boehner confessed to President Obama after he failed to stop a government shutdown in 2013 (Mayer, p. 434). He was replaced by Congressman Paul Ryan, who was elected with the support of the Tea Party–linked Freedom Caucus.

A House Speaker pleading for a billionaire for help in keeping the government afloat was atypical, but it starkly illustrates the subservience of the party's new conservative majority to its outside funders. After the 2012 election, Mayer wrote:

Hugely wealthy radicals on the right hadn't won the White House, but they had altered the nature of American democracy. They had privatized much of the public campaign process and dominated the agenda of one of the country's two major political parties. (Mayer, p. 408)

This shift was in part the result of the accumulation of the enormous wealth and political influence of the Koch family and its allies (Skocpol & Hertel-Fernandez 2016), but of a nest of other developments also contributed:

- First, the primary reforms of the 1970s that had weakened the weight of the central organizations of both parties and led to the rise of a "supercharged" primary electorate;
- Second, the campaign financing reforms of the 1970s and 2002 opened the gates to a flood of largely anonymous private money pouring directly into Republican election campaigns;
- Third, in its 2010 Citizens' United decision the Supreme Court opened the door to virtually unlimited and largely anonymous private funding of election campaigns.

All that money and all those troops had an inevitable effect on policy making. The Koch network was instrumental in defeating the Obama administration's cap-and-trade bill, which would have impacted the company's oil and gas interests (Mayer, ch. 8). It created an organization dedicated to whittling down and almost killing President Obama's Affordable Care Act (ch. 7). And, through the American Legislative Exchange Council and other decentralized groups, the Kochs created "what appeared to be a conservative revolution bubbling up from the bottom to nullify Obama's policies in the states" (Mayer, pp. 424–28).

But the Koch network was not always successful in its assaults on Obama and the Democrats. For one thing, as power shifted from central party professionals to what Mayer calls "rogue billionaires," top-down consensus was giving way to warring factions in the party (Mayer, p. 376). Party professionals, as La Raja and Schaffner remind us, are in it to win, and winning usually consists of making compromises, rolling logs, reaching out to moderate voters, and shifting ideological ground (La Raja & Schaffner 2015). Although the Kochs were flexible tacticians, their strategy of whittling down the regulatory state was based on rigid ideological convictions that came across as massive indifference to ordinary Americans.

Second, despite their obsessive preoccupation with secrecy, the insistent spread and enormous financial investments and rapacious politics of the network could not remain under wraps indefinitely. When, despite the millions poured into the campaign to make him a one-term president, Obama won the 2012 election, even the normally ebullient Charles Koch was chastened. "Our goal of advancing a free and prosperous America is even more difficult than we envisioned, but it is essential that we continue, rather than abandon, this struggle," he wrote in the *National Review Online* after the Republicans' defeat.[13] It was not long after this – following a close analysis of the election results – that the Charles Koch Institute announced a new "Well-Being Initiative" aimed at softening – but not reducing – the network's links to the Republican Party.[14]

CONCLUSIONS

In this chapter, I have made three interrelated arguments about movements, parties, and their relations to each other in the early twenty-first century:

> First, though there has clearly been an increase in movement-related politics over these two decades, the shift goes beyond the thesis of a "movement society" in the expansion of movement mentalities and movement tactics to groups beyond classical social movements. While the anti–Iraq War movement fit the traditional model of hybridity, neither the Koch network nor the Tea Party were classical social movements or traditional lobbying organizations, but they adopted familiar movement discourses and forms of action. The Tea Party movement shared many properties with "reactionary rightist" movements of the past, but it was built through a combination of grassroots organizing at the base and modern media and advocacy group intervention at the summit. Charles Koch, from the heights of the American capitalist system, saw himself acting on behalf of a movement and adopted both the uncompromising language and the organizational weapons more familiar from the history of social movements than from the repertoire of interest groups and lobbies. Had Lenin witnessed the strategic rigidity and tactical flexibility of the network that the Kochs built, he would have felt right at home.
>
> Second, the weakening of the classical party organizations that has occurred over the past few decades made these institutions vulnerable to the entry of the movements outlined in this chapter. Though the antiwar movement was able to coordinate impressive national and international demonstrations, it virtually vanished as a movement while Bush was still in power. The Tea Party gained greater purchase over the Republicans, combining grassroots mobilization with the prominence it gained from the sponsorship of national advocacy groups. As for the Koch network, while beginning its life with the classical abhorrence of parties typical of movements, its "tentacles" have surrounded the Republican Party from many angles and influenced its adoption of hard-right libertarian policies.

---

[13] www.nationalreview.com/corner/kochs-postpone-post-election-meeting-robert-costa
[14] In 2019 and 2020, Charles Koch reduced even further his group's ties to the GOP, unhappy with the Trump administration's policy stances. www.cnbc.com/2020/09/29/2020-presidential-election-why-koch-network-wont-help-trumps-bid.html

Third, while it would be an exaggeration to conclude from these trends that parties need to be redefined to include the internalization of these "outsiders," there is no doubt that parties and movements now share intimate connections, of which we have seen three variants in this chapter: *horizontal hybrids* like the antiwar movement, which could still be understood as a familiar form of division of labor between a movement and a party; *blended hybrids* like the Tea Party, which assailed the party system from the bottom and from the top through a combination of grassroots organizing, advocacy group pressure, and amplification by the media;[15] and *vertical hybrids* like the Koch network's imbrication with the Republicans, in which the former employed vast resources and organizational innovation to advance major changes in the latter's public policies.

It is too soon to decide whether these hybrid forms are part of a general trend or constitute transitional forms between past and future. What seems clear is that they laid the groundwork for a more direct insertion of a new movement into the Republican Party – the Trump movement – one that may crash and burn after Trump's loss of the 2020 election and the tragic events that followed or may have a lasting impact on the party system and on American democracy. We will turn to that movement and to the countermovement it triggered in Chapter 8.

---

[15] Another form of blended hybrid are the top-down controlled "grassroots" insurgencies created by professional organizations on behalf of big money funders. For this type of "invention of the grassroots," see Walker (2014).

PART IV

CONTEMPORARY CONJUNCTIONS

8

Trumpism and the Movements He Made[1]

The outcome of the 2016 election was unlike others in many respects, but its most important distinction was that – like the triumph of Lincoln in 1860s – it was not so much the success of a party but that of a movement. If we want to understand the unexpected success of Donald Trump in that election and the extraordinary loyalty of his "base" in the four years that followed, we will do best to see them as the result of a social movement. Trump started to claim that he represented a movement early in his campaign, when he told a New Hampshire audience that "The silent majority is back. We really are in a position we haven't been in a long time. The people are speaking. It's an amazing thing. *It's like a movement*" (italics added, quoted by Merciera, p. 188).

I am not the first observer to liken Donald Trump to a leader of a movement. "Trump," as Jennifer Merciera notes, "liked to describe his presidential campaign not merely as a 'campaign', but as a movement" (2020, p. 187). "More than other candidates," writes Arlie Russell Hochschild, "Donald Trump fits the classic description of a charismatic leader, as Weber defined it ... . Trump offers himself ... as the *personal messenger* of his followers" (Hochschild 2018). Many of the puzzles about the Trump administration, as well as its aftermath, can be traced to the fact that its leader saw himself as the leader of a movement and not of a party or a government.

This was a hybrid of plutocratic and populist components. As Paul Pierson wrote of it in 2017:

What has emerged in the United States [in 2017] is not populist governance but a peculiar hybrid – one quite distinct from what might emerge in other national contexts. Initially,

---

[1] This chapter draws upon the Introduction and chapter 9 of David S. Meyer and Sidney Tarrow, eds., *The Resistance: The Dawn of the Anti-Trump Opposition Movement*, 2018.

key features of the American setting played a critical role in amplifying the populist impulse, catapulting a populist candidate into a central political position. (2017: S106)

Some scholars have emphasized the "populist" face of Trumpism. When Trump lost the national election of November 2020, Mark Lander and Melissa Eddy wondered whether his loss meant a decline in global populism.[2] Others, like the historian Ruth Ben-Ghiat, insisted on the importance of the plutocratic elites who had joined his administration, "thinking that he can be controlled as he solves their problems" (Ben-Ghiat 2020: 13–14). As we will show, both were correct, but although Trump's support from organized business eroded toward the end of his mandate,[3] his populist base continued to support him, leading to the insurrection at the US Capitol in January 2021.

In Chapter 6, I argued that the insertion of the "long new right" into the Republican Party led to the partial "movementization" of that party. Trump's takeover of the GOP after his election in 2016 crystallized the movement elements within the party and provided them with a charismatic focal point. But it also led to some of the important incongruities that scarred Trump's administration. While Trump aided the rich by giving them enormous tax breaks and access to the White House, he also catered to his populist base by replacing free trade with protectionism, attacking people of color, castigating undocumented immigrants and Muslims, and demolishing the internationalist foreign policy that most conservatives had endorsed. These factors converged to bring out the contradictions in Trump's movement during his years in power.

Was there a dominant strain in this composite movement? "In the realm of rhetoric," writes Pierson, "right-wing populism remains robust. In actual government, the interests and concerns of plutocrats have typically prevailed" (2017: S106). With respect to Trump's policy agenda, Pierson's 2017 prediction proved to be prophetic. From the vast tax reform that benefited the very rich to the deregulatory program that stripped the administrative state of much of its regulatory capacity, to the opening up of national forest lands to oil exploitation, to the replacement of career civil servants with lobbyists and business titans: Trump and his enablers attacked the national state that has been built up since the New Deal.

But the populist elements in Trump's movement had continued purchase even as his support from business constituencies began to wane. In earlier collaborative work, I argued that collective claims fall into three categories: *program claims, standing claims,* and *identity claims* (Tilly & Tarrow 2015). Standing claims say that an actor belongs to an established category within a regime and deserves rights and respect (ibid., p. 110). As Parker writes, much

---

[2] www.nytimes.com/2020/11/10/world/europe/trump-populism.html

[3] This was especially true of the Koch network, whose leaders had never been happy with Trump but who were shocked by the events of January 6, 2020, into declaring that Republican lawmakers' behavior during the riots would "weigh heavily" in the network's future financial support. www.politico.com/news/2021/01/13/koch-network-capitol-riots-459143

of Trump's base experienced a loss of standing in American society – what he calls "status threat" (2021: 6–7).

Pierson's diagnosis of the plutocratic policies of the Trump administration mainly addresses the first two – program and standing claims – but elides an important part of movement politics – addressing identity claims. Identity claims declare that an actor exists. That actor may have existed before the episode began or it may be *constituted* in the course of the episode (Tilly and Tarrow, p. 111). Trump's populist constituency had roots in earlier particularist movements (Smith 2010); in the racialization of small government, anti-welfare ideology we saw in the long New Right; and in the strain of racial resentment found by Arlie Hochschild as Trump was coming to power, but he personalized these resentments and provided followers with a target for them in his claim to represent the "pure people" against a corrupt elite.

First, in contrast with his European parallels, Trump founded a populist movement within a party, one that could build on decades of right-wing incursions (Roberts 2018). He had an assist from the fact that he found himself at the helm of a movementized party, one in which the transactional elements of party politics coexisted uneasily with the ideological drive of the movements that had been absorbed into the party in previous decades.

Second, although Trump's particular brand of nationalism and racism found a ready audience in the Republican base he inherited, he added to it an almost unique ability to manipulate the media and a willingness to strip off the carapace of civility that had disguised the racist resentment he found in parts of the Republican base.

Third, Trump's "base" was not alone: Because of the incursion of a new wave of elected officials – many of them coming out of the Tea Party (see Chapter 7) into the party – Trump found an elite ready to do his bidding. No one who watched 121 members of the House of Representatives vote to overturn the certification of the votes in Arizona and Pennsylvania only hours after the Capitol had been invaded by a Trumpist mob in January 2020 could believe that his movement was a strictly plebeian one. As Lance Bennett writes of the January 6 coup attempt, "None of this could have happened without the majority of national Republican officials enabling Trump." But as Bennett also notes, "Nor could it have happened without the unwavering support of the large plurality of citizens who voted for him and then cheered his efforts to overturn the election."[4]

---

[4] Lance Bennett, "We the People? Time for Truth about Democracy in America." https://cjmd .com.uw.edu/we-the-people-time-for-tritj-about-democracy-in-america; also see Jeff Goodwin, "The Eighteenth Brumaire of Donald J. Trump." www.pwsc.us/conflicted-the-pwsc-official-blog/blog/the-eighteenth-brumaire-of-donald-j-trump?fbclid=IwAR0NuirjoSzaH7Dc_ZbsA4t-N-v2g2OCACYrug_YrAWUl-j3jkWkAXbwOMU

This was a conglomerate movement that, after winning the election in 2016, Trump was at pains to service and which he attempted to energize after his electoral loss in 2020. From his kind words for the Neo-Nazis who rampaged in Charlottesville in 2017, to his hostility to Mexicans, Africans, and African Americans, to his offensive comments about his political opponents, the president continued to play to this base. Why it remained loyal during four years of his erratic and corrupt administration is the first puzzle I will examine in this chapter. How the reaction to Trump's shrill politics shaped a countermovement after his 2016 election victory is the second; the relationship between the countermovement and the future of the Democratic Party is the third; and the fourth is the possible futures of the Trumpian movement after the coup attempt of January 2021.[5]

I   THE TRUMP MOVEMENT

There were many factors that helped observers understand Trump's unexpected electoral victory in the 2016 elections: the distortions of the electoral college; the inability of the "hollowed out" Republican Party to find a candidate who could represent its institutional interest; the weakness of Hillary Clinton as a candidate and her inability to mobilize enough votes among key Democratic constituencies to defeat him; the intrusion of a popular progressive competitor – Senator Bernie Sanders – whose candidacy cut into her support among younger voters; and "conjunctural" factors, like FBI Director James Comey's last-minute intervention in the campaign when he chose to cast doubt on Clinton's honesty. But it was Trump's rhetorical and organizational ability to electrify the base of the party that explains its electoral support for him in 2016 and its stubborn loyalty throughout his presidency.

Trump's determination to reinforce his populist base could already be seen in his inauguration speech in January 2017. Gesturing at what he called abandoned factories, rampant crime, and a failed education system, Trump pledged that his presidency would bring about change. "This American carnage stops right here and stops right now," he proclaimed on the steps of the Capitol, electrifying his base and leaving both Clinton and former president George W. Bush aghast.[6]

---

[5] I use the term "coup attempt" advisedly, following the revealing parallel between the incursion to the Capitol and the Eighteenth Brumaire of Louis Napoleon that Goodwin draws (see note no. 4) and that the coup was a coup within a riot, the latter an expression of Trump's larger movement within the Republican Party.

[6] Clinton's reflection on the speech is worth quoting in detail:

"I thought: Wait a minute. It's not rational but it's also not politics. It's not what a president does," said Clinton. She had hoped to hear Trump make an attempt to reach out to nonsupporters. "I hoped I would hear a little of that, I didn't hear any of that. And that carnage in the street and the dark dystopian vision. I was sitting there like just, wow. I couldn't believe it. And George

Trump was certainly trying to tap into the economic discontent that had been roiling important parts of the electorate, as inequality soared and jobs disappeared overseas following the financial crisis of 2007–8.[7] There was also evidence that the authoritarian instincts of many voters had "the largest effect on white vote choice in 2016 than in any prior election" (Knuckey & Hassan 2020: 1; also see Hetherington & Weiler 2009). Then there was "Trump's willingness to make explicitly racist and sexist appeals during the campaign" (Schaffner et al. 2018: 10).

The face of the Democratic leadership under Obama's presidency reinforced these appeals. For example, Obama had worked closely with Nancy Pelosi, the first woman to serve as Speaker of the House, and with Representative Barney Frank, openly Jewish, gay, and chair of the House Financial Services Committee. Obama also appointed record numbers of women and minorities to visible positions in his administration. His defense of Harvard Professor Henry Louis Gates, who was arrested on his front porch by a Cambridge policeman, convinced many conservatives that the president was opposed to the police. If you tended toward racial resentment, gender hostility, and authoritarian instincts before Obama came to power, the composition and politics of his administration would have reinforced those tendencies.

Even before Trump entered the scene, Republicans had learned that they could benefit from the anger of people driven by racial resentment. Starting in 2010, with the election of the first Tea Party candidates, the GOP began to play to a populist base that would prove dangerous, first to Democrats, but then to the traditional Republican elite. Individual-level characteristics, attitudes, and actions undoubtedly contributed to Trump's electoral success, but they elide the *collective mechanisms* that produced that result (Skocpol 2020: xxi–xxii). Trump took the elements of the New Right in the Republican Party and turned them into a *movement*, using an appeal to the same sector of American society that had nourished the rise of the Tea Party (Parker & Barreto 2013; McVeigh 2014) but stripping it of its civilized veneer. In seeking power, he combined the personal charisma of a movement leader with a diffuse organizational infrastructure in the mold of his populist predecessors in Europe and Latin America (Roberts 2018).

W. Bush says to me, 'Well, that was some weird shit.'" https://thehill.com/blogs/blog-briefing-room/news/326438-george-bush-after-inauguration-that-was-some-weird-s-t-report.

Clinton recorded these impressions in an interview with *Inside Hook* in December 2019. www.insidehook.com/daily_brief/news-opinion/hillary-clinton-reveals-george-w-bushs-reaction-to-trumps-inaugural-speech

[7] For a representative journalistic account, see Eduardo Porter, "Where Were Trump's Votes? Where the Jobs Weren't," *New York Times*, December 14, 2016. www.nytimes.com/2016/12/13/business/economy/jobs-economy-voters.html

A Charismatic Demagogue

In his historical study, *American Demagogues* (1954), Reinhart Luthin offered a list of characteristics that he had found in the public careers of selected American demagogues of the last century – those "masters of the masses" who, in their aspirations for political place and power, pandered to the passions and prejudices, rather than the reason, of the populace and performed all manner of crowd-captivating tricks, only to betray the people who had supported them. Like Huey Long, charismatic governor of and then senator from Louisiana, Trump applied a strategy of "bread and circuses" to wean his supporters from their traditional party affiliations with overheated rhetoric, vicious attacks on opponents, and policies aimed at appealing to their preferences and prejudices (Amenta et al. 1994). Like many of these earlier figures, Trump gave little attention to policy and more to "rallying" his base at set-piece demonstrations aimed at catering to their excitement at his presence.

Trump's efforts to amplify the preferences of his base meant that he often played fast and loose with the facts. "Followers forgive, one after another, flagrant flaws in such a 'messenger', because he is their messenger and he recognizes their suppressed, as they see it, deep story," notes Mercieca (ibid.). "Trump," writes Ben-Ghiat, "does not lie about one or two things. Rather, facts on any subject that conflict with his goals of power and profit are degraded through rumor and innuendo or simply altered or denied" (Ben-Ghiat 2020: 116). This meant that it did little good for Democrats or the media to expose his untruths or offer rational arguments in attempts to convince his supporters to rethink their loyalty. This aversion to fact-based arguments continued even after Trump's loss of the 2020 election by more than 7 million votes, when he claimed, without foundation, that he had only lost because the election was "rigged."

Appeals to racial resentment – which had lain beneath the surface of Republican strategy for decades – were brought to the surface in Trump's campaign. His 2019 declaration of a "national emergency" over the "invasion of our country with drugs, human traffickers, with all types of criminals and gangs," which reprised the language of previous demagogues, expanded the "southern strategy" from attacks on African Americans to the denigration of Latinos, Muslims, illegal immigrants, and other minorities (Ben-Ghiat, p. 86). As Doug McAdam wrote in 2018:

> The tumultuous onset of Donald Trump's administration, to say nothing of the president's outsize presence, has so riveted our attention that we're in danger of losing historical perspective . . . . Trump is only the most extreme expression of a brand of racial politics practiced ever more brazenly by the Republican Party since its origins in the 1960s. (McAdam 2018: 27)

Pollsters pointed to the dependence of Trump's appeal to non–college-educated working class voters. But when Brian Schaffner and his collaborators tested the effects of economic motives and education on Trump's support among white voters in 2016, class was dwarfed by the effects of sexism and racism. Controlling for an individual's attitudes on racism and sexism, these authors found that the education gap between Trump and non-Trump voters became far less significant (Schaffner, et al. 2018: 30). Employing a newer dataset, Parker found that whether assayed by education or income, class has mostly no impact on contemporary reactionary politics (2021: 13).

II A RHETORIC OF DIVISION AND MOBILIZATION

Although the press made much of Trump's tweets throughout his mandate, his rants and outbursts were not random. As in all populist movements, they revolved around the concepts of the "pure" people and the corrupt elite (Mudde 2004; Mudde & Kaltwasser, eds. 2012). But right-wing populism exhibits a third cornerstone, as David Snow and Colin Bernatsky argue in a thoughtful article. Drawing on the work of John Judis (2016), they point to the populist's need for a suspect non-elite group that functions as a "negative Other, that they use to frame the obstacles to the 'pure' or 'true' peoples' interests and rightful standing" (Snow & Bernatsky 2018: 3). As they write:

The anti-pluralism of right-wing populism takes the form of a Manichean project – that is, a dualistic worldview that provides clear contrast conceptions between "the People" and "the negative Others," and some configuration of enabling elites. (ibid., p. 4)

Trump's public style drew on some of the rhetoric of the Tea Party–backed members of the 112th and 113th Congress, whose attacks on opponents aggravated feelings of resentment, damaged the image of "establishment" politicians in the minds of voters, and normalized the uncivil rhetorical style that reached its nadir in Trump's campaign. As Gervais and Morris summarize the data they collected for their book, *Reactionary Republicanism*:

By the time the 114th Congress began in 2015 and would-be candidates began positioning themselves for the 2016 presidential election, conditions were ripe for an uncivil outsider, adroit with Twitter and willing to take advantage of (and further aggravate) high levels of resentment, to blaze a path to the Republican nomination, claim the White House, and effectively take over the Republican Party. (Gervais & Morris 2018: 65)

In a creative content analysis, Rachel Blum found a similarity between the subjects she found on Tea Party websites and Trump's rhetoric. Prominent among them were the media, American exceptionalism, law and order, foreign countries, and immigration (Blum 2017). What Trump added to the Tea Party repertoire was the rhetorical style and the tactical flexibility that allowed him to gain the active approbation of the right-wing social media and magnetized the attention of its competitors in the mainstream press.

But Trump's rhetoric went beyond the Tea Partiers' attacks on opponents. More than any of the right-wing movements that preceded his rise, his speeches were infested with lies, half-truths, and deliberate disinformation designed to enrage and mobilize his followers (Bennett & Livingston 2020). This was not lying for lying's sake: When Trump promoted the idea that Barack Obama was not born in the United States, he was able to gain the simultaneous attention of both the legacy press and a then-emerging "alt-right" media system:

This media amplification fed back through mainstream and alternative communication channels as a disruptive and disorienting reverberation, reaching mainstream audiences" (Bennett & Livingston 2018: 124; also see Bennett & Livingston eds. 2020).

In her 2020 book *Demagogue for President: The Rhetorical Genius of Donald Trump,* Jennifer Mercieca catalogued five rhetorical devices that Trump employed to attract his base and attack his opponents. These include, notably:

Ad hominem arguments, like his attacks on former President Obama with the false claim that he was not born in the United States;

Ad populum devices appealing to the wisdom of the crowd, as when he praised his followers for being wiser than the "corrupt political elites";

Misogeny, for example, attacking Fox News broadcaster Megyn Kelly, who asked him in a debate about his demeaning comments about women;

Reification, as when he attacked Hillary Clinton for what he called "playing the women's card"; and

Xenophobia, as when, in his first campaign appearance, he attacked Mexico for sending us bad people.

Many of these devices were designed to appeal to groups that existed well before Trump came on the political scene. For example, supporters of Men's Rights, Neo-Nazis, anti-immigrant groups, and right-wing websites like Breitbart "all supported Trump's denigration of women during the campaign, cheering him on through his most controversial moments" (Mercieca, p. 169). But critical to his strategy was the effort to create a movement around himself, pulling together these various strands of opinion and organization.

Violent Rhetoric and Even More Violent Mobilization

Trump's rhetoric did not systematically elevate violence to a virtue, but it did emit an air of macho masculinity that occasionally lapped over into encouragement of violence (Ben-Ghiat, ch. 6). Trump's encouragement of violence against protesters and his comment that police stop being "nice" to those they arrest were cheered by the more boisterous participants at his rallies. More significant, when Neo-Nazi thugs bearing torches attacked protesters in Charlottesville, he judged that there were "very fine people on both sides."[8] And when armed protesters demonstrated against Governor Gretchen Whitmer's lockdown policy to combat the coronavirus in Michigan, followed by similar demonstrations in Richmond, Virginia, Trump

---

[8] www.politifact.com/article/2019/apr/26/context-trumps-very-fine-people-both-sides-remarks

tweeted, in all caps: LIBERATE MICHIGAN![9] Those protests provided a template for similar armed protests in six other states and turned out to be a dress rehearsal for the attempted coup at the US Capitol on January 6, 2021.

Like many demagogic movements in the past, Trump's appeals coincided with spasms of violence. Although it is impossible to demonstrate a causal connection between the tenor of his campaigns and right-wing terrorism, there was a stunning increase in such incidents after 2016. Based on an extensive dataset collected by the Center for Strategic and International Studies (CSIS), Seth Jones and his collaborators found a significant increase in attacks by right-wing extremists in 2019 and during the first half of 2020. Defining right-wing terrorism as "the use or threat of violence by sub-national or non-state entities whose goals may include racial or ethnic supremacy; opposition to government authority; anger at women; and outrage against certain policies, such as abortion," they found that the most significant threat *"likely comes from white supremacists, though anarchists and religious extremists inspired by the Islamic State and al-Qaeda could present a potential threat as well"* (Jones, Doxsee & Harrington 2020).

Trump's advent also appears to have triggered a rise in hate crimes. In a carefully documented analysis, Griffin Edwards and Stephen Rushin showed that Trump's election was associated with a statistically significant surge in reported hate crimes across the United States, even when controlling for alternative explanations of these crimes. Using panel regression techniques, their analysis showed that counties that voted for Trump by the widest margins in the 2016 election experienced the largest increases in reported hate crimes (Edwards & Rushin 2019). These authors argue that it was not only Trump's rhetoric that triggered the rise in hate crimes, but its validation by his election (ibid., 2018).

Not only that: The growth of violent groups intersected with the growth of website-spawned conspiracy theories (Bennett & Livingston, eds. 2020). These emissions were not necessarily violence-producing (in fact, many were risible!), but toward the end of Trump's mandate, evidence began to accumulate that there was a linkage between conspiracy theorists and armed groups.[10] With the spread of the coronavirus pandemic, such groups began to mobilize at the local level.[11] The most prominent was the plot to kidnap Governor Whitmer of

---

[9] www.usatoday.com/story/news/politics/2020/04/17/coronavirus-trump-calls-liberate-virginia-michigan-minnesota/5152120002

[10] The juncture between the militia movements and merchants of disinformation was evident at a conference on Georgia's Jekyll Island in October 2020. There, well-known conspiracy theorists interacted with militia leaders like Stewart Rhodes, president of the Oath Keepers, which had acted as a vigilante squad at a number of Trump campaign rallies. Betsy Quammen, who specializes on both conspiracy theories and militias, commented: "As someone who's been studying militia maneuvering and conspiracy theorists, it's disconcerting to see these various groups uniting under a common banner of mistrust about coronavirus."

[11] The connections between the Q-Anon conspiracy network, violent far-right groups, and Trumpism have still to be adequately investigated at this writing. For a careful journalistic foray, see the analysis in *Politico* shortly before the 2020 election. www.politico.com/news/2020/10/15/qanon-trump-maga-movement-429739

Michigan and even put her on trial. Trump never disowned the plotters, and when the governor called him out for fomenting a climate of intimidation, he launched a verbal attack against her.

The connections between verbal and actual violence culminated in the attack on the Capitol on January 6, 2021. In urging supporters to attend the rally, Trump said it "will be wild." In addressing the crowd, Representative Mo Brooks declared that "Today is the day that American patriots start taking down names and kicking ass." The president's attorney, Rudy Giuliani, told the crowd that the fight over the certification of the elections would be a "trial by combat."[12] And in Congress, pistol-packing newly elected representative Lauren Boebert tweeted that "Today is 1776."[13]

When Trump urged his listeners to set off down Pennsylvania Avenue to demand that Congress support the objections to Biden's election, he could not have failed to notice that substantial minorities of the crowd were armed. Many of these militants were conspiratorial figures, some of whom were arrested following the January 6 insurrection, but Trump's public persona appealed to a much large number of ordinary Americans who had substituted identification with him for their identification with the Republican Party. In a Huffpost/Yougov poll reported in the *Washington Post* after the January 6 incursion into the Capitol, when asked if they considered themselves mostly a Trump supporter or mostly a supporter of the Republican Party, 66 percent of his supporters said they were more a supporter of Trump than of the party.[14]

How did this happen? Though much was the result of the personal bond established between the president and his following, we should not underestimate the influence of the intermediate groups that turned a generic right-wing ideology into support for Trump's movement. Among these were organizations associated with the Koch network, local churches, the National Rifle Association (NRA), groups that identified with the local police, and local Tea Party organizations. Sketching these links at the state and local level will provide evidence that Trump built his movement on a preexisting infrastructure and suggest that even if the movement he spawned passes from the scene, the themes he represented are likely to remain in American public space.

---

[12] For Trump's "will be wild" quote, go to www.nytimes.com/2021/01/06/us/politics/capitol-mob-trump-supporters.html; for Brooks' "kicking ass" statement, go to www.nytimes.com/2021/01/11/us/politics/republicans-capitol-riot.html; for the Giuliani quote, go to www.businessinsider.com/giuliani-claims-trial-by-combat-comment-game-of-thrones-reference-2021-1

[13] Boebert later tweeted Speaker Nancy Pelosi's location. www.dailykos.com/stories/2021/1/10/2008012/-Congress-member-declared-Today-is-1776-tweeted-re-Pelosi-s-location-during-insurrection

[14] Henry Olsen, "Opinion: New Poll: There Is No Singular Trump Voter," Washington Post, February 5, 2021. www.washingtonpost.com/opinions/2021/02/05/new-poll-there-is-no-singular-Trump-voter

III A DISPERSED ORGANIZATIONAL INFRASTRUCTURE

Since the foundational work of John McCarthy and Mayer N. Zald in the 1970s (1973, 1977), movement scholars have taught that "organizations deploy resources continuously, not just momentarily – and, over time, they can shift the balance of power in elections, public discussions, and governmental policymaking" (Skocpol 2020: xxi). Networks connect actors to one another to "help them concert their voice, plan activities and build collective resources" (ibid.; also see Diani 2015 and Diani & McAdam 2003). As a candidate, Donald Trump was such an outsized figure that the organizational infrastructure that helped to spread his message lay hidden in the background. This was less his own organization than what Bert Klandermans has called a "multi-organizational field" (1992).

Until recently, the few accounts of the Trump campaign organization focused on how poorly organized it was and on his dependence on the media. These generalizations are true, but much of Trump's ability to mobilize his base depended not on his official campaign organization but on a spectrum of preexisting organizations that occupied social space at the state and local levels. Some of these, like Tea Party groups and parts of the Koch network, we have already encountered; the Trump campaign was able to "socially appropriate" others with very little direction from above (McAdam et al. 2001). Among them, these groups constituted the kind of "blended hybrid" I described in Chapter 7.

Trumpian Republicanism: The Ultimate Hybrid

Theda Skocpol, Caroline Tervo, and their collaborators put forward a similar thesis, focusing less on conventional national-level organizations than on the grassroots infrastructure that helped propel Trump to victory (2020; see, especially, Zoorob and Skocpol, ch. 4). As Skocpol writes in the preface to their volume, the Trump presidential effort "made deals to activate well-established networks that could spread Trump's message across many states and localities, inspiring high turnout among conservative Christians and gun owners on Election Day" (Skocpol, p. xviii). Within states like North Carolina (Tervo 2020), Michigan (Marsh 2020), and Wisconsin (Hertel-Fernandez 2020), these networks combined grassroots and elite forms to create what I called, in Chapter 7, "blended hybrids."

Part of the reason for this success was the result of necessity. So weakened was the Republican central organization by 2016 that had the Trump campaign relied on that party's infrastructure, he would probably never have gained support from so many widely scattered places. I will draw on state-level studies from Skocpol and Tervo's volume to show how the campaign assembled support from a wide variety of groups and organizations that predated his appearance on the scene and that existed to advance aims other than his election.

Central to this infrastructure were groups associated with the Koch network. This may surprise readers who recall that the Koch brothers declined to support Trump in 2016 and were at odds with him over issues ranging from international trade to immigration to support for infrastructure (Skocpol 2020: 13). Central to these efforts were the widespread chapters of AFP. Created out of the breakup of Citizens for a Sound Economy, by the end of 2007, AFP "already had paid state directors installed in fifteen states encompassing almost half the total US population and their representatives in Congress" (Skopol 2020: 9). As we saw in Chapter 7, AFP has a highly developed federal structure, with "grassroots directors" in most of the states in which it is active. But make no mistake; like the Leninist organizations after which it was modeled, AFP's directors are selected from above and local efforts are centrally ordained and coordinated (ibid.). Thus, it is no surprise that AFP was at the center of Trump's 2016 electoral success in states as diverse as Wisconsin (Hertel-Fernandez 2020: 30), North Carolina (Tervo 2020: 57), and Michigan (Marsh 2020: 108).

It is well known that Donald Trump executed a "transaction" – for that is what it was – with the leaders of the Christian Right in order to attract evangelical voters. In exchange for his promise to oppose abortion, this thrice-married serial philanderer received commitments from within the Christian conservative elite to support his candidacy. What is less well-known is that the groundwork for this transaction was laid as early as 2011, when Trump asked televangelist Paula White to convene ministers to "pray together" to help him decide if he should run for president in 2012 (Zoorob & Skocpol 2020: 81). In the event, he decided against that effort, but ties between the Trump organization and Christian conservative groups continued to expand during Obama's second term in office.

Prior to the 2016 election, the evangelical Faith and Freedom Coalition carried out a massive mobilization campaign to garner support for Trump among its members. As Zoorob and Skocpol learned from their research:

Over the course of the election, organizers and volunteers from the group distributed thirty million voter guides, sent twenty-two million mailers, made fifteen million phone calls, ran twenty-six million digital ads, and canvassed more than one million religiously conservative households in twelve battleground states. (ibid., p. 83)

The peccadillos and the sexual abuses in Trump's history were not as well known at the time as would later emerge, but when the notorious "Access Hollywood" tape surfaced in the midst of the campaign, "redemption" became the name of the game for evangelical leaders. Megachurch preacher Jerry Falwell Jr. shrugged off the revelation: "We are all sinners," he declared. Praised as an "instrument of God" who had appeared to help Christians defend their faith in an increasingly secular world, Trump "provided rhetorical fodder for preachers, advocates, and [Christian] broadcasters sending a constant barrage of messages to congregants right through Election Day" (Zoorob & Skocpol, p. 84).

Somewhat less bizarre than the support that Trump received from the evangelical community was his support from two thematically and politically linked groups – gun enthusiasts and (largely white) police support groups (ibid., pp. 86–96). In states with large gun-owning populations, mainly in the South and the center of the country, it took little effort on the part of the NRA to convince its membership that a President Clinton would threaten their Second Amendment rights. The NRA spent more than $30 million in the 2016 election, most of it on the Trump campaign. It wasn't the NRA alone that helped Trump with gun enthusiasts; Zoorob and Skocpol point out that "nominally independent but officially sanctioned state NRA affiliates do lobbying and sponsor shooting contests, gun training and safety programs, community events, and youth programs" (ibid., p. 89). These local networks provided outlets for the NRA to spread its political preferences at election time.

Police support groups, such as the Fraternal Order of Police (FOP), were at first wary of Trump but came around to supporting him after the Republican convention decried a (largely fictitious) rise in violent crime under Obama. Trump himself visited numerous police lodges during the campaign, assuring FOP members that while he was the "law and order candidate," Hillary Clinton was "against the police" (Zoorob & Skocpol 2020, pp. 92–93). The Trump/police union alliance would become even closer in the wake of a spate of police killings of young black men and women during his mandate, culminating in the murder of George Floyd in Minneapolis in 2020 and the sometimes-violent protests against it. But none of these parts of the Trump infrastructure were as central as the activists he inherited from the Tea Party movement.

Tea Party Roots of the Trumpian Movement

We saw in Chapter 7 that the Tea Party did much to pave the way for Trump's electoral victory (Gervais & Morris 2018). Of course, the term "paving the way" admits of a multitude of meanings, ranging from the anodyne "came before" to the much more forceful term "caused to happen." Between these extremes we can imagine a spectrum of direct and indirect connections between Tea Party activists and the Trump movement, including the election of a cadre of Tea Party–supported members of Congress in 2010, many of whom later became the corporals and lieutenants in Trump's administration. It is no accident that the minority whip of the Republican Party in the House of Representatives, Kevin McCarthy, and Trump's final Chief of Staff, Mark Meadows, were both backed by Tea Party groups in the 2010 midterm elections.

When Trump intimated that he might run for president, his campaign was met with indifference from Tea Party activists, many of whom preferred the sunbelt politico, Ted Cruz, over a New York real estate wheeler and dealer.[15] But Trump's opposition to abortion, his fulminations against undocumented immigrants, and his red-blooded nationalism brought many Tea Partiers around to support his candidacy. His success in appealing to Tea Party supporters emerged from a Pew poll. As the Pew researchers concluded, "Republicans who had positive views of the Tea Party movement in 2014 or 2015 were among Trump's most enthusiastic supporters during the 2016 campaign. And, unlike Republicans who had mixed or negative opinions of the Tea Party, they continued to have very positive feelings about Trump through his first year in office."[16]

What was responsible for the shift of Tea Party supporters into Trump's orbit? Several campaign-linked factors converged to influence their recruitment. First, as Trump's Republican opponents knocked each other off in the primaries, he was able to play successfully for their supporters by appearing to be different from all the others with a common-man, outsider appeal. "He says what we're thinking and what we want to say," said a Trump supporter at a rally in Montana (quoted by Ben-Ghiat, p. 85). Second, Trump's conversion to an anti-abortion position helped him gain the support of practicing evangelicals throughout the South and West. Finally, his dismissal of African American voters ("What do you have to lose?") and his denigration of Mexican immigrants ("They send us rapists ... ") resonated with the racial conservatism of many Tea Party veterans.

But these general factors might not have produced a Trump victory in 2016, if not for the residues of the Tea Party networks at the state and local levels. Recall that, at its height, the Tea Party had almost a thousand local chapters. Although many of these groups went quiet in the years preceding the 2016 campaign, others remained active or were reenergized by Trump's rhetoric. In North Carolina, Caroline Tervo identified fifty-two Tea Party groups that still existed in forty-six of the state's counties in 2016. Many of these overlapped with the state's vigorous Christian right networks (Tervo 2020: 56). In Michigan, there were more than thirty Tea Party groups still active in 2016. By the end of the campaign, Tea Party–related congressional Republicans like Mark Meadows and former opponent Ted Cruz saw the writing on the wall and became fervent Trump acolytes. Tea Partiers were diverse sociologically and geographically, but Trump' naked racial nationalism and opportunistic opposition to abortion appealed to many of them.

The appropriation of these sources of support by the Trump campaign underscores the importance of the new forms of interaction between nonparty

[15] htttps://blogs.wsj.com/washwire/2016/09/22/tea-party-group-backs-trump-overcoming-earlier -doubts-about-his-ideas-proposals
[16] Pew Research Center, "Trump's Staunch GOP Supporters Have Roots in the Tea Party," May, 2019, p. 2.

organizations and electoral outcomes that we saw in the last two chapters. From the local and state extensions of the Koch network to associations linking Christian conservatives, gun owners, and police supporters to the more frankly political Tea Party networks, the Trump campaign profited from the proliferation and extension of social movements and movement-like affordances to a political campaign that had had no hand in creating them. Nowhere is this connection between electoral success and movement-like agents seen more clearly than in the wide spectrum of "new media" sources that supported the Trump campaign.

Digitizing Movement Organization

Like many earlier authoritarian leaders, Trump had a talent for the use of the media that helped bring him to power and supported his policies once he was elected. From the former journalist Benito Mussolini's use of newsreels to Adolf Hitler's mastery of propaganda to Italian Prime Minister Silvio Berlusconi's dominance of the TV networks, writes Ben-Ghiat (p. 95), "the strongman has turned politics into an esthetic experience, with him as star." Like Mussolini, Trump "spent hours every day reading the newspapers, looking to punish critics and anyone who did not praise him enough" (ibid., p. 101). We now know how much time Trump dedicated to his interchanges with Fox News, an exchange relationship that was starkly revealed when the latter was trounced by the president for an early announcement of Biden's electoral success in Arizona.[17]

Although both Mussolini and Berlusconi were masters of media manipulation (Ben Ghiat 2020), Trump was the first leader to take advantage of the most dramatic change in the relationship between movements and elections over the past few decades: the use of the Internet and social media in mobilizing support for campaigning (Bennett & Segerberg 2013; Earl & Kimport 2011; Karpf 2012; Schradie 2019). As Boczkowski and Papacharissi write:

> From the apparent disconnect of the agenda-setting media with a vast segment of the American voters to the deluge of fake news circulating on social media, and from the intensity of the confrontation between President Trump and these media to his constant use of Twitter to promote alternative – and often unsupported by facts – narratives, there is a sense that the matrix that used to tie politics, media, technology, and the citizenry in fairly predictable ways has moved far away from equilibrium (2018, p. 1).

I cannot add much that is new to a tidal wave of scholarly and journalistic attention to the role of the new media in shaping the ascent of Donald Trump. What needs to be emphasized here is not that "new media" have displaced "brick and mortar" movement organizations or the traditional tool of talk radio. The emphasis I have given to organizations and networks in this chapter may appear to reinforce such a dichotomy. But rather than substituting for collective action, such groups have become agents for *connective action*, to adopt the terminology of

---

[17] www.nytimes.com/2020/11/04/us/politics/trump-fox-news-arizona.html

Lance Bennett & Alexandra Segerberg (2013). It was the *interchange* between Trump's personal organization and the affordances of the new media that created and sustained Trump's movement with bonds of loyalty that went well beyond any modern candidate and his or her support base.[18]

Bennett and Segerberg argued that rather than displacing traditional "brick and mortar" organizations with digital platforms, access to the Internet has *combined* personal networks with organizations in recruiting people to take part in electoral campaigns and demonstrations (Bennett & Segerberg 2013: 172–73). As Bennett and Steven Livingston wrote in the wake of Trump's first election campaign:

> these visible, heavily trafficked and often networked media link in and out of broader networks of political foundations, think tanks, grass roots and Astroturf political organizations, communication professionals and political organizers. This complex set of organizations advances an agenda that mixes tax and regulatory benefits for the wealthy, with disinformation about climate change, immigration, refugees, government waste and ineptitude, and a host of other issues aimed at stirring political crowds. (Bennett & Livingston 2018: 129; also see Bennett & Livingston, eds. 2020)

For example, the demonstration that was organized at the Michigan state capital to protest Governor Whitmer's plan to lock down her state to combat the coronavirus was organized by a small number of informal right-wing groups, but the De Vos–funded nonprofit group Michigan Freedom Fund (MFF) paid for two Facebook ads that took users to the Facebook event page of the protest.[19] (Betsy DeVos, in case readers don't know her name, was the Secretary of Education in the Trump administration.) This was only one of a myriad of connections between Trumpian political organizations and more scattered, but more volatile, political groups whose actions verged on, and sometimes crossed, the frontier into political violence.[20] When the FBI went down the lists of people who had come to Washington for the "Save America" rally, they found dozens who were on the Bureau's "Terrorist Watch List" – many of them members of white supremacist groups.[21]

---

[18] Focusing on the victory of the Trump campaign, Robyn Caplan and Danah Boyd make clear that social movements in the form of online communities like 4chan, 8chan, Voat, reddit, and Discord "used these affordances to coordinate the spread of memes and messaging in support of their candidate, first during the primaries and then during the general election of 2016" (Caplan & Boyd 2018: 53).

[19] www.prwatch.org/news/2020/04/13562/devos-funded-group-organizes-protest-against-michigan-governor%E2%80%99s-stay-home-order

[20] www.theguardian.com/world/2020/sep/23/oregon-portland-pro-trump-protests-violence-texts?utm_term=092660321007cfe089614d125e471c09&utm_campaign=USMorningBriefing&utm_-source=esp&utm_medium=Email&CMP=usbriefing_email

[21] www.washingtonpost.com/national-security/terror-watchlist-capitol-riot-fbi/2021/01/14/0741228 14-55f7-11eb-a931-5b162d0d033d_story.html

IV THE CREATION OF A TRUMP-INSPIRED COUNTERMOVEMENT

What was happening on the ideological left as Trump was assembling a movement of "white supremacists, veterans, current and former law enforcement officers, a few elected officials, Christian evangelicals, and a motley crew of far-right conspiracy mongers?"[22] As we have seen throughout this study, movements often create their own antithesis, and this was clearly the case from the day after Trump's inauguration, when millions of women and men demonstrated against his administration. This was the beginning of what came to be called "The Resistance" (Fisher 2019; Meyer & Tarrow, eds. 2018; Skocpol & Tervo, eds. 2020), which energized the Democratic Party's campaign in the midterm elections of 2018 and contributed to Joe Biden's victory in 2020.

Movement/Countermovement Interaction

In their much-cited study, David S. Meyer and Suzanne Staggenborg examined the relationship between movements and countermovements during earlier cycles of contention (1996). Defining movements as "collective challenges by people with common purposes and solidarity in sustained interaction with elites, opponents, and authorities," they defined a *counter*movement as "a movement that makes contrary claims simultaneously to those of the original movement" (ibid., p. 1631). "Movements," they argued, have a "demonstration effect" for political countermovements – showing that collective action can effect (or resist) change in particular aspects of society. Movements thus create their own opposition, which sometimes takes countermovement form. Once a countermovement is mobilized, movement and countermovement react to one another (ibid., p. 1632).

In their article, Meyer and Staggenborg listed three conditions that promote the rise of countermovements: first, that the movement [it opposes] shows signs of success; second, that the interests of some populations are threatened by movement goals; and third, that political allies are available to aid oppositional mobilization.

Let us look briefly at how each of these claims applied to the creation of an anti-Trump movement:

Movement Success: Trump's electoral success was certainly a triumph for the movement he had stimulated. Although his legislative successes were modest, his efforts to unravel the administrative state (Rose-Ackerman 2017) and to remake the federal judiciary were highly successful.[23] Moreover, by trumpeting the success of business claims that more expert

---

[22] See Goodwin, "The Eighteenth Brumaire of Donald J. Trump," p. 1, in note no. 4.
[23] www.brookings.edu/blog/fixgov/2020/06/26/trumps-200th-judicial-appointment-less-than-meets-the-eye

observers considered dubious, Trump was able to shroud himself with an aura of success to low-information and low-interest supporters. His claim to have restored economic prosperity after six years of Obama administration era growth in employment was a public relations success, if not a triumph of economic management.

Threatened Interests: During Trump's years in office, the Trump presidency threatened the interests and values of vast sectors of the population, from African Americans to Latinos, to women, to businesses dependent on international trade, foreign policy elites, and to the LGBTQ community. Each major policy initiative – from the refugee ban to repeal of the Affordable Care Act (i.e., "Obamacare") to tax reform – appeared as a powerful threat to many sectors of the American population.

Available Allies: The "demonstration effect" that Meyer and Staggenborg referenced in their article helped Trump's opponents – despite various origins and commitments – to band together through a process that social movement scholars have called "intersectionality" (Fisher 2019: 52–53). If Trump did nothing else, he brought together a broad coalition of progressive Americans around a spectrum of claims that had more often divided than unified the progressive Left. But so outraged were Trump's opponents that these divisions were at least temporarily suppressed. Mobilization grew from the moment of Trump's inauguration in January 2017 to his electoral defeat four years later. This began with the widespread Women's Marches the day after Trump's inauguration, which illustrates how diffuse were the sources of the countermovement and how it came together (Fisher 2019 and 2020a and b).

The Centrality of the Women's March

Here is how the Women's Marches' organizers characterized their efforts: "On January 21, 2017," they wrote,

people of all backgrounds – women and men and gender nonconforming people, young and old, of diverse faiths, differently abled, immigrants, and indigenous – came together, five million strong, on all seven continents of the world. We were answering a call to show up and be counted as those who believe in a world that is equitable, tolerant, just, and safe for all, one in which the human rights and dignity of each person [are] protected and our planet is safe from destruction. Grounded in the nonviolent ideology of the Civil Rights movement, the Women's March was the largest coordinated protest in US history and one of the largest in world history.[24]

What is remarkable about this statement is not that it was exaggerated – which it was – but that it was very nearly true! Consider the claim that the march was "the

---

[24] www.womensmarch.com/the-march-1; quoted in David S. Meyer and Sidney Tarrow, "Introduction" to *The Resistance: The Dawn of the Anti-Trump Opposition Movement*, 2018, p. 1).

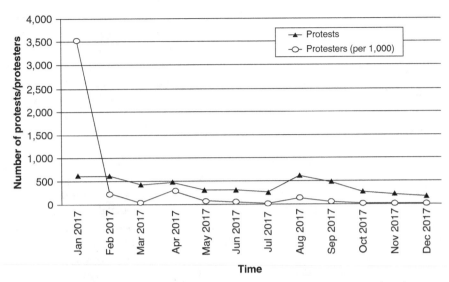

FIGURE 8.1 Crowd-sourced reports on participation in protest events after the 2016 election
Source: Unpublished data graciously provided by Chan Suh. Published in David S. Meyer and Sidney Tarrow, eds., *The Resistance: The Dawn of the Anti-Trump Opposition Movement*, Oxford University Press, 2018, p. 2.

largest coordinated protest in US history." A crowd-sourced archive of reports on participation in protest events following the election of Donald Trump tells the dramatic story. In the six-month period that saw thousands of protest events organized over a wide range of issues, the Women's March towered over the rest, both for the number of citizens participating and for the diffusion of the events it inspired, as Erica Chenoweth and Marie Berry show in their "Who Made the Women's March?" It was much broader than a march defined by gender, and its most important implication was to show how broadly distaste for Trump was diffused in the population. As Berry and Chenoweth note, after merely 9 weeks of organizing an estimated 4.5 million people were gathered in a mass demonstration around the world (2018: 76) as Figure 8.1 shows.

That march was only the beginning of a wave of rallies and demonstrations around the country. Fisher writes:

Since the 2016 election ... progressives of all stripes have had much to yell about, and they have come out in droves: marching, chanting, and calling their elected officials regarding efforts made by the Trump administration around a range of progressive issues. (Fisher 2019: 18–19)

The day of women's marches was followed by a series of national events with overlapping goals, beginning with a March for Science in April 2017, followed by a March for Racial Justice in October of the same year, a second Women's

March in January 2018, a National School Walkout, a March for our Lives, a Families Belong together March in July, and the protests against the Kavanaugh Supreme Court nomination in September (Fisher 2019, p. 23). Though none of them came close to the first Women's March in turnout or enthusiasm, participation ranged from an estimated 75,000 at the second Women's March to an estimated 800,000 at the March for Our Lives 2 months later (ibid., p. 34).

More remarkable than the breadth of the protests were the overlapping motivations of the protesters. Of course, the designated focus of each event was the most common motivation that participants gave for turning out. But many also reported being motivated by other reasons that spanned the progressive spectrum. Perhaps because of the actions of the Trump administration, "More than 40 percent of participants at the March for Science reported being motivated by women's rights ..., equality (45 percent), politics/voting (44 percent), President Trump (53 percent)." At the second Women's March, "the only motivations that received *less than* 50 percent were labor (46 percent) and religion (25 percent). These results clearly show," Fisher concludes, "that participants in the resistance in the streets are not aligning exclusively with one specific issue; rather, they are motivated by many intersecting and overlapping issues" (Fisher 2019: 51–52).

Who Were the Resisters?

Who were these people? Participants in the women's marches, Berry and Chenoweth found, were not particularly radical, were disproportionately white, were on average middle-aged, well educated, and more likely to be female than male. Their median age ranged from thirty-seven to forty-two, although this varied substantially across the different marches. Although most marchers associated themselves with the Democratic Party, others were independents or even Republicans who opposed Trump's agenda. A staggering proportion were first-time protesters (Berry & Chenoweth 2018: 85). And although the majority of protesters were there to support gender issues against a president who was a serial denigrator of women (Fisher 2019, p. 45), a broad range of organizations supported the march (Berry & Chenoweth, pp. 76–80).

These groups ranged from purpose-created groups like the Pussyhat Project, which shared knitting patterns for the pink hats that many of the marchers wore, to long-term advocacy groups like the National Organization for Women, the Sierra Club, and the National Bar Association, to labor groups like the AFL-CIO and the SIEU, to the Indivisible network that grew out of a website created by former Democratic staffers (Fisher 2019: 24–25; Brooker 2018; Han & Okawara 2018). In response to particular Trump administration moves, professional groups also took part in collective actions, beginning with the lawyers who came to the airports to oppose his refugee ban in early 2017

(Dorf & Chu 2018). Like the Trump network it was created to oppose, the Resistance grew out of many organizational tributaries.

In the months that followed the women's marches, the press and pundits focused – as they often do – on the radical opponents to Trump's presidency. On the far left, a small and loosely organized "antifa" movement responded to his election with violent outbursts, particularly in places like Portland, Oregon, which had developed a thriving radical culture. Trump's victory also produced a revival of Senator Bernie Sander's left-populist movement, which unified a large number of "Bernie-Bros" across the country. In New York City, a young Latina progressive, Alexandria Ocasio-Cortez, won the 2018 Democratic Party primary against a moderately liberal Democratic stalwart in New York City, alongside a scattering of other progressive women of color who helped the Democrats take control of the House after those elections. These left-wing currents were fastened on by the Trump campaign as "socialists and communists" who could be expected to destroy American freedoms were the Democrats to be elected in November 2020.

But the Resistance was actually an aggregate of a number of different streams of contention. As Hahrie Han and Michelle Okawara write:

The Women's March on Washington was just one of many new resistance groups that emerged in the wake of the 2016 election. From groups like Swing Left to Flippable, Wall of Us to Indivisible, and People Power to Daily Action, the outpouring of resistance after Trump was elected spawned a host of new networks, apps, and organizations. (Han & Okawara 2018: 231)

Not only that: Trump's election victory galvanized a number of existing organizations into action, increased their donor and membership bases and – in some cases, like the ACLU – led them to shift into more grassroots forms of activity.[25]

A Cycle of Contention

This maelstrom of movement activity raises a fundamental question: Given the vast range and diversity of the Resistance, was it simply an archipelago of unconnected progressive groups or was it an integrated "cycle of contention"? I use this term to indicate a sequence of heightened conflict across the social system, one that sometimes indicates a critical juncture – as in the New Deal and the 1960s – with a rapid diffusion of collective action from more mobilized to less mobilized sectors, a rapid pace of innovation in the forms of contention employed, the creation of new or transformed collective action frames, and a combination of organized and unorganized participation (Tarrow 2011, ch. 11).

[25] www.theguardian.com/us-news/2017/mar/09/aclu-people-power-freedom-cities-trump-immig ration-policies?CMP=Share_iOSApp_Other

The anti-Trump resistance showed all five of these properties of a unified cycle:

- *Heightened conflict across the social system*: Soon after his election, hundreds of thousands of ordinary people went out into the cold to protest – none more dramatically than the US Army veterans who rallied to the side of the Native Americans protesting against the Dakota Access pipeline on their ancestral land.
- *A rapid diffusion of collective action*: A broader range of claims was adopted on the part of women's groups that were originally mobilized against Trump's abuse of women in the great January 21 Women's March, as we learned from Dana Fisher's surveys and from other sources.[26]
- *Innovation in the forms of contention*: When Trump was first elected, the normally slow-moving and legalistic ACLU responded as it always has: "We'll see you in court," they warned the new administration. But by early March, the ACLU had launched a "People Power" network in what it called "Freedom Cities" to resist the new administration.[27]
- *The creation of new or transformed forms of protest*: In the face of the new administration's assault on undocumented immigrants, a large number of cities and counties declared themselves to be "sanctuaries" and ordered their police and sheriffs' offices not to cooperate with federal agents seeking to detain these immigrants.
- *A combination of organized and unorganized participation*:[28] The town hall protests against the Republican health-care repeal plans brought together experienced activists with ordinary people, many of whom had never protested before.

Ingenious efforts to unite these threads into a loosely coordinated national network were soon made. For example, after the 2016 election, a group of former congressional staffers published *Indivisible, A Practical Guide for Resisting the Trump Agenda*.[29] To their surprise, the online guide attracted the attention of thousands of viewers and what had begun as a "how to" guide turned into a network, one that used social media and email communications to highlight innovations and reforms in local, state, and national government.[30] Many of the local groups that sprang up out of the women's marches identified

[26] See Fisher 2020a and Adam Gabbatt, "Solidarity Sundays: Women Resist Trump with Monthly Activism Meet-Ups." *The Guardian*, March 31, 2017. www.the guardian.com/us-news/2017/mar31/trump-resistance

[27] www.theguardian.com/us-news/2017/mar/09/aclu-people-power-freedom-cities-trump-immigration-policies?CMP=Share_iOSApp_Other

[28] For a general rundown of the major groups that have formed nationally to contest the Trump administration, go to www.theguardian.com/us-news/2017/mar/09/the-resistance-now-key-players-donald-trump?CMP=Share_iOSApp_Other

[29] www.indivisibleguide.com

[30] www.cnn.com/2017/02/11/politics/indivisible-profile-trnd/index.html

themselves with Indivisible, but the composition, the goals, and the methods of the groups that constituted its "membership" were distinct from one another. They varied in how they framed their messages and in the forms of contention they employed, and they ranged from those that were part of the institutional landscape to those that were outside the gates of institutional politics. But that is exactly the point: They made up what Milkis and Tichenor call "a formative movement" with significant institutional and noninstitutional facets (2019), a variety of modes of action, and differential links to institutional politics (see Table 1.1). The anti-Trump movement also brought about a major development: overcoming one of the most enduring divisions of progressive social movements – between white people and people of color.

Race, Racism, and "Law and Order"

An early glimmer that the enduring issue of race would play a role in the Resistance took place before Trump's election with the killing of Trayvon Martin by a self-appointed vigilante in Florida and of Michael Brown by a police officer in Ferguson, Missouri. Soon after, when he was selling cigarettes on Staten Island, a man named Eric Garner was killed by a New York City policeman during an arrest. Most of the protests that followed these outrages were peaceful and were organized by the rising "Black Lives Matter" movement. But some were violent, like the riots that followed Michael Brown's killing in Ferguson, and the murder of two police officers in New York by a man who claimed to be responding to the killing of Eric Garner.[31] But it was the murder of George Floyd by a police officer on the streets of Minneapolis, Minnesota, in May 2020 that launched a national and international wave of protests around the theme of "Black Lives Matter."

George Floyd and Multiracial Resistance

The year 2020 was a terrible one for America's black community. Apart from the coronavirus pandemic and the economic shock it produced, which disproportionately affected people of color, the murder of a black man by a brutal white policeman on the streets of Minneapolis exposed the glaring nature of the racial cleavage in American society. Not long before, another African American named Ahmaud Arbery had been shot dead by two white men who pursued him in a van while he jogged through their neighborhood.[32] Not long after, a young woman named Breonna Taylor was killed in her bedroom in

---

[31] www.nytimes.com/2014/12/21/nyregion/two-police-officers-shot-in-their-patrol-car-in-brooklyn .html

[32] The murder was filmed by a third man who was later found to have been collaborating with the killers. www.usatoday.com/story/news/nation/2020/05/10/ahmaud-arbery-shooting-new-video -shows-georgia-jogger-did-nothing-illegal/3105123001

Louisville, Kentucky, by three police officers executing a "no-knock" warrant.[33] But the culmination of this string of killings came on May 25, when Floyd was arrested outside a store in Minneapolis where he had been suspected of trying to pass off counterfeit money.[34] Caught on a cell-phone camera with his hands manacled, Floyd appeared to be complying with the arresting officers. But moments later, he was on the ground next to a police cruiser. When he complained that he couldn't breathe, the policeman, Derek Chauvin, told him to stop shouting. As passersby pleaded with Chauvin to release him, Floyd cried out for his mother and died.

A video revealed the extent of the crime. Chauvin had kept his knee on Floyd's neck for more than nine minutes while three of his colleagues looked on. The officer was charged with second- and third-degree murder and second-degree manslaughter, while the other officers were charged with lesser offenses.[35] The murder led to a massive cycle of protest. Polls taken over the following weeks estimated that between 15 and 26 million Americans participated in demonstrations over Floyd's murder. According to the *New York Times*,[36] on June 6 alone, half a million people came out to protest in nearly 550 different places. This would make the wave of protest the largest in the country's history, according to scholars interviewed by the *Times*. "I've never seen self-reports of protest participation that high for a specific issue over such a short period," said Neal Caren, editor of the prestigious academic journal *Mobilization* – more than the 3 to 5 million people who had turned out to protest Donald Trump's inauguration four years earlier.[37]

Protests following police abuse had also occurred during the urban unrest of the 1960s. But in three respects, this new wave of protest was different:

First, the slogan of many of the protesters was institutional – a demand to "defund the police!" In a dozen cities, including Minneapolis, city councils voted reductions in police funding;[38]

---

[33] www.nbcnews.com/news/us-news/breonna-taylor-police-shooting-what-we-know-about-kentucky-woman-n1207841

[34] www.bbc.com/news/world-us-canada-52861726

[35] www.nytimes.com/2020/05/29/us/derek-chauvin-criminal-complaint.html

[36] Well worth reading is Larry Buchanan, Quoctrung Bui, and Jugal K. Patel, "Black Lives Matter May Be the Largest Movement in US History," New York *Times*, July 3, 2020. www.nytimes.com/interactive/2020/07/03/us/george-floyd-protests-crowd-size.html

[37] Erica Chenoweth and Jeffrey Pressman, "This Is What We Learned by Counting the Women's Marches," *The Monkey Cage*, February 7, 2017. www.washingtonpost.com/news/monkey-cage/wp/2017/02/07/this-is-what-we-learned-by-counting-the-womens-marches

[38] This happened in some of America's biggest cities, including New York, Los Angeles, Philadelphia, and San Francisco. The defunding bills included proposals to remove police as responders for "noncriminal" calls, homeless services, traffic enforcement, mental health emergencies, substance abuse, public transit, and other areas of social services. www.theguardian.com/us-news/2020/aug/15/defund-police-movement-us-victories-what-next?CMP=Share_iOS App_Other

Second, in part because a presidential election was imminent, the protests transitioned quickly into institutional politics. Across the country, city councils voted to remove, or to displace, statues of heroes of the Confederacy. Even the military began to study changing the names of bases named after Civil War generals. The impact soon spread to presidential politics, helping Biden to choose Kamala Harris, a mixed-race former attorney general from California, as his vice-presidential pick. And in the November presidential elections, a large proportion of voters told pollsters that – both positively and negatively – Floyd's killing and the attendant protests affected their votes.[39]

Third, and most important, the new movement was multiracial. Outrage at Floyd's murder spread from African Americans to white and Hispanic communities and to small towns and cities as well as to metropolitan areas. This was "a demographic mix that is far more varied than anything we have seen in recent years," wrote Doug McAdam soon after. Indeed, writes McAdam, the mix is "far more diverse than anything we saw during the heyday of the mass Civil Rights Movement of the 1960s."[40] This resonated to a degree with the co-occurrence of civil rights and the antiwar protesters during Nixon's 1968 campaign, but there was a sharp contrast. Though most of the 1960s' antiwar movement was white, the movement that arose in 2020 over police killings of African Americans was interracial. Poll results across the country showed growing minorities of white voters expressing sympathy for injustice against African Americans.

After Floyd's killing, Dana Fisher and Michael Heaney assembled a group of interviewers in New York, Washington, DC, and Los Angeles to survey pro–George Floyd protesters. To their surprise, as the New York *Times* reported, "White protesters made up 61 percent of those surveyed in New York over the weekend, according to the researchers, and 65 percent of protesters in Washington. On Sunday in Los Angeles, 53 percent of protesters were white. Many organizations and institutions embraced the protests, asking what the current moment demanded of them, or what changes could be made to advance social justice and racial equity."[41] As Doug McAdam, who has done some of the best work on the demographics of civil rights protests, observed of the wave of protests in the summer of 2020:

This fact brings us to the most important, and potentially consequential, difference between the current protests and any we've seen in recent years: the racial and ethnic

[39] www.nytimes.com/2020/11/07/us/black-lives-matter-protests.html. As could be expected, while Democratic voters were outraged by the killing and were enthused by the protests, Republican voters were stuck by the violence and looting that accompanied the protests in some cities.

[40] Doug McAdam, "We've Never Seen Protests like These Before," *Jacobin*, June 20, 2020. www.jacobinmag.com/2020/06/george-floyd-protests-black-lives-matter-riots-demonstrations

[41] For example, in the 2020 elections, five states had racial justice referenda on the ballot. www.nbcnews.com/news/nbcblk/racial-justice-ballot-these-5-states-november-n1243337

diversity of the current protest wave. Given this is an ongoing and young movement, it is hard to get a systematic handle on the demographics of the protesters, but there is simply no denying the diversity of those taking part (2020: 1).

How did Trump respond? Already in trouble with the electorate because of his chaotic response to the pandemic, he tried to use the George Floyd protests and the occasional violence they triggered to turn his campaign into a call for "law and order." Even before his election, Trump had been quick to respond to the swelling threat of the new black movement: "I have a message to every last person threatening the peace on our streets and the safety of our police," he warned. "When I take the oath of office next year, I will restore law and order to our country."[42] In taking this line, Trump followed the playbook of Richard Nixon during the 1968 campaign, when he had famously coined the term "the silent majority" for those he hoped to mobilize against the antiwar movement.[43] But Trump's racial appeals went further; he was willing to strip away the disguise that had hidden Republican racist appeals as, for example, when he warned suburban mothers that if Joe Biden was elected president, low-cost housing (*read*: minority) would be imposed on their communities.[44]

On July 8, 2020, following violent protests over Floyd's murder and accompanied by his Attorney General, William Barr, Trump marched out of the White House to St. John's Episcopal Church, which had been damaged by fire in previous days, waving a Bible. Because there were still protesters on the streets, the president ordered security forces to clear the square in front of the White House, employing tear gas to do so. Trump's photo-op in front of the church came after he delivered remarks at the White House in which he declared himself "your president of law and order" and demanded that state governors deploy National Guard units to "dominate the streets."[45]

In response to the repression of peaceful protesters on the streets of her city, Mayor Muriel Bowser renamed the square from which the protesters had been cleared "Black Lives Matter Plaza" and applauded the efforts by activists to paint the group's name down the middle of the street. "In America, you can peacefully assemble," Bowser said in remarks to the crowd. In New York City, protesters went a step further in linking the president to Floyd's killing, painting a similar message in front of Trump Tower. Mayor Bill de Blasio joined the

---

[42] Perry Bacon Jr., "Trump and Other Conservatives Embrace Blue Lives Matter Movement," *NBC News*, July 23, 2016. www.nbcnews.com/storyline/2016-conventions/trump-other-conservatives-embrace-blue-lives-matter-movement-n615156

[43] Angie Maxwell recalls that "When Nixon used the phrase in 1968, his goal was to occupy a middle ground of voters between Democratic nominee Hubert Humphrey and third-party candidate George Wallace, the segregationist governor of Alabama." Those were white voters who "liked their racism polite." Trump's appropriation of the term appeals more to openly racist voters.

[44] www.politico.com/news/2020/08/23/trumplow-income-housing-suburbs-400155

[45] www.npr.org/2020/07/17/892277592/federal-officers-use-unmarked-vehicles-to-grab-protesters-in-portland

activists in painting the letters "BLACK LIVES MATTER" on the street, adopting the language of patriotism to applaud the protesters. "When we say 'Black Lives Matter'," he pronounced, "there is no more American statement, there is no more patriotic statement because there is no America without Black America."[46] "Black Lives Matter" paintings followed on the streets of a number of other cities and around the world.

The Radicalization of Trumpism

Affronted by the protests and by the street painting of "Black Lives Matter" outside the White House, Trump fulminated but could do nothing against these symbolic acts. Republican officials, who had been following his dizzying navigations for the last three and a half years, had little to say about them either. But a spinoff of the Trump movement arose on the part of a spectrum of far right groups who were enraged by the chaos on the streets and by the apparent inability of the police to control it.[47] Some of these – like the so-called Proud Boys – were already in existence when Trump came into office but rose to become his ardent supporters when he urged them to "stand by and stand down," a clear signal that he did not want to lose their support for his reelection campaign and beyond.[48]

In the course of the campaign, convoys of vehicles filled with armed right-wing activists began to thread through the streets of cities where there had been racial justice protests, waving their guns and occasionally shooting paintballs at protesters. In many of these places, following the playbook from Charlottesville,[49] far right activists adopted the tactic of ramming protesters with their vehicles. As of early July, more than 100 Black Lives Matter protesters reported having been rammed while marching.[50] As the president fulminated about his desire to defend law and order during his increasingly frequent campaign rallies, his most ardent supporters threatened to turn the cycle of protest into a spiral of violence.

As in many cycles of contention, the attention of the public following Floyd's murder largely focused on evidence that the country was going through a crisis. And so it was, heightened by the tragedy of the coronavirus pandemic, the economy's attendant decline, and the president's increasingly erratic reactions. But beneath the radar, there were signs that the chaos and conflict of the summer and fall of 2020 were disguising deeper currents that might be fueling a galactic shift in American politics. This was first evident during the midterm

---

[46] www.theguardian.com/us-news/2020/jul/09/black-lives-matter-trump-tower-de-blasio?CMP=Share_iOSApp_Other
[47] www.nytimes.com/2020/08/30/us/portland-trump-rally-shooting.html
[48] www.nytimes.com/2020/10/02/opinion/trump-proud-boys.html
[49] www.bbc.com/news/world-us-canada-40912509
[50] www.usatoday.com/story/news/nation/2020/07/08/vehicle-ramming-attacks-66-us-since-may-27/5397700002

elections of 2018 and to the move from "the barricades to the ballot box" in both that year and in 2020 (McAdam & Tarrow, 2010).

V FROM THE "BARRICADES" TO THE BALLOT BOX

Bolstered by the upsurge of militancy following Trump's election, the Democratic Party won the 2018 midterm election by a whopping margin. While the Democrats lost 2 seats in the Senate, they gained 43 House seats, took control of 7 more governorships, and won 350 new state legislative seats. Among those elected to the House, 167 were women, compared to 89 in 2016, two of them the youngest women ever elected to Congress. Two others were the first Native American women elected to Congress, and two were Muslims. Among the total of newly elected Democrats, there were 23 people of color and 10 LGBTQ Americans. By any metric, this was the most diverse freshman class of any American Congress ever elected.[51]

The press was drawn to the election victory of an attractive young candidate, Alexandria Ocasio-Cortez, who came from an immigrant family in New York City. Arriving in Washington in early 2019, "AOC" allied with three other progressive women of color in a group that called itself "the squad." The press gave outsized attention to these four women, neglecting the fact that most of the Democrats who took seats from the Republicans in the 2018 election were moderates who had been elected from swing districts.[52]

Until these new Congress members had time to establish a solid voting record, the best way to calculate how radical or moderate the new cohort of congressional Democrats would be was by examining the endorsements they received from groups with different ideological perspectives. Based on the endorsements by one moderate group (New Dem PAC) and by three progressive groups (Our Revolution, Justice Democrats, and Brand New Congress), it seems clear that candidates who were endorsed by the moderate New Dem PAC both did better proportionately in both the primaries and the general election than those who were endorsed by of the more progressive groups. Table 8.1 summarizes these data from the lists of democratic candidates endorsed by these four groups in the 2018 election.

How much of the electoral shift in the 2018 midterms was the result of the mobilization of women politicized by the women's marches is not possible to say. But what is clearly true is that many of the women returning home from that event transitioned from marching in the streets to mobilizing in the districts (Fisher 2019: ch. 4; Putnam 2020). These were not the "usual suspects" of progressive politics nor were they veterans of earlier protests. From her follow-

---

[51] These data come from https://ballotpedia.org/Election_results,_2018

[52] The ideological composition of the "class of 2019" is calculated from the endorsements offered to different candidates by political action committees associated with the Democratic Party. The data were collected by the self-declared "modern center-left group, Third Way. For the complete analysis, go to www.thirdway.org/memo/2018-endorsement-scorecard

TABLE 8.1 *Endorsement of Democratic House candidates by four different political action committees, 2018 election*

Political action group	Number endorsed in 2018 primary	% of Endorsed candidates chosen	Numbered endorsed in 2018 election	% of Endorsed candidates elected
Moderate:				
New democratic PAC	37	86%	57	55%
Progressive:				
Our revolution	57	37%	35	14%
Justice democrats	74	31%	23	17%
Brand new Congress	27	30%	11	9%

Source: The data were calculated by the author from Third Way, which defines itself as a modern center-left group. For the complete analysis, go to www.thirdway.org/memo/2018-endorsement-scorecard

up interviews with women who had participated in the marches, Fisher found that a third had never participated in a demonstration before and that many had little or no contact with any of the formal organizations that had backed the march (Fisher, ibid., p. 47).

This was a new incarnation of the "amateur Democrat" movement that James Q. Wilson wrote of in the 1960s (1962), with the difference that these new activists were far more numerous and came out of a movement on the boundaries of institutional politics. As Lara Putnam, who studied many of these women's groups up close, writes:

Far beyond blue metropolises, rural and rust belt counties with one-twentieth of the population of Queens or Brooklyn also saw cases of drama and insurgence around county committee leadership elections. Grassroots activists had decided that a seat at the table was worth fighting for, even though the national party that put the tables out in the first place seemed not to think they mattered much at all. (Putnam 2020: 184)

White educated women's support for the Democrats continued to grow in the run-up to the 2020 election. Six weeks before that election, according to a *Washington Post–ABC* poll, Biden held a 65 percent to 34 percent advantage among likely female voters. Trump's lead among men remained about the same as it had been in 2016, but Biden's lead among women was more than twice as large as Clinton's had been four years earlier.[53] Beneath the dramatic headlines regarding police murders, street riots, countermovement violence, and Trump's threat to refuse to step down if he lost the election, the deep story of the 2020 election was the unlikely combination of an interracial coalition protesting in the streets and middle-class black and white women getting out the vote in the districts (Fisher 2019).

Will these forces constitute a new movement/party hybrid – like labor insurgents did in the 1930s and civil rights activists did in the 1970s? Or will they disappear into the now-successful Democratic Party like the veterans of the anti–Iraq War movement we met in Chapter 7? This story had not ended as these lines are written, but there are signs that in the multiple crises set off by the Trump presidency and continuing in the form of the movement he founded the loud and bombastic Donald Trump may have met his match from a mass movement of ordinary Americans coming together across class, race, and gender lines in a movement/party coalition that brings to mind earlier such coalitions in American history.[54] But did Trump's loss of the 2020 elections mean the end of Trumpism? On the answer to this question may hinge the future of the American party system and of American democracy, in general.

VI AFTERWORD: TRUMPISM AFTER TRUMP?

The invasion of the Capitol on January 6, 2021, was one of the most tragic days in American political history. Soon labeled by Senate Minority Leader Chuck Schumer and others "a day that will live forever in infamy,"[55] it is too soon to assess its long-term impacts on American democracy. But within the framework of this study, three features of the invasion of the Capitol stand out:

> First, it showed how truly dangerous a movement demagogue can be in a democracy when given the instruments of power. This was not only true of Trump's politicization of the Executive Branch (Mettler & Lieberman 2020: ch. 9) but of his ability to use his "bully pulpit" to mobilize an army of followers.
>
> Second, those followers were not simply an excitable "base," as they have been characterized by the press and much of the commentariat: They were both coup plotters and rioters[56] who came from *a social movement*, with the properties of many of the movements we have encountered in this book: an extreme ideological commitment; a nonrational attachment to

[53] www.washingtonpost.com/politics/poll-trump-biden-post-abc/2020/09/26/940ef678-ff7f-11ea-9ceb-061d646d9c67_story.html
[54] www.nytimes.com/2020/06/12/us/george-floyd-white-protesters.html
[55] www.radio.com/wcbs880/news/local/schumer-says-jan-6-2021-will-live-forever-in-infamy
[56] See Goodwin, cited in note no. 4, for the argument that the invasion of the Capitol is best seen as both a coup and a riot.

their leader; and especially a willingness to transgress the institutional routines of ordinary politics to make their claims.

Third – and here I return to the central message of this book – the Trump movement was at the same time both anti-political and highly political. Its anti-political nature was built on fealty to a leader who claimed to be an insurgent force on behalf of the "pure" people against the corrupt elite, but its political nature is that it was mobilizable for political purposes by that leader and served as a wedge to help him to gain the fealty of a good part of the Republican Party.

How likely is it that the Trumpist movement will remain vital? As this book goes to press, it is far too soon to tell. On the one hand, in the maelstrom of recriminations and arrests that followed the invasion of the Capitol, there were signs that the Trump movement, and possibly the Republican Party itself, was heading to dissolution. But on the other hand, a small majority of Republican voters continued to claim that the 2020 election had been stolen, long after its results had been certified.[57] Given the widespread conspiracy theories and calls for rebellion on social media following the attempted coup, the United States may be headed for a long period of political violence.

Trump may be gone, but his remarkable success in melding a significant portion of the Republican electorate to himself has major implications for the relations between movements and parties.

First, as we saw earlier in this chapter, Trump didn't need a well-organized political machine to get himself elected. His campaign infrastructure was largely made up of organizations that he did nothing to create and did not control, many of them emerging from the New Right and Christian Right movements of the preceding decades. The result may be that little of this infrastructure will be left behind when he is gone from the scene. Already, after the 2020 election campaign, campaign megadonor Charles Koch offered regret for the partisan ways of his organization. "Boy, did we screw up!" he declared to an interviewer.[58]

Second, the lack of a traditional organizational infrastructure made it unnecessary for Trump as president to expend resources maintaining it. Having won the presidency by the media and having governed through the media, his instinct as an ex-president will be to continue to rely on the media to transmit and amplify his message and attack his opponents. But this means that although he maintained a loyal – and indeed, a passionate – base after losing power, his "aura of specialness may dissipate as public opinion changes" (Ben-Ghiat, p. 13).

---

[57] www.washingtonpost.com/technology/2021/01/09/trump-twitter-protests

[58] www.economist.com/united-states/2020/11/19/charles-koch-offers-partial-regrets-for-his-partisan-ways

Third, Trump's bombastic appeals and his capacity to stir the fervor of conservatives of every stripe triggered the creation of an equally diverse countermovement. When the history of Trumpism is recorded in the history books, this countermovement may be forgotten. But its interaction with the Trump movement was one of the factors that led to the revival of the Democratic Party's campaign capacity and to Joe Biden's election. Whether it will endure after Trump's political demise is another question, one that depends very much on what happens to the relationship between his movement and the Republican Party and whether the latter will seek to return to the big-tent party of the past (Patterson 2020).

Much will also depend on how the Democrats respond to the opportunity afforded them by the end of the Trump presidency. Will the party work to delegitimize its opponents, as many Republicans claimed during the impeachment debate of early 2021? Or will it respond with an effort to reduce the polarization of the polity by encouraging the GOP to return to its older ways? Much depends on how the two main parties manage their relations with the movements that circulate on their margins. We will return to this question in the Conclusions after examining how three other countries – Italy, Chile, and South Korea – responded to their own crises of democracy.

9

Learning about America from Abroad

Until recently, few students of American politics asked where the United States fit on a spectrum of democratic resilience.[1] This largely derived from the fact that most Americans assumed that the United States was exceptional; that the system's institutional mechanisms – like the separation of powers and federalism – would protect it from democratic breakdown (Pierson & Schickler 2021); and that the norms that had grown up around these institutions would assure its stability. If you think your country is a paradigm of democratic functionality, why compare it to countries that have struggled to achieve democracy, have suffered democratic breakdowns, and where movements and parties have often been the source of democratic breakdown?

The recent dangers to democracy detailed in Chapter 8, however, make it clear that the United States may not be as "exceptional" as observers have thought. On January 6, 2021, an authoritarian leader urged an insurrectionary mob to execute a coup against his elected successor, recalling the coup d'état managed by Louis Napoleon in 1849.[2] As in Italy after World War I, a political "strongman" had taken advantage of extreme polarization to attempt to take over the state and turn it to his political advantage with the help of economic and political elites who thought they could use him for their own purposes (Ben-Ghiat 2020). And, as in Latin America in the 1990s, the results of neoliberal policies and growing inequality have brought many Americans to the brink of desperation (Roberts

---

[1] Overcoming this bias was one of the goals of the project called The American Democracy Collaborative, https://americandemocracycollaborative.org and of the volume in progress that it has produced, *Democratic Resilience: Can the United States Withstand Rising Polarization* (2021). I am grateful for my colleagues in the Collaborative for allowing me to be a fly on the wall of their proceedings, from which I have learned a great deal.

[2] See Jeff Goodwin, "The Eighteenth Brumaire of Donald J. Trump," at www.pwsc.us/conflicted-the-pwsc-official-blog/blog/the-eighteenth-brumaire-of-donald-j-trump?fbclid=IwAR1MrdMZ1rP-CqNHWE3k9VjvbVpTGA8eo8zoG15hFlsfUxZWPvHKsZBbZoY for this suggestive comparison.

2015). If Americans could think of their country as "exceptional" when it did not face major threats to democracy, perhaps the current crisis will lead them to turn to the lessons of other countries' experiences with democratic crises and transitions.

When we turn to these experiences, as I will do in this chapter, we quickly find that the relations between parties and movements were critical to the survival or failure of their democratic institutions. In some – like Italy after World War I – the polarization between movement subcultures impeded the negotiation of party compromises in the political system. In others, as in South Korea in the 1980s, a coalition of movements and parties overcame an authoritarian tradition and created a stable, though contentious, democratic regime. But in still others – as in Chile over the last three decades – movements were sidelined by party leaders who were concerned at the possibility of extremism, leaving the country prey to the discontents of extreme inequality.

From many of the episodes in this book, we have seen that party/movement relations advanced the democratic project. But the results of these interactions have not always had benevolent results for democracy. Unreconciled to the end of slavery, a vicious and violent "Redemption" movement with its instrument in the southern Democratic Party created an authoritarian redoubt in an entire region (Mickey 2015). Taking "legal" form and eventually tying its fortunes to the Republican Party, a white minority movement used the courts, the educational system, and ballot manipulation to hold back the democratic tide that was unleashed in the 1960s. Examining different forms of party/movement relations in other countries can help us to judge what kinds of relations are more likely to protect and advance democracy and which are more likely to lead to democratic decline.

Two trends – the first in academic research and the second in real-world politics – support the argument that Americans would do well to pay more attention to the role of movements and parties in democratic transitions elsewhere. The term "Third Wave of democratization" is generally ascribed to the political scientist Samuel Huntington (1991). Huntington wrote as the Soviet Union was crumbling, but the idea of a "Third Wave" rapidly became a common discourse in comparative politics.[3] This trend produced several generations of "democratization" studies, several scholarly journals, and a new specialty that some have called "transitology" (Bunce 1995). Some of this research was linked to the particular type of pre-transition system under examination. For example, transitions from state socialism were bound to be different than transitions from capitalist systems, however authoritarian they were. The interactions of parties and movements during the "Third Wave," as

---

[3] This can be seen in the more than 65,500,000 Google hits for the term in December 2020. For an N-Gram graph that demonstrates its rapid and continued diffusion, go to https://books.google.com/ngrams/graph?content=third+wave+of+democracy&year_start=1960&year_end=2019&corpus=26&smoothing=3#

well as previous failures of democracy (Linz & Stepan, eds. 1978), can help us to ask where the United States fits on a spectrum from democratic breakdown to democratic resilience.

The second factor is the reversal of the "Third Wave" in an increasing number of countries that had seemed to have made successful transitions to democracy. As Liliana Mason and Nathan Kalmoe write:

> The current political moment in American politics feels precipitous. We have whipsawed from an era of "hope and change" embodying multi-racial democracy into an era with a bigoted president who abuses his power for personal and political advantage, resulting in his impeachment. It is a wild time in American politics, with democratic norms and institutions tested on a nearly daily basis, and with some found to be worryingly weak. (2021)

In the remainder of this chapter, I want to show how the juncture of movements and parties has played out in three notable cases of democratic collapse, transition, and resilience. I will use these vignettes to highlight three themes of movement/party relations that have emerged from this book. Focusing on the failure of democracy in Italy after World War 1, I will examine the role of polarization and social sorting in obstructing democratic transitions; turning to South Korea in the 1980s, I will focus on movement/party coalition building in producing democratic transitions; and turning to the thirty-year transition to democracy in Chile, I will diagnose the effect of "pact making" with economic elites in maintaining the extreme inequality inherited from the dictatorship, leading to a major cycle of contention.

I ITALY IN 1922: A CASE OF PERNICIOUS POLARIZATION[4]

On the cusp of World War I, Italy appeared to be on a shaky but inexorable path to democratization. Born as a constitutional monarchy with a conservative "Liberal" ruling class in 1861, the country had moved slowly toward almost-full male suffrage in 1912. While the reform increased the electorate from slightly less than 3 million to 8,650,000, it left the electoral rules unchanged. Although it did increase the vote share of the Left (Socialists, Republicans, and Radicals), because of maneuvering by the elite, the reform left the parliamentary representation of aristocratic and traditional elites unchanged.[5]

We will never know whether the country would have continued its rocky path to democracy following the electoral reform because, in the years that followed, the

---

[4] I have adopted this term from Jennifer McCoy and Mural Somer's lively account in Robert Lieberman, Suzanne Mettler, and Kenneth Roberts' book *Democratic* Resilience (2021). The brief account in this section is based on a chapter in my earlier book, *War, States, and Movements*, 2015, ch. 2.

[5] On the limited effects of the electoral reform, see the excellent analysis of Valentino Larcinese, "Enfranchisement and Representation: Italy 1909–1913." https://sticerd.lse.ac.uk/dps/eopp/eopp32.pdf

political elite were consumed with the question of whether to enter the coming war and, if so, on which side to intervene – the country's traditional allies in the central powers or the Triple Entente of Britain, France, and Tsarist Russia. When Italy finally decided to enter the war on the side of the Entente, the long-awaited elections were put off until 1919, when suffrage was expanded to remaining male voters and the Socialist party – strengthened by its opposition to the war and enjoying the prestige of the revolution in Russia – emerged as the largest party against a center right that had been decimated by its disastrous conduct of the war.

There were a multiplicity of causes for the failure of democracy to take hold in Italy after World War I and for its collapse into the world's first fascist regime in 1922. The country had emerged from a devastating war and entered an economic crisis. A new and inexperienced electorate had been admitted to suffrage through an untested electoral reform. The parliamentary system was weak, and the king retained the power to appoint a prime minister who lacked a majority in Parliament. And thousands of workers and peasants had returned from the front with no jobs awaiting them. To this unstable mix, a wave of industrial and agrarian disorders added a destabilizing ingredient.

The war exacerbated these divisions. Under authoritarian Prime Minister Antonio Salandra, the government had canceled the elections, ruled largely by decree, and imposed military controls over the economy. It closed down newspaper coverage of the war, banned strikes, and sent recalcitrant workers to the front. The result of this authoritarian pattern of mobilization (Kier 2010) was that when industrial conflict erupted at war's end, it had a strong political component against a state that had taken the country into a war that the majority of Parliament opposed and had repressed the working class in doing so.

From 1918 on, a wave of class-based social protest swept across the country, triggered, in part, by the government's disastrous intervention in the war and in part by the economic aftereffects of that war. These factors have been carefully analyzed by historians of the failures of Italian democracy in that period,[6] but the structure of party/movement relations has been less well understood. Italy's parties had long been polarized, but the war had split each of its political families into pro- and anti-interventionist factions, divisions that intersected with its class conflicts. Table 9.1, based on Paolo Farneti's research (1978), reveals how fragmented the party system had become by war's end.

In addition to the traditional cleavages between left and right, at war's end, two new parties joined an already complex and polarized system: a small but volatile Communist Party (PCd'I) and a Christian Democratic Popular Party (PPI), which drew on the country's vast rural Catholic constituency and was

---

[6] The finest social scientific analysis of this failed transition is the landmark contribution by the late Paolo Farneti, "Social Conflict, Parliamentary Fragmentation, Institutional Shift, and the Rise of Fascist Italy." In Juan Linz and Alfred Stepan (eds.). *The Breakdown of Democratic Regimes*, 1978, ch. 1. The most accessible historical sources are Lyttleton, 1979 and 2002, and, for those who read Italian, Gentile 1995.

TABLE 9.1 *The intersection of left/right and pro-war/antiwar cleavages in Italy on the eve of World War I*

	Left	Right
Interventionists	Democrats Social Reformists	Right-wing liberals Right-wing Catholics
	Socialists	Nationalists Giolittian
Neutralists	Left Catholics	Liberals

Source: Paolo Farneti (1978). "Social Conflict, Parliamentary Fragmentation, Institutional Shift, and the Rise of Fascist Italy." In *The Breakdown of Democratic Regimes.* J. Linz and A. Stepan (eds.). Baltimore and London, Johns Hopkins University Press. II, ch. 1.

backed by the Vatican. The trade union scene was also changing: Though membership in the Socialist-linked General Confederation of Labor (CGL) reached two million members, it was challenged by the anarchist-linked Italian Syndicalist Union (USI), whose membership had grown to between 300 and 500 thousand (di Paola 2009).

The war and the revolution in Russia contributed to a realignment of the country's party system. First, the war both strengthened and radicalized the major left-wing party, the *Partito Socialista Italiana* (PSI); second, it weakened the "liberal" and conservative parties that had been running the country since before the war; and, third, the pre-war majority two-ballot system was replaced with a proportional list system of representation that brought hundreds of thousands of untested voters to the polls in an atmosphere of extreme polarization. When elections were finally called, in 1919, the PSI swept northern and central Italy, except for the Catholic northeast, where the PPI came first in the polls. It was only in the traditionally clientelistic provinces of the South and the two main islands that the liberal and conservative parties survived.

The *Biennio Rosso*

Italy had long had a contentious civil society, but nothing that had happened before the war came close to the militancy of the strikes during the two postwar years of the *biennio rosso*. Strikers in that period invented a new and challenging strategy: occupying the factories so as to prevent employers from locking the workers out (Spriano 1975). The core of the agitation came from among industrial and agricultural workers in the North. To many on the left, like the Marxist Antonio Gramsci, it seemed as if Italian peasants and workers could do what the Bolsheviks had done in Russia (Gramsci 1971).

But strikes, factory occupations, and land seizures also revealed a split between the Socialists and the CGL, on the one hand, and workers at the base, urged on by militant anarchist and syndicalist unions on the other. The CGL drew back from supporting the factory occupations for fear that they would carry grist to the mill of their competitors while factory committees pushed for them from the base. As militancy in the factories and in the fields rose, both the PSI and the unions temporized while militancy at the base rose. The result was that the *bienno rosso* came to a grinding halt, but not before terrorizing both industrialists and landowners with the prospect that Italy was headed for an Italian "October."

Movement/Countermovement Interaction

As the protest wave rose and fell, another movement – Benito Mussolini's Fascist movement – also arose out of the war with the support of a coalition of army veterans, peasants, small town thugs, wealthy landholders, and businessmen. The latter, like the conservative party leaders they supported, hoped to use the former leftist journalist to ward off the next wave of strikes and defeat the Socialists, who had taken over hundreds of municipalities in the elections. Combining vicious violence with calls for law and order, his *fasci di combattimento* – the military term that was deliberately chosen to evoke war – coagulated into a mass movement (Ben-Ghiat 2020).

The future *duce,* using his skills as a journalist (de Felice 2005), adopted a combination of populist and right-wing ideas to inspire his *squadre* to attack Socialist Party offices, chambers of labor, and *case del popolo* (houses of the people). He enjoyed loud support from landowners who were fighting off land occupations and quieter support from industrialists who hoped to use him to crush the unions. In October 1922, as his supporters were attacking Socialist municipalities across the North, Mussolini walked into power in the capitol after staging a theatrical "March on Rome."[7] At that point, democracy died for the next twenty-two years.

Polarization and "Social Sorting"

On his own, Mussolini was unlikely to have succeeded in subverting Italian democracy, but he attacked a party system that was divided between a Socialist and Communist Left, a Catholic Center, and assorted center-right parties. The Socialists were more concerned with holding off their opponents on the left than with negotiating with the non-Marxist parties to defend the parliamentary system; the Populist Party was anxious to open up political space for Catholics in a largely secular political class; and the Liberals, Democrats,

---

[7] To be more precise, the future *duce* arrived in Rome in a sleeping car while his squads of fascist thugs marched on city halls around the country.

Radicals, and Nationalists on the center right thought they saw in Mussolini a comical amateur who they could use to return to power (Levitsky & Ziblatt 2018).

Historians of this period have pointed to this extreme polarization to explain how a political adventurer with no governing experience could have destroyed a constitutional monarchy that was on its way to full democracy. But it was not polarization per se that permitted Mussolini to gain power but the combination of polarization – a *lateral* process – with the *political subcultures* in civil society – what I have called, following the work of Liliana Mason (1918), "social sorting."

Although Italy was widely thought to have a weak civil society, this was actually only true in the backward provinces of the South and on the two major islands (Putnam 1993; Tarrow 1967). Elsewhere, the society was both polarized *and* organized into competing subcultures (Trigilia 1986a and b). In the north and center, a plethora of organizations unified workers and poor peasants, offering them a variety of services through cooperative "houses of the people" (Kohn 2003), while a network of local Chambers of Labor instilled a class consciousness across occupational lines. In the northeast, the Catholic Church and the church-linked organizations around it offered similar identity-reinforcing mechanisms to the Catholic majority (Kalyvas 1996; Poggi 1967) and produced its own trade union movement in competition with the socialist and anarchist movements.

What was unusual about Italian civil society was not only that it was polarized between Marxist and Catholic parties, but that these parties were themselves internally integrated and socially sorted. The result was that when its political institutions were assailed by a political adventurer claiming to have a program that transcended Marxism and capitalism, the political subcultures at the base made it impossible for the parties and movements they represented to coalesce against the threat to democracy. What was seen on left and right as a threat to class interests was actually a threat to democracy, as the next twenty-two years of dictatorship would show. Partisan polarization and social movements together paralyzed the political elite, allowing a thuggish adventurer to turn a struggling democracy into a dictatorship.

II SOUTH KOREA IN 1987: DEMOCRATIZATION BY CONTENTIOUS COALITION[8]

The "Third Wave" of democratization provides us with more positive examples of party/movement interaction in transitions to democracy. But these cases were actually quite varied in their social support bases and in the mechanisms that

---

[8] This section is in debt to the guidance of Paul Y. Chang, Jai Kwan Jung, Sun-Chul Kim, and Chan S. Suh to a foreigner who came to Korea knowing next to nothing about the country's history, society, and politics.

produced successful democratization. For example, while students of "pacted democratization" in southern Europe and Latin America found little positive role for movements in transitions to democracy (O'Donnell, Schmitter & Whitehead, eds. 1986), other scholars found that social movements had positive impacts on the process (Bermeo 1997; della Porta 2020; Tarrow 1995). O'Donnell and his collaborators intuited that pacted transitions were unlikely to be highly democratic, but they argued that pacts between elites had the advantage of avoiding the excesses of democracy that risked bringing the military back into politics. We will turn to one of the outstanding cases of "pacted" transitions in Section III; here I will examine the case of South Korea in which the dominant mechanism was one of contentious interaction triggered by a coalition of social movement actors.

South Korea had a long history of elective authoritarianism dating to the foundation of its US-installed Republic in 1948 (Cumings 1997). From that time on, the Cold War and the looming threat of the North Korean Communist regime on its border gave advantages to authoritarian leaders coming from the military and to a Central Intelligence Agency (KCIA) that worked to suppress dissent. Although the United States – South Korea's major sponsor – never openly supported these authoritarian tendencies, neither did it encourage its allies to move toward competitive democracy.

A first effort to create an authoritarian state was foiled by a student rebellion in 1960, followed by a recurrent cycle of grudging reform and relapses into authoritarian governance. This led in the 1970s to revolts against President Park Chung Hee (Chang 2015) and then, in the mid-to-late 1980s, to a major wave of strikes and protests (Shin, et al. 2011).[9] This cycle of protest attacked the authoritarianism of the repressive Yushin Constitution that President Park had pushed through in 1972 (Chang 2015, ch. 1). As Jai Kwan Jung summarizes a long and tortuous process, "In South Korea, civil society has been the driving force for the breakdown of authoritarianism and the transition to democracy since the 1960s" (2020).

Like Italy, South Korea was a contentious society. Despite the draconian hand of the KCIA, the 1970s were marked by a series of protests and demonstrations that – in addition to students and workers – brought journalists, lawyers, and a vital Christian movement into cycles of protest against the regime (Chang 2017: chs. 3–5). As Paul Chang summarizes, "The politicization of Christians, journalists, lawyers, and other groups marked a critical juncture in the movement, reflecting growing discontent across a wider sector of society" (p. 145). "This contentious civil society formed a unified democratic coalition along with opposition political elites during the Chun Doo-hwan military

---

[9] These complicated decades are effectively summarized in Gi-Wook Shin, Paul Y. Chang, Jung-eun Lee, and Sookyung Kim, "The Korean Democracy Movement: An Empirical Overview" in Shin et al. 2011.

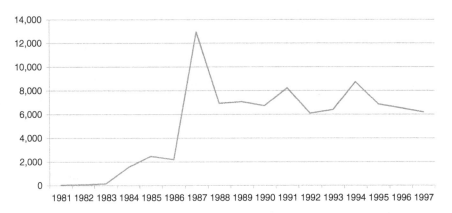

FIGURE 9.1 Number of public protests in South Korea, 1987–2002
Source: Sun-Chul Kim, *Democratization and Social Movements in South Korea: Defiant Institutionalization*, 2018, p. 5, Reproduced with the kind permission of the author.

dictatorship in the 1980s and eventually brought about the liberalization of authoritarian rule and the transition to democracy in 1987" (Jung, ibid.).

In 1987 and 1988, a wave of strikes and protests swept over the country. From Sun-Chul Kim's original dataset,[10] Figure 9.1 demonstrates the sudden emergence of the movement. In its magnitude, and in the presence of organized workers in the coalition, the Korean cycle looked not very different than the *biennio rosso* that had erupted in Italy between 1919 and 1921, but students and other nonworker groups had a profound influence on the movement for democracy because their presence forced it to adopt a coalitional structure.

There were two major differences between the Italian and the South Korean protest waves.

> First, although the *biennio rosso* was largely worker- and farm worker-based and bore the strong imprint of social class, the Korean cycle crossed class lines and was organized around the "master frame" of democracy (Snow & Benford 1992). Closely related to this was a human rights frame, one that was heavily influenced by the presence of lawyers in the movement and by the influence of the growing international human rights movement (Meyer et al. 1998). As a result, the courts and the call for the independence of the judiciary were important parts of the movement's claims and its repertoire of contention (Goedde 2011). While the

---

[10] Kim's data collection, guided by the tradition of protest event analysis in the United States, was based on police yearbooks and on a semi-automated reading of the Korea Integrated News Database system (KINDS) (www.kinds.or.kr) for the years 1990, 1994, 1998, and 2002. See Appendix 1 for Kim's description of his data-gathering procedures.

"usual suspects" of Korean protests – students and workers – were central to the protest cycle, "relatively docile segments of Korean society . . . joined the ranks of dissidents" (Shin et al. 2011).
Second, the different strands of the Korean movement were interlinked in a coalitional network. As Shin and his coauthors write, "the growth of coalitional organizations played a key role in the unprecedented 1987 protest cycle" (ibid.). "Democratization" was not the only demand of the movement – there were many sectoral and interest-group claims as well – but it served as a focal point on which most of the participants could agree. Writing in 2011, Jung noted that – in contrast to other Asian cases, like Taiwan – "in South Korea, a pro-democracy coalition of popular movements and opposition parties led massive protests during the initial phase of democratic transition" (Jung 2011: 386).

Although this was a movement-driven cycle, parties and movements worked together against the authoritarian regime. In his exhaustive study of "defiant institutionalization" in South Korea, Kim highlights the key brokerage role of the New Korean Democratic Party (NKDP) in the protest cycle. "For weeks in June 1987," he writes:

the NKDP operated as the central headquarter of the opposition, sharing information through leaflets and booklets, building ties between previously unconnected groups, and organizing mass demonstrations nationwide. With the successful orchestration of the June Uprising, the NKDP . . . elevated the united front tactic to the level of creed within the activist community. (Kim 2018: 4)

Importantly, the level of contentious politics never retreated to its pre-1985 level, even after a new constitution was passed.

After the (Democratic) Revolution[11]

Unlike the rapid death of the constitutional monarchy in Italy, the reforms instituted by the democratization movement in Korea led to the consolidation of democracy, but it did so through contentious interaction (Jung 2011; Kim 2018). Once instantiated, the pattern of reform though protest continued long after 1987. As Jung concluded from his comparison of South Korea and Taiwan, "The rise of movements in diverse sectors following the transition to democracy can be understood as the spillover of the full-scale mass mobilization that facilitated regime transition" (2011: 385).

This evolution was neither rapid nor painless. The constitution that was passed in October 1987 was actually the ninth revision of the document that had been adopted in 1948. Like that document, it contained a long list of impressively liberal provisions.[12] The most important was the reinstitution of

---

[11] This section is in debt to the research of Sun-Chul Kim (2018) and that of Chan S. Suh (2019).
[12] www.wipo.int/edocs/lexdocs/laws/en/kr/kro61en.pdfeave

direct election of the president, in contrast to the Yushin Constitution, which had given President Park almost unlimited power. But effective human rights reforms had to await the creation of a Human Rights Commission in 2001 (Kim 2018: 144–45).

One sign of how hard it was to transcend authoritarian rule was the slow pace of liquidating torture.[13] The government's use of torture was one of the triggers for the national uprising of 1987, when a college student, Park Jong-Chui, died under torture in police custody (ibid., p. 662). After the protest wave of 1987 ended, reports Chan S. Suh, "the reported cases of torture actually increased due to favorable legal environments for the victims and greater media freedom." Using a carefully researched dataset of arrests, prosecutions, and reports of torture,[14] Suh found that between 1988 and 1997, 138 cases of torture involving 330 victims were reported. Only in 1993, when Kim Young-sam, the first civilian president since the 1960s, came into power, did the number of torture cases begin to decline (Suh, p. 655).

What made the difference? A more liberal constitution emphasizing individual rights certainly had an impact. In addition, the international environment was becoming more hospitable to human rights (Suh, pp. 649–50; also see Meyer et al. 1998). But these are reasons *why* the use of torture declined; the real question is *how* it happened. My answer will not surprise readers of this book: It occurred through the interaction between parts of the social movement sector and political leaders like Kim Young-sam, who had come to power after a period of activism in the democratization movement. With the establishment of legal advocacy groups, such as Lawyers for a Democratic Society (*Minbyun*), human rights lawyers raised a collective voice against human rights violations (Suh, p. 665). As Patricia Goedde writes:

Formed within a year of the June 1987 uprising, *Minbyun* constituted a group of 51 lawyers who had been active as human rights lawyers during the preceding authoritarian rule . . . . In the span of two decades, *Minbyun* grew over ten-fold in membership and rose drastically in profile when one of its former members, Roh Moo Hyun, became president of South Korea in 2002" Goedde, 2011).

---

[13] Korean constitutions banned torture from the beginning, but these provisions were largely ignored by the national and local police, the Korean Central Intelligence Agency (KCIA), the armed forces, and the prosecutor's office (Suh 2019: 656). "Torture remained as a prominent repressive repertoire of the military governments that came to power through military coups in 1961 and in 1979. Under the military regimes of Park Chung-hee (1961 to 1979) and Chun Doo-hwan (1980 to 1987), torture methods were widely used to suppress political dissidents who were claimed by the government to be pro-communist and pro-North Korean supporters" (Suh, p. 653).

[14] For a description of the data collected and utilized by Suh, see his 2019 article, "More than Words."

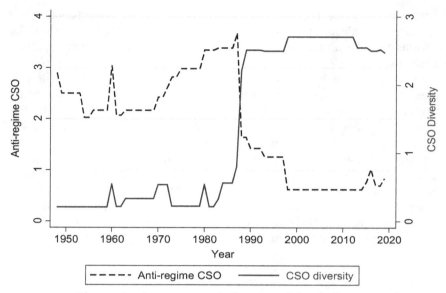

FIGURE 9.2 Change in the nature and diversity of South Korean civil society organizations
Source: Reproduced from original data collected by Jai Kwan Jung with his kind permission.

Soon after 1987, the democracy movement began to diversify into a number of strands (Jung, p. 385; Chang & Shin 2011; Kim 2018). Figure 9.2 from Jung's original analysis shows that from a diversity level of 0.31 before 1987, the diversity index rose to 2.59 after 1988 (Jung 2020: 3). But the democracy movement avoided dispersion through the continued use of the model of coalitional protest campaigns.

Coalitions also became institutionalized after the transition: Figure 9.3, reproduced from Kim's original work, shows a decline of the kind of informal coalitions that had piloted the 1989 campaign but an increase in the number of formal coalitions, a trend that continued into the new century. "The success of the 1987 NCDC coalition," Kim concludes, "furnished movement groups with an organizational model to emulate, and protest campaigns, with frequent government repression, provided the necessary stimuli for South Korean movement groups to act together" (Kim, p. 63). Coalition formation – to take a term from studies of protest repertoires – became "modular" (Tilly & Tarrow 2015: 12–13).

This is not to say that South Korean movements were passive adjuncts of the party system. On the contrary, as Shin and Chang write, "they remained as 'contentious and disruptive' as protest activities during the authoritarian era" (Shin & Chang 2011). It was their continued capacity to build coalitions around

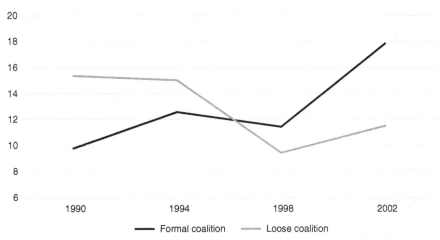

FIGURE 9.3 Changing trends of South Korean coalition formation, 1990–2002
Source: Sun-Chul Kim, *Democratization and Social Movements in South Korea; Defiant Institutionalization,* 2018, p. 62, reproduced with the kind permission of the author.

goals aimed at protecting democracy that made South Korea continue to prosper as a contentious democratic system. We saw the longevity of this tradition as recently as 2016–17, when a national movement of "candlelight protesters" gathered every week for almost half a year to protest the abuses of the country's then-President Park Geun-hye. That movement led to the impeachment of the president by a coalition of both organized and unorganized movement activists (Jung 2020). Cohering around a democracy frame, movements and parties built enduring coalitions that overcame their sectoral divisions and led to the consolidation of a contentious democracy.

III   PACT MAKING AND INEQUALITY[15]

Latin America is an important laboratory for examining party/movement relations because, as Marisa von Bülow and Sofia Donoso note, "the history of social movements [in Latin America] has always been one of simultaneously close and contentious interactions with state officials and political parties" (2017: 5). In particular, Latin America offers comparative evidence about the role of movement/party relations in transitions to democracy. On that

[15] This section is in debt to the contributions of Sofia Donoso and Marisa von Bulow and their collaborators in their edited book *Social Movements in Chile* (2017), to Patricia Hipsher for her "Democratic Transitions as Protest Cycles" (1998), to Juan Pablo Luna and David Altman for their "Uprooted but Stable" (2011), and to Ken Roberts for his many papers on parties and movements in Latin America and for his astute comments on an early version of this section.

continent, the neoliberal turn of the 1980s both challenged and restructured party systems. The stronger party systems were challenged from within but retained their basic configurations, while the weaker ones collapsed and gave rise to realignments led by social movements (Roberts 2018a).

Latin America was one of the original laboratories that produced the theory that "pacted transitions" are the royal road to democratic consolidation (O'Donnell, Schmitter & Whitehead 1986). But the Chilean case was unusual. After social movements played a central role in the mobilizations that helped bring down the dictatorship, an elite-pacted transition to democracy was forged with military and business leaders that gave them an effective veto over the policy process and limited vertical accountability (Luna 2016). As a result, inequality remained high; the parties of the center and left were unable or unwilling to meet civil society demands, which undermined the legitimacy of the political system and paved the way for increasingly massive protest waves.

Chile's experience of democratic transition was archetypical of "Third Wave" transitions in three ways:

> First, it was the earliest and the most determined example of a Latin American country to institute what later came to be called the "Washington Consensus." In the 1970s, under military rule, Chile instituted what Roberts calls "the four social pillars of the neoliberal model" (Roberts 2017): the liberalization labor markets and the installation of privatized delivery systems for social security, health care, and education. Using a combination of draconian legislation and harsh repression, and with the advice of a group of University of Chicago economists, the Chilean dictatorship executed a savage liberalization of the economy and all but destroyed the once-powerful trade union movement (Remmer 1980).
>
> Second, in the Chilean transition, both movements and parties were active in contesting the dictatorship. While a wave of movements pushed for reform through a broad repertoire of contentious action (Donoso & von Bülow, p. 6), a group of parties that had survived from the pre-Pinochet regime negotiated the transition and came to power through electoral means.
>
> Third, and most important, Chile was a poster child for the theory that democratic transitions are most successful when they take place through "pacted arrangements." In what Chileans called a "democracy of agreements," opposition leaders "negotiated a package of constitutional reforms with the military regime, agreeing to operate within a set of legislative and electoral rules that overrepresented conservative forces and placed serious institutional constrains on social and economic policy reforms" (Roberts 2017: 235; Siavelis 2016). The result was thirty years of pacted democracy and the survival of the extreme inequality carried over from the dictatorship.

For a decade or more after the military stepped down, Chileans breathed a sigh of relief that their model of a negotiated transition had avoided both violence from the extreme left and reaction from the conservative forces of the former dictatorship. During the 1990s, apart from isolated and local outbursts, social protest appeared to be in abeyance, dampened by a strong economic performance. Unlike neighboring Argentina, where the military staged a series of attempted coups, supporters of the former dictatorship either retired into private life or joined a new center-right coalition. As for the party system as a whole, it emerged as one of the most "institutionalized" in Latin America (Mainwaring & Scully 1995). But among them, enduring neoliberalism, the pacted nature of the transition, and the lack of accountability brought challenges that would explode after a decade and a half of apparently settled consolidation.

Neoliberalism and Its Resistance

Neoliberalism was, of course, a central feature of the "Washington Consensus" that was imposed on Latin American economies in the 1980s and 1990s. Where Chile's experience differed was that it was one of the first to make this transformation, and it did so under the control of one of the most ruthless dictatorships in the region. "Indeed," as Roberts writes, "Chile was the only country in the region that effectively completed the neoliberal reform process under military rule. Argentina and Uruguay started the reforms under military regimes in the '70s, like Chile, but their regimes collapsed in the economic crises of the early '80s, and it was left on the plates of new democratic regimes to complete the process of neoliberal reform in the '80s and '90s."[16] Because the Pinochet regime lasted from 1973 until 1990, there was plenty of time for it to tinker with the nuts and bolts of market liberalization to make it work effectively. Of particular importance for the future was the partial privatization of the national pension and health systems and of higher education.

Of course, the Chilean model also increased the degree of inequality in Chilean society, demobilized the party system, and destroyed the capacity of the labor movement to defend its members. From a level of unionization and a strike level that were among the highest in the region, the Chilean labor movement was constrained both by successive waves of legislation and by overt repression. As Karen Remmer summarizes, "[T]he government's policies disadvantaged, above all, the working class, which through various constraints and prohibitions on union activity lost an effective voice in private as well as public decision-making processes" (Remmer 1980: 291).

Protesters and Party Leaders

The Chilean economy had essentially completed the process of structural adjustment when the debt crisis of the 1980s forced the rest of Latin America to liberalize. When that crisis hit Chile, leading to a severe recession, a wave of

---

[16] In a personal correspondence with the author from Ken Roberts.

labor protest erupted. As Roberts summarizes, "A call by the copper workers federation for a day of protest triggered a massive three-year uprising against the dictatorship from 1983 to 1986, reversing a decade of highly coerced social quiescence" (2017a: 234). These labor protests rapidly widened into a broad cycle of contention involving women's groups, unions, and human rights organizations, increasingly relying on shantytown youths as the level of political violence rose (Schneider 1995).

The fact that resistance was so volatile and spread so rapidly across Chilean society gave pause to the Socialist and Christian Democratic party leaders who had seen social protest radicalize during the early 1970s, which had provided the military and its foreign supporters with the pretext to overthrow the Allende government. They remembered, for example, that Allende had "encouraged the formation of local mass organizations to provide a more mobilized popular base of support (as well as defense) and to serve as vehicles for 'mass' involvement in specific administrative programs – especially those directed toward the poor and working-class citizens to whom the government gave priority" (Goldberg 1975: 105). They were especially worried about the fact that the Communist Party – which had been the most active party in the protest movement, especially among shantytown youth (Schneider 1995) – had begun to advocate armed resistance and created an armed wing ready to engage in violent forms of resistance.

Determined not to offer provocation to the right, these parties led popular mobilization toward partisan and electoral forms of participation and created a number of informal institutions to engage conservative forces with their reforms (Roberts 2017). This gave conservative holdovers from the dictatorship the status of "veto players," "which included a tacit agreement that the president should negotiate with powerful economic actors and leaders on the right, such as business associations and producer groups, to craft agreements before legislation was introduced in Congress" (Siavelis 2016: 72).

The movement from protest to politics was facilitated by personal and organizational ties between party and movement leaders as many of the latter moved seamlessly into party and ultimately into governmental positions. Patricia Hipsher (1998) sees this progression as part of a classical protest cycle: "During the latter stages of transitions," she writes, specifically of the Chilean case, "when political parties return to the fore and confrontation is replaced by democratic cooperation and competition, movements tend to decline and become institutionalized, thus completing the cycle" (p. 154). This pattern of movements nudged aside and coopted by the parties was part and parcel of Chile's pacted model of democratization.

Pact Making and the Durability of Neoliberalism

Party leaders were not only anxious to tamp down the excesses of social movement activism and replace "confrontation" with "democratic cooperation and competition," but they were also at pains to assure conservative supporters of the dictatorship that their interests would be protected under the representative regime. As Roberts points out:

Although the *Concertaciòn* won a solid majority of votes to capture the presidency in 1989 – the first of four presidential victories that allowed the center-left coalition to govern the country for 20 years – conservative forces wielded a *de facto* legislative veto against major changes in the neoliberal model. (2017a: 236)

This meant that many of the privatizing reforms of the dictatorship would be continued into the post-transitional era and that reforms would be blocked by the effective elite veto over legislation (Siavalis, 72–73).

Having inherited a booming economy – albeit one with very high levels of social exclusion – the Christian Democratic (PDC) and Socialist (PSCh) parties that anchored the *Concertación* softened their criticisms of Pinochet's neoliberal model and steered a pragmatic course to induce business cooperation with the regime transition". (Roberts 2017a: 236)

The result was that the new democratic regime based its policies on acceptance of, and modest reforms of, the neoliberal political economy that it had accepted from the dictatorship, rather than either returning to the economic policies of the pre-Pinochet regime or setting off in new directions. It passed modest reforms, such as reform of the tax system and the expansion of educational opportunities, but the government persistently failed to diminish inequality of access to high-quality education (von Bülow & Bidegain 2015: 182). The Chilean model of "contested liberalism" limited the possibilities for transition to a more equitable political economy.

Contention after Pact Making

The Chilean model of pacted transition, modest reformism, and low levels of societal contention operated well for the first decade and a half after the fall of the Pinochet regime, but from 2000 on, a series of protest cycles threatened the equilibrium of the regime.

First, in 2001, a movement of high school students emerged based on "widespread disgruntlement with the quality of the school infrastructure and the authoritarian manner of many school directors, among other issues" (Donoso 2017: 74). Notable was the "horizontal" organization of the student movement and its leaders' desire to prevent its cooptation by the political parties by making student assemblies the locus of decision making (ibid., p. 75). This was followed in 2006 by the picturesquely named *Pinguino* movement, named for the black-and-white school uniforms the students wore. The students adopted the widespread practice of the sit-in and gained an unprecedented support level of 87 percent of the surveyed population for the students' claims (ibid., p. 77). The *Concertación* government under Michelle Bachelet proposed modest and ambiguous reforms, which neither satisfied the students nor gained their consensus.

A new student movement broadened the debate to the entire neoliberal model of education that the government had inherited from the dictatorship in 2011. Student leaders pointed to the vast profits that had come out of privatization and to the starving of the public education sector (ibid., pp. 78–83). The movement's contentious tactics were rooted in what Donoso calls "a profound distrust of existing political parties and the capacity of institutions to process the demands of the movement" (p. 83). As she concludes, the student activists' strategic focus and their continued use of street protest was "a response to their lack of affinity with the traditional left and an effort to construct a movement from below" (p. 88).

Students were not alone in challenging successive governments: As Somma and Medel's data show, during this period there were sharp increases in environmental, indigenous, labor, and regionalist protests. Particularly strident was the indigenous Mapuche movement, whose protest events rose to seventy a year by 2007, mainly on traditional Mapuche territory but also in the capital and in the rest of the country (Bidegain 2017: 111–12). In the environmental sector, an anti-dam movement that arose in Patagonia became the largest environmental campaign in Chilean history (Schaeffer 2017). Finally, although the labor movement was the sector most deeply affected by the Chilean model of development, Chilean labor activists have innovated by shifting an important part of its repertoire from industrial action to legal mobilization (Gutiérrez Crocco 2017).

The series of protest waves had a surprising effect on the previously stable Chilean party system. In 2012, a new party, *Revolución Democrática*, grew out of a number of movements that had come together in the wake of the protest wave of 2011. This was a movement party in the classical Latin American tradition, with the difference that it rose in the presence of two main party coalitions that showed no sign of going away. But in 2017, it led to the creation of a broader party – the *Frente Amplio*, which won an astonishing 20 percent of the vote in the presidential election of that year and twenty-one seats in Parliament, establishing itself as a third force. For the "institutionalized" Chilean party system, this was nothing less than a political earthquake.[17]

Why did these movements erupt after such a long delay? The reason is clear. As Somma and Medel put it: "Combined with the atomizing effect of a market society imposed during the dictatorship, 'demobilization from above' led to the fragmentation of collective action" (2017: 31) not only on the part of the working class but also students, pensioners, environmentalists, and indigenous groups. As governments stood aloof from civil society, either coopting former movement leaders or ignoring their claims, resistance to neoliberalism and to the constitution that "locked in" the neoliberal reforms became something like a master frame of civil society.

---

[17] I am grateful to Sofia Donoso and Maris von Bülow for filling me in about the importance of this "movement party."

An Institutionalized Party System?

In the 1990s, observers saw the Chilean party system as highly institutionalized (Mainwaring & Scully 1995). There are technical reasons why this image may have been overdrawn. Most studies of party institutionalization combine four dimensions: the stability and regularity of party competition patterns, the presence of deep party roots in society, a relatively high level of party legitimacy in society, and the presence of well-developed party organizations (Luna & Altman 2011: 1). The easiest of these variables to measure is the volatility of the party system, which, in Chile, was one of the lowest in Latin America. But other facets of "institutionalization" were either harder to measure or declined steadily as the system took root (ibid., p. 2).

Figure 9.4, drawn from the work of David Altman and his collaborators, reveals dramatically how, along a variety of measures, a party system that had begun with very high levels of participation rapidly began to lose voter participation and thus legitimacy among the population. This was especially the case among young people who came of age after the transition and had no

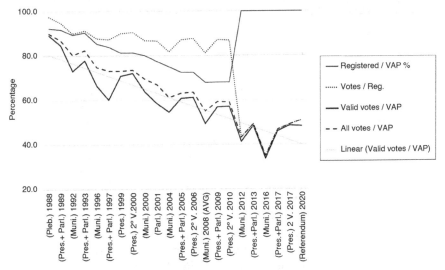

FIGURE 9.4 Electoral participation in Chile, 1988–2020

Note: VAP means voting age population. Registered/VAP percentage rises to 100 percent after 2010 because in the early 2010s, Congress passed a law that made registration automatic.

Source: The data through 2016 are based on David Altman and Rossana Castiglioni (2018). "Chile: el fin de una época política." In M. Alcántara, D. Buquet & M. L. Tagina (eds.). *Elecciones y partidos en América Latina en el cambio de ciclo*, (pp. 105–27). Madrid: Centro de Investigaciones Sociológicas (p.112), reproduced with permission. The more recent data were kindly provided to the author by Professor Altman.

identification with the parties and, of course, were at the core of the new cycles of social protest that would erupt after the turn of the new century.

Not only that: As the parties grew more deeply embedded in the state, their organizations hollowed out, giving way to personal machines in many areas. The parties' legitimacy also declined steadily; by 2010 more than 85 percent of Chileans did not identify with a party (Luna & Altman, p. 9; Siavalis, p. 76). Most important in the framework of this book, the parties had lost their roots in Chilean society. As Siavelis wrote prophetically in 2016:

> In the last five years, major issues have not been put on the table by political parties, but rather through the vocal demands of social movements. While *Concertatión* leaders often avoided controversial reforms or came to the table with incremental reforms, more substantial reform initiatives have been forced on the agenda by more assertive social movements and protests. (Siavelis 2016: 80)

While movement activity was most active in the educational sector, it was also stirring in gender relations, divorce, birth control, abortion, gay marriage, and in the Mapuche independence movement (ibid.). But nothing prepared Chileans for the massive protest wave of 2019–20, which was triggered, as many protest cycles are, by an apparently minor conflict before spreading to a number of other sectors and to the entire country.

No Son 30 pesos; Son 30 Años[18]

Like the 1968 French student revolution that began over the issue of dormitory parietal hours, the most substantial protest cycle in Chilean history since the fall of the dictatorship began in October 2019 over the decision of the government to raise Santiago bus fares by ten pesos and the subway fare by thirty pesos at peak hours. Although the increase was justified by technocratic criteria, students and other public transport users interpreted it as yet another blow to an economy that was the most unequal in Latin America. As described in the *Washington Post*, though the thirty years since the dictatorship had made Chile "one of South America's wealthiest countries," they also "created stark economic disparities and strapped many Chileans into debt."[19] The slogan "It's not 30 pesos; it's 30 years!" captured the frustration of the students: In one of the wealthiest countries in Latin America, 1 percent of the population controlled 26.5 percent of the nation's wealth, while 50 percent of low-income households controlled only 2.1 percent.

The students' protest against the fare increases spread quickly, first to the entire metro network of the metropolitan area, then to people who vandalized

---

[18] Translation: "It is not 30 pesos, it is 30 years!" referring to the three decades since the post-Pinochet government and to the 30-peso increase in metro fares that had been declared by the government. www.webyempresas.com/no-son-30-pesos-son-30-anos

[19] https://washingtonpost/com/nation/2019/10/21/chile-protests-santiago-dead-state-emergency

the city's infrastructure, and then to other Chilean cities like Concepción, San Antonio, and Valparaíso. On October 25, more than a million people took to the streets across the country to protest inequality and to demand the resignation of President Piñera. What had begun as a sectoral protest against public service fares rapidly transformed into a virtual insurrection.

The response to the protests and riots was even more viciously violent than usual. After President Piñera called a state of emergency, units of the national army were deployed. By December 28, 29 protesters had been killed, nearly 2,500 had been injured, and almost 3,000 were arrested. But with repression failing to contain the rebellion, on October 28, Piñera changed 8 ministers in his center-right government but declared that the country was "at war."

While not recognizing their responsibility for either inequality or for their institutionalized collusion with the right, the leaders of the enlarged *Concertación* – which now included the Communist Party – saw an opportunity to take advantage of the chaos and confusion surrounding the insurrection to call for major institutional changes. On November 15, the National Congress agreed to hold a national referendum to choose a constituent assembly that would rewrite the Pinochet-era constitution. After the vote was delayed because of the coronavirus lockdown, the election was finally held a year after the start of the protests and was approved on October 25, 2020, by a majority of 78.28 percent. As Figure 9.4 shows, after a steady decline in voter participation the turnout rose to 51 percent. A second vote to choose the citizens to form the constituent assembly took place in May 2021. Independents with little or no connection to the party system dominated the outcome, except for a movement party of the left that had grown out of the waves of protest.

IV   LEARNING FROM COMPARISON

What we have learned from these very different experiences of movement/party interaction in democratic crises that may be relevant to America's current crisis? In their incisive analysis of the threats to American democracy, Suzanne Mettler and Robert Lieberman lay out four of them, which, separately and together, have menaced the system (2020). The first, dating back to the dawn of the Republic, has been *polarization*; the second, most salient in the Civil War and in the 1890s, is *identity and membership*; the third, in the Great Depression, is *inequality;* and the fourth is *executive aggrandizement* (for their summary, see pp. 14–26). In their riveting book, these authors pinpoint the features of American political development on which variations in these four threats have turned: the separation of powers, the rule of law and its avoidance, and politicians who proved anxious to profit from any or all of the threats to aggrandize their positions.

Oddly enough, one feature is absent from this telescopic analysis of America's ills and virtues in confronting threats to democracy – social movements![20] Although the footprints of movements and activists can be found in the histories of all four of these threats, they can only be inferred from between the lines. In this final section, I want to rehearse the three cases of democratic transition we have scanned, pointing out how movement/party relations have affected in each one and trying to relate them to our major case – the interactions of movements and political parties in the United States.

Polarization and Social Sorting

Central to Mettler's and Lieberman's list of "threats" is a feature that we have seen throughout this book – polarization. In a companion piece written with comparativist Kenneth Roberts, these authors write:

Since polarization makes it difficult, if not impossible, to find common political ground, it can prevent democratic institutions from making important policy choices and responding to the critical issues of the day. Polarization, in short, can easily lead to democratic *gridlock and paralysis*. (Lieberman, Mettler & Roberts, 2021: 1, italics added)

Though the cases we have surveyed here all suffered from polarized societies, it was in Italy that polarization most closely corresponded to the situation of "gridlock and paralysis" that these authors describe in the United States today. But in contrast to authors who have seen left/right polarization as Italy's basic problem (Sartori 1966), it was the combination of lateral and vertical polarization that allowed a crass adventurer to seize power in 1922. By *lateral polarization*, I intend a great distance between ideological poles; by *vertical polarization*, I mean that different parties are "socially sorted" along the lines of race, ethnicity, gender, religion, and (especially in the Italian case), class (Lieberman et al., p. 18; Mason 2018). When these two dimensions of polarization combine – as they did in Italy after World War I – polarization becomes truly "pernicious" (McCoy & Somer 2021).

Enough has been said by others about the rising polarization in the United States to assume that this combination is a serious malady (Abramowitz 2017; Binder 2017; McCarty 2007). What our Italian comparison can add to this literature is the fact that polarization is neither a society-based nor a polity-based phenomenon, but a *relational* one that links center and periphery and impedes elites from shifting from the defense of their followers' interest to the defense of democracy. As we saw in Italy, and as Lieberman and his collaborators warn for America today:

non-elite social actors can play a central role in the process of partisan and ideological polarization. A wide range of interest groups, activist networks, and social movements have contributed to the realignment of the Republican and Democratic parties and the definition of their respective policy platforms, as each party came to be seen as the

---

[20] In fact, scanning the exhaustive index of their book, I found not a single reference to either "movements" or "social movements," to "activists" or "social activists."

primary representative of particular societal interests in the democratic arena (ibid., p. 16).

Social movements were active agents in democracy's demise in Italy in 1922. Had the Catholic movement looked beyond its goal of establishing a clerical beachhead in the state and had the Socialists worried more about preserving democracy than fighting off the insurgents to their Left, they might have united to defend the country's infant democracy from assault. It was neither the electorate nor the political parties but the subcultures consisting of unions, leagues, cooperatives, chambers of labor, churches, and Catholic Action sections that built and maintained the polarized subcultures that undermined Italian democracy and opened the space for a movement in the shape of a party to destroy it (Ben-Ghiat 2020).

How does the Italian case of a century ago help us to understand America's dilemma today? While the Democratic party developed as a collection of interest groups, the Tea Party movement "stitched together" diverse currents on the right flank of the Republican Party, "combining grass-roots mobilization with elite financial and organizational support from free market think tanks and advocacy networks" (Mettler & Lieberman, p. 16). These features were transferred out of whole cloth into the Republican Party. The result was that the GOP emerged as an ideologically fused and politically brittle party.

We saw this ideological brittleness in the aftermath of the 2020 election, when many Republicans continued to maintain, against all evidence, that the election had been rigged and demanded that Donald Trump should have a second term as president. Not even the invasion of Congress at the hands of a mob could shake them from their Trumpite fealty, as the majority of Republican members of the House returned to the floor to support "objections" to the certification of Biden's election. The Republicans had become a "movementized" party, one that will pay a price for its rigidity in the years to come. That may help the new Democratic majority in the short run, but the lack of a sane and settled center-right party cannot be good for American democracy.

Pactmaking: A Lesson About Bipartisanship

The second lesson that we can glean from our comparisons is that buying political peace at the cost of compromising principles is never a permanent solution to polarization. In Chile – as in other parts of Latin America – buying into the "Washington Consensus" produced deepened inequality and a continent-wide wave of social protest (Walton & Seddon 1994). The inequality brought on by the neoliberal turn was reinforced in Chile by the fact that it was adopted by a brutal dictatorship. But as we have seen, Chileans could not avoid the debt crisis that followed, which led to a wave of social protest on the part of, first, workers and then other groups that had suffered growing inequality under the dictatorship. That movement eventually forced the dictatorship to reverse course and allow a plebiscite that restored democracy in 1990.

But as we have seen, that democratic transition was a "pacted" one in which the social movements that had forced the regime to retreat were effectively suppressed by the parties that came to power in 1990. In fear of a reactionary resurgence, they opened breaches in the new regime for the conservative forces that had emerged from the dictatorship. Politics in post-dictatorship Chile was formally representative, but the country was actually run through informal institutions that allowed representatives of the old regime a quasi-veto over social and economic reform (Siavelis 2016), leaving civil society in the shadows. This *democracia de los acuerdos* assured a place for veto players in decision making – including the military, parties of the right, the business community, and large economic actors (ibid., p. 72). This protected social peace – as long as it lasted – but it left masses of the public effectively unrepresented, despite the fact that GDP per capita was increasing.

The United States is anything but a "pacted democracy." But with its soaring degree of inequality – especially in social provision – it is the Chile of the northern hemisphere. The wealth gap between rich and poor in the United States is the highest of any OECD nation,[21] and this before we include in the calculation the starved public sector under a succession of administrations that reduced social spending and deregulated the economy. While overall growth increased following the recession of 2007–8, its benefits have been skewed toward upper-income groups, and the size of the middle class has declined from 61 percent of the population in 1971 to 51 percent in 2019.[22]

Of course, rising inequality in the United States is not due to anything like the explicit "pact" that bound Chilean democracy to the social and economic policies inherited from the dictatorship. As Mettler and Lieberman point out, a great deal of the rising economic inequality in the United States is due to what might be called "sins of omission" (2020: 230). But there have also been "sins of commission" in the form of policies that benefit the rich and powerful business interests, like the dramatic reduction of the top marginal tax rate, the tax advantages for home purchasers, and the relaxation of the regulations on business since the Reagan administration.

These actions and inactions on behalf of a tiny sliver of the population "beg for an explanation." Mettler and Lieberman find it in the growth of the successful mobilization of the wealthiest Americans and major businesses over the past few decades (pp. 231–33). Part of the reason for this has been the increased amount of money in politics, especially since the Supreme Court's *Citizen's United* decision in 2010, but "the affluent have also grown more involved in highly visible politics, particularly through strategic political organizing" (p. 232). As I tried to show in Chapter 7, this was not simply an updating of the well-worn practices of lobbying but the adoption of methods of

---

[21] www.pewresearch.org/fact-tank/2020/02/07/6-facts-about-economic-inequality-in-the-u-s
[22] www.pewsocialtrends.org/2020/01/09/trends-in-income-and-wealth-inequality

political movement building updated to take advantage of modern organizing tools and links between national funders and their state and local acolytes.

We saw the success of this model of "vertical hybridity" in the network of organizations created by Charles and David Koch across the country (Skocpol & Hertel-Fernandez 2016). Back in the 1970s, Charles Koch saw himself as the progenitor of a movement – granted, an elite one with a high degree of ideological coherence and consistency. But, fortified with an extreme libertarian ideology and the support of an intellectual brain trust (MacLean 2017), the brothers built a movement that rose as the party system was being hollowed out. "Only with a movement," Koch declared, "can we build an effective force for social change."[23] It was its movement-like character and its adoption of the classical methods of extreme left movements that gave the Koch network its ability to reach into the Republican Party, ensuring that its interests would be protected.

Putting Democracy First

Although Italy's early experience with democracy was stillborn because movements and parties could not cooperate in its defense and Chilean democracy was hamstrung through the efforts of the parties of the *Concertación* to keep social movements at bay, our third case – South Korea – showed what can be accomplished by movements and parties through what Donatella della Porta calls "contentious democratization" (2016). In his book *Democratic Practice* (2019), Robert Fishman showed why Spain and Portugal – two countries that experienced democratic transitions on the same peninsula and at about the same time – varied so greatly in the inclusion of the economically underprivileged within the circles of the political community. In his research on both countries, Fishman showed how deeply democratic inclusion was shaped by the patterns of party/movement interaction – the first through a pacted democratization and the second through a contentious democratization.

In our brief examination of South Korea, we saw something very much like the Portuguese case that Fishman describes. We saw movements and parties forming recurring coalitions that resulted, first, in the democratic breakthrough in 1987 and then in a more "institutionalized" form of coalition building in the following decades (Kim 2018). Central to both phases of coalition building was the underlying master frame of construction and defense of democracy that these movement/party coalitions adopted.

Although most Americans value democracy in the abstract (Mettler & Lieberman 2020: 254), we have not always behaved in ways that would advance it. Leaving aside the downright antidemocratic movements that we have encountered in this book, Americans have often shown a willingness to

---

[23] Charles Koch, "The Business Community: Resisting Regulation." www.libertarianism.org/pub-lications/essays/business-community-resisting-regulation

place policy advantages ahead of the defense of democracy. Particularly in a period of deep polarization, in which a profoundly antidemocratic movement came close to seizing and solidifying power in the country, policy proposals and partisan differences need to be judged in the light of their impact on democracy. As Mettler and Lieberman conclude after their extended analysis of the threats to American democracy:

Any proposal or political choice needs to be evaluated in terms of whether it will diminish democracy or strengthen it .... We cannot take it for granted that democratic politics will endure if we do not pay careful attention to the democracy-enhancing (or democracy-eroding) consequences of the things we do in politics. (2020: 256)

What do these three stories tell us about the links between movements and parties during democratic crises? The Italian parties in 1922 were so tightly mortgaged to their social bases that they allowed a movement adventurer to seize power. Conversely, in 1987, South Korean movements and parties joined in a democracy coalition that defeated authoritarianism. In Chile in 2021, an imperfect "pacted democracy" was dislodged by a movement that achieved a constitutional convention which promises full democracy.

Where does the United States fit on this spectrum of movement/party interactions in democratic crises? The insurrection of January 6th – like the Italian one of 1922 – was effected by an antidemocratic movement in thrall to a charismatic demagogue. It was defeated but in its wake, parties and movements lack the unity of the Korean coalition for democracy. As this book goes to press, the Republican Party is still mortgaged to the Trumpist movement but a multiracial coalition for democracy may be taking shape. This takes us to our final considerations, on the relations between movements and parties in the future of American democracy.

Conclusions

In Chapter 9, I argued that once we shed the myth of American exceptionalism, we can see that the United States is marked by parallels with a variety of democratic experiences; with the "pernicious polarization" of post–World War I Italy; with the struggle to consolidate democracy amid deep inequality in Chile; and with the formation of a coalition for democracy in South Korea. In this final section, I will argue that the future of democracy in the United States will turn in many respects on how movements and parties navigate the shoals of a deep democratic crisis.

On January 15, 2021, a week and a half after the infamous invasion of the US Capitol, the *New York Times* published two front-page articles side by side. In the first, two of the *Times'* most experienced Capitol-watchers reported that Senator Mitch McConnell, the Senate's Republican majority leader, was reported telling advisers he believed that the Democrats' drive to impeach President Trump could help his party "purge itself" of Donald Trump and give it a chance to retake control of the Senate in 2022.[1] In the second, two other reporters surveyed Republican state and local leaders, like the chairman of the party in Nye County, Nevada, who posted a letter on the local committee website accusing Vice President Mike Pence of treason and calling the rioting in Washington "a staged event meant to blame Trump supporters."[2] Which was the real GOP: the senatorial leaders in Washington or the state and local officials in the same party?

---

[1] Nicolas Fandos and Cate Edmondson, "Parties Debate Where to Stand at Senate Trial," *New York Times*, January 15, 2021, p. 1. www.nytimes.com/2021/01/14/us/politics/impeachment-senate-trial-trump.html

[2] Lisa Lerer and Reid J. Epstein, "Beyond Washington, a GOP Totally Realigned," *New York Times*, January 15, 2021, p. A1. www.nytimes.com/2021/01/14/us/politics/trump-republicans.htm

I think that is the wrong question. Throughout this book, I have argued that the last half-century of American political development has seen the Republican Party, infused with the energies of the New Right and Christian conservatives and the ruthless untruth telling of such leaders as Paul Viguerie and Cliff White, becoming partly "movementized" – especially at the grassroots. The differences revealed in the two articles cited from the *Times* was an expression of that dichotomy. While the party at the summit has been hollowed out, its lieutenants and drill sergeants at its base are connected to the archipelago of white nationalists, evangelical Christians, and anti-black and anti-Semitic groups across the country that erupted at the Capitol a week earlier. As the chair of an Oklahoma County Republican committee asked just hours before the Capitol was invaded: "What the crap do you think the American Revolution was? A game of friggin' pattycake?"[3] While McConnell's was a typical expression of inside-the-beltway transactional politics, the rage coming from the Republican grassroots was archetypical of the ideological politics of a social movement. The fact that both came from within the same political family tells us much about the imbrication of party and movement politics in America today.

There is too much to be learned from more than 150 years of party/movement relations to be neatly encapsulated in a single moment of political conflict. Without pretending to either great depth or completeness, several main themes emerge from the episodes I have examined.

First, as the story suggests, if it was ever helpful to neatly divide political participation into the "articulation" and the "aggregation" of interests, it no longer is today. Movement politics were never entirely separate from party politics (remember the intersection of abolitionism and the Republicans in Chapter 2), but a series of historical processes have brought movements within the gates of institutional politics (Tarrow 2012) and affected parties to the extent that we find them increasingly engaged in movement politics (Borbath & Hutter 2020).

Second, political scientists and sociologists have written a great deal about "cycles of contention"[4] and, more broadly, about "critical junctures."[5] What is interesting about both of these literatures is that although parties and movements have left their footprints on most of these periods, we lack an overall picture of the interaction of these collective actors in their dynamics. Of course, movements and parties often arise at the start of such periods and decline or become institutionalized when they subside. Abolitionism and the agrarian movement are outstanding examples of the cyclical logic of movements

---

[3] Lerer and Epstein, cited in note no. 2.
[4] See Koopmans 2004; Mueller 1999, and Tarrow 2011 for empirical studies of cycles of contention.
[5] The critical junctures literature is effectively synthesized by David Collier & Gerardo Munck in their edited book Critical Junctures and Historical Legacies: Insights and Methods for Comparative Social Science, Rowman and Littlefield, 2022.

and parties in critical junctures. But even more striking was the role of long movements in these periods of change – that is, movements that arise long before the beginning of such periods and often endure long afterward.

Think of the women's suffrage movement, which we studied in Chapter 4: It had its roots in abolitionism and in temperance in the nineteenth century, rose to a peak in the years surrounding World War I, and went into "abeyance" in the following years but gave rise to a broader women's movement in subsequent decades. Or consider civil rights; it rose out of the campaign to stamp out lynching early in the twentieth century, struggled in the following decades to use the courts and party system to gain leverage for its claims, and only came into prominence in the mid-1950s and 1960s. Finally, think of the conservative movements we examined in Chapter 6: The "long new right" grew up over a thirty-year period and drew on diverse constituencies, but it came together in the Republican Party from which it has not strayed since.

Third, from the occasional encounter between movements and parties that we found in the nineteenth century, movement/party interactions became more routine in the decades that followed and have become fairly constant in recent years. When "political" abolitionists entered the Republican Party and cooperated with both President Lincoln and with "outsider" abolitionists, there was not even a language to describe that encounter in American political discourse. And when the agrarian movement/Populist Party "fused" with the Democrats in the 1896 election, observers saw it as no more than the common practice of politicians in the "party period" to bob and weave for short-term political advantage. Not even the suffrage movement's relations to the party system were well understood until recent analysts began to delve into its relations to parties at the state and local levels (see Teele 2018a and b).

It was only with the New Deal Democrats' interactions with the labor and civil rights movements that a true "anchoring" between parties and movements could be observed – the former decisive and immediate, the latter halting and drawn-out. The labor/Democratic alliance never flagged but with the decline of unionization and the thrust of an employer counteroffensive after World War II, it became less central to the party's coalition and, in fact, began to shed working-class votes to the Republicans. The civil rights/Democratic alliance was held back by racial animus until the 1960s, when the strength of civil rights protest pushed presidents Kennedy and Johnson to come down heavily on the side of the movement and has become a keystone of the party in recent decades.

A very different kind of anchoring emerged in the post-1964 fusion of the New Right and Christian conservatives with the Republicans, producing a party that was both sociologically narrow and ideologically structured. This – plus a new tone of belligerence and ruthlessness – prepared the way for the emergence of the Tea Party/Republican fusion in the 2010s and, ultimately, for the success of Donald Trump in capturing the party's leadership. Whether Trump's departure from the White House (but perhaps not from the political scene?) will draw his conservative followers out of the core of the party remains to be seen.

Fourth, as the ties between movements and parties were becoming more routine, the party system was hollowing out – in part as the result of structural trends common to all advanced democracies and in part through institutional shifts. At the same time, the partisan use of the executive by successive presidents has reduced the importance of parties as institutions even as the electorate and Congress were becoming more polarized (King & Milkis 2021). This hollowing-out process – added to the new forms of organization and funding available to interest groups – created space for hybrid forms of organization, like those we examined in Chapter 7, to take over an important part of parties' previous functions and importance. Since the 1960s, as we saw in the last two chapters, classical social movements have had to share the stage with new entrants – nonprofit organizations, politically savvy outsider groups, and deep-pocketed "policy demanders." Movement repertoires expanded into a surprising variety of forms, some familiar from the American past and others arising only in recent decades. The most remarkable was the so-called Koch network, which followed a classical Leninist logic of creating a battery of organizations, socializing a generation of activists, and supporting causes that went beyond electoral mobilization.

Finally, as movement/party ties were becoming more routine and more widely diffused, activists were learning how to use the repertoire of contention in new and disconcerting ways. Some movements – like Mothers Against Drunk Driving – were completely conventional (McCarthy & Wolfson 1992) while others – like the Occupy movement – literally refused to leave the streets. Between the two extremes, a number of movements combined conventional and contentious performances into "formative movements" as the civil rights movement had done a half-century before. Some of these movements attempted to promote their claims through the new affordances of the Internet and social media, but the most successful among them combined online and offline ways of connecting to supporters and expanding their reach (Bennett & Segerberg 2013; Schradie 2019; Tufekci 2017).

Lurking behind this telescopic survey of party/movement relations – but ultimately central to all of them – is the question of their impact on democracy. Those who believe, with Martin Luther King Jr. and Barack Obama, that the "arc of history bends towards justice" can cite the Civil War and Reconstruction, the passage of the Nineteenth Amendment, the New Deal, and the Great Society as evidence that movement/party relations led to democracy's expansion. This resonates with Charles Tilly's (2007) argument that social movements are an integral part of democratic transitions and with Donatella della Porta's claim (2020) that movements can save democracy today.

But skeptics can point to the opposite process, from the rollback of Reconstruction in the 1870s to the revival of the Klan at the turn of the century, to demagogues like Huey Long and Father Coughlin in the 1930s, and to the recrudescence of white supremacy during the Trump administration as examples of antidemocratic movements that have fought against hard-won rights. Theorists like Rogers Smith have argued that the American "liberal tradition" has had a counterpart in the illiberal tradition of racist and exclusionary politics since the founding (2010). And in his magisterial *Two Faces of American Freedom* (2010), constitutional expert Aziz Rana points out that although America is a republic, it was founded and remained a *settler's republic*.

I WHAT HAVE WE LEARNED?

Beneath these sweeping generalizations, what have we learned more specifically about the relations between movements and parties in the course of this book? First, that these interactions are deeply shaped by institutions; second, that they are both short- and long-term – with very different consequences; and third, that they frequently take the form of movement/countermovement interactions. Though all three of these findings are threaded through all of the chapters in the book, it will be worth citing particular examples to bring home their importance to American political development.

Movements, Parties, and Institutions

The movements we have examined in this book had very different relations to institutions. To some extent, these movements were formed by institutions; less frequently, their actions reshaped how institutions functioned. "Institutional movements" (see Figure 1.1) were by definition constrained by institutions. The women's suffrage movement was wedded to the ballot box from the beginning, despite the disinclination of women activists to get involved in politics. But the civil rights movement combined institutional with noninstitutional politics. Some movements, during some periods, avoided entanglement with parties, like the AFL under Gompers, which developed a species of "business unionism." In contrast, the newly born CIO was political from the first moment, forcing its more staid elder brother to engage in politics as well.

Federalism shaped many of the interactions we examined. For example, one-party rule in the South supplied white segregationists with a territorial authoritarian bulwark, but federalism also gave suffragists political leverage in western states where party organizations were weak and party competition provided them with openings for influence. Federalism also gave southern segregationists the constitutional argument of "states' rights" to use in opposing desegregation and voting rights for blacks. It was only by escaping the stranglehold of Jim Crow in the great migration that African Americans could become a significant voting bloc in the cities of the North.

Social movements have exercised choice in the institutions they confronted. When one institutional channel failed to work in a movement's favor, it could shift to another – as the temperance movement did in the nineteenth century when it shifted its focus from the state to the federal level and succeeded in gaining passage of the Eighteenth Amendment (Szymanski 2003). After being treated with indifference by Congress and the parties for almost a century, African Americans turned to the courts, but finding that court decisions were inadequate to solve their problems, they turned to a strategy that combined institutional and contentious actions.

Changes in institutional structure have crucially affected the strength and the direction of movement/party relations. We have seen how the universal adoption of the direct primary gave greater influence over nominations to grassroots activists, while campaign finance reform afforded greater influence to moneyed interests through PACs and newer hybrid organizations. Both innovations were adopted by party leaders with the stated goal of opening their parties to ordinary citizens, but in their implementation, both eased the entry of movement activists into the grassroots of weakened party organizations.

The institutional shift that had the greatest influence on both parties and movements was the expansion of the administrative state. As Desmond King and Sidney Milkis write, "Partisanship in the United States is no longer a struggle over the size of the State. It is an executive-centered struggle for the services of national administrative power." Despite rhetorical appeals to "limited government," since the late 1960s conservatives have sought to deploy state power as ardently as liberals did in the New Deal and the Great Society (King & Milkis 2021). The most obvious result was the shift in partisan conflict from parties to the executive, but it also shifted the focus of social movements from the legislature to the administration. One notable result was to increase the presence of movement activists within the administration, which both tempered how agencies operated and gave their movements allies inside the state (Lieberman 2005).

Short- and Long-Term Interactions

Many of the changes in movement/party relations we have examined took place over the short term – that is, they depended on the challenges and incentives posed by particular crises, on the availability of allies and ferocity of enemies, and on whether parties needed their support or could afford to keep them at a distance. But movements often influence the party system over the long term, for example, by creating or amplifying political identities that parties ignore at their peril. For example, when the Democrats reluctantly embraced women's suffrage under Woodrow Wilson, the Republicans had to follow suit despite the fact that many of their wealthy donors and their wives opposed votes for women. The slow and steady entry of African Americans into the Democratic party was not due to FDR's conversion to racial justice but because Democrats in northern cities and states recognized the growing importance of the black vote. Finally, although Ronald Reagan was basically an economic conservative and had no known religious fealty, he ushered Christian conservatives into the Republican Party.

The process began during the New Deal with union activists' relationship to the Democratic Party in the 1930s. Though they had previously engaged with party elites only at the state and local levels, during the Great Depression union officials turned to the national-level Democratic Party with the assist of legislative innovations like the Wagner Act and the creation of the first political action groups. In the earlier period, movements were generally lodged at the local level, which made it challenging for them to operate in national politics, as we saw in the inability of the farmers' movement to gain traction for their subtreasury plan. In more recent periods, even movements that were embedded at the state and local level – like the women's movement – created national organizations, like NOW, which took their claims to the national legislature and executive (Costain 1992). In contrast to the mass membership movements of the past, most of which grew out of the grassroots, many new movements were born nationally and failed to sink deep roots (Skocpol 2003).

Because civil rights has been such a "long movement," its connections to the party system have been more varied than that of most other movements. Beginning with their electoral ties to the Republicans, African American activists were held at arms' length by the Democrats for decades because of that party's unwillingness to risk losing the votes of white voters in the South. It was only after the Great Migration to the North, the uprooting of World War II, and the pressure of the Cold War that Democrats like Harry Truman came to recognize the electoral benefits to his party of African American votes. It was only when they faced the determined militancy of the "new" civil rights movement and the virulent reaction to it of southern segregationists, an enduring bridge was built between that party and the civil rights movement.

As we saw in Chapter 5, the juncture between civil rights and the Democrats was neither painless nor immediate. President Lyndon Johnson, who probably did more than any other president to expand citizen rights to African Americans, resisted the representation of black voters at his party's 1964 and 1968 conventions. It was the pressure of the direct action of black activists and their allies that forced Democratic leaders to fully integrate their party. But by that time, a younger, more militant branch of the movement arose, holding off black/white political entente in the movement sector for a generation.

The most complete linkage of a movement to a party – less an "anchoring" than a "merger" – was the insertion of the "long new right" into the Republican Party after the Goldwater defeat in 1964. While the Democrats were building a coalition of interest groups, Republicans fought off their minority status by bringing a sequence of determined conservative groups into the heart of the party. The fusion of these groups' ideology with traditional business-oriented small government thinking transformed the party into one that was increasingly guided by an ideological mission while the Democrats expanded their coalition by the accretion of a series of different interest groups.

Movement-Countermovement Interactions

A repeated finding of the book was how often movements made their own opposition. Beginning with the rise of anti-black vigilantism during Reconstruction to the triggering of an anti-women's suffrage opposition movement, to the growth of both legal and violent opposition to desegregation, to the success of the STOP ERA campaign, movement/countermovement interaction was one of the spurs to social change but also one of the threats to democratization.

David S. Meyer and Suzanne Staggenborg list three conditions that promote the rise of countermovements (1996): first, that the movement [it opposes] shows signs of success; second, that the interests of some populations are threatened by movement goals; and third, that political allies are available to aid countermovement mobilization.

All three of these factors combined in the countermovement of the Ku Klux Klan against African American rights during Reconstruction. That movement took mainly violent form during Reconstruction, but after the electoral deal of 1876, white rule was reinstituted by increasingly lily-white state legislatures, which passed a plethora of legal and semi-legal regulations designed to keep African Americans from the voting booth. Though fulminating about the denial to blacks of the Reconstruction amendments, Republicans discovered that they could assure their electoral future through a Northern/Western coalition of white voters in the name of ascendant capitalism.

The women's suffrage movement also triggered the organization of a countermovement in the form of the NAOWS. In the South, these women were worried that votes for women would disrupt a social order based on white supremacy, while in the North they were mainly the daughters or wives of wealthy businessmen who were convinced that giving women the vote would lead them to shed womanly properties and lead to unwelcome social legislation. That the NAOWS was a true countermovement was indicated by the fact that it was strongest where the suffrage cause was strong, for example, in Massachusetts and New York City. Women who opposed votes for women emphasized the dirtiness of politics and the wish to keep women in the home, where their purity would be unsullied by contact with machine politicians.

In the 1950s and 1960s, segregationists responded to court decisions on desegregation and to efforts to implement African American voting rights by creating new institutions, like the white Citizens' Councils, and with a resurgence of Klan violence. In the summer of 1964, when the bodies of three SNCC poll workers were discovered in an earthen dam in rural Mississippi, outrage over the atrocity helped to bolster northern support for the Civil Rights Act, which was passed by Congress in the same year. More consequential than the Klan were the Citizens' Councils that first grew up in the Deep South and diffused throughout the region. Although the Councils insisted on their legal vocation, they advanced polarization by putting pressure on moderate and integrationist groups and enforcing economic pressure against whites considered traitorous to southern values.

Perhaps the most successful countermovement in modern American history was the campaign of Phyllis Schlafly and the "STOP-ERA" movement she founded against the ERA, which was the most organic reform effort of the women's movement of the 1960s and 1970s. Combining the tried-and-true methods learned in her anti-Communist past with the support of religious groups, Schlafly turned back a near-successful state ratification process that put equal rights for women on the back burner for decades. When an anti-ERA plank was added to the platform of the Republican Party in the 1980 election, Schlafly's movement blended into the Republican Party politics out of which she had emerged. Schlafly herself was a true movement/party hybrid figure.

The most recent example of movement/countermovement interaction came with the Resistance to Donald Trump. In this period, we find evidence of all three of Meyer and Staggenborg's conditions for the formation of a countermovement. Trump's electoral success was a triumph for the movement he had stimulated, followed by Republican successes in a number of by-elections that followed. During his first two years in office, Trump threatened the interests and values of vast sectors of the American population, from African Americans to Latinos, women, businesses dependent on foreign trade agreements, and the LGBTQ community. Third, Trump's policy excesses and his outsized personality offered a focal point for various sectors of "The Resistance" to connect across racial and class lines. "Intersectional" alliances were already visible in the various marches that Dana Fisher investigated in a series of onsite protester surveys in 2017, but they expanded after the killing of George Floyd in May 2020.

Was the anti-Trump Resistance a true "formative movement," exhibiting institutional, semi-institutional, and contentious features (Milkis & Tichenor 2019)? Most important for our purposes, although the leftist fringe of the movement disdained party politics, as the 2018 and 2020 elections approached, the movement merged with the Democratic Party's electoral efforts. As we saw, many of the people who participated in the Women's March in 2017 went on to enter the grassroots level of the Democratic Party (Putnam 2020a and b). The most obvious result was the "blue wave" of Democratic victories in the 2018 midterms and a surge in support for Joe Biden from women, younger voters, and African Americans in the presidential campaign of 2020. Less obvious was that the Resistance as such disappeared into the Democratic Party, much as the "horizontal" hybrid of the antiwar movement disappeared into that party after Obama took office in 2008 (see Chapter 7).

II   MECHANISMS OF MEDIATION AND CONFLICT

This book not only pinpointed the number of times that parties and movements have intersected; it also highlighted the different mechanisms that have driven these interactions. Some of these mechanisms were unidirectional (e.g., how movements affect parties and vice versa) but others were reciprocal. Some of these took place mainly in the electoral arena while others engaged parties and movements in the central state. Some mechanisms had immediate effect – like the impact of movements on elections – but the most substantial relationships effected change in institutions and, at the margins, the character of American political institutions.

The Impact of Movements on Elections

The impact of movements on elections has taken several forms. First, movements can lend their electoral weight to parties but they can also bring new policy perspectives to a party's platform, as the civil rights movement did in the Democratic conventions of 1964 and 1968. Movements can also insert new performances into electoral competition, as the Wide Awake movement did in the election campaign of 1860. Third, movements can add their organizational heft to an election campaign, as the gun-rights and evangelical movements did in Republican campaigns from 1980 onward. Most dramatically, movements can *become* parties, as political abolitionists did in the 1850s and the agrarian movement tried to do in the 1890s.

But turning a movement into a party entails risks. First, it forces ideologically inspired militants to make pragmatic adjustments; second, it increases conflict within the movement over how completely to adopt the practices of electoral democracy; and, most important, it opens the movement to the entry of new recruits whose electoral goals can shift the movement from its core convictions. We saw such a derailment in the Populist Party's attempt to fuse with the Democrats in the 1896 election, which led to its adoption of the free coinage of silver as its central policy plank and lost it the support of many western farmers.

Movements make three kinds of claims on authorities, all three of which are visible in elections – identity claims, standing claims, and program claims. Identity claims declare that a particular actor exists; standing claims say that that actor deserves the rights and the recognition of recognized categories; program claims call for authorities to respond to their needs in certain ways (Tilly & Tarrow 2015: 110–11). Wholehearted engagement in elections is likely to weaken identity claims, shift standing claims, and broaden program claims from the movement's core commitments to policy claims that are likely to gain them a broader consensus.

The abolitionist movement and the radical faction of the Republican Party made identity and standing claims on behalf of African Americans but failed to agree on a program for what would happen *after* the Civil War. That lack of clarity explains a lot of the failures of Reconstruction as well as the failure to forge a consensus about the desirability of black enfranchisement. The women's franchise movement had an agreed-upon programmatic goal based on the desire for women's standing as equal citizens but divided over standing and women's identity. The civil rights movement came closest to developing a clear set of program claims, but divided over standing and itendity. As the movement shifted from South to North, a new generation of activists put forward more radical programmatic claims and insisted on a more distinct racial identity that appeared to exclude sympathetic white activists. Finally, the Tea Party movement had two distinct programmatic foci, libertarian and social conservative, and a desire for greater standing in a society they saw leaving them behind (Parker & Barreto 2013).

The openness and closure of electoral opportunities: Parties both open and close opportunities for movements at election time depending on their electoral needs and calculations. Recall that while the Republicans at the end of the Civil War attempted to create a new constituency from among the freed slaves, after the contested election of 1876 they drifted away from their interracial commitments and became the representative of northern business and midwestern farmers. That strategic shift not only closed off electoral opportunities to the African American population of the South – leaving it prey to resurgent racism in the region – but eventually shifted the major cleavage line of party competition from regional to class conflict.

Parties manage campaigns that offer movements legitimate opportunities to mobilize their supporters and attract new ones, give them a chance to insert their issues into the electoral agenda, and urge them away from disruptive and toward more conventional activities. Movements that enter election campaigns enliven elections and increase turnout, but they also close off other avenues of participation that lack an obvious electoral advantage. An example was the split between "absolute" and "political" abolitionists in the 1840s and 1850s, which brought the latter into the new Republican Party and isolated the former. When the balance rule was broken in 1854, it shattered the unity of both Democrats and Whigs and led to a critical election that opened the door to the influence of the previously shunned abolitionists.

Taking advantage of electoral competition: Competition for votes affords movement activists new leverage in the political system. For example, the suffragists of the late nineteenth and early twentieth centuries despised party politics but were not adverse to taking advantage of the opportunities opened by elections – as they did when the western states extended the vote to women. It was the greater competitiveness of western party systems that allowed the movement to gain the vote in that region sooner than in either the machine-dominated North or in the one-party South (Teele 2018a and b). But after the amendment passed, women voters turned out to be just as split on other issues as their male counterparts and continued to divide between those – like Alice Paul and the National Women's Party – who wanted nothing less than equal rights for women and reformers who sought incremental reforms in the workplace and in the home. It was only in the 1930s that women reformers found a home in the Democratic Party.

Civil rights activists were also deeply affected by competition for votes. Long stymied by disenfranchisement in the South and by their stubborn loyalty to "the party of Lincoln," they turned to the Democrats in response to the promise of the New Deal's social programs. Although Roosevelt was worried about the loss of southern support in Congress if he showed too much interest in black rights, many New Dealers forged an alliance with the movement that ripened during the last part of the 1930s, went on hold during World War II, and was revived during the Cold War (Schickler 2016; Dudziak 2000).

Party strength and weakness: Although strong parties can remain indifferent to movements' claims, weakened ones offer openings for movement activists. The appeal of adding women as a new voting bloc attracted the Republicans in the early 1920s. Weakened by eight years of Democratic rule under Wilson, party leaders worried about the unknown effects of the women's vote. As a result, they supported reforms pushed by the women's lobby. However, as women turned out to be both divided and low-turnout voters, by the mid-1920s, the party felt itself strong enough to ignore women's issues. By the mid-1930s, the women's movement had largely given up on the GOP and began its historic shift to the Democrats.

During a second period of party weakness, culminating in the crushing Goldwater defeat in 1964, the Republican Party opened itself to the entry of a succession of insurgent groups, from the Young Republicans after the disastrous Goldwater campaign, to the Christian conservatives in the 1970s, and the Reaganites in 1980 (Perlstein 2009; 2020). Once inside that party, these insurgents turned it into a more ideological instrument, making it fair game for the Tea Party insurgency to come, one that was based on a combination of racial resentment, economic libertarianism, and evangelical ardor. Although it was the most dramatic of these incursions – at least in the short run – Trumpism was but the latest in the sequence of movements that transformed the Republican Party from within.

III RECIPROCAL CAUSATION

Most of the research on movements' engagement with parties and institutions has attempted to chart movement impacts on them. But taking a longer view, the shape of movements has been deeply influenced by their interactions with parties and institutions. As movements affected parties, so too did parties influence the repertoires, the forms of organization, and the future of movements. We saw this first in how the new Republican Party enveloped part of the abolitionist movement, turning it into a party faction that would largely disappear in the wake of the Civil War. We saw it again in the collapse of the agrarian movement when it had hitched its wagon to the Democratic Party in the 1896 presidential election. We saw it during the New Deal, in which the Democrats used legislation and the administrative state to weld the insurgent CIO to the party. We saw it again in the 1970s when the adoption of the direct primary turned activists toward electoral politics.

Goal Displacement and Institutionalization

If there is anything approaching a sociological law in the study of social movements it is that, as they grow and mature, their original ideological and programmatic goals are to a degree displaced. We owe the extreme version of this theory to Robert Michels, whose book, *Political Parties*, coined the term "the iron law of oligarchy" (1962). Michels thought of this law as "iron" because he only examined the internal life of parties and movements; however, once we see movements in their relations with other actors, it is possible to see variations in the "iron law." Later scholars, like Zald and Ash Garner (1987), softened the image to one of "goal displacement."

Elections are the most important mechanisms in leading to goal displacement. Where independent movements are most solidly guided by their ideological orientations, when they decide to compete in electoral contests they are more likely to be influenced by transactional exchanges with parties. We saw this in the adoption by the Populist Party of the issue of free silver when it discarded much of the farmer-based message that had grown out of the agrarian movement. We saw it again when civil rights activists in the 1960s trimmed their sails to work with President Johnson to implement the War on Poverty, leading many to enter electoral politics.

But neither goal displacement nor movement institutionalization is deterministic. After the passage of the Nineteenth Amendment, the National Women's Party retained its deeply held conviction that nothing less than an ERA would secure women's place in society while its competitors in the movement spread out in support of a plethora of more concrete policy goals. Similarly, so central did ending abortion become to the Republican Party's platform after the party absorbed the Christian right that the issue could not be discarded in the decades after the late 1970s.

The "anchoring" of parties to movements has effects on both partners. Like much else in contemporary American politics, the process can best be seen in the wake of the 1960s. As McAdam and Kloos argued in their book, *Deeply Divided*:

As the 1970s dawned, both parties were shifting to accommodate the mobilized movement wings at their respective margins. The Democrats were contending with the increasingly radical movements of the New Left, while the GOP moved right to court racial conservatives and other disaffected elements of the former New Deal coalition. (2014: 25–26)

The result was the passage of direct primary reforms – what Byron Shafer called "the greatest systematically planned ... shift in the institutions of delegate selection in all of American history" (1983: 4). Without intending to do so, it gave grassroots activists the power to contest the candidate choices of party regulars. "In short," conclude McAdam and Kloos, "while reformers had sought to democratize the nominating process, the resulting system has proven to be the perfect vehicle for empowering the movement wings of the two parties" (ibid., p. 28).

Polarization and Social Movements

No one who reflects on the Civil War or the partisan conflicts of the New Deal and the 1960s can believe that polarization is a new phenomenon in American politics. But the advent of the Tea Party after the election of the country's first African American president contributed deeply to the country's current polarization – for example, "sorting" constituents into white, Protestant communities that voted together against communities of more multiracial and multiethnic Democrats. As Thomas Mann and Norman Ornstein prophetically wrote in 2012:

The GOP has become an insurgent outlier in American politics. It is ideologically extreme; scornful of compromise; unmoved by conventional understanding of facts, evidence, and science; and dismissive of the legitimacy of its political opposition.[6]

Mann and Ornstein are correct, but what their analysis elides is that a social movement – the New Right, with its mélange of economic libertarianism, religious fervor, and racial resentment – was the relational mechanism[7] between the old and the new Republican Party. Movements, as I argued in Chapter 9, can bring together disparate threads of opinion into movements for democracy, but they can also exacerbate conflicts and lead to polarization. The fact that American polarization is "asymmetric"[8] – that is, it is more deeply embedded on the right than on the left – tells us that the effect of the integration of the New Right into the Republican Party was to make that party increasingly impenetrable to new voting blocs and to Democratic incursions.

Trumpism was in many ways the culmination of these trends. Combining populist rhetoric with plutocratic elements, Donald Trump quietly carried water to the mill of traditional business groups while his shrill rhetoric and his revanchist social policies catered to the claims of his populist base. In some ways, Trump was

---

[6] Thomas E. Mann and Norman J. Ornstein, "Let's Just Say It: The Republicans Are the Problem," *Washington Post*, April 27, 2012. www.brookings.edu/opinions/lets-just-say-it-the-republicans-are-the-problem

[7] On the differences between dispositional, environmental, and relational mechanisms, see McAdam et al. *Dynamics of Contention*, 2001, ch. 2.

[8] Of the many efforts to understand this phenomenon, the clearest and most revealing is Jacob Hacker's and Paul Pierson's "Confronting Asymmetric Polarization." In N. Persily (ed.). *Solutions to Political Polarization in America* (Cambridge: Cambridge University Press, 2015), ch. 3.

only enacting the changes that previous generations of activists had imprinted on the party: the ruthless pursuit of opponents; the denigration of minorities and immigrants that was symbolized in his insistence on the construction of a border wall; and the crass language and take-no-prisoners methods that we first saw in the New Right. But in his ability to animate a mass base behind his person and his policies, he forged a movement that might endure beyond his passage from the political scene. Trump resembled one of the historical "strongmen" we find in the history of Europe (Ben-Ghiat 2020) more than the movement conservatives who rebuilt the Republican Party.

The "new" Republican Party no longer looks anything like "the party of Lincoln" or the moderate-to-conservative party of the 1940s and 1950s. It has become a movement party with strong links to extra-party movement groups that are – as we saw in the invasion of the Capitol in January 2020 – a real threat to democracy. I will return to the reality of that threat and to the potential countermovement against it in the final section of this chapter.

AFTERWORD

If we have learned anything from our accounts of party/movement relations in the United States, it is that movements – and their relations to the party system – have been central to every episode of democratization and de-democratization in American history. Once triggered by contingent events and gaining a mass following, movements have a way of taking root, and this was as true of the democracy-enhancing as of the antidemocratic movements we encountered in this book.

We saw the first kind of implantation in Chapter 4 in the longest lasting "long movement" in American history – the women's movement – which had its roots in abolitionism and has endured for more than a century despite periods of abeyance and defeat (Rupp & Taylor 1987). We saw it again in Chapter 5 in the labor and civil rights movements, which arose to gain rights for workers and African Americans and became the most enduring "formative movement" in American history. We saw the implantation of antidemocratic movements in the durability of anti-black terrorism after the Civil War, in the brief efflorescence of Father Coughlin and Huey Long in the 1930s, and in the rise of the John Birch Society that cropped up again after World War II. We saw it, finally, in the implantation and takeover of the Republican Party by the Trumpist movement after 2016.

With more than one-third of the American electorate believing fervently in the Trumpist message in the elections of 2020,[9] is it likely that the movement he founded will disappear from the scene?

---

[9] A reported 62 percent of Republican voters polled in a Monmouth University poll in November 2019 said that they would support him "no matter what." https://thehill.com/

Of course, voters are one thing; movements are another. As we have seen in this book, social movements generally arise on the outskirts of voting blocs, not from within their centers. This is particularly worrying with respect to the Trump movement, whose racist and white nationalist fringes arose as their hero held the White House. We still lack definitive data on these networks (but see Jones et al. 2020; Parker 2021), but what is nearly certain is that even – or particularly – if the Republican Party moves back toward the center after its misadventure with Trumpism, polarization on the right is likely to take a movement form, and possibly a violent one.[10] Donald Trump may be gone, but Trump*ism* may be here for a long time to come.[11] The dilemma for the Republicans is that if they move back toward becoming a more "normal" conservative party, that move may trigger a movement-led shift to the extreme right within the Trumpian base.

We also lack information on the future of progressive activism after the election of a moderate Democrat like Joe Biden. The struggle to unseat Donald Trump brought many activists who came out of the Resistance into the fold of the Democratic Party. Where they will go without their anti-Trumpian focal point is not at all clear. Some will no doubt remain embedded in the Democratic Party, like the antiwar activists we met in Chapter 7; others will return to private life after the exhaustion of years of mobilization. But it is likely that at least some progressive activists will return to movement activity, if only as a countermovement to what is likely to be the raging militancy on the right. That does not augur well for reducing the polarization that first emerged from the movement sector and then became lodged in the socially sorted party system of the decade of the 2010s.

As we learned from both the Italian and the Korean cases in Chapter 9, much will depend on how the parties manage their relations with the movement sector. Pursuing their purely sectoral interests, as Italian Socialists and Catholics did after World War I, will almost certainly feed into continued polarization. However justified was the rage of the Black Lives Matter movement after repeated killings of African Americans over the previous years, unless it broadens into a multiracial movement for democracy, it is bound to feed the countermovement of white supremacists who despise it. Only if the diverse sectors of what was born as "The Resistance" in 2016

---

homenews/administration/469058-poll-62-of-trump-supporters-say-nothing-the-president-could-do-would

[10] For scholarly reflections on the future of the Republican Party after Trump, see Patterson 2020 and Lemann 2020. While Patterson sees two main possibilities – neo-Trumpism and a return to a traditional Republican synthesis – Lemann sees three, which he calls "Remnant" (e.g., Neo-Trumpism), "Restoration," and "Reversal" scenarios (pp. 60–64).

[11] This is what Geoffrey Kabaservice, whose work I drew upon in Chapter 6, suggested in a *post mortem* on the 2020 election. www.theguardian.com/commentisfree/2020/nov/08/donald-trump-trumpism-republicans-democrats?CMP=Share_iOSApp_Other

come together around a democracy-enhancing multiracial frame will Americans be able to reverse the polarization that tore the country apart during the Trump administration and led to the attempted coup and insurrection of January 6, 2021.

Is there hope for a democratic renaissance after the democratic reversals of the Trumpian interregnum?. As Lara Putnam writes, for most of the activists who entered party politics after forming the core of the anti-Trump resistance, their "little-d democratic commitments were as important as their capital-D Democratic alignment" (Putnam 2020: 179). There is also hope that – if only to position themselves electorally – the Republicans will tame the movement stalwarts at their base and become something like the normal conservative party that America needs to maintain a stable two-party system. This book shows that if – as Martin Luther King Jr. said – "the arc of the moral universe bends toward justice," it will be because movements and parties can cohere around a project of democratic resilience.

References

Abramowitz, A. (2017). "Taking Polarization to a New Level: Racial Resentment, Negative Partisanship and the Triumph of Trump." Presented to the Annual Meeting of the American Political Science Association. San Francisco, CA.

Ackerman, B. (1998). *We the People: Transformations.* Cambridge, MA: Harvard University Press.

Alberoni, F. (1984). *Movement and Institution.* New York: Columbia University Press.

Aldrich, J. H. (1995). *Why Parties? The Origin and Transformation of Party Politics in America.* Chicago: University of Chicago Press.

Ali, O. H. (2010). *In the Lion's Mouth: Black Populism in the New South, 1886–1900.* Jackson, MS: University Press of Mississippi.

Almeida, P. (2010). "Social Movement Partyism: Collective Action and Oppositional Political Parties in Latin America." In N. Van Dyke and H. J. McCammon (eds.). *Strategic Alliances: Coalition Building and Social Movements.* Minneapolis and St. Paul: University of Minnesota Press, ch. 8.

Almeida, P., and N. Van Dyke (2014). "Social Movement Partyism and the Tea Party's Rapid Mobilization." In N. Van Dyke and David S. Meyer (eds.). *Understanding the Tea Party Movement.* Burlington VT: Routledge, ch. 3.

Altman, D. , and R. Castiglioni (2018). "Chile: el fin de una época politica." In M. Alcántara, D. Buquet, and M. L. Tagin (eds.). *Elecciones y partidos en América Latina en el cambio de ciclo.* Madrid: Centro de Investigaciones Sociológicas, pp. 105–27.

Altschuler, G. C., and S. M. Blumin (2000). *Rude Republic: Americans and Their Politics in the Nineteenth Century.* Princeton NJ: Princeton University Press.

Altschuler, G. C., and S. M. Blumin (2009). *The GI Bill: A New Deal for Veterans.* New York: Oxford University Press.

Amenta, E. (2005). "Political Contexts, Challenger Strategies, and Mobilization: Explaining the Impact of the Townsend Plan." In D. Meyer, V. Jenness, and H. Ingram (eds.). *Routing the Opposition: Social Movements, Public Policy and Democracy.* Minneapolis, MN: University of Minnesota Press, ch. 1.

Amenta, E. (2006). *When Movements Matter: The Townsend Plan and the Rise of Social Security.* Princeton, NJ: Princeton University Press.

Amenta, E. , et al. (1994). "Stolen Thunder: Huey Long's 'Share Our Wealth.' Political Mediation and the Second New Deal." *American Sociological Review* 59: 678–702.

Amenta, E., et al. (1999). "The Strategies and Contexts of Social Protest: Political Mediation and the Impact of the Townsend Movement in California." *Mobilization* 4: 1–24.

Anbinder, T. (1992). *Nativism and Slavery: The Northern Know-Nothings and the Politics of the 1850s.* New York and Oxford: Oxford University Press.

Andersen, K. (1996). *After Suffrage: Women in Partisan and Electoral Politics before the New Deal.* Chicago and London: University of Chicago Press.

Andrews, K. T. (1997). "The Impacts of Social Movements on the Political Process: A Study of the Civil Rights Movement and Black Electoral Politics in Mississippi." *American Sociological Review* 62: 800–19.

Andrews, K. T, (2002). "Movement-Countermovement Dynamics and the Emergence of New Institutions: The Case of 'White Flight' Schools in Mississippi." *Social Forces* 80: 911–36.

Andrews, K. T., and M. Biggs (2006). "The Dynamics of Protest Diffusion: Movement Organizations, Social Networks, and News Media in the 1960 Sit-Ins." *American Sociological Review* 71: 752–77.

Andrews, K. T., and S. Gaby (2015). "Protest Episodes: Shifting Actors and Targets in Local Movements." In J. Jasper and B. King (eds.). *Protesters and Their Targets.* Philadelphia, PA: Temple University Press, ch. 5.

Andrews, K. T., and K. Jowers (2018). "Lawyers and Embedded Legal Activity in the Southern Civil Rights Movement." *Law and Policy* 18: 10–32.

Anria, S. (2019). *When Movements Become Parties: the Bolivian MAS in Comparative Perspective.* Cambridge and New York: Cambridge University Press.

Arendt, H. (1966). *The Origins of Totalitarianism.* New York: Harcourt, Brace and World.

Aytac, S. E. and S. C. Stokes (2019). *Why Bother? Rethinking Participation in Elections and Protests.* New York and Cambridge: Cambridge University Press.

Azari, J. (September 2018). "Weak Parties, Strong Partisanship." Presented to the Annual Meeting of the American Political Science Association. Boston, MA.

Bailey, M. A., J. Mummolo, and H. Noel. (2012). "Tea Party Influence: A Story of Activists and Elites." *American Politics Research* 40: 769–804.

Balogh, B. (2009). *A Government Out of Sight: The Mystery of National Authority in Nineteenth-Century America.* New York: Cambridge University Press.

Bateman, D. A. (2018). *Disenfranchising Democracy.* New York: Cambridge University Press.

Bawn, K., et al. (2012). "A Theory of Political Parties: Groups, Policy Demands and Nominations in American Politics." *Perspectives on Politics* 10: 571–97.

Beckwith, K. (2003). "The Gendering Ways of States: Women's Representation and State Reconfiguration in France, Great Britain, and the United States." In L. A. Banaszak, K. Beckwith, and D. Rucht (eds.). *Women's Movements Facing the Reconfigured State.* New York: Cambridge University Press: 169–202.

Beckwith, K. (2008). "Conclusion: Between Participation and Representation." In C. Wolbrecht, K. Beckwith, and L. Baldez (eds.). *Political Women and American Democracy.* New York and Cambridge: Cambridge University Press, ch. 12.

Ben-Ghiat, R. (2020). *Strongmen: Mussolini to the Present.* New York: W. W. Norton.

Bennett, W. L., T. E. Givens, and C. Breunig (2010). "Crossing Political Divides: Communication, Political Identification, and Protest Organization." In S. Walgrave and D. Rucht (eds.). *The World Says No to War: Demonstrations against the War in Iraq.* Minneapolis and St. Paul: University of Minnesota Press, ch. 11.

Bennett, W. L., and S. Livingston (2018). "The Disinformation Order: Disruptive Communication and the Decline of Democratic Institutions." *European Journal of Communication* 33: 122–39.

Bennett, W. L., and S. Livingston (eds.) (2020). *The Disinformation Age: Politics, Technology, and Disruptive Communication in the United States*. New York and Cambridge: Cambridge University Press.

Bennett, W. L., and A. Segerberg (2013). *The Logic of Connective Action*. New York: Cambridge University Press.

Bensel, R. F. (1990). *Yankee Leviathan. The Origins of Central Authority in America, 1859–1877*. New York and Cambridge: Cambridge University Press.

Bensel, R. F. (2008). *Passion and Preferences: William Jennings Bryan and the 1896 Democratic National Convention*. New York and Cambridge: Cambridge University Press.

Bermeo, N. (1997). "Myths of Moderation. Confrontation and Conflict during Democratic Transitions." *Comparative Politics* 27: 305–22.

Bernstein, P. (2006). *The First Waco Horror: The Lynching of Jesse Washington and the Rise of the NAACP*. College Station, TX: Texas A & M University Press.

Berry, M., and E. Chenoweth (2018). "Who Made the Women's March?" In D. S. Meyer and S. Tarrow (eds.). *The Resistance: The Dawn of the Anti-Trump Opposition Movement*. New York: Oxford University Press, ch. 3.

Bidegain, G. (2017). "From Cooperation to Confrontation: The Mapuche Movement and Its Political Impact, 1990–2014." In Sofia Donoso and Marisa von Bulow (eds.). *Social Movements in Chile: Organizations, Trajectories, and Poliltical Consequences*. New York: Palgrave Macmillan, ch. 4.

Biggs, M., and K. Andrews (2015). "Protest Campaigns and Movement Success: Disaggregating the U.S. South in the Early 1960s." *American Sociological Review* 80: 416–43.

Binder, S. (2017). "Polarized We Govern?" In Alan S. Gerber and Eric Schickler (eds.). *Partisanship and Governmental Performance*. New York and Cambridge: Cambridge University Press, ch. 9.

Blum, R. M. (2017). "What Donald Trump's Rhetoric Borrows from the Tea Party." *Vox*. www.vox.com/mischiefs-of-faction/2017/2/9/14552930/trump-tea-party-rhetoric-immigrants-liberal-media (accessed February 7, 2021)

Blum, R. M. (2020). *How the Tea Party Captured the GOP: Insurgent Factions in American Politics*. Chicago: University of Chicago Press.

Boczkowski, P. J., and Z. Papacharissi, (eds.) (2018). *Trump and the Media*. Cambridge and London: MIT Press.

Boix, C. (ed.) (2009). *Oxford Handbook of Comparative Politics*. Oxford and New York: Oxford University Press.

Borbath, E., and S. Hutter (2020). "Protesting Parties in Europe: A Comparative Assessment." *Party Politics* 26: 1–13.

Borneman, W. (2014). *Iron Horses: America's Race to Bring the Railroads West*. Boston MA: Little, Brown.

Branch, T. (1989). *Parting the Waters: America in the King Years*. New York: Simon and Schuster.

Breckinridge, S. P. (1933). "The Activities of Women outside the Home." *Recent Social Trends in the United States: Report of the President's Research Committee on Social Trends*. US Government. New York: McGraw Hill.

Bremer, B., S. Hutter, and H. Kriesi (2020). "Electoral Punishment and Protest Politics in Times of Crisis." In H. Kriesi, J. Lorenzini, B. Wuest, and S. Hausermann (eds.). *Contention in Times of Crisis: Recession and Political Protest in Thirty European Countries*. Cambridge and New York: Cambridge University Press, ch. 10.

Brink, W., and L. Harris (1963). *The Negro Revolution in America*. New York: Simon and Schuster.

Brooker, M. (2018). "Indivisible: Invigorating and Redirecting the Grassroots." In D. S. Meyer and S. Tarrow (eds.). *The Resistance: The Dawn of the Anti-Trump Opposition Movement*. New York: Oxford University Press, ch. 8.

Brooks, C. (2016). *Liberty Power: Antislavery Third Parties and the Transformation of American Politics*. Chicago: University of Chicago Press.

Bullock, C. E., and R. K. Gaddie (2014). *The Triumph of Voting Rights in the South*. Norman, OK: University of Oklahoma Press.

Bunce, V. (1995). "Should Transitologists Be Grounded?" *Slavic Review* 55: 111–27.

Burnham, W. D. (1970). *Critical Elections and the Mainsprings of American Politics*. New York: W.W. Norton.

Button, J. W. (1978). *Black Violence : Political Impact of the 1960s Riots*. Princeton, NJ: Princeton University Press.

Cain, B., J. Ferejonn, and M. Fiorina (1987). *The Personal Vote: Constituency Service and Electoral Independence*. Cambridge, MA: Harvard University Press.

Campbell, A., P. Converse, W. Miller, and D. E. Stokes (1960). *The American Voter*. New York: Wiley.

Cantrell, G. (2020). *The People's Revolt: Texas Populists and the Roots of American Liberalism*. New Haven CT: Yale University Press.

Caplan, R., and D. boyd (2018). "Who's Playing Who? Media Manipulation in an Era of Trump." In P. J. Boczkowski and Z. Papacharissi (eds.). *Trump and the Media*. Cambridge and London: MIT Press, ch. 7.

Carpenter, D., and C. D. Moore (2014). "When Canvassers Became Activists: Antislavery Petitioning and the Political Mobilization of American Women." *American Political Science Review* 108: 479–98.

Carson, C. (1981). *In Struggle: SNCC and the Black Awakening of the 1960s*. Cambridge, MA: Harvard University Press.

Catsam, D. (2009). *Freedom's Main Line: The Journey of Reconciliation and the Freedom Rides*. Lexington KY: University Press of Kentucky.

Cebul, B., L. Geismer, and M. B. Williams (eds.) (2019). *Shaped by the State: Towards a New Political History of the Twentieth Century*. Chicago: University of Chicago Press.

Cebul, B., and M. B. Williams (2019). "Really and Truly a Partnership: The New Deal's Associational State and the Making of Postwar Politics." In B. Cebul, L. Geismer, and M. B. Williams (eds.). *Shaped by the State: Toward a New Political History of the Twentieth Century*. Chicago: University of Chicago Press, ch. 3.

Chang, P. Y. (2015). *Protest Dialectics: State Repression and South Korea's Democracy Movement, 1970–1979*. Stanford CA: Stanford University Press.

Chang, P. Y., and K. Lee (in press). "The Structure of Protest Cycles: Inspiration and Bridging in South Korea's Democracy Movement." *Social Forces*.

Chang, P. Y., and G.-W. Shin (2011). "Institutionalization and Diffusion." In G.-W. Shin and P. Y. Chang (eds.). *South Korean Social Movements: From Democracy to Civil Society*. New York and London: Routledge, ch. 1.

Charnock, E. (2020). *The Rise of the Political Action Committees.* Oxford and New York: Oxford University Press.

Chenoweth, E. (2017). "Trends in Nonviolent Resistance and State Response: Is Violence toward Civilian-Based Movemetns on the Rise." *Global Responsibility to Protect* 9: 86–100.

Chenoweth, E., A. Choi-Fitzpatrick, J. Pressman, F. G. Santos, and J. Ulfelder (April 2020). "The Global Pandemic Has Spawned New Forms of Activism – And They Are Flourishing." *The Guardian.* www.global-pandemic-has-spawned-new-forms-of-activism-and-theyre-flourishing

Chenoweth, E., and J. Pressman (February 2017). "This Is What We Learned by Counting the Women's Marches." *The Monkey Cage.* www.washingtonpost.com /news/monkey-cage/wp/2017/02/07

Clemens, E. S. (1997). *The People's Lobby. Organizational Innovation and the Rise of Interest Group Politics in the United States, 1890–1925.* Chicago: University of Chicago Press.

Clemens, E. S. (2020). *Civic Gifts: Voluntarism and the Making of the American Nation-State.* Chicago: University of Chicago Press.

Clemens, E. S., and J. Cook (1999). "Politics and Institutionalism: Explaining Durability and Change." *Annual Review of Sociology* 25: 441–66.

Cohen, M., D. Karol, H. Noel, & J. Zaller (2008). *The Party Decides: Presidential Nominations before and after Reform.* Chicago: University of Chicago Press.

Colburn, D. R. (2001). "Running for Office: African American Mayors from 1967 to 1996." In D. Colburn and J. S. Adler (eds.). *African American Mayors: Race, Politics, and the American City.* Urbana: University of Illinois Press, ch. 1.

Collier, D., and R. Collier (1991). *Shaping the Political Arena: Critical Junctures, the Labor Movement, and Regime Dynamics in Latin America.* Princeton: Princeton University Press.

Collier, D., and G. Munck (eds.) (2017). "Symposium on Critical Junctures and Historical Legacies." *Qualitative and Multi-Method Research.* Washington DC: American Political Science Association.

Collier, D., and G. Munck (2022). *Critical Junctures and Historical Legacies: Insights and Tools for Comparative Social Science.* Lanham Md: Rowman and Littlefield.

Corder, J. K., and C. Wolbrecht (2016). *Counting Women's Ballots: Female Voters from Suffrage through the New Deal.* New York and Cambridge: Cambridge University Press.

Cortright, D. (1975). *Soldiers in Revolt: The American Military Today.* Garden City, NY: Anchor Press, Doubleday.

Cortright, D. (1993). *Peace Works: The Citizen's Role in Ending the Cold War.* Boulder, CO: Westview.

Cortright, D. (2008). "A Peaceful Superpower: The Movement against the War in Iraq." In S. Chiba and T. J. Schoenbaum (eds.). *The Peace Movement and Pacifism after September 11.* Cheltenham England: Edward Elgar, 201–26.

Costain, A. (1992). *Inviting Women's Rebellion: A Political Process Interpretation of the Women's Movement.* Baltimore: Johns Hopkins University Press.

Cott, N. (1977). *The Bonds of Womanhood.* New Haven: Yale University Press.

Cowie, J. R. (2010). *Stayin' Alive: The 1970s and the Last Days of the Working Class.* New York: The New Press.

Cowie, J. R. (2016). *The Great Exception: The New Deal and the Limits of American Politics.* Princeton, NJ: Princeton University Press.

Crawford, A. P. (1981). *Thunder on the Right*. New York: Pantheon.

Cross, W. (1950). *The Burned-Over District: The Social and Intellectual History of Enthusiastic Religion in Western New York, 1800–1850*. Ithaca and London: Cornell University Press.

Cumings, B. E. (1997). *Korea's Place in the Sun: A Modern History*. New York: Norton.

de Felice, R. (2005). *Mussolini giornalista*. Milan: Rizzoli.

della Porta, D. (2016). *Where Did The Revolution Go?* New York and Cambridge: Cambridge University Press.

della Porta, D. (2020). *How Social Movements Can Save Democracy: Democratic Innovations from Below*. Cambridge: Polity.

della Porta, D., J. Fernandez, J. H. Kourki, and L. Mosca (eds.) (2017). *Movement Parties Against Austerity*. Cambridge: Polity.

della Porta, D., and M. Diani (2006). *Social Movements: An Introduction*, 2nd ed. Malden, MA, and Oxford: Blackwell's.

della Porta, D., and S. Tarrow (1986). "Unwanted Children: Political Violence and the Cycle of Protest in Italy." *European Journal of Political Research* 14: 607–32.

di Paola, P. (2009). "Biennio Rosso (1919–20)." *International Encyclopedia of Revolution and Protest*, Vol II. London: Blackwell's.

Diani, M. (2015). *The Cement of Civil Society: Studying Networks in Societies*. New York and Cambridge: Cambridge University Press.

Diani, M., and D. McAdam (eds.) (2003). *Social Movements and Networks: Relational Approaches to Collective Action*. Oxford and New York: Oxford University.

Dittmer, J., G. C. Wright, C. Dulaney, and W. Marvin (eds.) (1993). *Mississippi Movement: Essays on the American Civil Rights Movement*. College Station, TX: Texas A&M University Press.

Donaldson, G. A. (1993). "Who Wrote the Clifford Memo? The Origins of Campaign Strategy in the Truman Administration." *Presidential Studies Quarterly* 23: 747–54.

Donoso, S. (2017). "Outsider and Insider Strategies: Chile's Student Movement, 1990–2014." In S. Donoso and M. von Bulow (eds.). *Social Movements in Chile: Organizations, Trajectories, and Political Consequences*. New York: Palgrave-Macmillan, ch 4.

Donoso, S., and M. von Bulow (eds.) (2017). *Social Movements in Chile: Organizations, Trajectories, and Political Consequences*. New York: Palgrave Macmillan.

Dorf, M. C., and M. S. Chu (2018). "Lawyers as Activists: From the Airport to the Courtroom." In D. S. Meyer and S. Tarrow (eds). *The Resistance: The Dawn of the Anti-Trump Opposition Movement*. New York and Oxford: Oxford University Press, ch. 6.

Downs, A. (1957). *An Economic Theory of Democracy*. New York: Harper.

Du Bois, W. E. B. (1935). *Black Reconstruction in America: An Essay Toward a History of the Part Which Black Folk Played in the Attempt to Reconstruct Democracy in America, 1860–1880*. New York: Harcourt, Brace.

Du Bois, W. E. B. (2005). *The Illustrated Souls of Black Folk*. Boulder and London: Paradigm Publishers.

Dudziak, M. L. (2000). *Cold War Civil Rights*. Princeton NJ: Princeton University Press.

Dudziak, M. L. (ed.) (2003). *September 11 in History*. Durham, NC: Duke University Press.

Earl, J., and K. Kimport (2011). *Digitally Enabled Social Change*. Cambridge and London: MIT Press.

Edwards, G. S., and S. Rushin (2019). "The Effect of President Trump's Election on Hate Crimes." https://ssrn.com/abstract=3102652

Eisgruber, C. L. (2009). "The Story of Dred Scott: Originalism's Forgotten Past." In M. C. Drof (ed.). *Constitutional Law Stories*, 2nd ed. New York: Foundation Press, ch. 5.

Evans, S. M. (1980). *Personal Politics: The Roots of Women's Liberation in the Civil Rights Movement and the New Left*. New York: Vintage Books.

Everson, D. H. (1982). "The Decline of Political Parties." *Proceedings of the American Academy of Political Science* 34: 49–60.

Farneti, P. (1978). "Social Conflict, Parliamentary Fragmentation, Institutional Shift, and the Rise of Fascist Italy." In J. Linz and A. Stepan (eds.). *The Breakdown of Democratic Regimes*. Baltimore and London: Johns Hopkins University Press, ch. 1.

Fehrenbacher, D. E. (1978). *The Dred Scott Case: Its Significance in American Law and Politics*. New York: Oxford University Press.

Fetner, T., and B. G. King (2014). "Three-Layer Movements, Resources and the Tea Party." In N. Van Dyke and D. S. Meyer (eds.). *Understanding the Tea Party*. Burlington, VT: Ashgate, ch. 2.

Finegold, K., and T. Skocpol (1984). "State, Party, and Industry. From Business Recovery to the Wagner Act in America's New Deal." In C. Bright and S. Harding (eds.). *Statemaking and Social Movements: Essays in History and Theory*. Ann Arbor, MI: University of Michigan Press, pp. 159–92.

Fingerhut, E. R. (1976). "Tom Watson, Blacks, and Southern Reform." *Georgia Historical Review* 60: 324–43.

Fisher, D. R. (2019). *American Resistance: From the Women's March to the Blue Wave*. New York: Columbia University Press.

Fisher, D. R. (2020a). "The Diversity of the Recent Black Lives Matter Protests Is a Good Sign for Racial Equity." *How We Rise*. Brookings Institution, July 8. www .brookings.edu/blog/how-we-rise/2020/07/08/the-diversity-of-the-recent-black-lives-matter-protests-is-a-good-sign-for-racial-equity/?preview_id=900068

Fisher, D. R. (2020b). "The Original Women's Marches Are Still a Political Force." *The Washington Post*, November 3.

Fishman, R. (2019). *Democratic Practice: Origins of the Iberian Divide in Political Inclusion*. New York and Oxford: Oxford University Press.

Fitzgerald, M. W. (1989). *The Union League Movement in the Deep South*. Baton Rouge and London: Louisiana State University Press.

Flacks, R., and N. Lichtenstein (eds.) (2015). *The Port Huron Statement: Sources and Legacies of the New Left's Founding Manifesto*. Philadelphia: University of Pennsylvania Press.

Flexner, E. (1959). *Century of Struggle: The Woman's Rights Movement in the United States*. Cambridge, MA: Harvard University Press.

Foner, E. (1995). *Free Soil, Free Labor, Free Men: The Ideology of the Republican Party before the Civil War*. Oxford: Oxford University Press.

Foner, E. (2014). *Reconstruction: America's Unfinished Revolution*. New York: Harper Perennial.

Francis, M. M. (2016). *Civil Rights and the Making of the Modern American State*. New York and Cambridge: Cambridge University Press.

Frank, J. (2018). "Populism and Praxis," in C. R. Kaltwasser, P. A. Taggart, P. O. Espejo and P. Ostiguy (eds.). *The Oxford Handbook on Populism*. Oxford and New York: Oxford University Press, ch. 32.

Fredrickson, G. M. (1971). *The Black Image in the White Mind*. Middletown, CT: Wesleyan University Press.

Free, L. E. (2015). *Suffrage Reconstructed: Gender, Race, and Voting Rights in the Civil War Era*. Ithaca and London: Cornell University Press.

Frymer, P. (1999). *Uneasy Alliances: Race and Party Competition in America*. Princeton, NJ: Princeton University Press.

Funes, M. J. (ed.) (2016). *Regarding Tilly*. Lanham, MD: University Press of America.

Gallman, J. M. (1994). *The North Fights the Civil War: The Home Front*. Chicago: Ivan R. Dee.

Gamson, W. A. (1990). *The Strategy of Social Protest*. Belmont, CA: Wadsworth Publishing Company.

Ganz, M. (2009). "Organizing Obama: Campaign, Organization, Movement." In the Proceedings of the American Sociological Association. San Francisco, CA, August 8–11, 2009.

Garcia-Montoya, L., and J. Mahoney (2020). "Critical Event Analysis in Case Study Research." *Sociological Methods and Research*. http://doi.org/10.1177/0049124120926201

Genovese, E. D. (1972). *Roll, Jordan, Roll*. New York: Random House.

Gentile, E. (1995). *La Via italiana al totalitarismo*. Roma: Nuova Italia Scientifica.

Gerstle, G., N. Lichtenstein, and A. O'Connor (eds.) (2019). *Beyond the New Deal Order: US Politics from the Great Depression to the Great Recession*. Philadelphia: University of Pennsylvania Press.

Gervais, B., and I. Morris (2018). *Reactionary Republicanism: How the Tea Party Paved the Way for Trump's Victory*. New York and Oxford: Oxford University Press.

Gienapp, W. E. (1987). *The Origins of the Republican Party, 1852–1856*. New York and Oxford: Oxford University Press.

Gillion, D. Q. (2020). *The Loud Minority: Why Protests matter in American Democracy*. Princeton, NJ: Princeton University Press.

Gitlin, T. (1980). *The Whole World Is Watching: Mass Media in the Making and Unmaking of the New Left*. Berkeley: University of California Press.

Gitlin, T. (1987). *The Sixties: Years of Hope, Days of Rage*. New York: Bantam.

Giugni, M., D. McAdam, and C. Tilly (eds.) (1998a). *From Contention to Democracy*. Lanham, MD: Rowman and Littlefield.

Giugni, M., D. McAdam, and C. Tilly, (eds.) (1999b). *How Social Movements Matter*. Minneapolis: University of Minnesota Press.

Giugni, M., and S. Yamasaki (2009). "The Policy Impact of Social Movements: A Replication through Qualitative Comparative Analysis." *Mobilization* 14: 467–84.

Goedde, P. (2011). "Lawyers for a Democratic Society (*Minbyun*): The Evolution of Its Legal Mobilization Process since 1988." In G.-W. Shin and P. Y. Chang (eds.). *South Korean Social Movements: From Democracy to Civil Society*. London and New York: Routledge, ch. 13.

Goldberg, P. (1975). "The Politics of the Allende Overthrow in Chile." *Political Science Quarterly* 90: 93–116.

Goldfield, M. (1982). "The Decline of Organized Labor: NLRB Union Certification Election Results." *Politics and Society* 11: 167–210.

Goldfield, M. (1987). *The Decline of Organized Labor in the United States*. Chicago, IL: University of Chicago Press.

Goldfield, M. (1989). "Worker Insurgency, Radical Organization, and New Deal Labor Legislation." *American Political Science Review* 83: 1257–82.

Goldstone, J. A. (ed.) (2003). *States, Parties, and Social Movements*. New York and Cambridge: Cambridge University Press.

Goodheart, A. (2011). *1861: The Civil War Awakening*. New York: Knopf.

Goodwyn, L. (1976). *Democratic Promise: The Populist Movement in America*. New York: Oxford University Press.

Goss, K. A. (2013). *The Paradox of Gender Equality: How American Women's Groups Gained and Lost Their Public Voice*. Ann Arbor, MI: University of Michigan Press.

Gramsci, A. (1971). *Selections from the Prison Notebooks of Antonio Gramsci*. New York: International Publishers.

Greskovits, B. (2020). "Rebuilding the Hungarian Right through Conquering Civil Society: The Civic Circles Movement." *East European Politics* 34: 247–66.

Grinspan, J. (2016). *The Virgin Vote: How Young Americans Made Democracy Social, Politics Personal, and Voting Popular in the Nineteenth Century*. Chapel Hill, NC: University of North Carolina Press.

Grossmann, M., and D. Hopkins (2016). *Asymmetric Politics: Ideological Republicans and Group Interest Democrats*. New York: Oxford University Press.

Gusfield, J. (1986). *Symbolic Crusade: Status Politics and the American Temperance Movement*. Champaign Urbana: University of Illinois Press.

Gutierrez Crocco, F. (2017). "Coping with Neoliberalism through Legal Mobilization: The Chilean Labor Movement's New Tactics and Allies." In S. Donoso and M. von Bulow (eds.). *Social Movements in Chile: Organizations, Trajectories, and Political Consequences*. New York: Palgrave-Macmillan, ch. 7.

Hacker, J., and P. Pierson (2015). "Confronting Asymmetric Polarization." In N. Persily (ed.). *Solutions to Political Polarization in America*. New York and Cambridge: Cambridge University Press, ch. 3.

Hadden, J., and S. Tarrow (2007). "Spillover or Spillout: The Global Justice Movement in the United States after 9/11." *Mobilization* 12: 359–76.

Hahn, S. (2003). *A Nation under Our Feet: Black Political Struggles in the Rural South from Slavery to the Great Migration*. Cambridge MA: Harvard University Press.

Haines, H. H. (1984). "Black Radicalization and the Study of Civil Rights: 1957–1970." *Social Problems* 32: 21–43.

Hall, J. D. (2005). "The Long Civil Rights Movement and the Political Uses of the Past." *The Journal of American History* 91: 1233–63.

Hall, S. (1986). "Cultural Studies: Two Paradigms." In R. Collins (ed.). *Media, Culture, and Society: A Critical Reader*. Beverly Hills, CA: Sage, pp. 57–72.

Han, H., and M. Okawara (2018). "Constituency and Leadership in the Evolution of Resistance Organizations." In D. S. Meyer and S. Tarrow (eds.). *The Resistance: The Dawn of the Anti-Trump Opposition Movement*. New York: Oxford University Press, ch. 11.

Harris, K. (2012). "Change Is Not the Same as Progress: The Failures of the McGovern-Fraser Reforms in 1972." The Menlo School Roundtable. Menlo Park, CA.

Harvey, A. (1998). *Votes without Leverage: Women in American Electoral Politics, 1920–1970*. New York and Cambridge: Cambridge University Press.

Heaney, M. T., and F. Rojas (2014). "Hybrid Activism: Social Movement Mobilization in a Multimovement Environment." *American Journal of Sociology* 119: 1047–1103.

Heaney, M. T., and F. Rojas (2015). *Party in the Street: The Antiwar Movement and the Democratic Party after 9/11*. New York: Cambridge University Press.

Hertel-Fernandez, A. (2020). "Dissecting the Conservative Triumph in Wisconsin." In T. Skocpol and C. Tervo (eds.). *Upending American Politics: Polarizing Parties, Ideological Elites, and Citizen Activists from the Tea Party to the Anti-Trump Resistance*. New York and Oxford: Oxford University Press, ch. 2.

Hetherington, M. J., and J. D. Weiler (2009). *Authoritarianism and Polarization in American Politics*. New York and Cambridge: Cambridge University Press.

Hild, M. (2007). *Greenbackers, Knights of Labor, and Populists: Farmer-Labor Insurgency in the late-Nineteenth-Century South*. Athens, GA: University of Georgia Press.

Hipsher, P. (1998). "Democratic Transitions as Protest Cycles." In David S. Meyer and Sidney Tarrow (eds.). *The Social Movement Society. Contentious Politics for a New Century*. Lanham MD: Rowman and Littlefield, pp. 153–72.

Hochschild, A. (2018). *Strangers in Their Own Land: Anger and Mourning on the American Right*. New York: The New Press.

Hunter, W. (2007). "The Normalization of an Anomaly: The Workers' Party in Brazil." *World Politics* 59: 440–75.

Huntington, Samuel P. (1991). *The Third Wave: Democratization in the Late Twentieth Century*. Norman, OK: University of Oklahoma Press.

Hutter, S. (2014). "Protest Event Analysis and Its Offspring." In D. della Porta (ed.). *Methodological Practices in Social Movement Research*. Oxford: Oxford University Press.

Inglehart, R. (1990). *Culture Shift in Advanced Industrial Societies*. Princeton: Princeton University Press.

Inglehart, R., and P. Norris (2017). "Trump and the Populist Authoritarian Parties: The Silent Revolution in Reverse." *Perspectives on Politics* 15: 443–54.

Jacobs, M. (2019). "State Building from the Bottom Up: The New Deal and Beyond." In G. Gerstle, N. Lichtenstein, and A. O'Connor (eds.). *Beyond the New Deal Order: US Politics from the Great Depression to the Great Recession*. Philadelphia: University of Pennsylvania Press, ch. 2.

Jacobs, M., W. Novak, and J. Zeliger (eds.) (2003). *The Democratic Experiment: New Dimensions in American Political History*. Princeton NJ: Princeton University Press.

Jacobs, N. F., D. King, and S. Milkis (2019). "Building a Conservative State: Partisan Polarization and the Redeployment of Administrative Power." *Perspectives on Politics* 17: 453–69.

Jacobs, N. F., and S. M. Milkis (forthcoming). *What Happened to the Vital Center?* New York and Oxford: Oxford University Press.

Jacobson, G. C. (September 2011). "The President, the Tea Party, and Voting Behavior in 2010: Insights from the Cooperative Congressional Election Study." American Political Science Association Annual Meeting. Seattle, WA.

Jäger, A. M. M. (2020). "Populism and the Democracy of Producers in the United States, 1877–1925." PhD thesis, History Department, Cambridge University.

Jones, S., and C. Doxsee (2020). "The Escalating Terrorism Problem in the United States." *CSIS Briefs*. Washington DC: Center for Strategic and International Studies.

Judis, J. B. (2016). *The Populist Explosion: How the Great Recession Transformed American Politics. Columbia Global Reports*. New York: Columbia University.

Journal of American History (2019). "Interchange: Women's Suffrage, the Nineteenth Amendment, and the Right to Vote." *Journal of American History*, 106.

Jung, J. K. (2011). "Popular Mobilization and Democratization: A Comparative Study of South Korea and Taiwan." *Korea Observer* 42: 377–411.

Jung, J. K. (2020). *The Role of Civil Society in South Korean Democracy: Liberal Legacy and Its Pitfalls. EAI Issue Briefing.* Seoul: East Asia Institute.

Kabaservice, G. (2012). *Rule and Ruin: The Downfall of Moderation and the Destruction of the Republican Party.* New York and Oxford: Oxford University Press.

Kalyvas, S. N. (1996). *The Rise of Christian Democracy in Europe.* Ithaca: Cornell University Press.

Karol, D. (2014). "Political Parties in American Political Development." In R. Vallely, S. Mettler, and R. Lieberman (eds.). *The Oxford Handbook of American Political Development.* New York and Oxford: Oxford University Press, ch. 22.

Karol, D., and C. Thurston (2020). "From Personal to Partisan: Abortion, Party, and Religion among California State Legislators." *Studies in American Political Development* 31: 149–69.

Karp, M. (2016). *This Vast Southern Empire: Slaveholders at the Helm of American Foreign Policy.* Cambridge MA: Harvard University Press.

Karp, M. (2019). "The Mass Politics of Antislavery." *Catalyst* 3: 131–78.

Karpf, D. (2012). *The MoveOn Effect: Disruptive Innovation and the New Generation of American Political Associations. The Unexpected Transformation of American Political Advocacy.* New York and Oxford: Oxford University Press.

Katz, R. S., and P. Mair (1993). "The Evolution of Party Organizations in Europe: The Three Faces of Party Organization." *American Review of Politics* 14: 593–618.

Katz, R. S., and P. Mair (2009). "The Cartel Party Thesis: A Restatement." *Perspectives on Politics* 7: 753–66.

Katznelson, I. (2013). *Fear Itself: The New Deal and the Origins of Our Time.* New York: Liveright.

Keck, M. (1992). *The Worker's Party and Democratization in Brazil.* New Haven and London: Yale University Press.

Kennan, J. (1986). "The Economics of Strikes." In Ashenfelter and R. Layard (eds.). *Handbook of Labor Economics*, vol. 2. Amsterdam: Elsevier Science Publishers, pp. 1091–37.

Key, V. O. (1955a). *Politics, Parties and Pressure Groups.* New York: Thomax Y. Crowell.

Key, V. O. (1955b). "A Theory of Critical Elections." *Journal of Politics* 17: 3–18.

Key, V. O. (1984). *Southern Politics in State and Nation.* Knoxville, TN: University of Tennessee Press.

Keyssar, A. (2000). *The Right to Vote: The Contested History of Democracy in the United States.* New York: Basic Books.

Kier, E. (2010). "War and Reform: Gaining Labor's Compliance on the Homefront." In E. Kier and R. R. Krebs (eds.). *In War's Wake: International Conflict and the Fate of Liberal Democracy.* New York and Cambridge: Cambridge University Press, pp. 139–61.

Kim, S.-C. (2018). *Democratization and Social Movements in Korea.* Oxford and New York: Routledge.

King, B. G., and M. Cornwall (2005). "Specialists and Generalists: Learning Strategies in the Woman Suffrage Movement, 1866–1918." *Research in Social Movements, Conflict and Change* 26: 3–34.

King, D., and S. M. Milkis (2021). "Polarization, the Administrative State, and Executive-Centered Partisanship." In R. C. Lieberman, S. Mettler, and K. M. Roberts (eds.). *Democratic Resilience: Can the United States Withstand Rising Polarization*. New York: Cambridge University Press, ch. 11.

Kirby, D., and E. Ekins (2012). "Libertarian Roots of the Tea Party." *Policy Analysis*. Cato Institute.

Kitschelt, H. (2006). "Movement Parties." In R. A. Katz and W. Crotty (eds.). *Handbook of Party Politics*. London: Sage Publications, ch. 24.

Klandermans, B. (1992). "The Social Construction of Protest and Multiorganizational Fields." In A. Morris and C. McClurg Mueller (eds.). *Frontiers in Social Movement Theory*. New Haven: Yale University Press, ch. 4.

Klandermans, B. (2019). "How Citizens Try to Influence Politics: On Movements and Parties." Unpublished paper presented to the Closing Conference of the PolPart Project, Amsterdam.

Klinkner, P. A., and R. M. Smith (2002). *The Unsteady March: The Rise and Decline of Racial Equality in America*. Chicago: University of Chicago Press.

Knuckey, J., and K. Hasan (2020). "Authoritarianism and Support for Trump in the 2016 Presidential Election." *Social Science Journal* 57: 1–14.

Kohn, M. (2003). *Radical Space: Building the House of the People*. Ithaca and London: Cornell University Press.

Kousser, J. M. (1974). *The Shaping of Southern Politics: Suffrage Restriction and the Establishment of the One-Party South, 1880–1910*. New Haven, CT: Yale University Press.

Kriesi, H., et al (1995). *The Politics of New Social Movements in Western Europe*. Minneapolis and St. Paul: University of Minnesota Press.

Kriesi, H., J. Lorenzini, B. Wüest, and S. Häusermann (2020). *Contention in Times of Crises. Recession and Policical Protest in 30 European Countries*. Cambridge: Cambridge University Press.

Kryder, D. (2000). *Divided Arsenal: Race and the American State during World War Two*. New York and Cambridge: Cambridge University Press.

La Raja, R. J., and B. F. Schaffner (2015). *Campaign Finance and Political Polarization: When Purists Prevail*. Ann Arbor MI: University of Michigan Press.

Lemann, N. (1991). *The Promised Land: The Great Black Migration and How It Changed America*. New York: Vintage.

Lemann, N. (2020). "The Republican Identity Crisis After Trump," *The New Yorker*, October 23rd.

Lemons, J. S. (1973). *The Woman Citizen: Social Feminism in the 1920s*. Urbana: University of Illinois Press.

Lengle, J. L., and B. E. Shafer (1976). "Primary Rules, Political Power, and Social Change." *American Political Science Review* 70: 25–40.

Levitsky, S., and D. Ziblatt (2018). *This Is How Democracies Die*. New York: Penguin.

Lieberman, R. C. (2005). *Shaping Race Policy: The United States in Comparative Perspective*. Princeton and Oxford: Princeton University Press.

Lieberman, R. C., S. Mettler, and K. M. Roberts (2021). "How Democracies Endure: The Challenges of Polarization and Resiliance." In R. C. Lieberman, S. Mettler, and K. M. Roberts (eds.). *Democratic Resilience: Can the United States Withstand Rising Polarization?* New York: Cambridge University Press, ch. 1.

Lieberman, R. C., S. Mettler, and. K. M. Roberts (eds.) (2021). *Democratic Resilience: Can the United States Withstand Rising Polarization?* New York: Cambridge University Press.

Lijphart, A. (1968). "The Politics of Accommodation." *Pluralism and Democracy in the Netherlands.* Berkeley: University of California Press.

Linz, J., and A. Stepan (eds.) (1978). *The Breakdown of Democratic Regimes.* Baltimore and London: Johns Hopkins University Press.

Lipset, S. M., and S. Rokkan (1967). *Party Systems and Voter Alignments: Cross-National Perspectives.* Glencoe IL: The Free Press.

Luders, J. E. (2003). "Countermovements, the State, and the Intensity of Racial Contention in the American South." In J. A. Goldstone (ed.). *States, Parties and Social Movements.* New York and Cambridge: Cambridge University Press, 22–44.

Luders, J. E. (2010). *The Civil Rights Movement and the Logic of Social Change.* New York and Cambridge: Cambridge University Press.

Luna, J. P., and D. Altman (2011). "Uprooted but Stable: Chilean Parties and the Concept of Party System Institutionalization." *Latin American Politics and Society* 53, 1–28.

Lunardini, C. A. (1986). *From Equal Suffrage to Equal Rights.* New York and London: New York University Press.

Luthin, R. (1954). *American Demagogues.* Boston: Beacon Press.

Lyttelton, A. (1979). "Landlords, Peasants and the Limits of Liberalism." In J. A. Davis (ed.). *Gramsci and Italy's Passive Revolution.* London: Routledge, ch. 4.

MacLean, N. (2017). *Democracy in Chains: The Deep History of the Radical Right's Stealth Plan for America.* New York: Penguin.

Mahoney, J. (2000). "Path Dependence in Historical Sociology." *Theory and Society* 24: 507–48.

Mainwaring, S., and T. R. Scully (1995). "Party Systems in Latin America." In S. Mainwaring and T. R. Scully (eds.). *Building Democratic Institutions.* Stanford, CA: Stanford University Press, Introduction.

Mair, P. (2013). *Ruling the Void: The Hollowing of Western Democracy.* London: Verso.

Mair, P., and R. S. Katz (1997). "Party Organization, Party Democracy, and the Emergence of the Cartel Party." In P. Mair (ed.). *Party System Change: Applications and Interpretations.* Oxford: Oxford University Press, ch. 5.

Mann, T., and N. J. Ornstein (2012). *It's Even Worse Than It Looks: How the American Constitutional System Collided with the New Politics of Extremism.* New York: Basic Books.

Mansbridge, J. (1986). *Why We Lost the ERA.* Chicago: University of Chicago Press.

Markoff, J. (1996). *Waves of Democracy.* Thousand Oaks, CA: Pine Forge.

Marsh, S. (2020). "How Trump Flipped Michigan." In T. Skocpol and C. Tervo (eds.). *Upending American Politics: Polarizing Parties, Ideological Elites, and Citizen Activists from the Tea Party to the Anti-Trump Resistance.* New York and Oxford: Oxford University Press, ch. 5.

Mason, L. (2018). *Uncivil Agreement: How Politics Became Our Identity.* Chicago and London: University of Chicago Press.

Mason, L., and N. Kalmoe (2021). "The Social Roots, Risks, and Rewards of Mass Polarization." In S. Mettler, R. C. Lieberman, and K. M. Roberts (eds.). *Democratic Resilience: Can the United States Withstand Rising Polarization.* New York: Cambridge University Press, ch. 7.

Mason, L., and J. Wronsky (2018). "One Tribe to Bind Them All: How Our Social Group Attachments Strengthen Partisanship," *Advances in Political Psychology* 29, 257–77.

Matthews, D. R., and J. Prothro (1966). *Negroes and the New Southern Politics.* New York: Harcourt, Brace.

Mayer, J. (2017). *Dark Money: The Hidden History of the Billionaires behind the Rise of the Radical Right.* New York: Anchor Books.

Mayhew, D. (1986). *Placing Parties in American Politics: Organization, Electoral Settings, and Government Activity.* Princeton, NJ: Princeton University Press.

Mayhew, D. (2002). *Electoral Realignments: A Critique of an American Genre.* New Haven, CT: Yale University Press.

McAdam, D. (1983). "Tactical Innovation and the Pace of Insurgency." *American Sociological Review* 48: 735–54.

McAdam, D. (1988). *Freedom Summer.* New York: Oxford University Press.

McAdam, D. (1999a). "The Biographical Impact of Activism." In M. Giuni, D. McAdam, and C. Tilly (eds.). *How Social Movements Matter.* Minneapolis and St. Paul: University of Minnesota, ch. 6.

McAdam, D. (1999b). *Political Process and the Development of Black Insurgency, 1930–1970.* Chicago: University of Chicago Press.

McAdam, D. (2018). "Putting Donald Trump in Historical Perspective: Racial Politics and Social Movements from the 1960s to Today." In D. S. Meyer and S. Tarrow (eds.). *The Resistance: The Dawn of the Anti-Trump Opposition Movement.* New York and Oxford: Oxford University Press, ch. 1.

McAdam, D. (June 2020). "We've Never Seen Protests like These Before." *Jacobin.* https://jacobinmag.com/2020/06/george-floyd-protests-black-lives-matter-riots-demonstrations

McAdam, D., and K. Kloos (2014). *Deeply Divided: Racial Politics and Social Movements in Post-War America.* New York: Oxford University Press.

McAdam, D., and Y. Su (2002). "The War at Home. Antiwar Protests and Congressional Voting, 1965 to 1973." *American Sociological Review* 67: 696–721.

McAdam, D., and S. Tarrow (2010). "Ballots and Barricades: The Reciprocal Relations between Elections and Social Movements." *Perspectives on Politics* 8: 529–42.

McAdam, D., S. Tarrow, and C. Tilly (2001). *Dynamics of Contention.* New York and Cambridge: Cambridge University Press.

McCammon, H. J. (2012). *The US Women's Jury Movement and Strategic Adaptation: A More Just Verdict.* New York and Cambridge: Cambridge University Press.

McCammon, H. J., and K. E. Campbell (2002). "Allies on the Road to Victory: Coalition Formation between the Suffragists and the Woman's Christian Temperance Union." *Mobilization* 7: 231–51.

McCammon, H. J., K. E. Campbell, E. N. Granberg, and C. Mowery (2001). "How Movements Win: Gendered Opportunity Structures and the State Women's Suffrage Movements, 1866–1919." *American Sociological Review* 66: 49–70.

McCarthy, J. (1987). "Pro-Life and Pro-Choice Mobilization: Infrastructure Deficits and New Technologies." In M. N. Zald and J. McCarthy (eds.). *Social Movements in an Organizational Society.* New Brunswick: Transaction Books, pp. 49–66.

McCarthy, J., and C. McPhail (1998). "The Institutionalization of Protest in the United States." In D. S. Meyer and S. Tarrow (eds.). *The Social Movement Society: Contentious Politics for a New Century.* Lanham, MD: Rowman and Littlefield, pp. 83–110.

McCarthy, J., and M. Wolfson (1992). "Consensus Movements, Conflict Movements and the Cooperation of Civic and State Infrastructures." In A. Morris and C. M. Mueller (eds.). *Frontiers in Social Movement Theory*. New Haven: Yale University Press, 273–97.

McCarthy, J., and M. N. Zald (1973). *The Trend of Social Movements in America: Professionalization and Resource Mobilization*. Morristown, NJ: General Learning Press.

McCarthy, J., and M. N. Zald (1977). "Resource Mobilization and Social Movements: A Partial Theory." *American Journal of Sociology* 82: 1212–41.

McCarty, N. (2007). "The Policy Consequences of Political Polarization." In Paul Pierson and Theda Skocpol (eds.). *The Transformation of the American Polity*. Princeton: Princeton University Press, ch. 2.

McCarty, N., and E. Schickler (2018). "On the Theory of Parties." *Annual Review of Political Science* 21: 175–93.

McConnaughy, C. M. (2013). *The Woman Suffrage Movement in America*. New York and Cambridge: Cambridge University Press.

McConnell, G. (1953). *Decline of Agrarian Democracy*. Berkeley and Los Angeles: University of California Press.

McConnell, G. (1966). *Private Power and American Democracy*. New York: Alfred Knopf.

McCoy, J., and M. Somer (2021). "Pernicious Polarization and Democratic Resilience: Analyzing the US in Comparative Perspective." In R. Lieberman, S. Mettler, and K. M. Roberts (eds.). *Democratic Resilience: Can the United States Withstand Rising Polarization?* New York and Cambridge: Cambridge University Press, ch. 3.

McMath, R. C. J. (1975). *Populist Vanguard: A History of the Southern Farmers' Alliance*. Chapel Hill, NC: University of North Carolina Press.

McMillen, N. R. (1971). *The Citizens' Council: Organized Resistance to the Second Reconstruction, 1954–1964*. Champagn-Urbana: University of Illinois Press.

McVeigh, R. (2014). "What's New about the Tea Party Movement." In N. V. Dyke and D. S. Almeida (eds.). *Understanding the Tea Party Movement*. Burlington, VT: Ashgate, ch. 1.

Melucci, A. (1980). "The New Social Movements: A Theoretical Approach." *Social Science Information* 19: 199–226.

Mercieca, J. (2020). *Demagogue for President: The Rhetorical Genius of Donald Trump*. College Station, TX: Texas A&M University Press.

Mettler, S., and R. Lieberman (2020). *Four Threats: The Recurring Crises of American Democracy*. New York: St. Martin's.

Meyer, D. S. (1990). *A Winter of Discontent: The Nuclear Freeze and American Politics*. New York: Praeger.

Meyer, D. S., and C. Corrigall-Brown (2006). "Coalitions and Political Context: The Movements against Wars in Iraq." *Mobilization* 10: 327–44.

Meyer, D. S., and A. Pullum (2014). "The Tea Party and the Dilemmas of Conservative Populism." In D. S. Meyer and N. V. Dyke (eds.). *Understanding the Tea Party*. Burlington, VT: Ashgate, ch. 4.

Meyer, D. S., and S. Staggenborg (1996). "Movements, Countermovements, and the Structure of Political Opportunity." *American Journal of Sociology* 101: 1628–60.

Meyer, D. S., and S. Tarrow (eds.) (1998). *The Social Movement Society: Contentious Politics for a New Century*. Lanham, MD: Rowman and Littlefield.

Meyer, D. S., and S. Tarrow (eds.) (2018). *The Resistance: The Dawn of the Anti-Trump Opposition Movement*. New York: Oxford University Press.

Meyer, D. S., and S. Tarrow (2018). "War, Peace, and Social Movements." In D. A. Snow, S. A. Soule, H. Kriesi, and H. J. MacCammon (eds.). *Wiley Blackwell Companion to Social Movements*. London: John Wiley and Sons, ch. 2.

Meyer, J., J. Boli, G. M. Thomas and F. O. Ramirez (1998). "World Society and the Nation-State." *American Journal of Sociology* 103: 144–81.

Michels, R. (1962). *Political Parties: A Sociological Study of the Oligarchical Tendencies of Modern Democracy*. New York: Collier Books.

Mickey, R. (2015). *Paths Out of Dixie: The Democratization of America's Authoritarian Enclaves, 1944–1972*. Princeton, NJ: Princeton University Press.

Milkis, S. M. (1993). *The President and the Parties: The Transformation of the American Party System since the New Deal*. New York and Oxford: Oxford University Press.

Milkis, S. M., and D. J. Tichenor (2019). *Rivalry and Reform: Presidents, Social Movements, and the Transformation of American Politics*. Chicago, IL: University of Chicago Press.

Milkis, S. M., and J. W. York (2017). "Barack Obama, Organizing for Action, and Executive-Centered Partisanship." *Studies in American Political Development* 31: 1–23.

Miller, J. (1987). *Democracy Is in the Streets: From Port Huron to the Siege of Chicago*. New York: Simon and Schuster.

Minkoff, D. C. (1995). *Organizing for Equality: The Evolution of Women's and Racial-Ethnic Organizations in America, 1955–1985*. New Brunswick: Rutgers University Press.

Minkoff, D. C. (2016). "The Payoffs of Organizational Membership for Political Activism in Established Democracies." *Amercan Journal of Sociology* 122: 425–68.

Moore, B. J. (1966). *The Social Origins of Dictatorship and Democracy: Lord and Peasant in the Modern World*. Boston: Beacon Press.

Morgan, D. (1972). *Suffragists and Democrats*. East Lansing, MI: Michigan State University Press.

Morgan-Collins, M. (2021). "The Electoral Impact of Newly Enfranchised Groups: The Case of Women's Suffrage in the United States." *Journal of Politics* 83, pp. 150–65.

Morris, A. (1981). "Black Southern Sit-In Movements: An Analysis of Organizations." *American Sociological Review* 45: 744–67.

Morris, A. (1984). *The Origins of the Civil Rights Movement: Black Communities Organizing for Change*. New York: The Free Press.

Mudde, C. (2004). "The Populist Zeitgeist." *Government and Opposition* 39: 542–63.

Mudde, C., and C. R. Kaltwasser (eds.) (2012). *Populism in Europe and the Americas: Threat or Corrective for Democracy?* Cambridge: Cambridge University Press.

Munck, G. (2022). "When Causes Are Distant and Effects Persist: Rethinking the Critical Juncture Framework." In D. Collier and G. Munck (eds.). *Critical Junctures and Historical Legacies: Insights and Tools for Comparative Social Science*, ch. 5.

Neely, M. E. Jr. (1991). *The Fate of Liberty: Abraham Lincoln and Civil Liberties*. New York and Oxford: Oxford University Press.

Noel, H. (2012). "Which Long Coalition? The Creation of the Anti-Slavery Coalition." *Party Politics* 19: 962–84.

Noel, H. (2014). *Political Ideologies and Political Parties in America*. New York: Cambridge University Press.

Oakes, J. (2012). *Freedom National: The Destruction of Slavery in the United States, 1861–1985*. New York and London: W. W. Norton.

O'Donnell, G., P. Schmitter, and L. Whitehead (eds.) (1986). *Transitions from Authoritarian Rule: Prospects for Democracy*. Baltimore: Johns Hopkins University Press.

Offe, C. (1985). "New Social Movements: Challenging the Boundaries of Institutional Politics." *Social Research* 52: 817–68.

Orren, K., and S. Skowronek (2004). *The Search for American Political Development*. New York: Cambridge University Press.

Oshinsky, D. M. (1996). *Worse Than Slavery: Parchman Farm and the Ordeal of Jim Crow Justice*. New York: The Free Press.

Ostler, J. (1993). *Prairie Populism: The Fate of Agrarian Radicalism in Kansas, Nebraska, and Iowa, 1880–1892*. Lawrence, Kansas: University Press of Kansas.

Parker, C. S. (2009). *Fighting for Democracy: Black Veterans and the Struggle against White Supremacy in the Postwar South*. Princeton and Oxford: Oxford University Press.

Parker, C. S. (2021). "Status Threat: Moving the Right Further to the Right?" *Daedalus* 150: 56–75

Parker, C. S., and M. A. Barreto (2013). *Change They Can't Believe In: The Tea Party and Reactionary Politics in America*. Princeton, NJ: Princeton University Press.

Patterson, T. E. (2020). *Is the Republican Party Destroying Itself?* Seattle, WA: KDP Publishing.

Payne, C. M. (2007). *I've Got the Light of Freedom: The Organizing Tradition and the Mississippi Freedom Struggle*. Berkeley: University of California Press.

Perlman, S. (1928). *A Theory of the Labor Movement*. Philadelphia, PA: Porcupine Press.

Perlstein, R. (2009). *Before the Storm: Barry Goldwater and the Unmaking of the American Consensus*. New York: Nation Books.

Perlstein, R. (2020). *Reaganland: America's Right Turn, 1976–1980*. New York: Simon and Schuster.

Piazza, A., and D. J. Wang (2020). "Claim Specialization, Tactical Diversity and the Protest Environment in the Success of US Anti-Nuclear Activism." *Mobilization* 25: 93–114.

Pierson, P. (2017). "American Hybrid: Donald Trump and the Strange Merger of Populism and Plutocracy." *British Journal of Sociology* 68: S10–S119.

Pierson, P., and E. Schickler (2021). "Polarization and the Durability of Madisonian Checks and Balances: A Developmental Analysis." In R. C. Lieberman, S. Mettler, and K. M. Roberts (eds.). *Democratic Resilience: Can the United States Withstand Rising Polarization*. New York: Cambridge University Press, ch. 2.

Piven, F. F., and R. Cloward (1972). *Regulating the Poor*. New York: Vintage Books.

Piven, F. F., and R. Cloward (1977). *Poor People's Movements: Why They Succeed, How They Fail*. New York: Vintage.

Poggi, G. (1967). *Catholic Action in Italy: The Sociology of a Sponsored Organization*. Stanford, CA: Stanford University Press.

Porter, E. (2016). "Where Were Trump's Votes? Where the Jobs Weren't." *New York Times*. www.nytimes.com/2016/12/13/business/economy/jobs-economy-voters.html (accessed December 14, 2016).

Porter, J. R., F. M. Howell, and L. M. Hempel (2014). "Old Times Are Not Forgotten. The Institutionalization of Segregationist Academies in the American South." *Social Problems* 61: 576–601.

Posner, P. (2004). "Local Democracy and the Transformation of Popular Participation." *Latin American Politics and Society* 46: 51–81.

Post, C. (2011). *Political Marxism and the Rise of American Capitalism: Studies in Class Structure, Economic Development and Political Conflict, 1620–1877*. London: Brill.

Postel, C. (2007). *The Populist Vision*. New York and Oxford: Oxford University Press.

Prasad, M. (2013). *The Land of Too Much: American Abundance and the Paradox of Poverty*. Cambridge, MA: Harvard University Press.

Putnam, L. (2020a). "Middle America Reboots Democracy." In T. Skocpol and C. Tervo (eds.). *Upending American Politics: Polarizing Parties, Ideological Elites, and Citizen Activists from the Tea Party to the Anti-Trump Resistance*. New York and Oxford: Oxford University Press, ch. 8.

Putnam, L. (2020b). "Rust Belt in Transition: What Has Happened in Pennsylvania's and the Entire Rust Belt's 'Middle Suburb' Counties and Can It Be Reversed?" *Democracy Journal* 57. https://democracyjournal.org/magazine/57/rust-belt-in-transition

Putnam, R. D. (1993). *Making Democracy Work: Civic Traditions in Modern Italy*. Princeton: Princeton University Press.

Rana, A. (forthcoming). *Rise of the Constitution* Chicago: University of Chicago Press.

Rana, A. (2024). *Two Faces of American Freedom*. Cambridge, MA: Harvard University Press.

Remmer, K. (1980). "Political Demobilization in Chile, 1973–1978." *Comparative Politics* 12, 275–301.

Rich, J. (2019). "The Rise of Hybrid Social Movements." In J. Rich (ed.). *State-Sponsored Activism: Bureaucrats and Social Movements in Democratic Brazil*. New York and Cambridge: Cambridge University Press, ch. 7.

Roberts, K. M. (2015). *Changing Course in Latin America: Party Systems in the Neoliberal Era*. New York and Cambridge: Cambridge University Press.

Roberts, K. M. (2017). "Chilean Social Movements and Party Politics in Comparative Perspective: Conceptualizing Latin America's 'Third Generation' of Anti-Neoliberal Protest," In Sofia Donoso and Marisa von Bulow (eds.). *Social Movements in Chile: Organizations, Trajectories, and Political Consequences*. New York: Palgrave Macmillan, ch. 8.

Roberts, K. M. (2018a). "Political Parties in Latin America's Second Wave of Incorporation." In E. Silva and F. Rossi (eds.). *Reshaping the Political Arena in Latin America: From Resisting Neoliberalism to the Second Incorporation*. Pittsburgh: University of Pittsburgh Press, 211–21.

Roberts, K. M. (2018b). "Populism, Democracy and Resistance: The United States in Comparative Perspective. In D. S. Meyer and S. Tarrow (eds.). *The Resistance: The Dawn of the Anti-Trump Opposition Movement*. New York: Oxford University Press, ch. 2.

Rodgers, D. T. (2011). *Age of Fracture*. Cambridge, MA: Harvard University Press.

Rose-Ackerman, S. (2017). "Administrative Law, the Common Law, and the US Presidential System: The Republican Party Assault on Regulation." https://adminlawblog.org/2017/03/01/1

Rosenbluth, F. M., and I. Shapiro (2018). "Political Partisanship Is Vicious. That's Because Political Parties Are Too Weak." *Washington Post*, November 28.

Rosenfeld, S. (2018). *The Polarizers: Postwar Architects of our Partisan Era*. Chicago, IL: University of Chicago Press.

Rucht, D., and T. Ohlemacher (1992). "Protest Event Data: Collection, Uses and Perspectives." In M. Diani and R. Eyerman (eds.). *Studying Collective Action*. London: Sage Publications, pp. 76–106.

Rupp, L. J., and V. Taylor (1987). *Survival in the Doldrums: The American Women's Rights Movement, 1945 to the 1960s*. New York: Oxford University Press.

Sanders, E. (1999). *Roots of Reform: Farmers, Workers, and the American State, 1877–1917*. Chicago, IL: University of Chicago Press.

Sapiro, Virginia (2020). "The Power and Fragility of Social Movement Coalitions: The Woman Suffrage Movement to 1870." *Boston University Law Review* 100: 1558–611

Sartori, G. (1966). "European Political Parties: The Case of Polarized Pluralism." In Joseph LaPalombara and Myron Weiner (eds.). *Political Parties and Political Development*. Princeton, NJ: Princeton University Press, ch. 5.

Schaeffer, C. (2017). "Democratizing the Flows of Democracy: *Patagonia Sin Represas* in the Awakening of Chile's Civil Society." In S. Donoso and M. von Bulow (eds.). *Social Movements in Chile: Organizations, Trajectories and Political Consequences*. New York: Palgrave Macmillan, ch. 5.

Schaffner, B., M. McWilliams, and T. Nteta (2018). "Understanding White Polarization in the 2016 Vote for President: The Sobering Role of Racism and Sexism." *Political Science Quarterly* 133: 9–34.

Schattschneider, E. E. (1960). *The Semisovereign People: A Realist's View of Democracy in America*. New York: Holt, Rinehart and Winston.

Schickler, E. (2016). *Racial Realignment: The Transformation of American Liberalism, 1932–1965*. Princeton, NJ: Princeton University Press.

Schlafly, P. (1964). *A Choice Not an Echo*. Alton, IL: Pere Marquette Press.

Schlozman, D. (2015). *When Movements Anchor Parties: Electoral Alignments in American History*. Princeton and Oxford: Princeton University Press.

Schlozman, D., and S. Rosenfeld (September 2018). "The Long New Right and the World It Made." Presented to the American Political Science Association Annual Meeting. Boston, MA.

Schlozman, D., and S. Rosenfeld (2019). "The Hollow Parties." In F. Lee and N. McCarty (eds.). *Can America Govern Itself?* New York and Cambridge: Cambridge University Press, ch. 6.

Schmidt, C. (2018). *The Sit-Ins: Protest and Legal Change in the Civil Rights Era*. Chicago: University of Chicago Press.

Schneider, C. (1995). *Shantytown Protest in Pinochet's Chile*. Philadelphia, PA: Temple University Press.

Schradie, J. (2019). *The Revolution That Wasn't: How Digital Activism Favors Conservatives*. Cambridge, MA: Harvard University Press.

Schwartz, M. (1976). *Radical Protest and Social Structure: The Southern Farmers' Alliance and Cotton Tenancy, 1880–1890*. Chicago: University of Chicago Press.

Sewell, R. H. (1976). *Ballots for Freedom: Antislavery Politics in the United States, 1837–1860*. New York: Oxford University Press.

Sewell, W. H. Jr. (1996). "Historical Events as Transformations of Structures: Inventing Revolution at the Bastille." *Theory and Society* 25: 841–81.

Shafer, B. E. (1983). *The Struggle for the Democratic Party and the Shaping of Post-Reform Politics*. New York: Russell Sage Foundation.

Shefter, M. (1994). *Political Parties and the State: The American Historical Experience.* Princeton, NJ: Princeton University Press.

Shin, G.-W., and P. Y. Chang (eds.) (2011). *South Korean Social Movements: From Democracy to Civil Society.* London and New York: Routledge.

Shin, G.-W., P. Y. Chang, J-e Lee, and S. Kim (2011). "The Korean Democracy Movement: An Empirical Overview." In G.-W. Shin and P. Y. Chang (eds.). *South Korean Social Movements: From Democracy to Civil Society.* New York and London: Routledge, ch. 2.

Siavelis, P. (2016). "Crisis of Representation in Chile? The Institutional Connection." *Journal of Politics in Latin America* 8, 61–93.

Silbey, J. H. (1967). *The Transformation of American Politics, 1840–1860.* Englewood Cliffs, NJ: Prentice-Hall.

Silbey, J. H. (1977). *A Respectable Minority: The Democratic Party in the Civil War Era, 1860–1868.* New York: Norton.

Silbey, J. H. (1991). *The American Political Nation, 1838–1893.* Stanford, CA: Stanford University Press.

Sitkoff, H. (1981). *A New Deal for Blacks: The Emergence of Civil Rights as a National Issue: The Depression Decade.* New York: Oxford University Press.

Skocpol, T. (2003). *Diminished Democracy: From Membership to Management in American Life.* Norman, OK: University of Oklahoma Press.

Skocpol, T. (2020). "The Elite and Popular Roots of Contemporary Republican Extremism." In T. Skocpol and C. Tervo (eds.) *Upending American Politics: Polarizing Parties, Ideological Elites, and Citizen Activists from the Tea Party to the Anti-Trump Resistance.* New York and Oxford: Oxford University Press, ch. 1.

Skocpol, T., and A. Hertel-Fernandez (2016). "The Koch Network and Republican Party Extremism." *Perspectives on Politics* 14: 681–99.

Skocpol, T., and C. Tervo (eds.) (2020). *Upending American Politics: Polarizing Parties, Ideological Elites, and Citizen Activists from the Tea Party to the Anti-Trump Resistance.* New York: Oxford University Press.

Skocpol, T., and V. Williamson (2011). *The Tea Party and the Remaking of Republican Conservatism.* New York and Oxford: Oxford University Press.

Skowronek, S. (2009). "The Conservative Insurgency and Presidential Power: A Developmental Perspective on the Unitary Executive." *Harvard Law Review* 122: 2071–103.

Smelser, N. (1962). *The Theory of Collective Behavior.* New York: The Free Press.

Smith, R. M. (2010). "Understanding the Symbiosis of American Rights and American Racism." In M. Huilliung (ed.). *America's Liberal Tradition Reconsidered: The Contested Legacy of Louis Hartz.* Lawrence, KS: University of Kansas Press, 55–89.

Snow, D. A., and R. D. Benford (1992). "Master Frames and Cycles of Protest." *Frontiers in Social Movement Theory.* In A. Morris and C. McClurg Mueller (eds.). New Haven, Yale University Press, 133–55.

Snow, D. A., and C. Bernatzky (2018). "The Coterminous Rise of Right-Wing Populism and Superfluous Populations." In G. Fitzi, J. Mackert, and B. S. Turmer (eds.). *Populism and the Crisis of Democracy,* vol. 1: Concepts and Theory London: Routledge, pp. 130–46.

Snow, D., S. Soule, and H. Kriesi (eds.) (2004). *Blackwell Companion on Social Movements.* London: Blackwell-Wiley.

Snow, D., S. Soule, H. Kriesi, and H. McCammon (eds.) (2018). *Blackwell Companion on Social Movements*, 2nd ed. London: Wiley-Blackwell.

Somma, N., and R. Medel (2017). "Shifting Relationships between Social Movements and Institutional Politics." In S. Donoso and M. von Bulow (eds.). *Social Movements in Chile: Organizations, Trajectories and Political Consequences*. New York: Palgrave Macmillan, ch. 2.

Soule, S. A., and C. Davenport (2009). "Velvet Glove, Iron Fist, or Even Hand? Protest Policing in the United States, 1960–1990." *Mobilization* 14: 1–22.

Soule, S. A., and J. Earl (2005). "A Movement Society Evaluated: Collective Protest in the United States, 1960–1986." *Mobilization* 10: 345–64.

Spriano, P. (1975). *The Occupation of the Factories: Italy, 1920*. London: Pluto.

Stone, G. R. (2004). *Perilous Times: Free Speech in Wartime*. New York: Norton.

Suh, C. S. (2019). "More than Words: Legal Professional Activism and the Prevention of Torture in South Korea." *Human Rights Quarterly* 41: 646–71.

Szymanski, A.-M. E. (2003). *Pathways to Prohibition: Radicals, Moderates, and Social Movement Outcomes*. Durham: Duke University Press.

Tarrow, S. (1967). *Peasant Communism in Southern Italy*. New Haven: Yale University Press.

Tarrow, S. (1989). *Democracy and Disorder: Protest and Politics in Italy, 1965–1974*. Oxford and New York: Oxford University Press.

Tarrow, S. (1990). "The Phantom at the Opera: Political Parties and Social Movements in Italy in the 1960s and 1970s." In R. Dalton and M. Kuechler (eds.). *Challenging the Political Order*. New Haven: Yale University Press, 251–73.

Tarrow, S. (1995). "Mass Mobilization and Regime Change: Pacts, Reform, and Popular Power in Italy, 1918–1922 and Spain, 1975–1978." In R. P. Gunther, N. Diamandouris, and H.-J. Puhle (eds.) *The Politics of Democratic Consolidation: Southern Europe in Comparative Perspective*. Baltimore and London: Johns Hopkins University Press, ch. 6.

Tarrow, S. (2011). *Power in Movement: Social Movements and Contentious Politics*, 3rd. ed. Cambridge: Cambridge University Press.

Tarrow, S. (2012). *Strangers at the Gates: Movements and States in Contentious Politics*. Cambridge and New York: Cambridge University Press.

Tarrow, S. (2015). *War, States, and Contention*. Ithaca, NY: Cornell University Press.

Tarrow, S. (2018). "Rhythms of Resistance: The Anti-Trumpian Moment in a Cycle of Contention." In D. S. Meyer and S. Tarrow (eds.). *The Resistance: The Dawn of the Anti-Trump Opposition Movement*. New York: Oxford University Press, ch. 9.

Taylor, J. H. (1949). "Populism and Disfranchisement in Alabama." *Journal of African American History* 34: 410–27.

Taylor, V. (1989). "Social Movement Continuity: The Women's Movement in Abeyance." *American Sociological Review* 54: 761–75.

Teele, D. L. (2018a). *Forging the Franchise: The Political Origins of the Women's Vote*. Princeton, NJ: Princeton University Press.

Teele, D. L. (2018b). "How the West Was Won: Competition, Mobilization, and Women's Enfranchisement in the United States." *Journal of Politics* 80: 442–61.

Teles, S. M. (2008). *Rise of the Conservative Legal Movement*. Princeton, NJ: Princeton University Press.

Tervo, C. (2020). "Why Republicans Went Hard Right in North Carolina." In T. Skocpol and C. Tervo (eds.). *Upending American Politics: Polarizing Parties,*

Ideological Elites, and Citizen Activists from the Tea Party to the Anti-Trump Resistance. New York and Oxford: Oxford University Press, ch. 3.

Tilly, C. (1983). "Speaking Your Mind Without Elections, Surveys, or Social Movements." *Public Opinion Quarterly* 47: 461–78.

Tilly, C. (1990). *Coercion, Capital, and European States, AD 990–1992.* Cambridge, MA: Blackwell.

Tilly, C. (1993). *European Revolutions, 1492–1992.* Oxford: Blackwell.

Tilly, C. (1995). *Popular Contention in Great Britain, 1758–1834.* Cambridge, MA: Harvard University Press.

Tilly, C. (2006). *Regimes and Repertoires.* Cambridge: Cambridge University Press.

Tilly, C. (2007). *Democracy.* Cambridge: Cambridge University Press.

Tilly, C., and S. Tarrow (2015). *Contentious Politics,* 2nd ed. New York: Oxford University Press.

Tilly, C., and C. Tilly (1998). *Work under Capitalism.* Boulder, CO: Westview Press.

Touraine, A. (1971). *The May Movement: Revolt and Reform.* New York: Random House.

Trefousse, H. L. (1969). *The Radical Republicans: Lincoln's Vanguard for Racial Justice.* New York: Alfred A. Knopf.

Trefousse, H. L. (1991). *Historical Dictionary of Reconstruction.* New York: Greenwood Press.

Trigilia, C. (1986a). *Grandi partiti e piccole imprese.* Bologna: Il Mulino.

Trigilia, C. (1986b). "Small-Firm Development and Political Subcultures in Italy." *European Sociological Review* 2: 161–75.

Truman, D. (1951). *The Governmental Process.* New York: Knopf.

Truman, D. (1984–85). "Party Reform, Party Atrophy, and Constitutional Change: Some Reflections." *Political Science Quarterly* 99: 637–55.

Tufekci, Z. (2017). *Twitter and Tear Gas: The Power and Fragility of Networked Protest.* New Haven, CT: Yale University Press.

Tushnet, M. (2004). "Constitutional Hardball." *John Marshall Law Review* 37: 523–53.

Vallely, R. M. (2004). *The Two Reconstructions: The Struggle for Black Enfranchisement.* Chicago: University of Chicago Press.

Vallely, R. M., S. Mettler, and R. Lieberman (eds.) (2016). *Oxford Handbook of American Political Development.* New York and Oxford: Oxford University Press.

Van Cott, D. L. (2005). *Building Inclusive Democracies: Indigenous Peoples and Ethnic Minorities in Latin America.* New York and Cambridge: Cambridge University Press.

Van Dyke, N., and D. S. Meyer, (eds.) (2014). *Understanding the Tea Party Movement.* London: Ashgate.

Verhulst, J. (2010). "The World Says No to War." In S. Walgrave and D. Rught (eds.). *The World Says No to War: Demonstrations against the War on Iraq.* Minneapolis, MN: University of Minnesota Press, ch. 1.

von Bülow, Marisa, and Germán Bidegain (2015). "It Takes Two to Tango: Students, Political Parties, and Protest in Chile." In Paul Almeida and Aldo Cordera Ulate (eds.). *Handbook of Social Movements across Latin America.* New York: Springer, ch. 10.

Walgrave, S., and D. Rucht (eds.) (2010). *The World Says No to War: Demonstrations against the War on Iraq.* Minneapolis and St. Paul: University of Minnesota Press.

Walker, E. (2014). *Grassroots for Hire: Public Affairs Consultants in American Democracy.* New York: Cambridge University Press.

Walton, J., and D. Seddon (1994). *Free Markets and Food Riots: The Politics of Global Adjustment*. Oxford: Blackwell.

Wasow, O. (2020). "Agenda Seeding: How 1960s Black Protests Moved Elites, Public Opinion and Voting." *American Political Science Review* 114: 638–59.

Weaver, V. (2007). *Frontlash: Race and the Politics of Punishment*. Cambridge, MA: Harvard University Press.

Wechsler, B. D. (2002). "Black and White Disenfranchisement: Populism, Race, and Class." *American University Law Review* 52: 23–57.

Weingast, B. R. (1998). "Political Stability and Civil War: Institutions, Commitment, and American Democracy." In R. Bates, A. Greif, M. Levi, J.-L. Rosenthal, and B. R. Weingast, *Analytic Narratives*. Princeton, Princeton University Press, 148–93.

Weingast, B. R. (2002). "Institutions and Political Commitment: A New Political Economy of the American Civil War," Stanford CA, unpublished ms.

Weiss, L. (2014). *America, Inc? Innovation and Enterprise in the National Security State*. Ithaca and London: Cornell University Press.

Weiss, N. J. (1983). *Farewell to the Party of Lincoln: Black Politics in the Age of FDR*. Princeton, NJ: Princeton University Press.

Wills, G. (1992). *Lincoln at Gettysburg: The Words That Changed America*. New York: Simon and Schuster.

Wilson, J. Q. (1962). *The Amateur Democrat: Club Politics in Three Cities*. Chicago: University of Chicago Press.

Wineapple, B. (2019). *The Impeachers: The Trial of Andrew Johnson and the Dream of a Just Nation*. New York: Random House.

Winsboro, I. D. S., and M. S. Musoke (2003). "Lead Us Not into Temptation: Race, Rhetoric, and Reality in Southern Populism." *The Historian* 65: 1354–76.

Wolters, R. (1970). *Negroes and the Great Depression*. Westport, CT: Greenwood.

Zald, M. N., and M. A. Berger (1978). "Social Movements in Organizations: Coup d'Etat, Insurgency, and Mass Movements." *The American Journal of Sociology* 83(4): 823–61.

Zald, M. N., and R. A. Garner (1987). "Social Movement Organizations: Growth, Decay and Change." In M. N. Zald and J. McCarthy (eds.). *Social Movements in an Organizational Society: Collected Essays*. New Brunswick, NJ: Transaction Books, pp. 121–142.

Zald, M. N., and J. McCarthy (eds.) (1987). *Social Movements in an Organizational Society: Collected Essays*. New Brunswick, NJ: Transaction Books.

Zoorob, M., and T. Skocpol (2020). "The Overlooked Organizational Basis of Trump's 2016 Victory." In T. Skocpol and C. Tervo (eds.). *Upending American Politics: Polarizing Parties, Ideological Elites, and Citizen Activists from the Tea Party to the Anti-Trump Resistance*. New York and Oxford: Oxford University Press, ch. 4.

Index

Books in the Series (continued from p. ii)

Federico M. Rossi, *The Poor's Struggle for Political Incorporation: The Piquetero Movement in Argentina*

Chandra Russo, *Solidarity in Practice: Moral Protest and the US Security State*

Eduardo Silva, *Challenging Neoliberalism in Latin America*

Erica S. Simmons, *Meaningful Resistance: Market Reforms and the Roots of Social Protest in Latin America*

Sarah Soule, *Contention and Corporate Social Responsibility*

Suzanne Staggenborg, *Grassroots Environmentalism*

Sherrill Stroschein, *Ethnic Struggle, Coexistence, and Democratization in Eastern Europe*

Yang Su, *Collective Killings in Rural China during the Cultural Revolution*

Sidney Tarrow, *The Language of Contention: Revolutions in Words, 1688–2012*

Sidney Tarrow, *The New Transnational Activism*

Wayne P. Te Brake, *Religious War and Religious Peace in Early Modern Europe*

Ralph A. Thaxton Jr., *Catastrophe and Contention in Rural China: Mao's Great Leap Forward Famine and the Origins of Righteous Resistance in Da Fo Village*

Ralph A. Thaxton Jr., *Force and Contention in Contemporary China: Memory and Resistance in the Long Shadow of the Catastrophic Past*

Charles Tilly, *Contention and Democracy in Europe, 1650–2000*

Charles Tilly, *Contentious Performances*

Charles Tilly, *The Politics of Collective Violence*

Marisa von Bülow, *Building Transnational Networks: Civil Society and the Politics of Trade in the Americas*

Lesley J. Wood, *Direct Action, Deliberation, and Diffusion: Collective Action after the WTO Protests in Seattle*

Stuart A. Wright, *Patriots, Politics, and the Oklahoma City Bombing*

Deborah Yashar, *Contesting Citizenship in Latin America: The Rise of Indigenous Movements and the Postliberal Challenge*

Andrew Yeo, *Activists, Alliances, and Anti-U.S. Base Protests*

CPSIA information can be obtained
at www.ICGtesting.com
Printed in the USA
LVHW111800170822
726174LV00003B/162

9 781009 013963